RECORDED MUSIC IN AMERICAN LIFE

RECORDED MUSIC
IN AMERICAN LIFE

*The Phonograph and
Popular Memory,
1890–1945*

William Howland Kenney

New York   Oxford
Oxford University Press
1999

Oxford University Press

Oxford   New York
Athens   Auckland   Bangkok   Bogotá   Buenos Aires   Calcutta
Cape Town   Chennai   Dar es Salaam   Delhi   Florence   Hong Kong   Istanbul
Karachi   Kuala Lumpur   Madrid   Melbourne   Mexico City   Mumbai
Nairobi   Paris   São Paulo   Singapore   Taipei   Tokyo   Toronto   Warsaw

and associated companies in
Berlin   Ibadan

Published by Oxford University Press, Inc.
198 Madison Avenue, New York, New York 10016

Oxford is a registered trademark of Oxford University Press

Library of Congress Cataloging-in-Publication Data
Kenney, William Howland.
Recorded music in American life : the phonograph and popular
memory, 1890–1945 / William Howland Kenney.
p.   cm.
Includes bibliographical references and index.
ISBN 0-19-510046-8
1. Popular music—Social aspects—United States.   2. Phonograph—
Social aspects—United States.   3. Sound recording industry—United
States—History.   4. Popular culture—United States—History—20th
century.   I. Title.
ML3477.K46   1999
306.4'84—dc21   98-8611

9 8 7 6 5 4 3 2 1

Printed in the United States of America
on acid-free paper

to the memory of
Marie Isabelle (Gill) Kenney
& William Howland Kenney II

ACKNOWLEDGMENTS

In the lengthening interim between this project's opening hypotheses and its final chapter drafts, my curiosity grew steadily as I met and began learning from recorded sound archivists about the stunning number and range of phonograph records. It increasingly appeared to me that we historians had overlooked archival sources of unrivaled richness, diversity, and complexity. I started at the Library of Congress, where Sam Brylawski, director of the Division of Recorded Sound, became my invaluable guide. He and his colleagues Gene Deanna and Wynn Mathias then formed what seemed to me to be an exceptionally well-informed and professional archival team.

So, too, Dan Morgenstern, Ed Berger, Vincent Pelote, and Donald Luck of the Institute of Jazz Studies, Rutgers University, Newark, New Jersey, offered me their insightful commentary and friendly encouragement on this project, as they have on earlier ones. Calvin Elliker, director of the music library at the University of Michigan, ably assisted my research on the Edison surveys. Betty Obadashian of the Schomburg Center for Research in Black Culture guided my work on Harry H. Pace. Robin Van Fleet, senior manuscript librarian of the Moorland-Spingarn Research Center, kindly supplied copies of the correspondence between Harry H. Pace and Robert Vann. Amy Brown and Richard Shrader of the Southern Folklife Collection at the University of North Carolina at Chapel Hill guided my research into the origins of country music records, while Donald McCormick, curator of the Rodgers & Hammerstein Archives of Recorded Sound at the New York Public Library for the Performing Arts, helped me locate important documentation on early phonograph culture.

A 1993–1994 National Endowment for the Humanities Grant to University Teachers provided the necessary time to map out a research plan and begin to understand the primary sources in the several archives mentioned above. Dean Eugene Wenninger and his successor Dean M. Thomas Jones of Kent State University's Office of Research and Sponsored Programs helped to defray a significant portion of the expenses involved in my return visits to the archives.

My special thanks also go to Frank Field, associate director of the Kent State University Geneva Program, for helping me to secure in the fall of 1993 a pass to the Library of the United Nations, Geneva, Switzerland. Without that courtesy, I could not then have read all that microfilm of phonograph industry publications. Nina Kriz Leneman, chief of Readers' Services, United Nations Library, immediately grasped the goal of my project, and diplomatically overlooked its tangential relation to pressing United Nations business.

Several friends and colleagues took the time to criticize chapter drafts and to suggest further readings. Although the responsibility for all errors in this book is my own, I am indebted to Spencer Bennett, John Gennari, Victor Greene, Doris Kadish, August Meier, Henry D. Shapiro, Robert Swierenga, Nancy Walker, and Raymond Woller. I reserve special thanks for Richard Berrong's critical reading of the greater part of an early manuscript draft. Jonathan Crewe of the Dartmouth Humanities Institute suggested several exciting works on collective memory; Mark Tucker, Neil Leonard, James Collier, and Lewis Erenberg shared data from their own research; David Kyvig, professor of history at Akron University provided an occasion for me to speak to members of the University of Akron History Department about my evolving views of the phonograph. Herbert L. Hochhauser graciously consented to translate lyrics from records of Aaron Lebedeff. G. Phillip Cartwright, a jazz musician and educator who understands the power of recorded music, encouraged me to keep playing jazz and working on this project.

At different times, four editors at Oxford University Press took a hand in preparing this manuscript for publication. Sheldon Meyer saw some potential in my early chapter drafts and negotiated a book contract; Soo Mee Kwon guided the manuscript through the process of peer evaluation; while Jonathan Wiener and Jessica Ryan reviewed the final version. Thanks to all four for their faith in this further research on American music.

What eventually became a book began as I started to think about the influential role that the phonograph has played in my own life. I soon realized that I wanted to acknowledge and evaluate the paths to musical experience that it has opened to me. Thanks to the research that I have been able to undertake, I now understand better how and why I came so to embrace the recorded music of my parents' generation.

On this project, as on earlier ones, I take great pleasure in acknowledging my gratitude to Françoise Massardier Kenney for her encouragement and her critical readings of several chapters. She has carefully protected my research and writing time, sometimes at the expense of her own. So as not to unduly load the musical dice, we try to make a variety of recorded music available to our daughter Mélanie Massardier Kenney. Sharing her reactions to it enriches our resonant circle.

Hudson, Ohio   W.H.K.
October 1997

CONTENTS

A gallery of photos appears after page 108.

INTRODUCTION

*Recorded Music and
Collective Memory*

In memory, everything seems to happen to music.
> —Tennessee Williams,
> *The Glass Menagerie*

M ost people would admit that the phonograph[1] and recorded music have had an impact on life in the United
States. Americans' enjoyment of records has evolved into a major phenomenon: by 1902 the Victor Talking Machine Company had assets of
$2,724,016 which grew to $33,235,378 in 1917. Despite several difficult periods, record sales have soared over the long run, taking off in the
mid-1950s: they totaled $199,000,000 in 1954 and by 1977 we were pur-
chasing $3 billion worth of recordings a year at retail prices and playing
them on 75 million domestic playback machines.[2] The numbers alone
give pause and oblige us to consider that turntables and records may have
been more than clever distractions.

Most would as quickly acknowledge that records played a dominant
role in spreading a taste for popular and vernacular music styles—jazz,
blues, hillbilly, rock and roll—and a variety of other styles of popular
music. The mere mention of these stylistic labels and those that subsequently replaced them in popularity usually suffices to demonstrate the
cultural significance of the phonograph. Clearly, people of divergent
tastes have not only bought and listened to recordings but participated
in associated social and cultural movements as well. But important questions about this larger social and cultural context remain unanswered:
where did these style categories come from; how did they come to be
defined; what did they mean to those who bought and listened to the
records; and what, if anything, may they be said to reveal about the cultural life of the United States?

This book takes a step toward answering these latter questions by taking a closer look at the interplay between recorded music and social, political, and economic forces in the United States from 1890 to 1945. These two dates frame a formative period in commercialization of the phonograph: the first commercial recordings went on the market in 1890. Early in the twentieth century, after trials with cylinders, flat discs that turned at 78 revolutions per minute became the dominant form in which recorded sound reached the public. During the "78 rpm era" that this book describes, a small number of the many companies that made records overwhelmingly dominated music recording and distribution. Around the time of World War II, on the other hand, a whole series of new forces—a long, bitter struggle between music publishers and broadcasters, the strike of the American Federation of Musicians against the record companies, recording in radio studios, the advent of acetate disc cutters and magnetic tape—helped independent companies proliferate, and from a groundswell of major postwar culture changes, radio disk jockeys and the independent record companies produced the rock-and-roll revolution.[3]

From 1890 to 1945, the era of the phonograph's rise and decline as the dominant medium of popular recorded sound, the historian can readily document, in a way that is not possible thereafter, the give-and-take between the record business and major social patterns in the United States. Phonograph trade journals, reflecting the supremacy of New York City in the nation's music trades, detailed the goals, values, and major adjustments to the market of the few companies that dominated recording and distribution. The rise after 1945 of the independents (small, specialty labels), the geographical dispersion of recording, and the disappearance of trade papers like *Talking Machine World* and *Phonograph Monthly Review* makes documentary continuity and synthesis of record company goals and activities more difficult.

Unlike a handful of mindful collectors and writers on recorded sound, historians largely have forgotten about what was early known as "the talking machine," partly because the numerous famous modern inventions like the telegraph,[4] the telephone,[5] the radio,[6] movies,[7] the automobile,[8] and a host of domestic appliances that crowded into the early years of this century served as camouflage; the phonograph, which had begun to sell successfully as a clocklike, spring-driven machine, did not involve electrical power so much as the more familiar mechanical power, and can be thought to have had, therefore, a more modest influence on the popular imagination.

Moreover, this error of forgetting about the phonograph and recorded sound was the more readily made as the phonograph industry itself steadily disguised the machine that dispensed the sounds. Contemporary collectors and phonograph buffs treasure the up-front aura of the early machines with their soaring trumpet and "morning glory" horns, but those dramatic technological instruments were soon replaced by record players made to look like furniture, pianos, overnight bags, and suitcases.

Recorded sound devices were eventually miniaturized and hidden behind walls and ceiling tiles. The phonograph seemed to disappear as it became ever more ubiquitous.

Similarly, the phonograph's years of greatest historical influence lasted from 1890, when the first commercial recordings were placed on the market, to the late 1930s, when radio, which had arrived on the market in 1922, began to get the upper hand. Before the mass marketing of radio and the subsequent absorption of the phonograph companies by radio and movie conglomerates, the phonograph had competed only with music boxes and the player piano in supplying mechanized musical entertainment for consumption in American households. The record companies and the radio networks actually allied near the end of the 1920s in a manner economically beneficial to both: disguised as "electrical transcriptions," the phonograph record became the staple of radio broadcasting while the radio became a primary medium of publicity for the phonograph record. Still, the corporate absorption of the record companies only increased as the industry also merged with moving-picture empires and then with music video companies. A. J. Millard has called the resulting vast business conglomerates "empires of sound," and these powerful multinational conglomerates can make locating the core work of producing records more difficult.[9]

Cultural analysis of the phonograph and recorded music has languished as writers and scholars alike have favored the study of the technology in its many changing forms. This has had the effect of diverting attention from the ways that Americans interacted with recorded sound technologies, both in producing recorded music and in consuming it.[10] Recording machines may seem simply to reproduce what's out there to be recorded, but decisions about who to record, when, where, why, and how are influenced by a variety of factors. Consequently, historian of information-age invention Steven Lubar insists: "Recording is never value free. The producer is always making decisions about what the record should sound like."[11] So, too, are record listeners, who tend to select from the variety of recordings on the market, listen selectively to the ones they have chosen, interpret them as they wish, and pressure record companies by refusing to buy ones they don't like.[12]

This problem of aesthetic value in recorded music has been a vexing issue in the history of the phonograph. Prior discussion has minimized the diversity of different musical cultures that recorded sound stimulated, and Roland Gelatt, author of the best book on the medium, cast the phonograph into a struggle between "enduring" and "less enduring" sounds. Despite his smoothly ironic stance toward the industry's tendency to talk opera while recording blues (he admitted that even Victor produced three times as many popular as operatic discs), Gelatt made no bones about where he stood: the story of the phonograph held interest for him because of its association with "the artistry of Caruso, Melba, Beecham and Casals." Those, he wrote, who preferred popular composers and performers were free to disagree.[13]

Although Gelatt's tastes probably reflected the country's official musical values during the Cold War era in which he wrote, the recording business was far more populist and pluralistic than either the country's official musical values or the phonograph's elegant historian would openly admit. Moreover, even were we to grant his claim that operatic and symphonic records acted as a saving remnant of musical value, that would be an elevation of aesthetic judgment over historical description of past recording policy. Subsequent writers—Herbert Gans,[14] Serge Denisoff,[15] Lawrence Levine,[16] M. Gottdeiner,[17] and D. Hebdige[18]—have explored the influence of nonmusical forces in raising to a dominant position certain American musical styles and tastes. This greater awareness of the ways in which diverse musical cultures interact with their social and historical context has revolutionized music studies in this country and inevitably has raised new questions about the phonograph's history.

Since the history of recorded European concert hall music received preferential treatment in Gelatt's study of the phonograph during the years before World War II, I have focused on other, more vernacular and popular kinds of recorded music in this book. In the process, I have set aside the argument that recorded sound has spread upon a long-suffering nation a deadening blanket of cheap popular noise, as Allen Bloom,[19] Theodor Adorno,[20] and other critics would have it. To argue that the phonograph has had this or that particular, uniform influence, whether it be the redemption of a musically vulgar nation through recorded European concert hall music or the desecration of a purer musical vision by commercialization, oversimplifies the historical experience of the phonograph. More important, such blanket criticisms have been made at the expense of any understanding of the actual cultural processes by which recorded music has been made, packaged, marketed, purchased, "consumed," experienced, and interpreted.

The phonograph spread a taste for operatic and symphonic music to those who could never have heard them in performance, but it also spread different sorts of jazz, blues, country, and a variety of ethnic musical styles to a large number of groups who could not have otherwise heard them. The phonograph and the recording industry therefore expressed not so much the high culture consensus that dominated Gelatt's vision, or even a degraded popular taste, as a far more diverse set of cultural sensibilities in which various sorts of people found pleasure. If, as the primary sources clearly reveal, women, ethnic and racial minority groups, and those in other ways subordinated to the power structures that produced the phonograph also discovered deeply satisfying resonance in recorded music, something must be said about those more popular or vernacular dimensions of the phonograph's cultural history. The aesthetics of the musical patterns or schemas engraved onto sound recordings may not necessarily provide their primary "meaning"; that also can be found in the processes of their commercial production, promotion, and popular and critical reception. In other words, the machinery alone did not transform society, as A. J. Millard would have it; instead, powerful but constantly changing social and cultural patterns produced the phonograph in the first place and influenced its subsequent development.[21]

Despite their underlying assumptions of technlogical determinism, a small number of perceptive cultural historians have cleared paths toward a fuller understanding of recorded sound in its social and cultural context. Daniel Boorstin, one of the most influential interpreters of the American national experience, emphasized the technology's power to change lives. He saw it in much the same light as the camera, telegraph, telephone, and television, all of which contributed to making the experience of life, as he put it, "fungible," in other words repeatable, replayable "in a series of closely measured, interchangeable units."[22] The sense that each of life's moments was unique and irrecoverable gave way to the idea of recording and replaying them, Boorstin wrote. While he agreed that the phonograph did encourage a more democratic appreciation of concert hall music, as Gelatt also emphasized, Boorstin believed it also created popular fashions in music on a new scale, possessing the power "both to enrich musical experience and to trivialize it" with, for example, Muzak machines, among other things.

Boorstin's prescience about the cultural impact of the phonograph matched that of his entire synthesis of the impact on American life of what he called "mass-producing the moment." His ideas concerning the cultural impact of the media included the potentially useful notion of "consumption communities" that he likened to fellowships of consumers that transformed mass-produced consumer goods into vehicles of community. He thought of these taste subcultures as quick to form, nonideological, democratic, public, vague, and rapidly shifting, indeed, representative of all that was new about consumption-driven societies.[23]

Perhaps because he aimed not just at the phonograph but at the more distant and ultimately less visible target of the American democratic experience, Boorstin stopped short of actually exploring the cultural processes that created many different phonographic "consumption communities." A closer look at this cultural pattern in its historical perspective indicates that recorded music proved the focus for active recorded sound cultures, what might be called "circles of resonance"[24] or group sensibilities in which listeners shared, debated, analyzed, and fought, often passionately, over their personal patterns of empathy and appreciation for what they heard in grooves of 78 rpm recordings. Many Americans found ways of expressing important dimensions of their personal lives through their involvement with recorded sound.

In order to uncover the significance of phonographic activities in the cultural history of the United States, this book pinpoints three interrelated processes of recorded music in society. The first and most readily documented involves what culture studies scholars have called the "political economy of culture." Here I explore how different ways of financing and organizing cultural production influence the products to which the public is given access.[25] Primary sources such as phonograph industry trade publications detail how the goals and values of phonograph and record companies shaped the kinds of recorded music sold to the public. The pages that follow, for example, explore how record producers framed and designed the sounds of ethnicity and race.

A second process of recorded music in society, one about which far fewer primary sources exist, involves patterns in the audience reception of phonographs and sound recordings. To what extent the listening public could be said to have passively assimilated or actively interacted with what the record companies had prepared for them ultimately reflects upon questions surrounding the power of the media over our lives in this country. Between 1890 and 1945, the give-and-take between representatives of the record companies and the public evolved with such complexity that it cannot be said that the industry as a whole simply imposed its musical tastes upon America. On the contrary, as the first chapter demonstrates, meaning in recorded music arose out of the relationships between specific records or groups of records in a given style category, the musical and cultural gestures to which they referred, and the reactions of record listeners.[26]

The third major process by which meaning comes to adhere to recorded music involves analysis of selected musical inscriptions produced by the recording companies in order better to understand how they generated meaning. To avoid the pitfall of isolated musical analysis of recorded musical texts, I have tied my descriptions of the musical content of selected records as closely as possible to what can be known about the work of record producers and that of the musicians and vocalists who cooperated with them. In so doing, I think it is possible to find some fairly complex answers to the question of whether recorded music, by its very commercial nature, can be "authentic." I argue that recorded music resulted from mixing several different, widely recognized stylistic gestures, what can also be called familiar musical patterns and sequences, with just enough new and therefore unexpected innovations to attract listeners' emotional and critical attention and, significantly, corporate profits into the bargain. In order to sell, records had to present musical patterns that corresponded enough to widely shared expectations so that they could be at least within the realm of what the public would consider "authentic," while at the same time introducing and blending "unauthentic" surprises.

A cultural history of the phonograph also must include overt recognition that the machine's power involves music as well as technology, and an exclusive focus on the latter misses in a fundamental way the phonograph's importance. Early referred to as the "talking machine" by its primary American inventor, who thought of it as a preserver of the human voice, the phonograph soon delivered primarily singing voices and came to specialize in the power of music, instrumental as well as vocal, performed in the past—recorded music that, before being sold, had been mediated not just by the machinery but by the phonograph company employees and the musicians they had chosen to make music in their studios. Focus must be redirected, therefore, onto the process of making, selling, and listening to the music provided by phonographs and records.

The phonograph and recorded music need to be reinterpreted in light of work that explores the ways in which music can stir our emotions and our memories, as Leonard B. Meyer[27] and Charles Keil[28] have demonstrated. Whether in the composed forms of European concert halls or in the aural folk traditions, musical styles function as sets of learned expectations; Meyer, thinking primarily in terms of notation has used a linguistic parallel to music, "the possibilities presented to us by a particular musical vocabulary and grammar condition the operation of our mental processes and hence of our expectations. . . ." In any given piece of music, the melody, rhythmic pattern, and harmonic progression of chords all communicate, individually and collectively, structures of sound. Taken as a whole, such genre-specific forms of sound repetition act like linguistic formulas in which harmonic "grammar," syntax, and vocabulary provide the aural memories for making sense of experience. Music, in this case recorded music, also stimulates strong emotions attached to related past experiences and thereby makes those past experiences more accessible to the listener's consciousness. We feel, and therefore remember, past experience through, among other things, musical repetition.[29]

During the period under consideration, phonograph records sounded and resounded a variety of different musical genres prepared for what were seen as relatively identifiable markets. In being exactly repeated upon command, the musical grammar, syntax, and vocabulary of these styles or structures of recorded sound took on the characteristics of musical, cultural, and psychological habit, and, as such, of forms of culturally constructed and coded aural knowledge. Inevitably, then, the phonograph, not unlike the slide projector, moving picture projector, and VCR, offered a technological aid to remembering. Phonograph records "froze" past performances as engraved sound pictures: 78 rpm records offered Americans memories of memories.

Recorded music, moreover, played an important role in stimulating and preserving what has been called "collective memories." Since music recordings circulated in the form of commercial commodities designed to appeal to large numbers of Americans, collective listening patterns arose between 1890 and 1945. Record companies designed and issued various categories of records for what they recognized to be powerful (and many numerically less powerful) demographic units of American society. In the process, the genre-specific harmonic and rhythmic schemas on records helped to generate collective aural memories through which various groups of Americans were able to locate and identify themselves amid the many changing sounds with which the United States has been made to resound.[30]

Recorded musical performances from the past stimulated collective memories that vastly enriched the historical experience of this country by setting in motion emotions, fantasies, and memories that helped Americans reenvision themselves simultaneously in different spheres of their country's and their own past, present, and future. This idea of collective memories, introduced in 1950 by the publication in French of sociologist Maurice Halbwachs's *La Mémoire Collective*, emphasizes the interpenetration of social group and individual memories. Each social group seeks to maintain its identity by focusing attention on the resemblances between its past and present. Changes over time are reinterpreted as similarities through selective remembering, and a blurred image of apparent group unity will tend to dominate the recollections of its members.

Halbwachs further argued that just as groups encourage individuals to think in terms of group continuity over time, so too collective memory generates impressions of stopped time in which favored images of the past resist change. Because he understood language and spaces (places) to be the primary vehicles for collective memories, Halbwachs had little to say about the role of either the phonograph or recorded music in memory's work. His concluding essay called "The Collective Memory of Musicians" concerned the difficulty musicians have in remembering music but focused primarily on the role of written musical symbols in helping individual musicians to remember. Halbwachs admitted that those who could read music formed a minority of society and argued that even for that minority the recollection of music also involved a "schematic model," as when one hums a remembered trace of the musical piece, as well as written music.[31]

Halbwachs no more than mentioned recorded sound and did not emphasize the role of reiteration through recorded music, which, by his own logic, strengthens, clarifies, and enriches the remembered traces. His explanation of the formation of collective memories can help us understand how the phonograph functioned in shaping those memories. Sociologist Edward Shils, for example, has edged much closer to the aural mode of the phonograph in his insistence that societies preserve themselves through the perpetual reenactment and resaying of their communications. Members of social groups repeat what they can remember about what they themselves said or did before. Shils believed that this oral/aural repetition, led by memory, preserved the past into the present and future.[32]

Similarly, Walter Ong's work on the characteristics of oral/aural and literate cultures, which can be seen to parallel, in some respects, the work of Halbwachs and Shils, emphasized that oral cultures remember through the repetition of metrically structured verbal and/or musical formulas. Compared to literate cultures, oral ones create a stronger sense of group spirit and tend to value more strongly a sense of sacred, inner harmony with group members through shared repetition of rhythmic patterns. In order to remember, thought patterns must come in heavily rhythmic, balanced patterns, in repetitions or antitheses, in alliterations and assonances, in epithetic and other formulary expressions. . . ." For groups who communicate aurally, "redundancy, repetition of the just said, keeps both speaker and hearer surely on track."[33] The work of Ong, among others, has been taken in directions that lead more directly to recorded music. The internal structures in folk music and folk lyrics that steer the mind toward recollection recently have been labeled "multiple constraints" on variations in recall.[34] Music, poetics, narrative structure, and imagery all help people who are trying to remember by reducing memory's possible choices for any given musical or verbal signifier. Record listeners begin to "remember" through familiar musical and lyric patterns, their minds then moving on to related styles and even moments of past personal experience that they associate with music.

Here, at the juncture of social repetition and collective memory, the phonograph played a more important cultural role from 1890 to 1945 than the discourses on either recorded sound or on memory have recognized. Although isolated scholarly voices have called for greater recognition of the media "as sites of the creation of social memory and as a body of available materials for its study,"[35] recorded sound has not yet received such consideration. The phonograph's repetitive function acted as a major aid to memory by resounding the patterns of sensibility embedded in commercialized musical formulas from the past. Americans reexperienced and recalled the melodic, harmonic, and rhythmic structures of the past as well as something of the surrounding social and cultural contexts from which they had emerged. The phonograph and recorded sound, therefore, served as instruments in an ongoing process of individual and group recognition in which images of the past and the present could be mixed in an apparently timeless suspension that often seemed to defy the relentless corrosion of historical change. "Record buffs" formed varied communities of memory in response to discs that had been artfully contrived for them.

In exploring the cultural significance of recorded music, I hope this book will help to temper what the French historical essayist Pierre Nora has described as a fundamental conflict between history and memory. The historiographical emphasis of professional historians brings with it a dedication to secular, intellectual detachment from particular patterns of past life, one in which treasured islands of personal recollection drown in an ocean of constant change.[36]

In this book, the consideration of recorded music in history is an attempt to reenvision how the phonograph and record makers and their customers interacted to create and then maintain popular collective memories. On one side of the confrontation of history and memory, recorded music has had much more to do with the way many people relate to the past than we historians have realized. On the other side of the same conflict, the champions of phonographs and records may discover that their publications and collections, which have done so much to establish a history of recorded sound, have more to say about the history of the United States than even they may have realized.

RECORDED MUSIC IN AMERICAN LIFE

I

TWO "CIRCLES OF RESONANCE"

Audience Uses of Recorded Music

Reimagining the historical influence of the phonograph and recorded music in American life can begin with a reconsideration of Evan Eisenberg's description of domestic consumer phonograph culture. Eisenberg imagined domestic interactions of Americans with the phonograph as "ceremonies of a solitary," ritualistic observances in which the listener summons forth the sound of voices and musical instruments of his or her own choosing. The phonograph creates an impression of "private music" possessed by the record buyer, creating "a private structure of time to set against public time." Record listening, he argued, contributes to a hermetic world walled by favorite recorded sounds. The talking machine thus fragmented the unifying role of live music in late nineteenth-century social rituals and, by commodifying music, turned the Victorian "Cathedral of Culture" into a "supermarket."[1]

This may be true in some ways, but putting it that way ignores all those many individuals who were playing the same thing on their phonographs at any given time in the past. Moreover, Eisenberg's hypothesis has minimized the number of different, more active, shared ways in which people interacted with recorded music. In addition merely to listening passively to records while alone in their homes or rooms, many people also enjoyed shared patterns of musical activity and participated together, for example, in public juke box listening and dancing cultures, formal and informal record collector groups, and fan organizations; and, more important, they sing and play musical instruments in recording studios, direct recording sessions, scout for talent, choose which recordings to issue, take an active role in the recording process, publicize records, write about them critically, and actively study and play along with them in their homes. To emphasize solitary receptivity denies the phonograph's power to stimulate new musical "arts related to the creation of new associations of people in society,"[2] or, in other words, new musical cultures.

For the historian, a more accurate image of the phonograph's past would involve not just the individual alone with his "talking machine," but large numbers of individuals around the country and indeed the world, "alone together," actively using their phonographs to replay as they wished commercially mediated musical messages. As a point of departure, this different vision allows us to begin to see that phonographs, far from promoting only "ceremonies of the solitary," paradoxically encouraged widely shared patterns of popular behavior, thought, emotion, and sensibility.

Two dimensions of the phonographic experience contribute to the social and cultural dimensions of its history: it can introduce new musical experiences, as when many Americans first heard ethnic music, African American blues, country, and jazz on records, and it can resurrect and repeat older, more familiar ones. For example, although every record is by definition an engraved historical document, some records will inevitably amaze and otherwise move many people with sounds that they had not anticipated. In its turn, the phonograph's repetitive function then turns that novelty and the complex elements of music into an enhanced sense of mastery, creating shared patterns of musical recognition and discrimination.

Recorded music's power to resound musical patterns does much to fortify circles of shared popular experience. Although it is entirely possible to use record players very casually, they can introduce and reinforce powerful emotional responses. Moreover, this memory machine then can repeat recorded messages until they have become deeply assimilated parts of the listener's personal emotional and cultural life. Although he has not mentioned the phonograph, it has functioned as one of what French writer and editor Pierre Nora has called *instruments de la mémoire*, machines through which memories can be stirred, stimulating recollections that arrest the process of forgetting, that immortalize the dead, and that reintroduce into the present powerful emotions concerning past experiences.[3] Nora associates memory primarily with *lieux*, places such as cemeteries, museums, archives, and the like, as well as *rites*, rituals and ceremonies. But in exactly and repeatedly reproducing music from the past, phonograph records inject and reinject the emotional power of past musical performances into the present.[4]

Certain kinds of records, the "hearth and home" recordings produced in the second decade of this century by Thomas A. Edison, Inc., the different ethnic recordings marketed at about the same time on many labels, the African American country blues records pioneered by the Paramount label in the 1920s, and southern hillbilly records of that same decade had the power to awaken powerful emotions capable of stimulating recollections and dreams of departed family members, kin, hearth, soil, rural and agricultural activities, cultural community, past lifestyles, and special family mentalities.

Other sorts of records, more reflective of urban environments—hot dance, jazz, classic blues, and popular recordings—introduced and then perpetuated musical expressions of youthful energy, social daring, and erotic mating rituals. Phonographic memories of music associated with such highly charged youthful experiences "inflected the construction of identity in the present"[5] by allowing people to not only replay and reexperience the music and the emotions but to reexperience (and ultimately reassess) them within the changing contexts of their lives.

Although a few celebrated critics have excoriated popular recorded music as musically trivial, we should not therefore dismiss its impact on individual and social memory. Relatively little documentation exists on audience reception of recorded music, but unusually ample documentation does allow us to compare two different but interrelated patterns of audience reaction to phonograph records in the United States between 1890 and 1945. This descriptive comparison will underscore the power of the phonograph to revive in the present sounds from the past and will demonstrate that while the cultural process was much the same in each case, the actual musical and cultural content of these phonograph cultures could differ dramatically. Whatever the musical style, phonograph records functioned as rhythmically patterned, melodically repetitive, harmonically redundant mnemonic devices.[6]

The first circle of popular resonance to phonographic sound, just one of many divergent phonograph cultures, emerges from the analysis of responses by a group of 2,644 Americans who filled out a survey undertaken in 1921 by Thomas A. Edison, Inc.[7] The second pattern of phonographic culture—circles of jazz resonance—first emerged at about the same time, flourished in tension with Edison's consumers, and died in the depression, only to be revived once it was over.

While just one clearly demarked mode of consumption, the 1921 Edison survey responses have been largely overlooked despite the fact that evidence on audience attitudes and patterns of reception and use of phonograph records has been difficult to find. Studies usually rely on sources supplied by those who produce, rather than consume, the mediated messages.[8] Each of the major media developed trade magazines that provide fascinating data on what the manufacturers wanted their wholesalers and retailers to think. Any attempt to generalize from those sources to customer thought and behavior, however, involves pure speculation.

For this reason, the 1921 Edison survey returns provide rare primary source documentation from those who were actually using the phonographic equipment. The Edison Company claimed to have sent out as many as 20,000 copies of a questionnaire asking Americans in 43 states to list their "favorite tunes."[9] Their often laborious answers sometimes ranged far beyond the details of record issue numbers and unexplained lacunae in the Edison record lists: many took the occasion of the survey to explain how and why they simply would not have been able to live without their record players and their records. Hissing three-minute acoustical recordings or not, Edison's invention definitely touched many of his customers where they lived.

Many of the survey returns complained about the company's failures to meet market demands. Respondents whose comments indicated extensive musical knowledge complained about the lack of famous recording stars and the general thinness of operatic and symphonic repertoire on Edison discs. Some customers who preferred popular music lamented the slowness of the company in getting its records out to the public. By the time many popular items appeared on the Edison label, the public had already begun to tire of them. Many phonograph buffs who seemed particularly interested in the technology complained that Edison records produced too much scratchy surface noise and tended to warp.

Edison, Inc. took the time to respond to many of their customers' complaints, stapling carbon copies to the individual survey responses. Significantly, many customers revealed their sense of sharing a bond with the phonograph's inventor himself, addressing their responses directly to "My Dear Mr. Edison." Many a customer personalized her phonograph machine by referring to it as "My Edison." Company responses to returned surveys were handled, however, by employees, who invariably indicated that they had found the customers' suggestions mostly helpful and had forwarded them to the appropriate department. This gave the impression that Edison, Inc. responded to its customers in a democratic fashion, but we shall see that this was more an illusion than reality.

The survey had been undertaken in part at least to test the results of an experiment designed by a group of psychologists headed by Dr. W. V. Bingham of the Carnegie Institute of Technology. Bingham's group believed that music stimulated human emotions and they wanted Edison records to push the right emotional buttons. They classified the music on 135 Edison records into twelve categories ranging from recordings to "Stimulate and Enrich Your Imagination" to those that brought "Peace of Mind," "Joy," "Wistfulness," "Good Fellowship," "More Energy," "Love," "Dignity and Grandeur," "Tender Memory," "Devotion," a "Stirring" of the spirits, and a stimulation of "Childish Fancy." The company announced that its experimental program to record music that engendered such "moods" as these was designed to "harness this . . . power of music to the service of man."[10] Were this analysis correct, of course, a more systematic approach to assuring record sales would also result.

Edison, Inc.'s emotional utilitarianism involved an attempt to identify and then appeal to the emotions of large numbers of Americans. The plan proceeded from a belief in collective emotional patterning; the Edison team ran tests on three other psychologists—two women and a man—whom they claimed were "experts in introspection." Two of the test listeners were musicians who had studied music. The other lacked musical training but liked music and possessed "a keen ear for what is good."[11] Edison discs were played and each listener noted what emotions had been engendered.

Having described the producer's position and intentions, one still must investigate the public's reactions to the products they consumed. The Edison survey returns give us a broad measure of consumer attitudes toward the company's policies and products: they overwhelmingly affirm that studies of collective thought and behavior have overlooked the influence of recorded music in stimulating the kinds of collective emotions that permanently shaped group identities. The emotions of those who used Edison phonographs and records in their homes took on highly patterned and widely shared configurations. Clearly, common emotional patterns of meaning, set in motion and reconfirmed by sound recordings, did exist and often reached a level of self-conscious reflection. These patterns of meaning existed on at least two levels: first, a general awareness of the tendencies, resistances, tensions, and fulfillments embodied in Edison's recordings; and second, a more objectified, self-conscious reflection on the meaning of his recorded music.[12]

All of the emotional reactions predicted by Edison's team of psychologists turned up in the survey responses, but the coolly detached tone of the Edison team summoned forth many agonizing popular responses. Edison Diamond Discs certainly did stimulate emotions: ones that reached far more deeply into the sensibilities and aesthetic dimensions of American collective memory than the curmudgeonly inventor likely appreciated.

The 1921 Edison survey returns document a broad range of different public reactions to the phonograph and to recorded sound. Some customers enjoyed the way recorded sound stimulated images of exotic cultures and geographical locations; others appreciated most what they regarded as novel sound effects; some listened hard for virtuoso feats of instrumental technique; many liked anything recorded by certain artists; a goodly number focused on recordings of a particular instrument or type of voice; some listened only to certain styles of recorded music; a minority rejected the entire question, as in the case of one man who insisted: "My favorites in music can hardly be tabulated. They vary in order as one's mood differs one day with another. Circumstances, company, spirits, even the time of day, I find, shifts my desire and directs the record I choose." Some merely remarked that while the phonograph provided a pleasant diversion, they were far too busy to think more about it than that.

This diversity of popular public attitudes toward Edison's recorded sounds represents an important corrective to overly simplified, unitary interpretations of "the" influence of phonographic technology. The Edison survey responses confirm for the phonograph what Claude S. Fischer has written about the social impact of the telephone in this country:

> . . . while a material change as fundamental as the telephone alters the conditions of daily life, it does not determine the basic character of that life. Instead, people turn new devices to various purposes, even ones that the producers could hardly have foreseen or desired. As much as people adapt their lives to the changed circumstances created by a new technology, they also adapt that technology to their lives.[13]

Amidst the variety of responses, many rural and small-town Americans, those who took the time to write narrative comments on the survey returns, sent back powerful messages that linked recorded sound to the intense emotions of personal and family life. That this should be so will come as no surprise to those who have studied the kind of music that Edison favored: in one sense, respondents merely repeated back to Edison what he would likely have wanted to hear, but without something like the survey returns it is impossible to document patterns in the popular impact of recorded sound in America.

Many customers recalled and reaffirmed familial love and family identity by replaying recordings of music that they felt pointed to particular departed family members. Respondents preferred "old music well rendered," music that "takes us back to Grandfather days," tunes that brought "memories of home," old tunes that "take us back to the days of childhood." A striking number of Edison's customers wrote that the emotions stirred by their favorite records brought back treasured memories of their grandparents, parents, husbands, wives, and departed sisters, brothers, and children.

Although a few who filled out the form obviously knew a great deal about music and records, some obviously knew little about either of them and laboriously penned simple messages of loss, sorrow, and reaffirmation. The majority of those who took the time to write narrative comments liked old Anglo-American parlor songs and what many of them called "heart songs" of the sort written by Stephen Foster, Thomas Paine Westendorf, and H. P. Danks and other nineteenth-century Anglo-American popular composers: "Swanee River," "Annie Laurie," "My Old Kentucky Home," "The Rosary," "Carry Me Back to Old Virginny," "Silver Threads Among the Gold," "Abide with Me," "Rock of Ages," "Lead Kindly Light," and "The Old Oaken Bucket."[14]

The survey responses frequently contextualized the meaning discovered in these recordings by reference to ragtime and jazz, newer styles that had jarred the respondents' habitual, automatic patterns of aesthetic attention. Under the dual pressures of new recordings that they disliked and the need to respond to the Edison questionnaire, they declared their special loyalty to Edison's tastes and made it clear that they, too, disliked jazz and even ragtime.

Taken together, these songs, and the dozens of others written and published in the same vein, comprised one-half of the nineteenth century's popular music (minstrelsy, also recorded by Edison, constituted the other half). Derived from British, particularly Scottish, origins but adopted and Americanized in the United States, parlor songs, which reflected social ambitions before the Civil War, came to have a very broad democratic appeal by 1860.[15] Their peacefully flowing melodies, subdominant harmonies, and gentle rhythms bathed lushly romantic lyrics describing lost love, "hallowed visions of home,"[16] and bittersweet emotions about the loss of an earlier, better world. These recorded songs stimulated what some psychologists have called "self-defining memories," vivid, intense recollections that linked together into a kind of "script" of the central themes of the listeners' lives.[17]

According to the survey returns, many people who listened to recordings of these refined folk-inspired parlor songs simultaneously experienced grief over the deaths of loved ones and a sense of their psychic resurrection. One individual listened again and again to "When You and I Were Young, Maggie," "I think, because my Mother loved it and sang it." Another replayed the "two songs sung at my Mother's funeral services." As one man wrote in explaining his preference for "I'm in Heaven When in My Mother's Arms": "I loved Mother as well as one could love and I had to part from her about two months ago never to see her in this world again and songs of mother are always sweet to me."

But memories stimulated by Edison's recorded music involved as well emotions that mothers/wives felt for lost fathers/husbands. Powerful sentiments of loss and grief sometimes boiled to the surface of survey responses. One woman wrote that she liked a certain folk song: "Because it used to be sung by a loved one. It recalls a loved one who is no more. I love it because the one I loved, loved it. It is as dear to me as my little one who [also] loves it."

A tune like "I'll Take You Home Again, Kathleen," one that Edison requested be sung at his own funeral, seemed to many respondents to express the happiness that departed parents had felt with each other. Another man enjoyed replaying an old popular song that he associated with "my brothers before we were all married and away from home." Whatever their gender, family members recalled each other through recorded music, finding in its familiar melodic, harmonic, and rhythmic patterns confirmation of emotional expectations from remote, but ever present, musical memories.

Edison's team of psychologists believed that recordings of beloved hymns and religious songs, so difficult to distinguish from parlor songs, would put listeners in the proper mood "for true devotion,"[18] and many who wrote about their reactions explained that recorded religious music, like "Rock of Ages" and "Abide with Me," simultaneously communicated feelings of loss and of comfort associated with the passing of a close family member. As a female correspondent who preferred Catholic religious music put it:

> I really can't find words strong enough to express my love for my Edison. I have had my life made worth living since it came into my home. I am a poor widow with five children. My husband died 2 years ago this month. My baby was only ten days old. I know the comfort his invention has given me is beyond explanation. It is the best tonic I ever had.

Many others assuaged their grief with Edison discs of sacred music, praising the sense of "peace and assurance" and "precious comforting promises" that they conveyed. A woman from Chicago wrote: "My Edison has been the most comfort I ever had in this world—my little son and the Edison and my great trust in God and my mother."

This recurrent sense of resurrection, rejuvenation, and renewed hope leavened what might otherwise degenerate into despondency and depression. Although one might be tempted to interpret recorded music as expressive of nostalgia, regret, and a maudlin longing for a lost past, that is not how the memories stimulated by recorded music functioned. Edison's listeners may have felt some of these things sometimes but only as parts of more extensive and complex emotional experiences that allowed them to work through and perhaps resolve unpleasant memories of past experiences. The process of phonographic remembering included a growing sense of mastery over powerful memories of the past as the listener repeatedly summoned forth the music that stimulated the emotions linked to memory.[19]

Survey responses described Edison's phonograph and records as instruments in an ongoing process of renewing and reshaping personal memories of a fundamental kind. According to psychologists of what is called "autobiographical memory," the emotional intensity associated with a memory is a function of its meaning at the time of its recall, not at the time the recollected event took place. A memory may gain or lose power according to the individual's ongoing experiences.[20] In 1921, Edison's mass-produced sound recordings stirred strong emotions linked to familial identity among Americans for whom the jazz age and jazz records seemed to trumpet upsetting and bewildering social change. Under a veritable siege of the sounds of urban, industrial life, many Americans communed with their memories of a more tranquil time of family continuity through time.

Edison must have understood the connections between music, emotion, and memory and he had predicted that an important market awaited recordings of traditional nineteenth-century melodies. He was right. But his experiment did not overtly anticipate the powerful associations of these melodies with home and family. The genteel airs of Stephen Foster, rooted in Irish and English folk tunes, ran strongly to what American music historian H. Wiley Hitchcock has called "hearth and home" songs, concert and stage music for the rising middle class.[21]

Edison brought to these simple, strophic, major mode melodies artful concert hall interpretations by such operatic singers as Frieda Hempel and Anna Case and concert violinist Albert Spaulding. This combination of folk melody and art performance communicated an emotional power beyond that which might have been generated by an untrained, vernacular voice. Singing or playing musical instruments in the home generated familial participation and emotional interaction, but records usually brought more art to the music, art that drove home to that earlier generation of small-town Americans the full power of nineteenth-century folk songs.

In the homes of Edison's customers, sound recordings also intertwined with interfamilial relations. Many female respondents revealed that they strengthened family ties in those tired irritable hours late in the afternoon when relations became brittle. One mother got her children to dance to "The Home Dances." Another revealed that: "We have all moods of music. Some one looks *blue* or a little peeved [and] I go in and start "Henry Jones Your Honeymoon is Over" and at once everybody smiles and the white flag waves." A man wrote that he and his wife enjoyed playing "When I'm Gone You'll Soon Forget" after having "a row." One of Edison's racier customers liked "Dardanella" and "Laughing Trombone" as "they make old Folks young and young folks crazy." Another female correspondent used the phonograph to help keep her family happy and summed up her experiences by saying:

> Our little son, a year old, often during the day points till I put a piece on for him. Our two little girls love the dance pieces. We love our machine so much. If we had to part with any piece of furniture in our home, we would give our bed up before we would part with our Edison.

This intriguing hint that recorded sound could mean more to a married woman than the bed she shared with her husband raises the possibility that phonograph records, like popular culture in general, played a role in the relations of dominance and subordination built into family life.[22] Men and women answered Edison's survey in about equal numbers, but the image of woman as wife and mother played a particularly powerful role for those who associated Edison recordings of old-time American folk songs with the family. In great measure, this association had long been built into the Victorian concept of woman as "angel of the household."[23] As wife, the Victorian middle-class female was encouraged to soothe her tired, harassed husband with her keyboard skills at the parlor piano; as mother, she likewise edified and refined her children with music of "the best sort."[24]

Evidence from the 1921 Edison Survey indicates that the phonograph participated in a popularizing and social broadening of this nineteenth-century tradition among people with little or no instrumental or concert hall experience. Phonograph industry publications indicate that females dominated the market for phonograph records.[25] Husbands often left enough discretionary money in the family's weekly budget to allow their wives to purchase a record or two. If they couldn't soothe their mates with their piano virtuosity, wives could always slip an appropriately calming and/or uplifting record on the parlor phonograph. As a result, many, both men and women, who responded to the Edison survey tended to associate recordings of old-fashioned melodies with mother, wife, family, and household, reaffirming, by extension, both social and cultural continuity through their emotional recollections.

The sense of collective family and cultural identity that Thomas Edison's hearth-and-home records helped to build intertwined with periodic renewals of a sense of national pride. All of the companies,

Edison, Inc. included, issued large numbers of records of military-style concert bands, and many respondents associated these recorded sounds with patriotic emotions. One man listed "our best American marches," while another simply declared that "I like 'America' and 'The Star Spangled Banner' because I am a good American." Several men thought proudly of past wars and their own roles in them when they listened to recordings of certain military marches. One woman wrote that she cherished her Edison recordings of "Just as the Sun Went Down" and "On the Banks of the Wabash, Faraway" ". . . because I heard them during the War with Spain and I never hear one but what I'm thankful for the *quick work we done.*"

As chapter three indicates, phonograph records also functioned to mediate between a sense of immigrant cultural identity and pride in being American. The children of immigrants often recalled their parents' struggles when listening to recordings of "foreign" music. Edison, Inc. did not reach out to more than a few of the largest European ethnic groups—Spaniards, Mexicans, Germans, Scots, and Irish, for example—and some who had bought an Edison phonograph resented this fact. "While I was born in this country, my parents came from Poland and we live in a Polish settlement and for the old people I would like to get some old folk songs. Why don't you make them?" Several replied to Edison's survey with rousing calls for Bohemian records. Others questioned why Edison did nothing with Greek and Italian music. Clearly, then, Edison's records did not offer a broad spectrum of different ethnic musical styles.

While promoting all sorts of minstrel and vaudeville music, Edison, Inc. adopted a self-professed highbrow policy when recording foreign music, selecting what it called "first class records" and "the best songs" sung by stage stars "of refinement."[26] The company sounded defensive when describing its recording policy in this area:

> There is no reason why a music lover should not be attracted by the melodies of a foreign people when rendered by recognized artists and when such numbers are recorded as representing the best compositions of that people.[27]

Edison recordings of "foreign" music, therefore, filtered it through a complex veil of social and cultural assumptions.

The children of those immigrant groups that Edison recognized felt that they put themselves back in touch with their parents' immigrant culture. "My Mother and Father are German and I love German singing."

> My parents came from two old countries of Europe 50 years ago . . . and . . . gave up much. The Largo movement from Dvorak's Symphony of the New World seems to me to embody in its haunting fascinating melody their feelings.

Whether or not immigrants themselves would have recognized their former musical culture in the nationalized ethnic musicality of phonograph records is uncertain. None of the survey respondents characterized themselves as recently arrived immigrants. Ethnic records may have better served the needs of immigrants who had spent enough time in the United States to have participated in the process described by Lizabeth Cohen in which "small societies with narrow European orientations and purely local constituencies stabilized themselves by merging with other related societies or joining large fraternals organized around [European] national populations—Poles, Czechs, Italians, Jews—rather than particular villages or regions."[28] This cultural process evolved during the 1920s and by the end of that decade the nationalization legacies of World War I and the tendency of Americans to treat foreigners as members of national groups had overcome local and regional European loyalties.

Nationalized cultural identities of immigrant groups living in a foreign land find encouragement from the host culture. Many in the receiving culture cannot be bothered to learn about the particular local, regional, sectarian, and dialect identities of "foreigners," while immigrants and their children often find it easier to act in ways that other people expect.[29] The idea that all immigrants belonged primarily to foreign national cultures, as opposed to a foreign town or regional cultures, took its origin in the attitudes of Americans toward immigrants. As one phonograph industry trade paper put it: "a Neapolitan Italian regards a Sicilian language record, if not with distaste, at least with complete indifference. He would not buy such a record under any circumstances."[30] Ethnic records, therefore, represented a series of musical and cultural compromises with the variety of immigrant backgrounds; listening to them in the present "renovated and selectively appropriated" the sounds of the past, while promoting a distinctively American experience of ethnicity.[31] Edison made German, Scotch, and Irish records, ignoring the powerful religious, local, regional, and dialect traditions within such larger units, a form of cultural and musical reductionism practiced by Victor and Columbia on their far wider variety of ethnic records.

Such records clearly pleased many who answered Edison's 1921 survey. Mrs. William Murray of Colorado wrote: "These old Scotch songs [like "Annie Laurie"] bring to this household remembrance of Bonnie Scotland in bygone years." "I'm Irish and love Irish airs," wrote another, describing in the process how she represented herself to herself. A third reported: "We are only poor working people, but good [Irish] music is something to live for." Several males believed that records of their particular ethnic music served well to entertain and create a sense of common culture when inviting others of that ethnic group into their homes.

The returns from the 1921 Edison survey on the one hand overwhelmingly confirm that the phonograph became a mass-produced "private" shrine at which to summon forth spirits that allowed listeners momentarily to escape from the ravages of time into a domain in which dead loved ones seemed to live once again. Individuals answered Edison's questions, speaking more often for themselves alone than for their entire family or social circle; yet contrary to Eisenberg's hypothesis about the shattering of Victorian culture, Edison's records stirred the kinds of memories that for significant numbers of Americans reinforced, rather than shattered, the Victorian sense of cross-generational continuity in family, community, ethnicity, and nationality. The kind of social and psychological isolation that Eisenberg describes may well be more common among record collectors than among people unconcerned about possessing every record ever made in a given genre. If Edison's customers listened alone, they listened alone together.

Edison's records and his customers' reactions to them offer evidence of the powerful musical and cultural resonance that one phonograph company set in motion among its customers. Despite his unprecedented reputation, Edison's musical influence stopped far short of nationwide dominance. Edison, Inc. had long shared the market with Victor and Columbia, and the production of more diverse recorded sounds accelerated at the time of World War I when the original patents granted to Edison, Victor, and Columbia began to expire. New labels such as Okeh, Gennett, Vocalion, Brunswick, and Paramount began catering to new markets, producing a greater diversity of recorded sounds, associated with blues, jazz, and hillbilly.[32] Hearkening to Victor's 1917 recordings of the Original Dixieland Jazz Band, other companies began making records designed to sell to the urban working class, African Americans, and dance-crazy youngsters fascinated by the big city's dance halls and cabarets.

Many younger Americans of different ethnic backgrounds treated jazz records as invitations to daring open-ended experiences and reveled in their bright, swaggering musical language, one that seemed to defy traditional conventions of both popular and concert hall performance. Labeled as "vulgar," "illicit," and "out-of-control" by the gatekeepers of traditional musical culture, jazz records for that very reason appealed all the more to significant numbers of young Americans. As a result, from 1917 to 1945, jazz, blues, and hot social dance records contributed mightily to the process of creating new popular music cultures and more recently minted collective American "memories."

The relationship between jazz record customers and their records tended to be more active than that of Edison's listeners with theirs. Rather than sitting dreamily about, young record listeners with at least minimal musical training began an active aural study of recorded jazz performance techniques, turning their consumption of industrial recordings into the production of new jazz expressiveness.[33] The aspiring young white high schoolers who gathered in the western Chicago suburbs during the early 1920s, for example, provide a most clear-cut example of popular recorded jazz cultures. These self-styled members of the Austin High School Gang—Jimmy McPartland, Bud Freeman, and Frank Teschmacher—discovered hot dance music records at the local soda shop near Austin High School, turning an attentive ear to those by Paul Whiteman, Art Hickman, and Ted Lewis.[34]

One day, however, a record salesman slipped in some of the Gennett label's sides by the New Orleans Rhythm Kings, a white jazz band then playing at Friars' Inn in downtown Chicago. The youngsters "went out of our minds. Everybody flipped. It was wonderful." After one afternoon of repeated listening to these records, the young whites decided to try and imitate the NORK. They all wheedled musical instruments from their parents and started to meet in each other's family apartments to rehearse.

> What we used to do was put the record on—one of the Rhythm Kings', naturally—play a few bars, and then all get our notes. We'd have to tune our instruments up to the record machine, to the pitch, and go ahead with a few notes. Then stop! A few more bars of the record, each guy would pick out his notes and boom! we would go on and play it. Two bars, or four bars, or eight—we would get in on each phrase and then all play it.

After several months of this aural phonograph-centered apprenticeship, the youngsters had built up a repertoire of a dozen or so tunes and began "playing out" at school dances and the like. So it was that young Americans created whole worlds for themselves from phonograph records, stubbornly turning their initial adolescent impressions of what were only industrial commodities into a lifelong pursuit of jazz mastery and recollection.

Out in Davenport, Iowa, in a white-painted Victorian home, Leon "Bix" Beiderbecke, a shy German-American youngster, had shown a prodigious talent for playing "with improvements" anything he had once heard on the family's parlor piano. When in 1917 the Original Dixieland Jass Band recorded for Victor, some of their sides made it onto the Beiderbeckes' windup parlor phonograph: "Little Bickie," as he was then called, was never to be the same.

While he had resisted his mother's injunctions to practice the piano, he now practiced for hours a day, setting up the family phonograph just to the left of the piano and pushing the turntable speed lever back to its slowest point to pick out, note for note, the phrases of cornetist Nick LaRocca.[35] After enough practice, he could return the speed lever to its normal position and play along with the ODJB records. Upon returning from parties, his parents frequently found their son huddled over the graphophone in isolated concentration. They never did understand what was happening to him, either not seeing or not caring that their son had created for himself some personal space within the family as well as a growing sense of personal identity. Records led Beiderbecke to intense musical practice and then to shared performance experience with like-minded apprentice musicians. Years later, upon returning home to rest from his work in the nationally famous Paul Whiteman band, Bix found that his parents had never even bothered to open the packages of his own recordings with which he had thought to impress them. Bix Beiderbecke was a cardinal example of the power of the phonograph to create swiftly spinning new musical worlds that young and immensely talented Americans interpreted and used in creative ways. His parents remained telling examples of the dangers of taking the phonograph for granted.

Phonograph records also moved many youngsters to want to collect jazz records and to write about the music engraved on them. In the years just after the worst of the depression, for example, increasing numbers of young, college-age, white, middle-class males, turned back their attention to those hotly agitated recorded musical memories from the Roaring Twenties, creating for their own and for coming generations an influential published dialog on the meaning of jazz. This rebellious new jazz criticism, strongly dependent upon recorded music, at least at the start, thereby placed a social and intellectual distance between the listener and the musical performer. They created a canon of what they regarded as artistically significant jazz recordings.

In sharp contrast to the passive acceptance of many Edison listeners, the sympathetic vibrations among the new jazz record collectors and commentators touched off dynamic patterns of consumer activity. More than any other single American, Marshall Stearns provided leadership for the new breed of college-age jazz writers and collectors of jazz records who were to have a major impact on defining the cultural and musical significance of recorded jazz.

Stearns, who founded the Institute of Jazz Studies at Rutgers University, provides an outstanding example of some record collectors' active, intellectual engagement with recorded sound. Born in Cambridge, Massachusetts, in 1908, he graduated with a B.S. degree from Harvard in 1931 before attending Harvard Law School for two years. Much to the chagrin of his father, a member of the Massachusetts State Legislature and a friend of Calvin Coolidge, the younger Stearns quit law school in 1934 to enroll in the English Ph.D. program at Yale where he received his doctorate in 1942 after teaching at the University of Hawaii and Indiana University. While a graduate student, Stearns, in order to make up for the lack of any recognition of jazz in higher education, "consulted with" sociologist of race Melville J. Herskovits, George Herzog in Cultural Anthropology, and Henry Cowell, Roger Bass, and John Kuypens in Musicology.[36]

Throughout his years in higher education, Stearns pursued his fascination with jazz, hoping "to facilitate the universal progress of swing music, backed by the conviction that it is a worthy cultural object of study."[37] To this end, he founded the Yale Hot Club, a group of jazz record collectors, and affiliated clubs sprang up at Princeton, Dartmouth, and Syracuse, organizing jazz concerts and promoting jazz through campus newspapers. Stearns soon began writing a column entitled "Swing Stuff" in *Variety*. Thereafter, he also wrote articles on jazz for *Down Beat*, *Metronome*, and *Tempo*. Stearns therefore founded the organized movement in the United States to use phonograph records in a systematic study of jazz and swing.

Stearns soon discovered an invaluable ally in Milton Gabler, who, in 1935, along with John Hammond, organized a federation of campus hot clubs called the United Hot Clubs of America devoted to the appreciation and reissue of earlier jazz recordings. In 1936, Gabler, who had fallen in love with records of Louis Armstrong, Red Nichols, and Duke Ellington while working in his father's record store, opened his own Commodore Record Shop on West 42nd Street in New York City; it quickly became a "shrine" for jazz musicians and record buffs.[38] At the same time, Gabler started his own independent Commodore record label devoted to inter-racial jazz recording. With the cooperation and guidance of Marshall Stearns and John Hammond, Gabler began reissuing jazz records from the 1920s as "classics" of the genre on the U.H.C.A. label.

As cultural historian Neil Leonard has argued so effectively, a religious devotion no less intense and lasting than that of the neo-Victorians to whom Edison, Inc. catered deeply penetrated the intellectual ambitions of jazz record aficionados. Recorded music styles may have differed significantly, but the emotional resonance of recorded sound itself remained much the same whatever one's particular taste. Edison's devotees traced their shared musical memories back to England and Scotland via Stephen Foster and the members of the United Hot Clubs of America traced their shared musical memories back to Gennett's recordings of Joseph "King" Oliver's Creole Jazzband and Louis Armstrong's Hot Five and Seven recordings for the Okeh label.

As the negative comments of the Edison survey returns indicate, "jazz" records created a potent modernist countermemory that flourished in tension with the neo-Victorian sensibilities of Edisonian popular culture. Records acted to immortalize the early instrumentalists and bands selected by aficionados and stimulated a new form of historical writing about America's musical and cultural past. As John Gennari has shown,[39] two schools of thought emerged among the first generation of jazz writers about the importance of jazz to America's national identity: one, an American school of jazz writing that included Frederic Ramsey, Jr., Charles Edward Smith, Rudi Blesh, Sidney Finkelstein, John Henry Hammond, Winthrop Sargeant, Otis Ferguson, and Alan Lomax; the other, a European school of jazz writing led by Andre Coeuroy, Robert Goffin, Hugues Panassie, Charles Delaunay, and Leonard Feather.

The rise in the late depression years of a group of Americans who were to devote their lives to jazz writing took its origins in an appreciation of jazz, blues, and hot dance band records. Nat Hentoff discovered "a fierce wailing of brass and reeds, a surging, pulsing cry of yearning" one day while walking through Boston's Kenmore Square. The powerful music came from a record of Artie Shaw's "Nightmare" playing on a phonograph in Krey's department store. The young and poor Jewish American youngster turned to buying records of Shaw, Ellington, Armstrong, and Billie Holiday even though his family possessed no phonograph on which to play them. Rather, Hentoff followed the activities of the jazz musicians in *Down Beat* magazine and savored the heated discussions about the music that animated his peers.

Many swing fans found meaning in the records themselves. The very act of gaining ownership of a valued jazz record became an integral part of the meaning that a fan attributed to the music. Collecting records became an enduring passion, an intellectual preoccupation, and a way of life. Dan Morgenstern, now director of the Institute of Jazz Studies at Rutgers University in Newark, New Jersey, first got interested in his mother's and his aunt's jazz-inflected dance band records as a youngster during the depression years in Vienna and became "a child of the Swing Era."[40] As World War II approached, jazz became increasingly popular, acting for many, but especially for youngsters like Morgenstern, as a gesture against Nazism.

For Morgenstern, records had a socializing as well as a musical function, for they led him to contacts with a number of like-minded youngsters in Austria, Denmark, and Sweden. Sometimes, older boys revealed the secrets of records that he had yet to find on his own. By the same token, knowledge of records earned Morgenstern the respect of older youngsters. A friend his own age introduced him to alto saxophonist Benny Carter's records.

When at age 16 Morgenstern began collecting seriously—reading the pioneering books on jazz, comparing notes with other collectors, and finding his way to sources of records—he became adept at what he later believed to have been 78 rpm record culture. In a time before widespread record reissues, one was forced to hunt down copies on one's own. This necessity led to a detailed knowledge of the secondhand bookstores, junk shops, flea markets, and sidewalk browser bins where the occasional jewel awaited. Once he immigrated to New York City in 1947, Morgenstern quickly found his way to the 6th Avenue shops between 40th and 50th streets and the 7th Avenue stores below Union Square. He and other collectors would meet to talk about jazz at Big Joe's, a record store walk-up on 47th Street between 6th and 7th Avenues. Jerry Wexler similarly remembered the "shadowy streets" and "dark alleys" under the elevated subway tracks in Harlem, the Bronx, Queens, and Brooklyn that were breeding grounds for the kind of furniture stores that sold used phonographs and records.[41]

Moreover, 78 rpm records, when they are compared to the extended and long-play albums that came later, created a more highly focused listening experience. One purchased two short musical performances, rather than twelve to sixteen of them, and therefore listened more closely to each performance. When one side or the other turned out to offer the significant musical material, one often played and replayed just that part—the solo statement or the exciting ensemble passage—until it was nearly worn out.

Morgenstern had plenty of company in his involvement with jazz records. Walter Schaap remembered not just the music on his favorite swing record, but also the particular circumstances under which he discovered a used copy of it. He learned when to hang around the soda foutains' juke boxes as the records were changed; he could buy some for 10¢ and even if the latest popular hit turned out to be badly worn, the other side, sometimes a great jazz instrumental performance, could remain in mint condition. He came to judge the depth of his acquaintances' knowledge of jazz by the signs of wear on their records.[42] Critic and writer Ira Gitler measured his maturity by his increasing ability to make judicious purchases of jazz records. Russell Sanjek went door-to-door in Harlem looking for vintage 1920s jazz and blues records. During the 1930s, Chicago jazz aficionado "Squirrel" Ashcraft, later head of contract services for the CIA, combed the south side of Chicago for old jazz and blues records. The young Martin Williams, who was to become perhaps the most influential of all the jazz writers, cherished the hours he was able to spend in Ross Russell's Dial record shop in Los Angeles while on shore leave from the navy.

Where Edison's records had exerted a dominant power linked to ongoing memories of the paternal family, respect for the past, and veneration of Victorian values, the jazz, blues, and dance records produced by Columbia, Okeh, Vocalion, Brunswick, and other companies were welcomed within the family by sons, daughters, and grandchildren who used them to negotiate their own individual sense of identity and social space both within the family and then beyond it. Eldridge Johnson and Thomas Edison succeeded in inserting the phonograph into the domestic life of a broad spectrum of Americans, but it turned out to serve more than the interests of the heads of families.

The grooves of phonograph records sometimes stimulated and gave expression to a host of ill-defined emotions that surged below the surface of middle-class family life. Descriptions written by jazz writers about their early lives sometimes suggest that tensions revolving around questions of authority and submission played an important role in their powerful reactions to records. The young Leonard Feather developed a strong and growing interest in records just as he felt most acutely his "resentment of forced attitudes," a way of describing the strict religious and ethnic conformity expected by his parents. In retrospect, he believed that his subconscious rebellion against social and religious values had "started early." When he skipped synagogue for jazz concerts, his father's displeasure was unable to stem the growth of his son's record collection.[43]

As his father's displeasure mounted, the young Feather found himself increasingly attracted to American popular culture. A saxophone-playing school chum accompanied him to Levy's record shop in whitechapel, a Jewish district in London's East End. There he heard Louis Armstrong's "West End Blues" for the first time:

> I was hooked. Though I was not to realize it for many years, this episode in the listening-room of a record shop, not long before I turned fifteen, would determine the pattern of my life.

"West End Blues" provided a sense of direction, a lifestyle, an obsessive concern with every aspect of jazz, as nothing had before. All that mattered from that moment was the next record release or the latest transatlantic news item.[44]

So too, Martin Tudor Hansfield Williams, son of similarly upper middle-class parents who never listened to records and expected great professional achievement from their son, insisted on trying to impress his mother with jazz records played on his own bedroom phonograph. Both she and his father remained completely unmoved by them, convinced that their son was throwing his life away on socially unacceptable music. Similarly, Marshall Stearns's father "was really horrified" upon learning that his son had gone from listening to jazz records to palling around with jazz musicians.[45] Record producer Bob Thiele's mother "was positive her son had developed an incurable mental condition" when he began to listen seriously to jazz records.[46]

The phonograph's power spread the taste for blues, jazz, and hot dance music well beyond American shores. In Europe, collecting American records took on new levels of continental political meaning from the context of European life in the 1920s and 1930s. Charles Delaunay, son of French modernist painters Robert and Sonia Delaunay, invented the field of serious jazz discography, producing his first reference work in 1936 and culminating his lifelong labors with the *New Hot Discography* that appeared in 1948. Delaunay heard in Louis Armstrong records a distant sound of basic human significance that he juxtaposed to the rampant commercialism of America's show business establishment.

At the same time, Delaunay treasured American jazz records as the saving remnant of modern artistic genius in the Franco-American battle against German fascism. He and other members of the Hot Club de France carefully buried what they regarded as their priceless American and European jazz records to keep them out of German hands and sheltered from German bombs. From his vantage point, America, thoroughly corrupted by its rampant materialism, had still produced Black jazz records of timeless significance.

While living at a substantial distance from the actual people of color who made jazz records, many European lovers of jazz records developed intense feelings of admiration for such Black instrumentalists and band leaders as Sidney Bechet, Louis Armstrong, Count Basie, Duke Ellington, and later for Miles Davis, Charlie Parker, Charles Mingus, and others. The power of artfully played music itself joined with the phonograph's intensely focused repetitions to stimulate moments of recognition that wedded the alienation of youth to empathy with African American suffering and renewal.

Among the fanatical French devotees of recorded jazz, none played a more prominent historical role in the ongoing interpretation of records than writer Hugues Panassié, who, like most French people, had relatively few occasions to interact with African Americans but nonetheless developed through his exposure to jazz records a fervid devotion to "authentic" Black music. In his autobiography, Panassié recalled first being attracted to the phonograph in his family's Gironde chateau when he was five or six years old: the family's old Pathé machine, on which the tone arm started near the center and then moved outward toward the disc's edge, "was very beautiful; it fascinated me."[47] The young Panassié passed whole days listening to the latest dance records, particularly after falling ill with polio. In order to keep his left leg from more debilitating atrophy, he was given extensive social dance lessons in the tango, one-step, fox-trot, and Charleston. One of the better French jazz saxophonists, Christian Wagner, gave him saxophone lessons and brought him the records of Bix Beiderbecke, Frank Trumbauer, and Fletcher Henderson.

The chance actually to meet and hear in person one of the artists on his records of Chicago Jazz brought Panassié to L'Ermitage Mouscovite, a Parisian club where Chicagoan Milton "Mezz" Mezzrow was playing alto saxophone. The young Panassié fell under the spell of the older, self-assured, assertive American who passionately insisted upon the superiority of records made by Louis Armstrong to all the records Panassié had collected up to that time. Panassié, being white and French, came to defer to the older white American jazzman who lived among African Americans in Harlem and doggedly espoused their cause. Some years later, Panassié traveled to New York and promoted a series of recording sessions designed to bring what he understood to have been "the old New Orleans style" of jazz back to life. In this way, a primitivist circle of resonance, created and maintained by whites involved in Black music, crossed and recrossed the Atlantic.[48]

Less socially and ethnically distanced from the greats of early jazz, African Americans who wrote about records tended to be working newspapermen with regular columns devoted to show business in general in the leading Black newspapers. Journalists like Dave Peyton of the Chicago *Defender* noted new record issues by Black jazzmen within much longer and more detailed descriptions of live performances and a broader range of professional activities.

As Paul F. Berliner has convincingly demonstrated, by World War II and perhaps earlier, African American involvement with jazz records greatly contributed to creating a tradition of African American jazz performance. People "could listen to jazz all day long" on the juke boxes of Cleveland's neighborhood restaurants and bistros in the 1940s. Many gathered in record stores to catch the latest sounds, but the homes of some musicians looked like record stores. Some developed cooperative record-sharing "extended families" who circulated records from house to house. Children often involved themselves closely with their parents' record collections, strengthening family ties by learning to sing or hum often-played numbers from the older generation's record collections. When relations between parents and children became difficult, some children used jazz records to create a world of cherished musical "friends."[49]

The phonograph therefore exerted a powerful cultural influence and awakened listeners to music that they otherwise could not have heard in their own communities. The often repeated argument that records extended the experience of the world's most beautiful music to those outside the rarified social circles that traditionally had enjoyed it should not be limited to one musical category such as "classical music." The phonograph communicated many different styles of music that sounded excitingly fresh and unpredictable to many different groups in American society.

The experience of listening to phonograph records was capable of inspiring intense emotional reactions that sometimes endured throughout lifetimes of experience. Not simply solitaries, phonograph record lovers listened "alone together," discovering in mediated engravings of past musical expressiveness parallel avenues to shared social and cultural circles of resonance, ones that led them to active forms of musical knowledge and involvement. These circles of phonographic resonance demonstrate important patterns of popular consumer reaction to the recorded sound. It is time now to retrace the phonograph's deep involvement in popular culture.

2

"THE CONEY ISLAND CROWD"

The Phonograph and Popular Recordings before World War I

Amid the roar of the 'L' trains, the clatter of wagons and carts, the babble of voices and and hucksters' cries . . . came the music of the talking machine.

—"On the Bowery,"
Talking Machine World, 1919

[M]ost manufacturers would prefer to record only the highest class of music, but they aim to supply the market with what is demanded, and popular songs and talking records are good sellers. The manufacturers are not in business for the benefit of their health, nor as music educators pure and simple.

—"On the Bowery,"
Talking Machine World, 1911

In the 1890s, before the phonograph industry had time to erect what became in the nineteen teens a tidy facade of domestic bourgeois respectability, another largely forgotten world of coin-operated cylinder machines spun forth raucous worlds of popular entertainment. This other, earlier, and formative phonographic world, so suggestive of the juke box circles of the 1930s, provides ample evidence that the industry planted strong roots in turn-of-the-century popular culture.

The phonograph's inventor had not especially encouraged this context for his machine. In 1877, Thomas A. Edison had invented a functioning prototype of a "phonograph": a machine that recorded and played back his own voice. The inventor had had a practical idea in mind; he had been trying to discover how to store telegraphic messages for later retransmission at a higher rate of speed. The first working phonograph had given even the level-headed scientist and inventor reason to pause: he later remarked that upon hearing his voice reemerge from the machine "I was never so taken aback in my life." That marvelous and unprecedented experience of a "talking machine" would soon astound and captivate the entire country, encouraging optimistic and in some important ways intimate relationships with technology. Many Americans would soon learn to use recorded entertainment as a significant new means of holding reminders of the past in suspension with reactions to the present.[1]

The phonograph, it should be recalled, entered American life in a number of different guises, first as an office dictation machine, then as a forerunner of what came in the 1930s to be called the "juke box," and ultimately as a home entertainment device. Most Americans first encountered the new sound technology during the 1890s in the form of "automatic phonographs," a clever redesign of Edison's original invention that had been able to both record and play back. The automatic phonograph reserved the recording function to the company and could only play back commercially manufactured records. Single-cylinder phonographs, at first powered by heavy and unwieldy batteries and later by spring-driven motors, played and replayed one two-minute recording when someone inserted a nickel in the slot. Such automatic phonographs came with either one or several pairs of listening tubes. These listening devices enhanced the thin, scratchy sound of the early cylinder machines and also served to forestall criticism of the phonograph for polluting the environment with noise. More important, the ear tubes gave the listener the impression that the music and entertainment he or she heard was inside his or her own head, thereby deepening the social and psychological impact of their introduction to recorded sound.[2]

Automatic phonographs were pioneered at the grass roots level. In 1888, a firm called North American Phonograph Company headed by Philadelphia investor Jesse Lippincott, purchased Edison's patents and created thirty-three semi-independent, geographically defined subsidiaries primarily to lease phonographs as office dictation machines. Unhappily, the cylinders and phonographs manufactured at that time did not prove sturdy enough for constant office use. What people choose to do with machines is just as important as what the machines do to them, and stenographers of that day seem to have seen the new contraptions as a threat to their profession and therefore may have sabotaged them. Moreover, the idea of renting rather than selling these machines limited profits by increasing the overhead expenses of the phonograph companies. When, therefore, the office dictaphone business proved a major disappointment, those working in the regional affiliates cast about for some other profit-making venture and began to transform the phonograph into a vehicle of entertainment and diversion.

The process of redefining the talking machine moved from the ground up. Louis Glass, the little-known general manager of North American Phonograph Company's West Coast subsidiary—the Pacific Phonograph

Company—set up two coin-operated cylinder playback machines with multiple listening tubes in the Palais Royale Saloon in San Francisco on November 23, 1889. He patented the coin device that controlled each pair of listening tubes. Each of his first two machines had grossed more than $1,000 in nickels by May 14, 1890. Glass reported on these activities at the 1890 convention of local phonograph companies, emphasizing the money to be made, the relative lack of maintenance costs, and the encouraging way in which saloon habitues developed the habit of playing coin-operated phonographs. Any man who put a nickel in one machine was highly likely to try the other one and to repeat the pattern night after night.[3]

Soon thereafter, the Columbia Phonograph Company, under the leadership of two court reporters—Edward D. Easton and Roland F. Cromelin—also branched out on its own and pioneered the recording of popular musical entertainment. So, too, the Ohio Phonograph Company, also a regional affiliate of North American, turned, under the local leadership of President James L. Andem, to developing a musical entertainment market on the local level.[4]

To encourage popular acceptance of the new talking machines, these "automatic phonographs" or "coin-ops" were set up with a cylinder-reading apparatus that resembled a small metal lathe in a locked glass case set upon a pedestal. Often, an announcement card, a stylized painting of the title of the recorded material, usually a song, had been mounted above the phonograph casement. As the customer listened to the one featured recording, he could watch the needle's progress as the cylinder turned inside the glass case. The U.S. Phonograph Company of Newark, New Jersey, advised that "cabinets be kept highly polished, the glass clean, the machines bright, and announcement cards fresh and interesting, the tubing white."[5] Customers were supposed to enjoy watching the machine and its movements while listening to the recorded music.

The relatively small automatic phonographs that played one cylinder were placed in a variety of public places where large numbers of Americans gathered: in train stations, ferry boat landings, trolley waiting rooms, shopping districts, carnivals, circuses, amusement parks, hotels, lunch rooms, cafes, and saloons—semipublic places that did not collect an admission charge.[6] At the outset, automatic phonograph owners or the persons who had leased such machines for $125 a year (they could be purchased for $250) rented the necessary space, sometimes by paying a percentage of the coin machine's earnings to those who owned it.[7] As the automatic phonograph's popularity grew, the owners and managers of hotels, restaurants, and saloons offered free space to coin-in-the-slot operators, since the automatic phonographs themselves helped to attract the public into their establishments.

Coin machine entrepreneurs hired young men to make the rounds of the machines daily, repairing broken ones, replacing worn-out cylinders, removing the variety of foreign objects—slugs, foreign currency, gum, pebbles—all too often discovered in the machines. As a schoolboy, the

young Frederick William Gaisberg, later a leader in the recording industry, installed dozens of these machines in saloons, restaurants, and beer
gardens and was occasionally berated by an irate bartender when the
machines accepted money without playing the cylinder.[8]

During the 1890s, the fledgling phonograph companies hit upon the
idea of "phonograph parlors," arcades located near centers of urban
public transportation and filled with coin-operated sound machines.
These phonograph parlors solved the problem of having only one recording to offer and focused popular public attention on the phonograph as
a glamorous auditory experience of commercialized popular music culture. They also exploited more fully the valuable observation that people
tended to move from machine to machine enjoying a variety of short
musical distractions. According to the Edison Company, few people
visited a phonograph parlor without spending at least 10¢ and often 25¢
or more.[9]

The phonograph parlors of the 1890s introduced short samples of the
sounds of American popular music into the public urban world of "cheap
amusements," commercialized entertainments like the concert saloon,
musical hall, vaudeville theater, dime museum, and burlesque hall that
flourished in the emerging bright-light neighborhoods of American
cities.[10] The cylinder recordings they supplied to the slot machines were
intended to reflect and improve upon the shared public leisure patterns
of urban working-class neighborhoods. Coin-ops provided the opportunity for masses of individuals in crowded public places to escape into a
few intensely focused moments of bright, optimistic, and ultimately reassuring urbane musical entertainment that also contained a variety of
revealing commentaries about the modern urban world.[11]

The industry went out of its way to associate the experience of the
phonograph with the glamour and electrical excitement of the swiftly
approaching twentieth century. In 1893, the Columbia Phonograph
Company opened a phonograph parlor on the ground floor of its office
building at 919 Pennsylvania Avenue, in Washington, D.C. Passersby
were attracted by a dazzling room filled with "fifty, sixty, or even as many
as one hundred" slot machines, the walls lined with mirrors "lavishly"
illuminated with electric lights. The automatic phonographs had been
arranged along the walls or "grouped back to back in the open floor space
to allow visitors to make their way from one machine to another." People
lined up to take their turns at individual machines while others waited
on the sidewalk outside.[12]

Despite the inventor's reputation for opposing the use of his invention
for entertainment purposes, Thomas A. Edison's National Phonograph
Company eventually opened its own phonograph parlor in New York
City's Union Square. Early in this century, the NPC ran thirteen such
sound parlors in a variety of American cities and claimed that two hundred thousand people visited them on holidays. The Union Square parlor offered nearly one hundred Edison coin-slot phonographs; they were
said to remain "in constant operation . . . as a continual stream of young,

old, poor and well-to-do flow through the brilliantly lighted doorways." As the Edison Company put it, "rural . . . folks visiting the city are attracted by the glamour and glare of these places."[13]

While willing to note that the coin-op business existed and even that it served to sustain the struggling industry at a crucial early moment in its long history, most historians and chroniclers of the talking machine have treated its recordings as a regrettable embarrassment. Since neither the machine nor its recordings yet echoed the music of the conservatory, concert hall, or *soirée musicale*, Roland Gelatt, for example, simply dismissed the era of coin-op recording. But emphasizing that the era of the automatic phonograph was not "high brow" says too little about what it was. Automatic phonographs provided forms of popular commercial entertainment that suspended visions of an earlier rural and agricultural America within urban, commercial perspectives more in touch with contemporary sensibilities.

The automatic phonograph's ancestors in the world of entertainment—the minstrel show and vaudeville theaters—had proliferated in the nineteenth century but had never become as ubiquitous as the nickel and penny slot machines. Carefully placed in the most public places where the largest number of people congregated, the automatic phonographs were designed to attract and provide entertainment to transient people who roamed the streets, waiting rooms, saloons, vaudeville theaters, and movie houses of urban America, often with only a few coins in their pockets. Thus the founding era of the coin-operated phonograph business developed a new socially democratic type of popular entertainment enterprise that seemed, like electricity itself, the movies, and show business, to define what was "modern" about the modern world.

Automatic phonographs, for example, were often intermixed with a variety of other slot machines, specializing in the sounds of the new modern world. When the nickel-operated phonographs were interspersed with other types of coin-operated machines that accepted pennies, the resulting attraction was labeled a "penny arcade." Phonograph entrepreneurs often invested in selling postcards, movies, baseball equipment, photographic equipment, bicycles, motorcycles, roller skates, vacuum cleaners, sheet music, games of all sorts, and fishing rods.[14] They often sold or leased not only automatic phonographs but "talking scales," player pianos, and a wide variety of slot machines that printed cards, told fortunes, tested muscular strength, and sold candy, chewing gum, hot peanuts, towels, and soap.[15] Such machines were often leased or sold at cost so long as the customer signed a contract for the goods that the machines purveyed.

The class-conscious Edison National Phonograph Company, which went into the business of making coin-operated phonographs but ostentatiously refused to service them thereafter, took advantage of pricing wars with Columbia to set-up "penny vaudevilles . . . poor people's theaters." In Buffalo, New York, for example, twenty-eight Edison automatic phonographs were lined up next to the kinetoscope peephole motion picture machines in the vestibule of Vitascope Hall, the first "deluxe" motion picture house in the city. New York City's Union Square presented "Automatic One Cent Vaudeville," "the greatest nickleodeon" in the country.

The exciting sounds of the urban nickleodeon and penny arcade reached large numbers of Americans. One 1907 estimate claimed that an average of 100,000 people per day or 36.5 million people per year visited Chicago's "five cent theaters."[16] In New York City during the same year, the police department reported that more than 400 penny arcades "and similar places where phonographs, moving pictures, and mechanical pianos furnish the entertainment" enlivened the street scene. One arcade entrepreneur estimated that a fortune awaited anyone lucky enough to own an arcade on the main thoroughfare in any city of 15,000 or more inhabitants.[17] The average coin-operated phonograph took in about $50 a week, an excellent return on the original investment.[18]

The coin-op business served as advertising for the phonograph, encouraging public admiration for "the machine with a soul" while whetting the public taste for recorded entertainment. As early as 1896, Edison introduced a sturdy cylinder model intended for home use—the Edison Standard Phonograph—selling for $20. This stimulated Columbia to market a take-home "Eagle" cylinder model one year later selling for only $10, the equivalent of one U.S. gold eagle coin; and so the phonograph began its nearly 100-year history as a constantly changing form of home entertainment.[19] Compared to later price schedules, the earliest home machines cost very little and would have been available to masses of Americans.

The Columbia Phonograph Company also produced the greatest number and variety of popular music entertainment records made for both coin-operated phonographs and the new flat disc machines that Columbia marketed early in 1901–1902. A survey of record company catalogues indicates that all of the companies offered more military-style marching band music than any other single type of musical recording before World War I. The sales of military-style concert wind ensembles must have been excellent, for they dominated all record catalogs before 1910.[20] This martial style of music, with its numerous brass instruments that recorded well, found fitting visual expression in the sharply angled listening horn of the cylinder phonograph.

That recordings of military-style instrumental music should lead all other types comes as no surprise: over twenty years ago, historian John Higham described the popular spiritual reaction in the America of the 1890s against "the growing restrictions of a highly industrialized society." Americans looked to "break out of the frustrations, the routine, the sheer dullness of urban-industrial culture" and to be "young, masculine, and adventurous." This spirit encouraged a "muscular," manly, martial spirit in music and found encouragement and symbolic leadership in the public persona of President Theodore Roosevelt.[21] As Rupert Hughes described the music of John Philip Sousa: "The music is conceived in a spirit of high martial zest. It is proud and gay and fierce, thrilled and thrilling with triumphs. . . ."[22] Industry publicity promised that buyers of recorded military marching music would discover that "something swells up inside you and you wish you were going to war or doing something daring and heroic."[23] Record and phonograph salesmen encouraged potential customers to remember that the music recorded by the United States Marine Corps Band formerly had been reserved for the ears of the President of the United States alone.[24]

This musical style functioned, moreover, as cultural historian Neil Harris has argued,[25] as a "culture of reassurance" to a wide variety of Americans of all classes who felt threatened by industrial America's increasing social, economic, and political unrest and violence. Military-style wind ensembles recalled for many people, who were otherwise bitterly divided by class and economic interests, a united national spirit; the public band concert had functioned as "a ritual testifying to the unspoiled benevolence of national life," march tunes "aural icons for the era's patriotism and commercialism."[26] The phonograph spread these sensibilities far beyond the reach of the traditional band concerts, carrying reminders of the sounds of band concerts and mixing short patriotic musical recollections more thoroughly than ever before with other patterns of commercialized urban entertainment.

A study of company catalogs reveals how pervasive recorded military-style music was in this period and also how the genre provided a framework or structure for the public's assumptions about a wide range of perceptions less directly associated with a military frame of mind. For example, the United States Marine Band, Patrick S. Gilmore's Band, The Columbia Band, Issler's Band, and other prominent recording outfits waxed not only a very large number of concert-style marches, incorporating a variety of stylistic variations from the nineteenth century, but also recorded other musical styles.[27] A typical list of "march music" records usually included a variety of social dance music subspecialties labeled "waltzes," "polkas," "galops," "yorkes," "schottisches," "cakewalks," and "ragtime." No composer credits were included for such social dance numbers, so that they were thought to supply a generic need for mostly traditional social dance steps.

The military wind ensemble instrumentation and group sound also defined the 1890s' approach to recorded instrumental virtuosi. Columbia catalogs included lists of cornet, trombone, piccolo, and even clarinet solos by the stars of the leading military and concert wind ensembles. In part, these recordings may have been suggested by the difficulty with which late nineteenth-century recording technology encompassed the wind ensemble. Military bands were reduced in size to twelve to fifteen instruments for recording purposes and, of course, their selections had to be radically truncated to fit the two-to-three-minute recording time limit. Whatever the cause, recordings of solo wind instrument virtuosi from the military bands further encouraged a public taste for wind instruments rather than stringed ones whose sound carried poorly through the early recording apparatus. People also became accustomed to listening to records in order to admire virtuoso instrumental solos.

Military band ensembles recorded a wide range of the patriotic anthems of European countries, so that listeners in the penny arcades and railroad stations heard the "Airs of All Nations" as filtered through military and patriotic sensibilities. In like manner, the first records of operatic overtures and melodies were recorded by the bands of Sousa, Issler, and Gilmore, who gave them a martial instrumental interpretation. Most surprisingly, given the musical ambitions of the genre, military wind ensembles also recorded popular novelty numbers from turn-of-the-century minstrel shows and vaudeville: "All Coons Look Alike to Me," "Whistling Rufus," "Mammy's Pumpkin Colored Coons," "Smokey Mokes," and "You've Got to Play Ragtime." Indeed, one scholar insists that "Sousa's Band was the first [marching band] organization to bring this music to the attention of the nation."[28]

The early record company catalogs indicate that military bands did bring together the stirring marches—"the [marching and dance] music of the people"—with transposed variety show and popular vaudeville hits and foreshortened selections from light opera, opera, and famous instrumental solos from European concert hall music. The marching band created a broad traditional instrumental musical consensus, a popular middle-class sound redolent of the band concert rituals of small-town America. Its repertoire contained elements of both working-class and upper-class musical traditions and it interpreted the entire range of musical styles for American audiences. As Walter Benjamin[29] and Evan Eisenberg have emphasized,[30] however, the phonograph changed the context in which musical messages were sent and received, lifting them out of the ritualized social contexts and transforming them into commercialized memories. The coin-op and early home phonographs began this process: gone from the experience of martial music were the carefully arranged and impeccable military uniforms, white gloves, and printed programs of Sousa's Marine Corps Band in concert, with the haughty all-powerful bandmaster conducting an elaborate program of inspirational music. In exchange for a small coin, a two-minute, fragmentary reminder of one or more pieces of military-style music issued from a machine located in a milling public or semipublic space where most people had nonmusical matters on their minds. Always aware of his public performances as theater, Sousa no doubt understood and lamented this destruction of the aura of his carefully staged live performances.

In a more positive sense, the early phonograph created a new infiltration of urban society in general with recollections of the small-town band concert. These short reminders of the "proud," "gay," and "thrilling" military band sensibilities briefly shut out the depression and tedium of everyday life. Such recorded musical sensibilities could be mixed in memory with contemporary sorts of activities and thoughts, two minutes of recorded music leaving a lingeringly proud, gay, and thrilling mood among ticket buyers, "hot dog" eaters, and street cleaners.

Despite the popularity of marching band records, the marriage of nascent recording industry and military wind ensemble was not altogether successful. Part of the problem was technical: the recording aparatus of the nineties could absorb only a wind ensemble reduced to half of its normal size. Similarly, most compositions had to be edited down to a brief two-to-three-minute segment, nowhere near enough time to capture an entire performance structure of the march tradition. The artistic ambitions of military-style wind ensembles soared well beyond the range of the humble cylinder phonograph.

All of these problems contributed to John Philip Sousa's outspoken and comprehensive criticism of the phonograph. Sousa never conducted recording sessions by the United States Marine Corps Band or even those of his own Sousa's Concert Band. First, the widely admired band leader sharply criticized the lack of copyright protection for composers such as himself whose compositions were widely recorded for sale by other bands without any copyright compensation. In 1906, Sousa urged the Joint Congressional Committee on Patents to adopt a new law to protect composers from profiteering record companies that defended themselves by saying that their product did not take the form of the musical notation that characterized the original compositions. When the Copyright Act was finally passed in 1909, its provisions for "mechanical royalties" from the record manufacturers to the music copyright holders were not established retroactively, and Sousa therefore never saw any royalties for the many records of his works made before 1909.[31]

But Sousa's criticisms went well beyond his own economic perspective. He, like the German sociologist of music Theodor Adorno after World War I, feared "a marked deterioration in American music and musical taste, an interruption in the musical development of the country." He proudly estimated that the American working class owned more pianos, violins, guitars, mandolins, and banjos than in all the rest of the world; but once they started listening to the phonograph, America's children would stop practicing and music teachers would be driven out of business.[32] These were criticisms that would continue to ring in the ears of phonograph leaders for years to come.

The popular recordings made by vaudeville-style vocalists, comedians, and instrumentalists before World War I emerged more directly than the military band tradition from the urban working-class world of popular entertainment into which the fledgling phonograph introduced itself when the anticipated profits from the dictaphone business were not forthcoming. The Columbia Phonograph Company openly embraced the world of popular entertainment, recognizing the insights of "showmen at fairs and resorts," who, according to Frederick Gaisberg, demanded records of popular songs and instrumental numbers.[33] The Edison Company and Victor Talking Machine Company both worked to brush their own involvement in "lowbrow" recordings under an imported rug of European operatic music. In fact, the determinedly "highbrow" Victor Talking Machine Company executives scornfully referred to their own

Black Label popular recordings as "Coney Island stuff." The popular entertainers responsible for those recordings proudly embraced the label and referred to themselves as "the Coney Island Crowd."[34]

Phonograph entrepreneurs first noticed many of the popular music recording artists of the pre–World War I era as these entertainers worked in railroad stations, on ferryboats, and in "beergardens and street corners," the same sorts of places where the coin-in-the-slot phonographs were to be located. Frederick Gaisberg discovered several performers in these kinds of environments. Singer Billy Golden, the first cylinder recording star, whose "Turkey in the Straw" was a best-seller, had been born in Cincinnati, Ohio, along with Pittsburgh the cradle of blackface minstrelsy. As a child, he sang and danced on the steamboats that traveled from St. Louis to New Orleans. He knocked around the South, acquiring what was then called a "rich Mississippi twang," and started on the minstrel stage in a blackface act at sixteen. George W. Johnson, the first African American recording star, had been born into slavery and subsequently became a wandering minstrel entertaining on ferry boats.[35] Similarly, vocalist Billy Murray's father, Patrick, was a blacksmith while his mother, Julia Kelleher Murray, had come to the United States from County Kerry, Ireland. Billy sang in honky-tonks, medicine shows, and small-time vaudeville before becoming a major recording star.[36] Baritone vocalist and comedy artist Len Spencer rebelled against his parents' middle-class values and lived among the sporting set in the District of Columbia's tenderloin district, a stone's throw from the White House.[37]

John H. Bierling (1869–1948), a tenor in many different vocal duets and quartets during the late nineteenth century, described how urban street singers in New York City moved into the recording business. A member of the first vocal quartet to be recorded, he went on to make hundreds of records before vocal difficulties drove him out of the business in 1913, at which time he became a record company executive.[38] Bierling was brought up "down in the old Fourteenth Ward—born and raised there; around Spring Street and the Bowery. Four of us fellows used to 'barber shop' on Saturday night and Sunday—good old fashioned melodies and sentimental ballads."[39]

In 1892 George J. Gaskin, also a tenor and a group member who went on to a long recording career, told Bierling about "a man named [Victor Hugo] Emerson who was manager of a concern over in Newark, New Jersey called the U.S. Phonograph Company, who wanted a good quartet to make some records for him." The group recorded in "a loft over some meat packing house about 50 by 100 and 20 feet, littered with machine boxes and barrels . . . piled-up everywhere."[40] Bierling, Gaskin, and the quartet were all signed by other recording firms and made hundreds of recordings of street singing.

In addition to thousands of straight popular song records, three different types of popular recordings characterized the work of the Coney Island Crowd: the "rube" or "hick" encounters the big city and modern world; a variety of comical portraits of Gay 90s Bowery types; and what turn-of-the-century recording companies considered to be the comical dimensions of ethnic and racial stereotypes. Each of these kinds of music and popular entertainment records placed what the record producers and recording artists seem to have intended as benevolent, heart-warming sketches of a variety of socially marginal farmers, immigrants, racial minorities, and bar flies against the context of middle-class conformity and assurance.

The recorded rube or hick character took a positive cast in its first incarnation by the amazingly popular Cal Stewart (1856–1919), called the "emperor of rural comedians" in Columbia Phonograph Company advertising. Stewart got his start at seven years of age, playing "a little pickaninny part in the Hidden Hand" and went on to do every sort of dialect character. Stewart's recordings of "Uncle Josh Weathersby" featured the drolly old-fashioned reactions of a stock New England farmer character to an expanding urban industrial world. Beginning in 1884, Stewart, "a large framed, fleshy, fat faced good natured" man began doing "Yankee Storyteller" routines; they came to include recordings like "Uncle Josh Weathersby's Visit to New York" (Col 33116) that satirized the crazy modernity of urban ways, and "Uncle Josh and the Labor Union" (Col 3601), a more overtly conservative political satire in which the farmer has to employ a "horse-turner's union" to turn his plow horse around at the end of each row.[41] The haymakers' union would stack the hay but a separate removers' union must carry it to the barn, and so on, in this nineteenth-century satire of twentieth-century ways. Cal Stewart's popular recording was entitled "Uncle Josh Buys an Automobile." The Uncle Josh records were still appearing in the last half of the 1920s and helped listeners to hold in suspension images of nineteenth-century white rural America and the urban twentieth century.[42]

In addition to their power to entertain, Cal Stewart's Uncle Josh Weathersby recordings communicated cultural information to a variety of immigrants milling around the public and semipublic spaces in American cities at the turn of the century. His humorous monologs functioned as cultural survival kits in recorded sound, allowing European and rural American immigrants who inserted their nickels into the slots to laugh at both Uncle Josh's bumpkin blunders and his buoyant rural perspective on the juggernaut of American urban life. Uncle Josh's humor must have appealed strongly to the thousands of recently arrived migrants to the city, catching and then enhancing, as he did, the lingering rural perspectives in their newly urban lives.

The tension between country and city, such a vital ingredient in early twentieth-century American sensibilities, took on a much more overtly urban working-class perspective in the recordings of Len Spencer and Ada Jones, who took on the roles of young people from the Bowery in New York City. The Bowery, located in lower Manhattan, was, according to Luc Sante,[43] stamped early on with the brand of "an idyllic spot gone to seed." Here a cross-section of urban society found diversion in "groggeries, flophouses, clip joints, brothels, fire sales, rigged auctions, pawnshops, dime museums, shooting galleries, dime-a-dance establishments, fortune-telling salons, lottery agencies, thieves' markets, and tattoo parlors, as well as theaters of the second, third, fifth, and tenth rank." The coin-operated phonograph should be added to the list.

The "Bowery Kid" emerged in post–Civil War vaudeville as a descendant of "Mose" the "Bowery b'hoy," the minstrel stage character of the 1840s, who was a "compound of East Side swell, gutter bum, and volunteer fire laddie," according to Richard Dorson.[44] The late nineteenth-century Bowery Boy formed a positive comic stereotype of the young, often Irish but usually mixed ethnic "street arab," an uneducated but resilient, tough-talking fellow who, according to the lyrics of one Len Spencer record of 1907 called "Kid From the Bowery" (Col 3786), was "light on his feet" and "fast with his dukes," pronounced "these" as "dese," "world" as "woild," and girl as "goil." The Bowery Boy's language became known as "New York talk" thanks to Edward Townsend's *Chimmie Fadden* and Stephen Crane's *Maggie*. His style, according to Luc Sante, included "the pearl grey or brown derby tilted over one ear, the suit in loud checks with a tight coat, worn over a pink striped shirt, with a flaring box overcoat thrown on top in the winter."[45] The Bowery Boy walked with a swagger known as the "hard walk" that became a dance step as well and was associated closely with "spieling," the tough dance described by historian Kathy Peiss as separating inner city workers from small-town decorum.[46]

The phonograph's leading "Bowery Boy" artist before 1910 was Leonard Garfield ("Len") Spencer, one of the most prolific of the early recording stars. Born in 1867 in Washington, D.C., where so much of the history of the phonograph began, Spencer came by his street culture through rebellion against his family's middle-class values. His mother, Sara Andrew Spencer, was a leading advocate of woman suffrage while his grandfather had originated the Spencerian handwriting method. Len worked in the family school but rebelled against their values and, like many another "Bohemian" rebel,[47] joined the sporting crowd where he was reputed to be a good poker player. Frederick Gaisberg later recalled seeing Spencer at an outside table on Pennsylvania avenue surrounded by Black and white customers as he wrote out calling cards in the ornate Spencerian script ending in matching doves. At some point thereafter Spencer's face was seriously disfigured by a razor slash, and the idea of a stage career, if indeed he had ever envisioned one, became problematic.

Len Spencer's booming baritone voice carried well on the early acoustic recordings, however, and he built an impressive career as a recording artist beginning with the short stentorian announcements that introduced the performer and material and moving on to performing vocal and comedy numbers alone and with a number of other artists. Jim Walsh, the leading expert on early recording stars, recognized Spencer as "the great originator of the phonograph"[48] who made thousands of different cylinders and discs. Records like "The Vagabonds" (Col 3786) and "Panhandle Pete's Patrol" (Vic 2063) cast a wry and comically sentimental glow on the ill-fated lives of New York's Lower East Side hoboes and bums. Listeners to these records would have assembled an imaginative world of charming and musically inclined social outcasts blithely living on the edge of self-destruction.

Len Spencer was a remarkably versatile performer who did rube numbers ("Reuben and Rachel"), Irish character sketches ("Sweet Peggy Magee"), Jewish specialties ("The Original Cohens"), animal imitations ("A Barnyard Serenade," "Knausmeyer and His Dog Schneider," "Daybreak at Calamity Farm," "A Scene at a Dog Fight"), and, as Leonard G. (not Len) Spencer, even recorded famous speeches by the leading American politicians of the day. He opened his own pioneering show business booking agency that he called The Home of Mirth, Melody and Ideas in New York's theater district.

Spencer's best work, however, found him paired with Ada Jones, whom James Walsh calls "the most popular female recording artist and one of the most popular regardless of sex in the world" during the first decade of this century.[49] Jones was the leading lady of the phonograph before World War I at a time when men overwhelmingly dominated all facets of the upstart industry. She created her own marvelously compelling interpretation of "Maggie," the Bowery Girl, often paired with Len Spencer's or Billy Murray's "Chimmie," but just as often snapping out the streetwise one-liners alone, bringing the songs to life with her bright, piercing alto voice. With all those male voices on the early popular recordings, Ada Jones's voice stood out.

As described by Luc Sante, the Bowery Girl of the vaudeville stage was "clad in a tight jacket with corseted waist, a long, somewhat bedraggled skirt, a nondescript hat perched on top and perhaps ornamented with a feather, typically a broken one."[50] Ada Jones recreated the sounds of the Bowery Girl's social worlds and attitudes for phonograph listeners and also cast her character amid the bright lights of the big-city amusement enterprises. Her records, like those of Len Spencer, demonstrated attractive, energetic, and stylish ways of being poor but proud and having a good time on the streets.

Very little is known about Ada Jones's early life. Born on June 1, 1873, in Oldham, Lancashire, England, where her father operated a public house known as The British Flag, Jones moved with her family to Philadelphia by 1879, started a stage career as "Little Ada Jones," and began her recording career in 1893–1894 on brown wax cylinders made by Thomas Edison, Inc. They were the earliest known commercial recordings of a female singing as a solo artist.[51]

Vocalist Billy Murray later claimed that he "discovered" her singing in Huber's Palace Museum, a dime museum at 106–108 East 14th street in Greenwich Village. He instantly concluded that she had what he called "pep," "ginger," "tabasco," and "spice." Jones's brightly good-humored personality came through the sound of her voice and she cheerfully impersonated Black women, German maidens, cowgirls, country damsels,

Irish colleens, Bowery tough girls, newsboys, and grandmothers. With Len Spencer, Ada Jones cut her recording of "Pals," a "Chimmie and Maggie" Bowery sketch that made her famous. "Pals" set the pattern for a series of such records variously titled "Peaches and Cream," "Jimmie and Maggie at the 'Merry Widow'," "Jimmie and Maggie at the Ball Game," and "Jimmie and Maggie at the Hippodrome." Two of her most popular solo records were "The Bird in Nellie's Hat" and "Just Plain Folks."[52]

Ada Jones's exceptional popularity among the early recording stars took its impetus from swiftly changing gender patterns in turn-of-the-century American cities. Historian Joanne J. Meyerowitz has described the urban social world from and to which Ada Jones sang, emphasizing the sharp increase in single working-class females living apart from their families in cities like turn-of-the-century Chicago and New York. She argues that "emerging [urban] popular culture industries like movies and cabarets used a newer image of vibrant, sexual 'women adrift' to titillate audiences and sell urban vitality." The phonograph records made by Ada Jones with Billy Murray and Len Spencer provided a channel for the romanticization and communication of these images to people of all classes. If, as Meyerowitz argues, middle-class and upper middle-class females adopted what she calls "blueprints of 'sexy' behavior" from working class models, phonograph records in general and those of Ada Jones in particular played a major role in the process.[53]

For example, Ada Jones cut a series of records of songs framed by audio sketches in which the Bowery Boy and Bowery Girl enjoyed and commented upon the rough-and-tumble urban leisure-time enterprises. In "Blondy and Her Johnny at an East Side Ball" (Vic 16265–B), for example, Jones and Spencer created a sound portrait of the human types, music, and camaraderie found at the Bowery dances organized by neighborhood social groups with political interests.[54] In their Bowery records, Jones and Spencer created recorded images of the bright light enterprises and stylishly saucy characters who enjoyed them. In Jones's solo record "Coming Home from Coney Isle," she sang and talked about her working-class character's blithe enjoyment of a day's trip by trolley car to and from Coney Island, complete with belligerent ethnic stereotypes, fist fights, Chimmie and Maggie routines, a drunk, and general hilarity.

Ada Jones was more aware of the cultural implications of her work than any of the other early recording artists. She enjoyed playing off popular against high culture, as in the Jones and Spencer recording of "Shakespeare in Travesty: Anthony and Cleopatra," and in "Jimmie and Maggie at the Merry Widow" she burlesqued both her adopted Bowery Girl accent and the affectedly upper-class accents of audience members discussing the play at intermission, sharply contrasting upper-crust pretensions with working-class wisdom. In a world of swiftly passing one-liners, her hardy deformation of a society lady's decolletage as "de cold tea," stands out. When Chimmie explains that the Hippodrome is a dance hall, she quickly replies, "Oh, I'm hip."

Ada Jones's portraits of urban working-class women emphasized their buoyant independence and unsentimental freedom from Victorian propriety. The image she created, for example, of a young woman whose boyfriend is stolen by and then married to her mother relies for its power on the ingenue's brightly knowing manner in singing "And Now I Have to Call Him Faaather." Jones offered working-class listeners a dry-eyed rejoinder to the Victorian sentimentalization of the family.

In an outspoken article, widely reprinted in the recording trade publications, Ada Jones spoke out forcefully in defense of both her work and her materials. She insisted that she sang "the everyday songs for everyday people." As she put it:

> My work has brought me a profound respect for my profession. I have come to take a delight in interpreting the songs that are born of the people. They express the real sentiments of the times with far greater fidelity than the productions of cultured and educated musicians who look to other countries and other times for their themes and inspirations.

Interpreting the phonograph as the voice of the people, Ada Jones continued:

> I believe that the world is enriched by the melodies and sentiments that come from the masses. Only a fragmentary portion of either classical or popular music becomes immortal, and fully as much "popular" music survives as does classical. I like ragtime because I feel that it is typically American. It is alive, virile, dashing, and stimulating.[55]

To reverse a saying that would become popular in the industry around World War I: Ada Jones made records for the masses, not the classes.

Several Ada Jones records focus on female problems, everyday situations seen from a woman's point of view. For example, Jones's solo records include "You Ain't the Man I Thought You Was" which voiced a complaint common to many women, while "I'm a Woman of Importance" reflected a basic matter of self-esteem. "Don't Get Married, Ma!" played upon the fears of a female child whose single mother contemplated marriage to a disagreeable man. Ada Jones tried to record numbers that would communicate something important to women as well as men in an amusing, entertaining manner.

Most of the pioneer popular recording artists also recorded ethnic comedy, reminding listeners of the vocal mannerisms and dialects of stereotyped ethnic stage characters; the content of these fictitious characters is depressingly familiar, coming frequently from the well-established conventions of the minstrel show and vaudeville. Columbia advertising explained to record salesmen that minstrel records "include an overture with bones and characteristic dialogue between the interlocutor and the end men, interspersed with laughter and applause, and end with the song given in the title accompanied by the orchestra and vocal quartette."[56]

The traditions of the minstrel stage lived on in the 1890–1910 craze for "coon songs," the most popular form of racial humor whether on stage, in sheet music, or on records. Nearly all of the great stars—Len Spencer, Ada Jones, Billy Golden, Billy Murray, Arthur Collins, Byron Harlan, George W. Johnson, Bert Williams—recorded this kind of material; Arthur Collins specialized in it. As developed on the early phonograph records, most ethnic humor served to reaffirm the reigning white-Anglo-Saxon-Protestant social class and racial hierarchy while interpreting ethnic characters in what was intended to be a patronizing but benevolently humorous manner. The resulting ethnic sound portraits affirmed WASP superiority over the variety of peculiar and preposterous "outsiders" who inhabited urban areas and the South while according such humorous figures plenty of native wit and buoyancy.

The biggest recording star of racial stereotype was Arthur Collins (1864–1933), "one of the half dozen most popular singers on record," according to Jim Walsh.[57] A large white man weighing well over two hundred pounds, Collins studied voice in Philadelphia and even sang with a touring opera group before appearing with the St. Louis Summer Opera. He began recording in 1898 and so continued, specializing in "coon songs" (he preferred to call them "Ragtime Songs") for twenty years thereafter. His greatest hit was his recording of "The Preacher and the Bear" in which an African American is treed by a bear, predictably pratfalls out of the tree after the obligatory expressions of terror, but lives to sing about the incident by dispatching the bear with his pocket razor.

Collins's recordings of turn-of-the-century racial humor often contain this combination of nasty paternalistic condescension and begrudging admission of a basic human buoyancy that defied racialization. Despite its triply offensive title, his recording of "Coon, Coon, Coon" actually develops a bathetic portrait of the pain experienced by Black people at being treated as inferiors on the basis of physical characteristics. The lyrics to "All Coons Look Alike to Me" speak from the perspective of a black woman who is rejecting the attentions of a black man. The cruelty of Collins's work lay in his distanced white gaze upon non-white cultural traditions, a lofty nineteenth-century Victorian perspective upon supposedly lesser people whose ways appear too exotic to be taken seriously by all those who share the entertainer's background. The element of grudging admiration comes from a recognition of the suffering of the Black race and their underlying resiliency. Sometimes, however, as in Collins's recordings of "Down in Monkeyville," the derogatory labels and stereotypes overwhelm all other elements and we are left with a recorded time capsule filled with blatantly racist information.

In this light, the records made by George W. Johnson, the first African American on wax, take on special cultural significance. Johnson, born into slavery in 1846/7, came north in 1873 and began to attract public attention as a whistler and vagabond entertainer on excursion boats and ferries. He is said to have made records on tinfoil in 1877, the first, extremely perishable medium of sound recording in this country. In 1892, Johnson recorded "The Whistling Coon," "Laughing Song," "Laughing Coon," and "Whistling Girl" for the New Jersey Phonograph Company, an Edison subsidiary. He went on to remake these sides again and again for a large number of companies. Fittingly, Johnson recorded a fifth number, "The Mocking Bird," but only for the Berliner Company.[58]

Frederick Gaisberg claimed that George Johnson "achieved fame and riches" with his records, thanks to his "low-pitched and fruity" whistle that sounded like a contralto voice, and his "deep-bellied, lazy like a care-free darky" laugh.[59] What may be just as important, although none of the sources seem to take notice of it, is Johnson's ability to produce an entertainment commodity that fit the general expectations of minstrel show and coon song traditions without actually requiring that he sing lyrics that would be humiliating to either himself or African Americans in general. In this, George Johnson becomes the first of many Black performers in the long history of the phonograph to creatively adapt and transform minstrel traditions, "momentarily dominating 'by the superior powers of grace and invention' a world that attempted to 'drain every atom of life and feeling' out of them."[60]

The popularity of minstrel-influenced records, coming as it did so late in the history of the stage genre, took on added significance from the conflict-torn social and economic fabric of America in the 1890s. At a time when social class relationships and the working agreements between capital and labor trembled under the onslaught of widespread strikes and economic conflict, a time when African American immigration into northern American cities got under way, a revealing amount of symbolic racial oppression appeared with the coon song craze.[61] Arthur Collins's many records symbolically recalled the historical system of racial oppression rendered so much more brutally in the era of southern white vigilantes and lynchings.

The specific contribution of the phonograph to this phenomenon was, once again, to disseminate dying minstrel and vaudeville stage traditions into the very world of modern communications that would kill them. The automatic phonographs and inexpensive early domestic models took minstrel stereotypes out of their theatrical context, removing their visual signals, and intermixed their sounds more pervasively in a variety of public social contexts and more deeply into collective popular sensibilities. Without the visual cues that indicated that racial humor was just a stage act, coin-op and home listeners might have more easily concluded that they were listening to actual African Americans. In the process, of course, the early phonograph also intermixed a powerful new form of white racism with the popular leisure experience of the new machine age.

Listening to the popular entertainment records of the last decade of the nineteenth century and the first decade of the twentieth does not confirm Eric Lott's argument that the "language of revolt and the language of amusement were impossible to separate."[62] On the contrary, records of Len Spencer and Ada Jones communicated a proud working-class attachment to richly complex patterns of popular culture without ever making reference to the bitter conflicts between capital and labor or rich and poor during the 1890s. Their recordings communicated "the sometimes contestatory character of plebeian culture" outside of any concrete or active political structure.

Although the recording activity of the early popular phonograph artists retained close ties to minstrelsy and vaudeville, the early recording stars were not vaudeville stage stars. Billy Golden and Billy Murray did have successful vaudeville careers, but most of the stars of the cylinder days were not popular on stage; nor were their recordings merely reproductions in sound of their stage performances. Rather, the careers of the "Coney Island Crowd" generally began with the earliest recording era and remained deeply involved with the particular problems and possibilities of the early recording and playback machines.

In a negative sense, several of them were forced by circumstances into something—they could not have known what, at first—other than live onstage performance. Len Spencer, of course, had his facial scar; Ada Jones was epileptic;[63] Billy Murray had suffered from tuberculosis and Bright's Disease, although it is not clear that these diseases would have denied him a stage career.[64] Recording artists did not have to be seen by the public nor to perform on stage, and recording must have represented an important career opportunity to them.

This latter reality served to define a new breed of popular recording artists. Stage performers could, after all, fluff a line and cover the error with any of a number of visual, verbal, and/or musical tricks. The phonograph focused everything on the recording artist's voice, timing, and an accurate recollection and pronunciation of the lyrics. The first requirement of the phonograph vocal artist before the introduction of electrical recording in 1924 was, of course, a powerful voice, one that cut sharply with a penetrating, distinctive vocal sound. Stage artists needed these same qualities, among many others, but phonograph artists relied much more heavily upon them.

Powerful tenor voices tended to record well, for example, particularly those with a nasal edge. Tenor Billy Murray is said to have had a certain "'ping' to his voice that cut sharp into the wax."[65] "Few women's voices recorded well in the old days" so that most popular phonograph artists were male. Ada Jones, who possessed a strong, bright, lively contralto voice, was the major exception to this rule. Clear and precise enunciation was important, too, becoming even more so when the comedians were recording their dialect materials. Sharp-edged sibilants were difficult to pick up in the early days.[66] Billy Murray recalled that he had been taught to "round out our vowel sounds," otherwise reproduction would be flat and unsatisfactory. Stage performers, he felt, could get away with sloppy vowel pronunciation but not the recording artist.[67]

Those who specialized in recording were performers who could accept and work within strict time limitations—two, three, and four minutes—before World War I. The vocalist and instrumentalist had to go over the material to be recorded and cut it to fill the time requirements. The usual procedure for recording a popular song was to perform the verse only once and the chorus twice.[68] Often studio pianists came to specialize in rearranging published songs to fit the recording limit.[69] The pacing and tempi of performances had to be carefully calculated in advance and painstakingly respected during recording. As Billy Murray put it: "We are taught to keep perfect time. Stage performers are not held strictly to the limit as we are. You can't play with rests and pauses to suit your own musical tastes. The selections have to be timed to fill a certain period, and any deviation throws things out." As Ernest L. Stevens, a seasoned recording studio pianist, remembered: ". . . I'd go through the song first, make tests, and then I'd time it with a watch. I'd know exactly the tempo, how long to play it and what to put into it. It would take me, maybe, four or five hours to work out an arrangement."[70]

All of the early recording artists also had to come to grips with the recording horn, a megaphonelike cone that protruded from the wall into the studio. Seasoned stage performers trembled when faced with its threatening impersonality. As Richard Jose, contratenor and composer of "Silver Threads Among the Gold," put it: "You are locked all alone with the band in a big bare room, your back to the musicians and your face to a blank wall out of which protrudes the horn."[71] Ernest Stevens, who played piano on more than six hundred Edison recordings, "shook like a leaf" on the six hundredth, just as he had on the first.

During the thirty-four-year period of acoustical recording, singers had to learn at what distance to place themselves from the recording horn. As one trade publication explained: "The phonograph singer, like the baseball player, and the horse jockey, must be an exact judge of distance" from the recording horn.[72] If one stood too near or too far from the horn, the relative value of the tones was destroyed and one had to start all over again. As one pioneering vocal artist put it: "The distance between lips and horn is determined not just by the height of the note but also the way of attacking it. Intensity must be retained for soft caressing tones, not lighter, just less volume."[73] The machine just couldn't wait for the artists: "two raps signaled that the artist begin and it must be at once." Care had to be taken not to turn either to the left or to the right while singing, as would have been natural on the vaudeville stage, but rather to sing directly into the horn,[74] otherwise the reproduction would consist of "a confused medley of harsh, grating, unintelligible sounds."[75] Vocalists either learned to lean into the horn for their softer passages and away from it when singing more loudly, or they relied on a recording assistant to push and pull them.

What bothered all of the early recording artists most was the immortalization of their every imperfection. "The cruel recorder brings out and exaggerates one's least defects."[76] Female voices seem to have suffered most from the early mechanical recording devices. The higher notes tended to become distorted, leading to "blast," a screeching sound. The lower and softer notes did not record well either. The least bit of hoarseness and any sign of vocal fatigue became painfully apparent on the recordings. As a result of all these problems, many vocal artists found recording a trying experience. Even the great Ada Jones admitted that recording was exhausting: ". . . the nervous strain that you must not make a single mistake . . . to make one means that you must make the record over again."[77] By the same token, the machine would faithfully record whatever noise it heard after the recorded performance had ended: ". . . you can't even let a breath out after the last note—you must close your lips on it and wait for the little whir within the horn to cease."[78]

Finally, those who steadily built careers as the first stars of the popular recording industry proved that they possessed a kind of physical and mental stamina not required of stage stars. Until the commercial introduction of the Edison "gold moulded" cylinders in 1902, the necessary technology did not exist to mass-produce copies from original recorded cylinders, although the recording artist could be placed before several recording machines, each of which made a single original recording. The "gold moulded" process introduced the system of a master cylinder from which copies might be made. Before 1902, the recording artist might perform his or her number twenty times into five recording machines in order to create enough cylinders to supply the demands of the coin-slot industry. The early stars proved resilient enough to inject repeatedly that all-important "pep" into a tedious and exhausting series of repetitions.[79]

All of these complex and subtle interactions with the early recording apparatus went into the making of a successful popular recording artist. In fact, many an established concert stage star, well convinced of his or her artistic worth, found the technical limitations of commercial recording too ludicrous to bother overcoming. The established operatic star Yvonne de Treville ordered her first records destroyed and waited several more years until she heard some more "lifelike tones coming from those weird little wooden birdhouses" to allow records of her singing to be released.[80] She and other opera stars credited improving technology with their increased willingness to record, but astronomical recording fees proved persuasive as well. People like Len Spencer, Ada Jones, George W. Johnson, and Billy Murray, on the other hand, earned a far more modest fee per recording but eagerly etched out their careers nevertheless.

While their era lasted, the "Coney Island Crowd" saturated urban America with popular music, dialogs, and monologs that offered attractively robust portraits of white working-class street life. Their records offered listeners a series of amusing and buoyant reminders of popular urban types, interpreting popular culture as a variety of working-class social roles that emphasized urban survival techniques and the enjoyment of commercialized leisure enterprises. For those who listened in the Union Square penny arcade, the records of the Coney Island crowd brought back to mind an awaiting world of popular amusements and a series of social types and personality styles appropriate to their enjoyment. For those who listened in the small-town drug store, the same records created enticing and glamorized advertisements for the cheap amusements of urban street life. For the younger sons of wealthy Victorian businessmen, the Coney Island Crowd offered stolen glimpses of the unbuttoned world of the masses swarming in the normally forbidden neighborhoods of the mysterious city.

The Coney Island Crowd continued to make disc recordings intended for domestic use up to World War I. By the time of that international upheaval, they were quite elderly, however, since most of them had been born during or soon after the Civil War. The automatic phonographs and phonograph parlors had come under attack from the keepers of America's cultural hierarchy. Urban reformers, particularly in New York and Chicago, focused public attention on the potential dangers risked by unsupervised youth who hung around the nickelodeons and penny arcades pumping coins into kinetoscopes and coin-op phonographs and supposedly imbibing dangerously jaunty attitudes toward sex and violence.

Vastly influential attempts within the phonograph industry to transform the coin-op into a "true musical instrument" that would bring "high class music" into the parlors and sitting rooms of middle- and upper middle-class America accompanied the attacks of urban reformers on the automatic phonograph. The talking machine was quickly entering an entirely new transformative period that would pull its spinning memories out of the amusement parks and enshrine them next to the family piano.

3
"HIS MASTER'S VOICE"

The Victor Talking Machine Company and the Social Reconstruction of the Phonograph

It is advertising which has made the talking machine so popular . . . instead of losing time in waiting for the people to become acquainted with the charms of the talking machine in the ordinary way, the creative forces . . . have accomplished in 10 years what would have taken half a century.
—*Talking Machine World*, 1915

In the early days of the industry, the chief work of the pioneers was to overcome the fixed prejudices of the people, especially the prejudices of what is termed the "high brow" element, who professed to find nothing of merit in the talking machine.
—*Talking Machine World*, 1919

The history of the phonograph clearly demonstrates important ways in which economic and cultural forces have shaped technological inventions. In 1877, Thomas A. Edison invented a machine that recorded and played back sound; to what uses such a machine could best be put and what form it would take in serving them remained open questions whose answers emerged from the pressure of cultural and economic forces on the basic principles of sound recording and replay. Edison, after all, guessed wrong about both the primary function of his invention and about its form, clinging stubbornly to the concept of office dictation machines and continuing to make records in cylindrical form long after discs had proven to sell better. Edison certainly invented the first functioning prototype of the phonograph, but others subsequently patented major improvements and, in the process, reinvented and reconstructed the phonograph and recorded sound.

44

The fledgling phonograph entered a socially and politically volatile America, and perhaps for that reason the politics of culture helped to transform it all the more rapidly from a modest instrument of popular culture to a purveyor of genteel musical culture with which men and women of refinement might vanquish the vulgarity of the swarming masses. Powerful leaders in the phonograph business did not want the talking machine to be what, by 1890, it had already become—a medium of popular culture. They worked intensely to transform it into "a high class musical instrument" in order to maximize sales and overcome bitter criticism.

In some senses phonograph technology did determine the broad outlines of sound recording from the popular music in the 1890s to opera in the 1910s.[1] The early acoustic machines recorded the human voice better than they did violins, so that both popular vocal and "operatic" records preceded instrumental symphonic ones. The early recording machines could not adequately record either the high or the low ends of the vocal range: both sopranos and basses awaited improvements in recording technology while tenors, baritones, and contraltos made recorded history. In some cases, therefore, the first companies simply recorded and subsequently sold whatever recordings they had the technological ability to make; they started in 1894 with raucous "vaudeville trash" that was thought to merit little if any audio fidelity, and progressed inevitably, thanks to improved sound technology, to grand opera and finally in 1915 to symphonic music.

Much depends upon the definition of "opera record." While many featured arias from operas, many others presented operatic voices interpreting traditional and folk songs in the public domain. The Rumanian soprano Alma Gluck recorded several of Stephen Foster's hearth-and-home ballads and her dialect version of "Carry Me Back To Old Virginny" (Vic 6141) sold a million copies. The most prolific in this regard was the Irish-American tenor John McCormack who recorded numerous Irish folk songs. Many "opera" discs actually presented a curious mixture of genres that made them the more accessible.[2]

Long before they were actually able to record operatic and symphonic music with any appreciable fidelity, industry spokesmen envisioned a dominant role for their "talking machine" as an "active agent in the spread of civilization."[3] No matter what the range and variety of sounds actually recorded, the first great companies in the industry—Edison, Columbia, and particularly the Victor Talking Machine Company— eagerly sought the middle- and upper middle-class markets that offered leisure-time income far beyond the more limited means of urban workers. In inserting the phonograph into the homes of middle-class Americans, even those industry leaders like Edward Easton of the Columbia Phonograph Company General, who promoted popular music, touted the "high brow" line.

After ten years of popular music recording in the 1890s, the rollicking era of the early coin-operated automatic phonograph was buried beneath an overwhelming new publicity campaign focused on what trade papers referred to as "music of the highest class"[4]—operatically interpreted music. This new policy formed the dominant theme of industry publications and was interwoven with appeals to traditional Victorian social and aesthetic values. All of the great pioneers of the phonograph industry—Thomas A. Edison; Emile Berliner, inventor of the flat disc; Edward Easton; and Eldridge Reeves Johnson, founder and director of the Victor company—agreed that their invention should become a permanent part of every American home. As a result, improvements to the original design of the phonograph and to records were guided by the Victorian era's association of the home with "an oasis of calm" at which the wife/mother provided, among other things, refined and uplifting music with which to rejuvenate her hard-working husband and edify, enrapture, and improve the memories of her children, imparting a sense of proportion, good taste, high moral purpose, and brotherly and sisterly affection through inspiring music.[5]

Inventors, therefore, rushed to patent a series of improvements to the brassy trumpet phonograph of the 1890s, new designs that would transform that raucous and vulgar machine into a real "musical instrument" that, like the parlor piano, could become a focal point in the musical life of the proper American home. Sound had to be made louder, clearer, and fuller through improvements to studio recording machines and home playback instruments. The phonograph itself had to take on a less industrial appearance.

More than any other individual, Eldridge Johnson transformed the lowly phonograph into an angel of domestic spiritual uplift. Johnson invented major improvements—a spring-driven motor with a governor that ensured a constant turntable speed, an improved sound box, a tapered tone arm design, the method of recording on wax blanks and from them creating both higher-quality masters and pressings with quieter surfaces, the first 10-inch discs superior to any then on the market, a disc with a recessed center area to hold a paper label, and, most important, a record player, which he called the Victrola, with the sound horn and all movable parts enclosed.[6] Just as important, Johnson's unsurpassed entrepreneurial skills countered the social and artistic derision of the guardians of America's art music establishment.

One of America's unsung industrial tycoons, Eldridge Reeves Johnson was born in Wilmington, Delaware, on February 18, 1867; his subsequent life personified the search for gentility that he imposed upon the talking machine business. The future inventor and communications magnate was born to Asa S. Johnson, a rural Delaware carpenter, and Sara Caroline Reeves [Johnson], who died two years after giving birth to him. After his mother's death, his widower father decided that his son needed a mother figure, and he was sent away to live in Kent County, Delaware, with his late mother's sister, Elizabeth, who was married to Daniel Johnson, a "hell-fire" lay preacher. After several years of his aunt's moral severity and her husband's interminable sermons, he returned to live with his father and his stepmother, Fannie Smith.[7]

The young country boy's life on Delaware's eastern shore continued with his education at Dover Academy, but his grades were very poor. He did manage to graduate in 1882 with "his heart set upon going to college because that is where gentlemen went, and above all things he wished to be a gentleman."[8] The Director of Dover Academy had decided that the young Johnson was "too God damned dumb to go to college." Instead he was twice banished, apprenticed in a Philadelphia machine shop and "condemned to labor with his hands."[9]

Ironically, despite his shame at having hands "calloused and disfigured by oil and carbon black in the seams and under his fingernails," Johnson proved a gifted machinist with a flair for making practical improvements to the inventions of others. For example, his first invention—an automatic bookbinding machine—involved, like his later more famous ones, practical improvements to the metal stapling principles already established by someone else, in this case by John Scull, son of Johnson's machine shop partner. Johnson made the bookbinder into "a good commercial proposition" and quickly established himself as sole proprietor of his own machine shop, the Eldridge R. Johnson Manufacturing Company.[10]

In 1895 a representative of the Berliner Gramophone Company, founded by Emile Berliner, inventor of the process for recording and playing back on flat discs, approached Eldridge Johnson about improving a toy hand-driven phonograph. As Johnson later wrote:

> The little instrument was badly designed. It sounded much like a partially educated parrot with a sore throat and a cold in the head. But the little wheezy instrument caught my attention and held it fast and hard. I became interested in it as I had never been interested before in anything. It was exactly what I was looking for. It was a great opportunity and it came to me as it can never come to any other man in the talking machine business again.[11]

Between 1895 and 1904 Eldridge Johnson patented many technical improvements to the hand-driven toy phonograph and also proved himself to be a masterful businessman and corporate pioneer. Never allowing his attention to drift away from "practical" and "good commercial" inventions, he immediately patented, manufactured, marketed, and established his own exclusive legal control over the sale of his improved phonographs and disc records.

Johnson's major advantage over the vicious competition in the early phonograph business lay in his exceptional business skills. In 1901, the industrial pioneer convinced those interested in commercializing the sound reproduction inventions of Emile Berliner to drop their opposition and join with him in the phonograph business. Johnson then incorporated his strengthened patent position into the Victor Talking Machine Company of Camden, New Jersey. He retained 60 percent of the company's stock and dominated the phonograph industry from 1901 to 1926 when radio drove him out of the business.

Johnson named his Victor Talking Machine company for his legal victories over the competition, and in response to a court injunction against his using any word such as "phonograph" or "gramophone" with "phon" in it. He built his Camden, New Jersey, plant into "a healthy town, a plant of 10 city blocks with 10,000 employees, private railroads, waterworks, printing plant, fire department, orchestra, hospital, restaurant, and a stock of African mahogany."[12] He paid his workers well but drove them hard, employed plain clothes detectives to ferret out union organizers, and insisted on a policy of piecework. The one attempt to unionize the Victor factories ended when the Camden, New Jersey, police removed the sit-down strikers.[13]

Unlike the inventor Emile Berliner, on whose flat disc principle the Victor company was largely built, Johnson showed exceptional legal and financial insight by incorporating his recording and phonograph operations, issuing 20,000 shares of common stock and 5,000 shares of preferred, trading 40 percent of the company shares to Berliner in exchange for the German inventor's invaluable patents, and reserving 60 percent of Victor stock for himself. Shares of Victor Talking Machine stock rose to such breathtaking heights that those of Johnson's gifted and dedicated partners who took payment in stock rather than cash became very wealthy men.

Eldridge Johnson brought an old-fashioned elitist industrial order out of the continuing patent litigation and intensified corporate competition that followed upon Victor's incorporation. On December 8, 1903, he negotiated an end to immensely expensive court battles with his major rival, the Columbia Phonograph Company General, by devising a pooling of both companies patents and a cross-licensing of each other's products. Under this agreement, the two dominant corporations in the American phonograph field divided what was clearly a ripe market between themselves, with Thomas A. Edison's National Phonograph Company a distant third, and effectively closed out further competition during the life of the original phonograph patents.[14]

Under United States law, those who secured patent rights to inventions also received exclusive rights to their marketing. The patent conveyed "the right to full, reasonable, and exclusive use" of the invention. When, as often happened, a new company copied and marketed a patented invention, it could be sued for patent infringement. Johnson kept a number of skilled attorneys on retainer, and patents, therefore, became an economic weapon wielded by Victor to dominate national and world markets. Issued for an effective term of seventeen years, a patent could not be renewed except under extraordinary circumstances, however. It therefore behooved the patent-holder to act swiftly and decisively to exploit his advantage before the patent expired.[15]

As *The Phonograph*, a trade publication, later described it: "The talking machine business [is] one of special privilege based upon patents."[16] The Victor Talking Machine Company used its exclusive patent rights to take all dimensions of the phonograph business under its control. For example, at his Camden, New Jersey, plant, Johnson manufactured all of the parts, motors, turntables, tone arms, needles, horns, and cabinetry involved in his product. He subcontracted nothing. Victor also exercised vast powers over the sale of its products, contracting with "jobbers," regional wholesale purchasing companies that resold phonographs in bulk to retailers within their region. Under Victor's sales contracts, jobbers agreed not to sell Victor phonographs at less than a price set by the manufacturer. Victor's jobbers refused to sell to retailers who undercut the manufacturer's stipulated prices.

Victor tried to create a marketing system that would allow the company to control prices once patents expired. Victor attached a "license notice" to each phonograph on which it announced in convoluted legalese that Victor "licensed" (the verbs *sell* and *buy* were not used) its patent right to use the machine "for demonstration purposes" only. Licensed wholesalers might assign "a like right" to licensed retailers once a minimum "royalty" had been paid. Legal title to the machines remained with the manufacturer. In 1917, the Supreme Court of the United States in the case of *R.H. Macy Co. v. Victor* declared this particular license system had not been designed in order to secure to Victor "full reasonable and exclusive use of its invention" but rather as "a disguised attempt to control the prices of its machines after they have been sold and paid for." Victor abandoned that license system and soon thereafter also renounced before the Federal Trade Commission its reliance upon "tying contracts" that obliged buyers to use only Victor needles, sound boxes, and records with Victor phonographs.[17]

Price-fixing, or what Eldridge Johnson preferred to call "the standardization of fair prices,"[18] assured the manufacturer of an acceptable profit margin on each sale, as well as money with which to fund research on further improvements to the product. As such, it played an important role in plans to "break into the cultivated class with the phonograph."[19] For example, Johnson did not want discount stores and mail-order houses selling his product because he believed that their intense sales competition would drive down prices and ultimately reduce the quality of the machine as well. Rather, he favored retailing a well-made machine "at a fair price, one fixed [by the manufacturer] at a certain proportion to the cost of production," and ideally by agreement with the most prestigious central-city department stores—Wanamaker's in Philadelphia and Altman's in New York City—and small neighborhood stores associated with high-quality goods and licensed to sell Victor phonographs, phonograph supplies, and records.

Given the phonograph's honky-tonk past, backers of the high-priced talking machines did not want sales handled like five-and-ten-cent-store transactions. To draw attention away from the mechanical nature of their product, sales personnel were encouraged to talk about the phonograph "as a musical instrument of the highest type."[20] When referring to their "shops," the word "stores" was to be avoided, and in referring to operating phonographs they should say: "'The Edison is playing Spaulding's violin number. The Columbia is singing Barrientos' Mad Scene.'"[21] "He who sells the world's most sought instrument with which we embellish our drawing rooms, adorn our reception halls and the verandas and solariums of our country homes [should not be called] 'dealer' but 'a Merchant.'"[22] Phonograph "merchants" should refer only to "distributors," never jobbers or wholesalers. Their instruments performed "selections"; one amassed a library of selections, not a "collection." An excellent way to redefine public perceptions was to control the marketing process.

In order to obliterate the sound of the cheap nickelodeon and penny arcade, worlds that America's wealthy would have nothing to do with,[23] Johnson both improved the surface of his records, removing much of the hiss, and changed the music offerings on them by instituting a much-heralded series of operatic recordings—Victor's "Red Seal" records—introduced in 1903 by performances of Enrico Caruso. On April 30, 1903, the first Victor Red Seal recording session in a small studio in Carnegie Hall initiated a long series of operatic celebrity recordings that sold at $5 apiece. As the leading trade publication proudly put it, "The talking machine is spreading what used to be known as music 'for the classes, not for the masses.'"[24]

But a significant portion of what passed for "opera" records actually presented folk, semipopular, and popular songs interpreted in operatic style by famous opera stars who lent their cultural prestige to nonoperatic music. Caruso, for example, recorded O'Reilly's "For You Alone" in 1910, de Capua's "O Sole Mio" in 1916, and George M. Cohan's "Over There" in 1918 for Victor. Amelita Galli-Curci waxed Moore's "The Last Rose of Summer," Bishop's "Lo, Hear the Gentle Lark," "The Gypsy and the Wren" by Benedict, and Stephen Foster's "My Old Kentucky Home" for Victor between 1917 and 1928. Many other examples can be cited, especially from among the records of tenor John McCormack.[25]

To an important degree, Victor imposed its own "high class" gloss on opera, which was not considered especially high class in Italy, for example, when compared to symphonic or chamber music. Many of the Red seal records featured operatic voices singing nonoperatic music. At the same time, Victor, which made more money on its high-priced records and top-of-the-line phonographs, needed to appeal to people who had money.

To further the phonograph's transformation, Victor introduced a much more solid, durable, substantial-looking and expensive machine, the sort of purchase that "the cultivated class" might make for their homes. Johnson, for example, introduced in the United States an idea first generated in England of improving the appearance of the machine by adding "gilded Greek columns to the corners of the box which housed the motor" and using only "polished mahogany."[26] Suddenly, phonographs were physically and aesthetically transformed to resemble icons of high culture.

Victor's arch rival, Columbia, also labored to rebuild their own "squeaky toy"[27] into a traditional cultural icon. Victorian musical sensibilities responded to the piano, of course, as most expressive of the role of music in the home.[28] All of the phonograph manufacturing companies aspired to the status of the great piano manufacturers and indulged in a good deal of self-congratulation when Steinway and Sons finally agreed to carry a line of expensive talking machines.[29] Columbia took this obsession to its ultimate conclusion by marketing in 1907 the Columbia Symphony Grand, a talking machine in the shape of a small grand piano,[30] but its principal competitor claimed that "Victor is the Steinway of talking machines."[31]

This physical transformation of the phonograph reached its most successful form in Eldridge Johnson's "Victrola," the phonographic answer to the parlor piano. The name, reportedly devised by Johnson himself, represented an elision of "Victor's viola" but, at the same time, when combined with the company name, suggested the sound of "Victoria." First marketed in 1906, this record player—4 feet high, 20 inches wide, 22 inches deep, weighing 137 pounds, and built in solid mahogany with gold-plated metal parts[32]—erased Edison's aesthetic offense of offering the better sort of people pure musical beauty from a "soulless mechanism" that resembled an industrial lathe with a trumpet attached. By directing a wooden sound horn downward through the standing "piano-finished" mahogany console itself, thereby hiding the older intrusive metal trumpet bell and turn-table motor from view, and placing a hinged cover over the top to hide the machinery and mute some of the hissing sound of the needle passing through the record grooves, Victor produced an unintrusive piece of Victorian furniture worthy of refined middle-class parlors, and, in its more gilded and ornate reincarnations, upper middle-class parlors as well. Johnson advertised the Victrola as "a standard musical instrument. It presents all the Victor repertoire of high class music in an attractive setting. It is elegant and artistic in appearance. . . . It appeals to the best class of people."[33] Photographs were widely reprinted to prove that President and Mrs. William Howard Taft had bought a Victrola for the White House.[34]

The Victrola's Victorian-style cabinet provided an answer to a major problem in the adjustment of the phonograph to the middle-class American home. After the novelty of the initial purchase had worn off, usually in six months or less, the housewife had been left with what she considered an ugly machine in her living room with its even uglier records strewn across the floor.[35] The Victrola's restyled cabinet offered shelf space for storing the records and Victorian camouflage for the industrial machine.[36] Shelves for records suggested an entire world of parallels with book shelves: customers now were to be encouraged to think in terms of amassing "a musical library"; each new record would become an addition to "his library of music," rather than just another chunk of industrial detritus. Customers were taught to think of record purchases as an artistic responsibility.[37]

In 1914, Columbia took the campaign of cultural camouflage several steps further by designing, manufacturing, and marketing the "Regent," a flat table-model phonograph cabinet. Other companies like Sonora and Aeolian swiftly introduced their own cabinets in period designs. This led to a growing profusion of cabinet styles that disguised the machinery in Gothic, Hepplewhite, Queen Anne, Chinese Chippendale, and Louis XVI styles.[38]

Having offered the public a new kind of phonograph and a different "high class" form of records to play on it, Eldridge Johnson's Victor Talking Machine Company worked hard to eradicate older public conceptions. No other industrialist and no other industry relied more heavily on public advertising than Victor. According to Roland Gelatt's pioneering study, advertising "became almost a mania with Johnson. By 1912, Victor's annual advertising budget was to surpass $1.5 million."[39] As Johnson himself put it: "advertising increases the turn-over at less cost than by any other method."[40] Victor advertising also carried the price fixed by the company for the machine being promoted. Opponents claimed that Victor thereby "fool[ed] the public into thinking that its product is worth more than it in reality is."[41]

Victor's first double-page spread appeared in the *Saturday Evening Post* on November 19, 1904. It paraded three photos of its high-priced operatic stars but only one photo of its popular stars. This famous ad marked a beginning to a continuous, long-term advertising campaign designed to change the way the public thought about the phonograph. Victor advertising hammered home the "high class" interpretation of its phonograph and its records. Color advertisements typically showed a tuxedoed or white-tied male and his refined and evening-gowned female companion gracefully seated in their Victorian-furnished parlor before their piano and their Victrola. Often their elegant sitting room appeared to be filled with costumed opera stars, and in some ads readers could identify Enrico Caruso, Emma Calve, Pol Plancon, and other Victor operatic stars. Accompanying text emphasized that "the young couple is surrounded by these intimate friends willing and eager to entertain them."[42] In pre–World War I phonograph advertising, the talking machine became a charged symbol of middle-class social and economic power. The beautiful young couple's economic status found expression in their elegant dress and their substantial furniture, which, of course, included the cleverly disguised phonograph. The music emanating from their Victorian machine, so redolent of the opera stage, further emphasized class relationships in American musical culture. Sometimes the visiting, costumed opera stars appeared as tiny little figures, sitting and standing about the room, while the regally seated life-size beautiful young couple, a look of absorption on their faces, gazed into the middle distance toward their phonograph.[43] The symbols of Victorian domesticity completely dominated the crowd of recording stars. In another Victor ad in which the costumed opera stars appear life-size, they and their hosts studiously avoid one another's eyes and appear to concentrate on the sound of Enrico Caruso's voice.

In commodifying music, phonograph industry advertising emphasized the power that a phonograph purchase conveyed to the buyer. Trade magazine copy could become quite explicit about this dimension of the phonograph experience. When radio came onto the market, Louis Sterling, founder of the British Columbia Graphophone Co., Ltd. and mid-1920s savior of the American Columbia company, affirmed that "the phonograph still remains the one and only instrument which gives the public at all times the music it wants . . . and makes that music available whenever it is desired."[44] One early advertisement assured the reader that "What you want is your kind of music. Your friends can have their kind."[45] With a phonograph purchase, the customer bought a form of individual control over the cultivated, refined, and complex world of music, without controlling who or what was recorded, where, when, or how. Advertising copy showed the generic elegant couple standing formally to receive properly deferential opera stars who bowed and shook hands as they filed by in costume. The couple graciously presented the recording stars to their guests "after dinner." The recording stars, socially unacceptable due to their humble social origins, risqué morals, and questionable nationalities, apparently made their own dinner arrangements.

At the same time, the company bent every effort toward improving the social and aesthetic image of its phonograph records. Less could be done with the records than with the talking machine to reduce their intrusively technological appearance. The record companies had to convince the public to fill empty spaces in their living rooms with objects made from "powdered shellac, rotten rock [coal], and lamp black."[46] The preferred approach was to camouflage them—first, of course. with labels and then with "sleeves." Labels typically featured ornate and old-fashioned gold-colored script. Victor's Red Seal label actually combined red and gold and suggested the opulent decor of the Metropolitan Opera. The paper envelopes or sleeves, invented by Arthur D. Geissler, both protected the record grooves from harmful scarring and acted like the dust jacket of a book, covering up the monotonous black grooves as a dust jacket covered the visually uninteresting binding. In addition to avoiding the ugly physical reality of records, Victor sleeves redirected attention to the voices engraved into them.[47] As one advertisement put it:

In France, genius is crowned by election to the French Academy. Members of this brotherhood of the great are known as the French Immortals. In the world of recorded music, there is a similar distinction in becoming a famous Victor artist. None but the chosen few can win this laurel.[48]

Another tactic involved linking label colors to price schedules for phonograph records. Colors and designs of record labels were used to rank different types of recorded sound according to their cultural prestige. The Victor Red Seal label indicated European operatic singers; records carrying that symbol sold for around $2 apiece for a one-sided disc. The price could rise to $3 for a Dame Nellie Melba record and $5 for a Melba-Caruso record or ones by Adelina Patti.[49] Blue and purple labels symbolized popular celebrity recordings by nationally known vaudevillians like Harry Lauder and George M. Cohan and cost from 75¢ to $2. Black-labeled band and comedy records usually sold for 75¢.

Advertising worked to convey the notion that buyers gained a powerful symbol of wealth and social power. A Victor advertisement from July 1912 cleverly associated the phonograph customer with individuals of great wealth: "Maybe you can't go to the great pleasure parks and seaside resorts where Sousa, Pryor, and Victor Herbert perform. . . . No matter. . . . You can take them to your summer home, your yacht, and out on your lawn."[50]

The social and cultural values that Johnson brought to sound recording found symbolic expression in the so-called Nipper logo that he patented and placed on all Victor products. This painting of a small white fox terrier with black markings sitting in front of a phonograph and apparently listening to a record carried the legend "His Master's Voice" and was sold by its creator, Englishman Francis Barraud, to Johnson's British affiliate, The Gramophone Company, Ltd., and later repainted to show a Victor phonograph.

As the enduring symbol of Johnson's new dispensation in the phonograph business, the logo of "His Master's Voice" or "Nipper" expressed, as Marsha Siefert has argued,[51] "the technological and cultural meanings of 'fidelity' in the dual sense that the voice is reproduced accurately enough for Nipper to recognize, and Nipper, by his rapt attention, displays loyalty to that voice." The picture actually contains two revealing inconsistencies: first, and most significantly, the dog could only have been listening to his master's voice if his master were a "recording star." The phonograph companies reserved the recording function of the phonograph to themselves, thus exercising control over their consumers.[52] Second, and perhaps less important, the painting shows the turntable braking mechanism in the On position.[53]

The misleading suggestion that talking machine buyers might themselves control the sounds that they replayed on their machines symbolically denied reality, but the Nipper logo in other ways symbolized the power relationships of the phonograph business as Eldridge Johnson pursued it. If he did not treat the public like dogs, he did exercise enormous legal and corporate power over the kinds of sounds that the public could buy; and he used that power to reinforce upper middle-class cultural values and to uplift the untutored masses to "better" standards of musical taste. Nipper, unlike Johnson and the Victor Company, did not know how the sound related to the machine, but neither did most human listeners! Those who look at the Nipper logo may enjoy a false sense of superiority over the confused animal, who may suppose that his master is actually inside the horn or the box; but the vast majority of those who bought Victor phonographs and records knew about as much as Nipper about how the sound effect had been created or why they had actually bought it. As such, "Nipper," whom phonograph executives might have wished to think of as Pavlov's dog, furthered advertising's general policy of encouraging a sense of public incompetence in the face of technology.[54]

Early advertising and trade publication copy sometimes creatively rearranged the Barraud concept in ways that emphasized the power conveyed by the phonograph to render some people receptive, passive, and lost in music.[55] In one variation, instead of a dog, two tiny red-headed children sit before a phonograph placed on an imported oriental rug. In a Japanese take-off, a sitting monkey cups his ear to a talking machine.[56] One cover design on an Edison publication showed a bevy of beautiful Victorian ladies sitting together on the beach listening to a phonograph. The logo read: "A Man's Voice, Anyhow."[57] Another Edison ad showed a handsome, serenely self-assured young couple in formal attire standing behind their machine while their African American and Irish-American domestic servants stood in front of it apparently enraptured by the sounds that had been chosen for them. The logo claimed that "One touch of harmony makes the whole world kin."[58] In every case, the phonograph's power, wielded by white middle-class and upper middle-class owners, transfixed the weak and the disenfranchised.

Victor's corporate symbol acted as an important metaphor for the extension into the realms of early twentieth century sound of what historian Alan Trachtenberg has called the "incorporation" of American culture.[59] The Victor Talking Machine Company, controlled by Eldridge Johnson, the Columbia Graphophone Company, owned first by the Dodge family and then by the DuPont family of Delaware,[60] and the weaker Thomas A. Edison Inc., dominated by the inventor, ruled the dissemination of recorded sound in the United States during the first twenty years of this century. They succeeded brilliantly in making the phonograph into something that many middle-class Americans wanted to listen to in their homes, and they claimed that they improved the musical tastes of the nation.

The Nipper trademark also carried an appropriately down-to-earth American quality with it. In England from 1898 to 1909, the Gramophone Company, Ltd. used as their registered trademark the symbol of an angel writing with a quill on a disc. The angel, so redolent of museums and the history of European painting, provided a symbol appropriate to musical art. To portray a dog on talking machine labels reflected the more mundane world of the machine shops out of which Edison, Berliner, and Johnson had brought their machines. Victor's Eldridge Johnson, for example, refused to have anything to do personally or socially with his recording stars.[61]

Indeed, as soon as he was able (he first became a millionaire in 1902), Johnson made himself over into a Philadelphia gentleman. He and his wife, Elsie Reeves Fenimore, moved from a modest double house in North Philadelphia to the old Baird estate near Merion Station on the Main Line. In good business tycoon fashion, Johnson bought this estate, whose main hall was two stories high, without consulting his wife. He traveled to Europe often to confer with his British affiliates and see the sights. He made a hobby of expensive guns and big-game hunting, bought a 171-foot-long yacht, and collected rare porcelain and books such as the final draft of Lewis Carroll's *Alice in Wonderland*. The man who made Victor showed no personal interest in listening to the sounds with which he filled the parlors of America.

During the first two decades of this century, the big three phonograph pioneers gathered their enormous financial powers behind a new definition of the talker and of its owners. The talker represented musical culture as "the antidote to unruly feeling, to rebellious impulses, and especially to such impulses showing themselves with more frequency, as the years went on, among the lower orders."[62] Linking the phonograph with wealth and property on the one hand, and with surrender, self-denial, and subordination to the world of high musical culture on the other, transformed its image into an instrument of social control and reform. As one early industry publication explained:

> The musical phonograph operates upon man's nervous system in two opposite ways: first, by subduing undue or ill-directed emotion, and regulating the general action of the mind; next, by stimulating the spiritual faculties and awakening those perceptions which lead to the infinite.[63]

Any attempt to describe the full range and intensity of the spiritual and psychological experience of recorded music must remain incomplete, but social and cultural historians have described the sensibilities of late Victorian middle-class Americans at the turn of the century in ways that can clarify the enormous appeal of the phonograph. According to T. J. Jackson Lears, for example, a waning nineteenth-century "Protestant ethos of salvation through self-denial" encountered a more "therapeutic ethos stressing self-realization in this world."[64] Many Americans experienced an inner emptiness and a sense of unreality in a swiftly industrializing and urbanizing society; they longed to be "liberated" from sterile repression and hungered for an "intense experience" of "radiant, wholesome living." The business elite in general and Eldridge Johnson in particular seized upon this shared pattern of emotions and, in a movement that has not been sufficiently appreciated, offered in the experience of phonographs and Red Seal records a spiritual transcendence of the sterility of modern life.

The phonograph, no matter how artfully linked to the piano, was an article of consumer culture, however, not Victorian self-discipline. Try as they might to lead the public to associate the talker with the parlor piano, the equation remained deeply flawed. As ably described by cultural historian Craig Roell, in *The Piano in America*, the piano required unremitting toil, sacrifice, and perseverance on the player's part.[65] It emphasized work, duty, and effort, all of which epitomized the extension of Victorian virtues into the twentieth century. Nothing in the world was worth having or doing unless it meant pain, difficulty, and effort.

The weakness in the phonograph's ties to Victorian musical culture found emphatic expression in music publications. Alice Clark Cook, for example, declared that although "no finer or more fundamental education of the soul" could be found than music, one found wisdom in playing musical instruments, not in listening to the phonograph.[66] While "the fingers, the ear, the memory, power of concentration, patience, precision, feeling and imagination" grows as one works at his instrument, "the mere listening to a machine becomes often nothing more than an idle habit." In making music too easily available, the talking machine would ultimately encourage indifference: "mental muscles become flabby through a constant flow of recorded popular music." The phonograph could become like "a loquacious brook—babbling at teas and receptions"; people commonly adopted an external air of polite attention to its sounds, while their minds, in reality, enjoyed "a complete and comfortable vacuum."

This very effortlessness was presented as an asset. The phonograph sounded the most beautiful music in the world without any effort. In many advertisements, the man of the household, who more often than not had bought the phonograph,[67] sat back and allowed his wife to choose the records, wind up the machine, and set the tone arm into place. Her discrete manipulation of this machine would give her the power to "sooth her angry hubby when he comes home and his dinner is burned." According to an industry publication, Walter Rothwell, conductor of the St. Paul Symphony, and music critic Walter Damrosch agreed that "mutual knowledge and fondness for higher music by husband and wife will sooth domestic conflicts."[68]

The core disdain of the high-culture music establishment for the phonograph as a cheap distraction refused to go away. As early as 1906, John Philip Sousa predicted that the phonograph's technological legerdemain would destroy the active pursuit of music in this country. As he put it:

> I foresee a marked deterioration in American music and musical taste, an interruption in the musical development of the country. . . . [There are] more pianos, violins, guitars, mandolins, and banjos among the working classes of America than in all the rest of the world, but once the talking machine is in a home, the child won't practice.[69]

Sousa really had two interrelated criticisms: first, the phonograph encouraged a passive relationship to the world of music; second, it transformed what he believed to be the intensely human and interpersonal world of music into a soulless machine.

The industry carefully responded to these telling criticisms. Admitting that it might be true that the younger generation was "disinclined toward personal effort" and would no longer practice the piano for six to eight hours a day, a dedication that had been "viewed as indispensable in persons of taste and culture by the older generation," and also true that piano sales had begun to slump, amateur music making, whether by the daughters of America on family parlor pianos or by street-corner barbershop quartets had always tended to be of uncertain quality. Phonograph records of the most gifted musical artists in the world would vastly improve the dismal sound of the country's amateur musicians.[70] All of that late-Victorian keyboard effort had generally produced only a belabored musical mediocrity. According to his son, Fenimore, Eldridge Johnson even refused to allow his wife, Elsie, an amateur pianist, to perform in his presence.[71]

Another damaging criticism of the phonograph claimed that it diminished literacy by encouraging Americans to live in a world of sounds.[72] Here trade responses distinguished between general literacy and musical literacy, focusing upon the former and insisting that, unlike the automobile and the movies, the phonograph encouraged Americans to stay home "and be inclined to enjoy a good book along with good music." The talking machine made the home a more attractive place. Such "refinement in the home creates a demand for books." About musical literacy, the industry made no comment whatsoever.

Without directly addressing the important question of the phonograph's influence on reading and writing skills, the Victor Talking Machine Company cleverly took the high road in defense of its national cultural influence. The company created an Educational Division headed by Mrs. Frances E. Clark, who defined her mission as "serving the children of America and building business for Victor dealers through work in the schools teaching millions of children to think of the Victor."[73] The company produced a ruggedly constructed "School House" model for educational use.[74]

A two-page Victor ad of 1918 emphasized the educational potential of its product in helping to teach roller-skating, calisthenics, kindergarten games, penmanship, maypole dancing, typewriting, something called "girls' classes in rhythmic expression," wireless telegraphy to the Army and Navy, and French to the doughboys, all of this in addition to the history of music. The company bragged that its phonographs and records could even "vitalize" the study of history, literature, and geography.[75]

Victor stressed that the phonograph brought a combination of social discipline and cultural meliorism to the rural schools. Anne Pike Greenwood, a schoolteacher in Milner, Idaho, reported that her students had been unable either to sing or to march before she started to use the talking machine in her classes, and consequently, "their youthful enthusiasm came out in most objectionable ways." Then she saw "a picture of a roomful of quiet, orderly children receiving instruction in 'Parsifal,'" with the aid of a Victor talking machine. The phonograph brought order to her classroom and led to the formation of an orchestra, the organization of a literary society, and even a nonsectarian Sunday School. The beneficent influence of the Victrola spilled over into "community singing . . . the blessed habit of community effort, getting together, and an all-together pull for the common need, a common purpose, and a common good."[76]

The core of Victor's self-proclaimed educational campaign could be found in its Red Seal recording program that vastly strengthened the influence of European musical culture in the United States. Victor's successful recording executive, Calvin Child, signed practically every star of the Metropolitan Opera to a Red Seal contract; his company became the foremost American distributor of opera-influenced vocal recordings. Attracted by extremely lucrative recording contracts, the cream of the European operatic stage voyaged to New York to record and perform.[77] Caruso, for example, earned $8,000 in 1906 for recording four arias plus an equal sum per year in royalties from them.[78] In 1912, he earned close to $90,000 from his recording activities.[79] He made the Victor Talking Machine Company into a major force in the popularization of operatic-style singing in America; Victor in turn "increased his fame immeasurably" and made Caruso into a "personality," described in the newspapers as one capable of drawing people who had never attended an operatic performance to his concert recitals.[80]

Victor's long-lived and comprehensive Red Seal recording program clearly distinguished the firm from its competitors and justified its highbrow self-promotion. Columbia, for example, first tried to follow Victor's initiative, and in the spring of 1903 recorded a series of arias by contralto Ernestine Schumann-Heink, sopranos Suzanne Adams and Marcella Sembrich, and baritones Antonio Scotti and Jean de Reszke.[81] Columbia President Edward Easton quickly abandoned "operatic" recording when these initial efforts sold poorly. Columbia's catalog contained primarily more popular material.

Whatever its ultimate cultural influence might be, Victor insisted that its Red Seal records opened up operatic musical culture to the masses.[82] The company worked to coordinate its Red Seal promotions with concert and public appearances by touring vocal stars. Record dealers created window displays at least one week in advance of the local appearance of a particular opera star and prepared invitation-only "Red Seal Concerts" for musicians and music teachers. At these recitals of recorded music, audiences were impressed with the high artistic quality of Victor Red Seal records and were invited to attend the upcoming concert.[83] Urban and regional associations of talking machine dealers organized concerts and ran advertising that emphasized the desire of record owners to see and hear opera and instrumental stars "sing and play just as they do when making records for their millions of admirers."[84] Dealers, of course, sold tickets for such concerts but also organized lectures on opera, the development of music, and the history of particular musical instruments.[85] "Victorizing" the city of Pittsburgh brought an oversubscription to a 1917 Caruso concert and stimulated sales of Red Seal Records.[86]

The trade liked to claim that "talking machines have made the opera stars, not opera stars the talking machine."[87] The "success achieved by the great operatic stars, both in concert and in opera, must unquestionably be attributed to the tremendous educational value of the talking machine." The "impresarios of Grand Opera . . . were brought to realize that the influence of the Victor was being felt in the box offices."[88] Phonograph records promoted concerts, song recitals, and festivals. Even during periods of depressed theatrical business, operatic recitals flourished. One industry spokesperson summarized the impact from 1904 to 1913 of the talking machine on opera:

> When there were not over 30 cities where a famous diva could attract a paying audience 10 years ago, not more than 5 or 6 musical celebrities could get enough bookings to build a tour. Today there are as many as 60 well-known vocal and instrumental soloists who can attract an audience representing between $1,500 and $6,000 at each appearance.

It seems safe to concede that the phonograph educated thousands of Americans to opera singers. In one sense, it surely increased public awareness of opera singers, if not opera in general: three-minute 78 rpm recordings lifted vocal stars and their truncated arias from the surrounding cultural and musical context of opera performance. One cultural historian of opera in America emphasizes the exaggerated social snobbery and conspicuous consumption of the Metropolitan Opera's "diamond horseshoe," the thirty-five boxes owned by "the top tier of the social hierarchy in New York City"—the Morgans, the Vanderbilts, and the Knickerbockers—who ruled the Metropolitan Opera.[89] The social cachet of opera on the East Coast made opera goers out of certain wealthy nonmusic lovers.

Thousands of socially unpretentious Americans, people who would not have been welcome in the Metropolitan's Diamond Horseshoe, bought operatic-style music on phonograph records during the first three decades of this century and learned to enjoy arias and folk songs in surroundings in which the phonograph itself was the only symbol of social status. Their listening minds may have imagined worlds of opulence and refinement, but the opera house, the costumes, the make-up, the melodrama, the audience, and the libretto were missing.

In their places came the European operatic voices in three-minute fragments of vocal musical culture reified and recontextualized in middle-class America as works of recorded musical art. Without an English-language libretto, most record buyers could not even understand the lyrics. The experience of recorded "operatic" sound, therefore, would have counteracted the alleged tendency of East Coast opera goers to enjoy the dramatic spectacle as much as or more than the music.

Victor's real impact on the highbrow element of America's cultural hierarchy was to create a new domestic medium for middle-class consumption of operatic music, one that bypassed the socially intimidating world of the eastern opera houses and created for millions of Americans the possibility of domesticating operatic music. This recorded medium promoted vocal art over dramatic acting and the individual star performer over the libretto. For many record buyers, if not the opera buffs in New York City, Victor Red Seal records served to promote attendance at recitals by touring operatic stars, rather than at fully staged performances of entire operas. In one sense, therefore, it is true that records fragmented the opera performance, but record sales spread the experience of listening to operatic music to untold thousands who would not have otherwise been exposed to it. Record royalties brought a new prosperity to vocal stars and enhanced the status of performers such as Enrico Caruso, whose social origins had been modest, in his dealings with the power elite that ruled the Metropolitan.[90]

The Victor Talking Machine's publicity campaigns suggested that middle-class Americans would find richer and fuller domestic lives by listening to its records of Enrico Caruso, momentarily losing their tired and bored selves by discovering a diffuse and imaginary state of spiritual well-being.[91] The very purity of Victor's three-minute arias and folk songs, shorn as they were of the trappings of opera houses, promised domestic spiritual renewal through the passionate and masterful voice of Caruso, the glinting brilliance of Geraldine Farrar, and the pure weightless quality of John McCormack. Though fleeting, such moments of intense feeling brought a vibrancy and exaltation to ordinary lives, calling forth from a middle-class American audience short epiphanies of imported passion, excitement, sorrow, and longing.

Victor's October 1905 trade publicity, if no other ad thereafter, fully exposed the hypocrisy of its high-culture pretensions, at least as a description of the company's overall recording policies. Victor recorded and marketed three times as many popular Black Label discs as Red Label records. In 1917, the company was the first to issue records by the famous Original Dixieland Jazz Band, discs that announced the arrival of the "Jazz Age." The company's trade advertisement also raised the possibility that Victor promoted its Red Seal records only to camouflage its expansion of the phonograph's tawdry past. As Johnson, who wrote many ads himself, put it: " . . . *there is good advertising in Grand Opera*,"[92] especially when you actually had Alma Gluck singing "Carry Me Back to Old Virginny" (Vic 6141) and Irish-American tenor John McCormack emoting on "Dear Little Shamrock."

In marketing three times as many popular music records as Red Seal discs, and in creating its own recorded mixture of genres on many of its "opera" records, Victor actually promoted the dissemination of American popular music far more than it did European concert hall music. As the trade put it: "The quick profits for the dealer are in the sale of popular song [which could include Red Seal records] and dance records."[93]

Louis F. Geissler, Victor's general manager and head artist and repertory man, put it differently: "This record game, if worked properly, is the biggest end of the talking machine business. The Victor company sells more in dollars and cents in records by far than they do in machines."[94]

Victor offered a number of rationalizations for its Black Label recordings. First, the company argued that its educational mission would eventually improve popular musical tastes, diminishing the necessity of catering to musical morons. The talking machine would "exercise a beneficent influence in making America really musical, . . . inculcating a love of the best music among young people. . . . People who only know music hall songs can be educated."[95] Most of the responsibility for making the public appreciate Red Seal records rested on the shoulders of retail sales clerks who needed to be educated in operatic and symphonic music.[96] Customers "should be compelled to listen to records under the careful guidance of salesmen."[97] After buying his or her popular hit record, the customer should be "lured" into listening to "some of the higher class records."[98]

Sales personnel, however, reportedly failed in the educational mission outlined for them by the phonograph trade papers. The talking machine dealer was accused of "falling down lamentably in his high duty as music's representative—a duty that is fast becoming a civic obligation."[99] Such pontificating could not erase the fact that Victor jobbers eagerly supplied their dealers with popular dance and vocal records. In 1913, for example, at the height of the Turkey Trot and Tango dance craze, Victor quickly sent out a list of new dance records and urged that "dealers take advantage of the current desire for this type of dance to reap a profitable harvest . . . by means of an active solicitation of their clients' needs and wishes."[100]

Those involved in sales discovered quickly enough that "people don't like to have their tastes questioned in music or anything else. The businessman who prefers ragtime, prefers ragtime. He doesn't want Metropolitan opera." Sales personnel had to *serve* the customer, not lecture him.[101] Retailers, like record manufacturers, after all, were "not in the business for their health, nor as musical educators pure and simple." The vast majority of those in the industry "aim to supply the market with what is demanded, and popular songs and talking records are good sellers."[102]

Victor produced at least three times as many popular records as Red Seal ones and, under Eldridge Johnson, powerfully reinforced the middle-brow levels of America's popular musical culture, filling the parlors of the nation with its particular middlebrow blend of popular, folk, and operatic music. Before World War I, Victor recorded many of the Coney Island Crowd, as well as its many different military wind ensembles, ragtime banjoist Vess L. Ossman and his star Victor successor Fred Van Eps, and Neapolitan and Florentine string trios and quartets.

Victor's middlebrow influence emerged most clearly in its role in the dance craze that began sweeping the nation around 1910.[103] Under John

S. McDonald, chief artists' manager until 1920, Victor championed the white dance bands that played in the leading racially segregated big-city hotels and carriage-trade cabarets. This same policy continued under McDonald's successor Edward T. King, who ruled the recording of popular music in Victor studios from June 1920 to November 1926, when Victor finally began recording African American jazz artists, seven years after the first Gennett jazz releases.[104] Despite introducing the Original Dixieland Jazz Band, the company had not followed up on its popular success, disassociating itself from jazz, with its attendant reputation for moral laxity. As *Talking Machine World* put it in 1919, two full years after Victor's introduction of the Original Dixieland Jazz Band: "The future of our industry lies in encouraging the sale of high-priced goods and the best records. It does emphatically not lie in pushing cheap machines and jazz records."[105] Indeed, Victor lagged behind Columbia and the newer and smaller companies in recording blues and jazz. In 1926, however, the company finally began a highly successful program of recording such African American musicians as Jelly Roll Morton, Bennie Moten, McKinney's Cotton Pickers, and many more. In the realms of vernacular music, nevertheless, Victor is remembered for having pioneered the recording of white southern country-and-western or hillbilly music.[106]

This Victor recording policy was a consciously designed reaction to the transformation of the record business when the original patents upon which Victor had founded its business expired. In 1916, three new companies—the New York Recording Laboratories, Aeolian, and the Otto Heinemann Phonograph Supply Company—entered the business and subsequently introduced three new record labels—Paramount, Vocalion, and Okeh, respectively, into competition with Victor, Columbia, and Edison. Of these new firms, only Aeolian tried to compete with Victor for the Red Seal market. The Paramount and Okeh labels introduced what admirers of Victor's Red Seal ads would have considered "Low Brow" "Race Records" of African American jazz, blues, and popular music. Victor followed suit only five years later at the time of Eldridge Johnson's sale of the company.

Instead of jazz bands or blues shouters, from 1917 to 1926 Victor promoted a musical synthesis of jazz with late Victorian sentiment and propriety. Victor's greatest popular dance band recording star was Paul Whiteman, whose 1920 recording of "Whispering"/"Japanese Sandman" (Victor 18690) sold over 1,250,000 copies in the next five years.[107] Whiteman, who was billed as "The King of Jazz" at His Master's Voice, went on to record a highly original synthesis of jazz and social dance music with sophisticated "symphonic" arrangements. He capped his career with the celebrated February 12, 1924, concert at New York City's Aeolian Hall at which he introduced George Gershwin's "Rhapsody in Blue," with the composer at the piano. Here was a technically sophisticated style of recorded popular music appropriate for the elegant parlors of America, one that frequently edged over into a concert style too rhythmically complex for dancing.[108]

Whiteman's was the most successful of several white hotel orchestras that dominated Victor's dance records from 1917 to 1926. The Benson Orchestra of Chicago, a large pool of white professional dance band musicians sent out by their leader, Edgar Benson, to work in the most expensive hotels, recorded prolifically for Victor, bringing to their discs the polished professionalism that came from holding a privileged position in Chicago's dance band business. Benson recordings often swung nicely and sometimes featured the outstanding alto saxophone stylist Frank Trumbauer. Beginning in 1924, Victor also waxed other hot hotel dance bands, such as the Coon-Sanders Nighthawks and the Jean Goldkette Orchestra.

Orchestras like these came to enjoy privileged positions at Victor, where recording executives gave them the latest hot-selling sheet music to make into hit records. Since the record companies were legally bound to pay royalties to sheet music publishers and since the white hotel dance bands usually included at least twelve musicians, recording them was relatively expensive. Smaller jazz bands performing original materials cost less to record but usually did not enjoy the white bands' long-term relationship to the record maker.[109]

Thus, after introducing the jazz age with its subsequently regretted recordings of the Original Dixieland Jazz Band, Victor issued thousands of Black Label records of white society dance orchestras, reinforcing a middlebrow position in America's cultural hierarchy. In 1926, Eldridge Johnson sold his company for $28,175,000 to two New York banking houses. With his retirement and the several successful examples of "Race Record" series produced by other companies, Victor began to feature a carefully selected number of the most sophisticated Black bands.

Victor retained its devotion to the middle ground in popular music by white and Black bands. During the depression, the company turned to Whiteman, East Coast society orchestra leader Eddie Duchin, and Britain's popular bandleader Ray Noble. The company also took the lead in fashioning the Swing Era with its recordings of the Benny Goodman Orchestra.

The Victor Talking Machine Company, therefore, reinforced the upper and middle levels of an American musical hierarchy in recorded music. This aesthetic stance influenced the initial desire to make records abroad and the subsequent program of recording within the United States for sale to this country's immigrants. In each case, a strong Eurocentric impulse influenced the sorts of records made and the particular shape given to what was a more democratic and multicultural dimension of the phonograph industry. The following chapter traces that further development within the phonograph's national influence.

4

THE PHONOGRAPH AND THE
EVOLUTION OF "FOREIGN"
AND "ETHNIC" RECORDS

Cultural stereotypes in the United States constrained the involvement of immigrants with recorded music while simultaneously opening limited avenues of opportunity, especially for those from continental European nations. Just as Victorian tradition considered females particularly musical and, therefore, apt consumers of recorded music, so it taught that Europeans had invented and most skillfully developed the traditions of concert hall music that had been grafted onto the artistic life of the United States. The phonograph industry therefore quickly turned to recording "foreign" European concert hall vocal artists. Surprisingly enough, this colonial attitude eventually led the recording industry to a variety of multiculturalism dominated by European musical traditions.

The swift transformation of the phonograph into a highly touted medium for the appreciation of transplanted and transformed European vocal music encouraged recordings outside the United States for sale to customers living both here and abroad.[1] During the last years of the nineteenth century, American phonograph pioneers had eagerly plunged into the creation, development, and control of European markets for their product and therefore exported phonographs and phonograph parts abroad and recorded and pressed in Europe commercial recordings for use on talking machines carrying American patents. In 1898, Frank Dorian established a factory for Columbia in Paris and two years later another at Wandsworth, England, outside of London.[2] In 1898, William Barry Owen established in London, on behalf of Emile Berliner, the Gramophone Company, Ltd., which adopted the Victor trademark in 1900.[3]

The importation into the United States of "foreign records" of European artists became a regular practice of the recording industry, interrupted (but not ended) by the two world wars. A second, culturally distinct, ethnic recording concept accelerated during World War I, that of recording for American ethnic customers the music of European immigrant musicians living in the United States. The second of the two approaches produced "ethnic records" and involved a fascinating process of cultural reconstruction in tailoring non-American musical and theatrical traditions to fit both the experiences of American immigrants and their children as well as the new sound medium.

Both foreign and ethnic records severed the experience of music from the particular web of cultural ceremonies that it had known; each approach also ascribed a unified musical nationalism upon the village and regional musical traditions of immigrants; ethnic phonograph records intensified a more self-conscious, modern, and commercialized experience of aural culture.[4] The industry appears to have groped its way toward changing definitions of non-American records. Before they began recording abroad, the early companies marketed renditions of European art and folk music which had been Americanized through the musical organizations that performed them. By 1894, the United States Marine Band, for example, recorded large numbers of German and Italian polkas, marches, schottisches, and patriotic, folk, and operatic pieces that had been written down and arranged for wind ensemble.[5] In this way, phonograph records filtered European musical traditions through the distinctive sound of the military wind ensemble and its association in American minds with patriotic moments in small-town band concerts and parades. The unfamiliar, exotic cultural elements were thoroughly intermixed with familiar American sounds so that foreign culture could be presented from a reassuring American perspective.

Relatively few Americans would have been aware of the inordinately large role played by European immigrant musicians in America's military-style marching bands at the turn of the century. The growing popularity of band music after the Civil War created an unprecedented demand for good instrumentalists. The relative absence of music schools and conservatories in America opened an avenue of opportunity for European-trained immigrant musicians. John Philip Sousa, the son of a Portuguese immigrant trombonist, hired as many as forty foreign-born musicians among the fifty performers in his concert wind ensemble.[6]

A similar process of cultural filtration and disguise extended to the records of "foreign" music made by the salaried record company studio orchestras and vocal groups in America. Even though most Polish-Americans, for example, were not from the wealthy or educated classes, the Columbia Polish Orchestra in the United States churned out arranged orchestrations of the sort of music found in the Polish concert halls. When vocal parts were added, they were performed by conservatory-trained voices.[7] In the same manner, in 1905 the Edison Company made cylinder recordings of Hebrew music performed by the Edison Military Band. Company publications reassured readers that its band could adopt the "characteristic style" of whatever national music it recorded.[8]

From the start, therefore, record companies tended to market what can be called "crossover" styles, music that was at once identifiable as somehow reflective of a particular national or cultural group and yet still likely to appeal to record buyers who were not members of that group. The mechanism involved was, of course, economic, since record companies were in the business of selling as many records as possible.

This principle can be distinguished in several types of "ethnic" records: the operatic and wind ensemble definitions of the musical ethnicity of European peoples existed side-by-side with more popular sound portraits of theatrical immigrant stereotypes in the "descriptive" recordings of ethnic vaudeville humor. The many records made from the late 1890s to World War I by the "Coney Island Crowd," discussed earlier in chapter 2, as opposed to the popular immigrant entertainers who were to treat many of the same themes from a non-American perspective during the 1920s, typed immigrants into familiar comic characters. People of foreign birth were cast in a popular urban working-class context, their supposedly foreign characteristics as immigrant groups juxtaposed to the reigning WASP culture so as to heighten the sense of contrast and elicit laughter primarily from those who thought of themselves as not having those characteristics, but inevitably also from immigrants themselves. The earliest recorded versions of minstrel and vaudeville ethnic humor rarely if ever wielded ethnicity as a direct criticism of WASPs or of American life.

But when around 1900 the industry awoke to the potential profits in selling "foreign" records both abroad and in the United States, they saw American immigrants in a more positive light than Anglo-Saxon humor had allowed. Between 1865 and 1917, more than 25 million immigrants entered the United States. Most were eastern- and southern Europeans. In 1900, 13.5 percent of the population of the United States was foreign born, and during the next thirty years 3.5 million Italians, 2 million Russians, including many of Jewish origins, 2.5 million from Austria and Hungary, and nearly 1 million Germans migrated to the United States. In 1910, 700 foreign-language daily newspapers with a combined circulation of 5 million catered to immigrant readers. The record companies estimated that nonnative speakers of English amounted to about one-third of the total market for phonograph products. American companies were to issue at least 30,000 different 78 rpm records aimed at foreign-born communities between 1900 and 1950. Many more were designed for sale in Europe but distributed in the United States as well. Clearly, economic motives impelled greater attention to "foreign" and "ethnic" recordings.[9]

The direct ancestors of both European concert music discs and American ethnic records, ones that were made abroad by Americans with the intention of representing the music of non-American cultures, were those recorded at the behest of phonograph disc inventor Emil Berliner by his assistant Frederick Gaisberg in 1898 in Europe. Some were sold abroad and others exported to the United States. Without explaining why, Gaisberg and his team headed straight to the opera houses in the musical capitals of Europe—Leipzig, Vienna, Budapest, Milan, Madrid, St.

Petersburg, and Warsaw—eager to record the greatest stars of continental European vocal music.[10] After setting up recording and marketing operations in London and a record-pressing plant in Hanover, Gaisberg and his brother Will moved on to Russia for more recording. From Europe, American sound engineers moved around the world.

A mixture of American-born and immigrant executives dominated the pioneer recording industry. Some of the most influential leaders were themselves immigrants. Disc inventor Emil Berliner had emigrated from Germany, as did Otto and Adolph Heinemann, who revolutionized popular and ethnic music with their Okeh label of the 1920s and their imported Odeon records originally made by the Lindstrom Company. Anton Heindl of Columbia Records, who changed the course of ethnic recording during World War I, hailed from eastern Europe. Lieutenant Gianni Bettini, the pioneer of the opera cylinder business, was Italian. Thomas A. Edison and Eldridge Johnson, on the other hand, were home grown.

No matter how deeply some of these men may have involved themselves in recording popular music for the automatic phonographs, they subsequently proved eager to record European operatic music. Such records would prove attractive to American devotees of "serious" music, whether or not they were interested in non-American cultures or could understand the words, and to many emigrants from European countries living in the States as well. In this way, a "high brow" cultural synthesis muted any potential tensions between immigrant ethnic identity and turn-of-the-century American patriotism by providing a shared experience of a European musical culture that was commonly accorded a powerful redemptive spiritual value in the United States.

Victorian high culture values encouraged the admiration of European art music.[11] So long as the imported foreign music was considered to be "of the best sort," it presented no threat to upholding the spiritual value of musical art. On the contrary, as one trade paper remarked, such operatic music might help to redeem a musically primitive and notoriously materialistic America. The idea that "the average foreigner has a greater appreciation of music than an American . . ." runs like a refrain through industry publications.[12]

In selling to the American market, however, the word "foreigner" and "immigrant" might also conjure among America's elite phonograph customers images of dirt and poverty; the European concert hall factor consequently required special emphasis. An Edison Company publicist made the problem explicit: "There is no reason why a music lover should not be attracted by the melodies of a foreign people when rendered by recognized artists and when such numbers are recorded as representing the best compositions of that people."[13] Americans would define standards of artistic recognition and compositional quality.

The recording industry trade papers emphasized that their "foreign records" appealed across social, educational, and cultural differences, no matter how deep and abiding those divisions might be. According to *Talking Machine World*, Italian immigrant workers digging up the pavement on a New York City street enjoyed operatic sounds coming from music storefronts, just as much as did someone like Walter Damrosch, the famous conductor, who listened to it on an expensive phonograph in his home.[14] So, too, Polish records by Warsaw's leading artists were intended for sale to "those who love fine music as well as those who understand Polish."[15] And these were only the most prominent of several different ways in which early recording policies served to create a new medium for a Euro-American high cultural consensus in a diverse world.

The pressures felt by recording company executives to prove the value of their "musical instrument," combined with beckoning world markets, produced not just recordings of art music, but middle- and lowbrow musical traditions recorded by concert singers. Columbia Records, for example, sold discs of Polish folk songs, comic selections, and opera made "by leading artists from the Warsaw theater and opera,"[16] thus creating a musical synthesis of lowbrow music with highbrow performances.

This synthetic definition of "ethnicity" continued to influence the recording of non-American music as the companies moved beyond Great Britain and continental Europe and into the Latin American market. Columbia opened a recording studio in Mexico City in 1904 and Victor installed its own a year later. By 1915, Victor had recorded in Buenos Aires, Santiago, Montevideo, Lima, Rio, and Trinidad. In the 1920s, record-pressing plants operated in Mexico and Argentina.[17] But Latin American recordings showed the influence of the same concert hall sound.

Typically, the Edison company provided a stark example of this power to define acceptable ethnic music for those living both in foreign countries and in America. The company announced in 1909 that it was about to issue "first class records in the Spanish language," in this case "the best songs of the Argentine and Uruguay Republics."[18] Baritone Alfredo Gobbi was employed to render "quaint and picturesque . . . *gaucho* songs [but he] is not a gaucho. He is a man of refinement, an intense lover of the customs and traditions of his country." Gobbi and his wife specialized in gaucho materials that they sang in costume in "the leading theaters of the Argentine, Uruguay, Spain, Brazil, Paraguay, Chile, and Paris." Clearly, the phonograph filtered Latin American vernacular music through a concert hall prism.

Columbia used the same approach one year later in recording and marketing "the first and only set of native Colombia[n] records . . . for sale only by dealers in the United States of Colombia, S.A." Recorded in New York City by the Uribi Brothers, "one of whom was selected by the Colombia[n] government to be sent to Europe and educated in the famous conservatories at public expense," these sides represented an explicit intention to make records "superior in a musical sense" since the recording of "Indians" in Chile, Peru, and Bolivia had proven too "crude" and "harsh."[19] Such records as these might have been retailed from Jose

Tagini's stores "in the leading streets of Buenos Aires."[20] In the same vein, industry publications insisted that the "average Mexican" and even more particularly those living in isolated mountain valleys, haciendas, and mining camps preferred "classical and operatic music" to any folk or popular styles.[21]

Mexican recordings also provided examples of another pattern in the process of cultural filtration that conditioned the recorded music offered for sale to those living both within and outside of the United States. The National Phonograph Company's Mexican expert traveled across the border in 1904 and made 300 records "of national airs and marches as rendered by two wind ensembles paid by the [Mexican] government."[22] Similarly, Columbia employed the Municipal Band of the Argentine Republic to record Argentinian tangos that enthralled American buyers.[23] Thus phonograph representatives continued to associate the idea of national musical traditions with official, military-influenced musical organizations as well as concert hall performances.

The European influence in early foreign recordings also found encouragement from the kinds of international business contacts that American phonograph executives forged when creating and supplying foreign markets. Passing first through Great Britain, where the first European operations were organized, each of the companies then moved to the Continent, and then to Latin America and Asia. In 1904, Columbia made its Italian records with the help of a former member of the Anglo-Italian Commerce Company of Milan and Genoa. The company subsequently relied upon a successful Italian immigrant phonograph dealer in Buenos Aires to decide what to record in that part of the world. Madame Gina Ciaparelli led a 1905 Columbia expedition to Spain where she identified for the company "several of the leading opera and concert singers . . . and . . . Spanish artists whose fame extends throughout Europe." Columbia prided itself on giving its customers throughout the world "the records locally in demand." Consequently, "Mexican music" tended to be music that talking machine dealers in Mexico City selected. Not surprisingly, given the North American and European precedents, the music recorded in 1904 favored "Spanish and Mexican marches, waltzes, schottisches, polkas, and mazurkas, with a good selection of danzas and jotas.[24]

The Spanish language bridged the cultural divide between European musical perspectives and those in the leading Latin American countries. In their determined search for worldwide markets, the record companies, however, soon encountered levels of cultural and linguistic diversity beyond anything they had been able to imagine or felt that they could sell. Even Columbia, the most aggressive of the companies recording "foreign" music, wished aloud that Spanish and Italian music and cultures might suffice for all of Europe. As the company put it:

> As all languages seem to have once been contained in an ancient universal tongue and all of the hundreds of languages and dialects to have emanated, by gradual degrees, from the Aryan, so all mod-

ern music seems to have proceeded from the Spanish and Italian schools . . . they seem to have been almost identical in the beginning. The music of the great composers in Russia, Germany, [and] France stems from the Spanish and Italian groundwork.[25]

Operatic and symphonic music might create a Euro-American cultural consensus, but such genres proved unable to reduce the world's linguistic and cultural diversity.

Frederick Gaisberg concisely summarized the classic cultural problem as he experienced it in 1902 soon after arriving in Calcutta, India, on a recording expedition: "We entered a new world of musical and cultural values. One had to erase all memories of the music of European opera-houses and concert-halls: the very foundations of my musical training were undermined."[26] In India, Anglo-Indians, the sort of cultural go-betweens who had guided past recording expeditions in Europe and Latin America, "were living on another planet for all the interest they took in Indian music. They dwelt in an Anglo-Saxon compound of their own creation, isolated from India."

Because Gaisberg's own musical tastes did not apply to India, he turned to Calcutta's "various important entertainments and theaters in Harrison Road," recording professional theatrical entertainers and vocalists who performed at parties and fêtes. Some of them featured "most unconventional" Indian renditions of western songs. Goura Jan, a celebrated singer of Jewish-Armenian extraction who could sing in twenty languages and who sang her version of "Silver Threads Among the Gold" for Gaisberg, charged 300 rupees per evening and wore elaborate costumes, even at her recording sessions, that offered "a tempting view of bare leg and a naked navel."

According to Gaisberg, "it was practically impossible to record the voice of a respectable woman," and all of the female singers he recorded came from "the caste of public women." As a result, recorded "Indian" music tended to contain a bias toward professional popular show business rather than traditional "folk" music. In fact, Gaisberg noted that the phonograph business inherently favored show business. He and his entourage found "traditional music" in India "static," and once they had recorded traditional festival and wedding songs there was "no traditional music left to record." The phonograph seemed to exacerbate the problem, because new Indian artists began to learn by imitating records produced by the American companies.[27]

Folk music favored traditional repertoires and performance styles. Professional entertainers, on the other hand, recognized the need to take the music out of its cultural context. The American recording companies helped pry folk musicians from their traditional surroundings by refusing to record in people's homes, where music might remain too much within its customary ceremonial and ritual context. Instead, native talent was obliged to come to the foreign company's European-style hotel room in order to record.[28] In this way, vocalists and musicians came to understand the need to sing and play musical instruments in order to divert and entertain audiences with fresh recorded materials and inventive interpretations.

The phonograph record business was built on entertaining audiences with constantly changing musical variety acts. Because India did not seem to encourage enough musical variety, Gaisberg and his staff "founded training centers in Calcutta, Delhi, Lahore, Madras, and Rangoon and engaged musicians to train artists." The scheme worked, and every year thereafter India churned out two-to three thousand songs in most of the six hundred dialects and languages. In the process, the recording executive solved the problem of the exorbitant expenses engendered by working with traditional folk musicians "who had to be trained over long periods before they developed into acceptable gramophone singers."[29]

Moving on to Japan during the first week of 1903, the German-American recording pioneer discovered the "progressive urge and a greater variety of effects" that had been missing in India. His procedures were the same: contacts through a bilingual European resident, an Englishman married to a Japanese woman, a recording studio in a European-style hotel room, and extensive talent searches in theaters and teahouses. Although he noted that this recording expedition produced "six hundred titles covering every variety of the national music," Gaisberg emphasized how eagerly the Japanese "grafted our culture on their tree"; they had "not even made use of their own national idioms for a new growth combining the two colors."

The phonograph and its records nevertheless did become a medium for Japanese musical culture and eventually provided important profits for the Columbia Phonograph Company, among others. In 1911, Columbia established a Japanese subsidiary called the Nipponophone Company with its main plant in Kawasaki. Russell Hunting, Jr., son of the pioneering popular recording artist, was named head of the Nipponophone recording department. After several years of difficulty in adapting phonograph recording practices and Japanese musical cultures to one another, Hunting managed to produce discs of Japanese music.[30] In addition to records, this international extension of American enterprise sold mainly table model phonographs to Japanese families who demanded records of their classical drama Kabuki, classical singing Nagauta, a variation of Nagauta called Gidayu, and Biwa vocal music. Naniwabushi, stories sung with accompaniment, turned out to be the best-sellers. All of these Japanese styles sold records in addition to the more Americanized jazz-like music by Japanese composers and musicians playing on foreign instruments.[31]

Cultural adjustments were required on the Chinese mainland as well. In Shanghai, where a George Jailing (whose Chinese name was Shing Chong) and the important music house of Moultrie & Co. acted as cultural go-betweens, and in Hong Kong and Canton where Gaisberg also recorded extensively, the German-American "suffered" through what sounded to him like the "paralyzing" "clash and bang" of Chinese instrumental music. "Tea-house girls" proved easier for him to record, except when he attempted to "push one singer closer to the horn"; "she turned on me like a viper." Everywhere they went in the Far East, the American recording expedition tended to catch most successfully the sounds of professional entertainers.

As a result, the different "foreign" or "ethnic" recorded musical memories actually possessed not only a common thread of commercialized popular culture but also a westernized professional influence. As Gaisberg remarked: "Outside of the Treaty Ports, the gramophone never achieved in China the vogue it enjoyed in Japan."[32] Import-export companies located in New York City, San Francisco, and Vancouver eventually supplied records made in China for the larger Chinese-American communities in the States.[33]

Where entertaining music records could not be fashioned, where markets for phonographs and records could not be built, records could be made only for anthropological study and classification. The recording companies' encounters with Native Americans, for example, demonstrated the cultural attitudes and technological requirements that shaped what were sometimes mistakenly referred to as "sound photographs" into commercially recorded entertainment. In 1912, Columbia undertook a recording expedition to Hawaii to record the "native music of foreign islands" and found the venture "fraught with complications and expenditures of time, money, and patience."[34] First they had to calculate the prospective demand for such records and then locate what seemed to them to be the best native talent. Then, tricky decisions awaited on the best material to record. Finally they had to determine how much recording to do.

But the most difficult part was "to teach the native talent to render their selections with the perfect accuracy necessary for recording." All the tricky arts of recording performance learned by the "Coney Island Crowd" back in the large East Coast cities—timing, pronunciation, pitch, memorization, acceptance of "the horn"—had to be taught to folk singers and musicians whose "knowledge of physical laws controlling the recording process is usually not even elementary." Columbia "surmounted" all these cultural barriers, according to trade publications, and marketed a selection of "pure Hawaiian music rendered by a number of native glee clubs, singers, and instrumental soloists." Pekka Gronow's major study of ethnic recordings, however, underlines that throughout the twenties and thirties most Hawaiian records were made primarily for sale to non-Hawaiians and often presented non-Hawaiian artists.[35]

Various official governmental expeditions recorded Native American music, particularly under the presidency of Theodore Roosevelt. But the resulting cylinders and discs were not marketed, since an extremely limited Native American market existed for them and extensive study was required before Americans could appreciate them. Rather, they became data in the Smithsonian Institution and university archives. In March 1913, at the time of a "Great Gathering of Indian Chiefs in New York," records made of Indian songs were much praised and a phonograph industry publication expressed the hope that "they might someday form the basis of a characteristically American opera."[36] Similarly, one month later, the secretary of the interior appointed New York composer Geoffrey O'Hara to travel throughout the West to record Native American music "in order not only to preserve it but also to transcribe it note for note."[37] For the time being, Native American music was not considered a marketable commodity; hopefully it could be transposed into a more recognizable form at some later date.

Since former citizens of European countries dominated the immigrant population of the United States, the music of their countries dominated the foreign and ethnic records marketed by American record companies. According to a study of foreign record merchandising and national census figures in the mid-1920s, Mexican records outnumbered those of any other nationality, followed in descending order by Italian, Polish, Hebrew, German, Hungarian, Bohemian, Russian, and Greek discs.[38] Some companies had signed outstanding artists of a particular national origin and therefore produced more records of that nationality than immigrant population figures would have justified. Some immigrant groups, such as Italians, Poles, Hebrew-Yiddish, and Hungarians, seem to have shown more interest in recorded music than others. But European dominance was overwhelming; even Mexican records showed the major influence of Spanish vocal and instrumental artists. In the United States, the sounds of ethnicity were European as were the immigrants.

From the start, when describing marketing strategies, recording industry publications tended to lump all immigrant groups (and all generational and age groups within them) together. Columbia, the most aggressive of the ethnic recording companies, divided its catalogs into separate categories: an "A" series of American popular records and an "E" series of foreign records. The company issued about 6,000 foreign records in the latter series.[39]

Recordings served as commercialized musical memories among "immigrants" or "foreigners" within the United States, who were said to be "literally starving for amusements. With no theaters except one or two in the larger cities, few books in their native tongues," they would eagerly buy records in their own language.[40] Recorded music, the trade publications averred, would provide "a retreat to one's homeland" and reinforce Old World values and a sense of self worth.[41] Immigrants were said to be psychologically needy and "longing for the beloved airs of their native land, sung in their mother tongue."[42]

According to record company publications, phonograph and record retailers had to be convinced of the viability of immigrant demand. Such customers appeared to be poor and they had difficulty communicating with the sales clerks. The trade journals therefore reassured retailers that whatever their appearance, the average foreigner had "a greater appreciation of music than an American."[43] "Given a thousand Americans and a thousand Europeans of equal financial standing, you would do a far bigger business in records and Victrolas with foreigners than with the Americans."[44] Since immigrants often lived in serious poverty, dealers usually sold to them on installment plans that provided for small weekly payments. No matter how poor, the average foreigner tended to be "clannish and live within a small circle as a rule and keep in close touch with one another. When they get a good thing, they pass it along."[45] One immigrant customer would likely bring in several more in short order. The Victor Company predicted, for example, that one or two Greek customers would spread the word rapidly and create numerous loyal Greek customers, thankful for having found a way to purchase "a piece of 'home.'"[46]

Moreover, the phonograph trade believed that appearances of poverty notwithstanding, the foreign-born were wealthier than they appeared. They saved and "hoarded" their money, and it was "up to talking machine dealers and all retailers to get this foreign money into circulation" so that the foreigners "won't hoard it and go back to the other side and spend it there." When one considered that there were an estimated sixteen million foreign-born individuals living in the United States, the possibilities multiplied.[47]

Still, many a phonograph dealer "whose customers are mainly Americans and who is American himself will take care not to mix poor foreign-born residents with the high-class American trade."[48] As a result, the foreign record department was best "located in the basement or in a part of the store away from the regular phonograph department." Picturing immigrants in general as people without English language skills, trade publications assured retailers that they "are sensitive about their lack of American manners, language, mode of living, and bustle." Therefore foreigners were eager to avoid unnecessary contacts with Americans and they preferred "this [basement] arrangement and the store finds it advantageous."[49] Many phonograph dealers complained, nevertheless, that they had so much "American material" that they had "no time to waste on dead material."[50]

The industry struggled with problems in retail sales. In order to sell to non-English-speaking immigrants with any effectiveness, it was thought that sales clerks ought to be able to speak at least one foreign language, and hopefully more. *Talking Machine Journal* blithely described the foreign record departments in the basements of the largest downtown Pittsburgh department stores like Kaufmann's as a place where "sales persons competent in eight or ten languages" conversed with foreign-born steel mill workers. Such workers "love music and have talking machines in their homes." When the mills were operating steadily, the demand for foreign records was "very brisk."[51]

Company publications sometimes paradoxically reassured retailers that there was "no need to speak foreign languages at all to sell foreign language records."[52] The companies distributed special catalogs of foreign records with each nationality's section identified with the flag of that nation. When a non-English-speaking customer entered the store, the salesperson had only to proffer a major company catalog; the customer would scan the list of records in his native language and point to those he wanted. The salesperson would then step over to the numerically organized record shelves and pull the records that carried label numbers corresponding to those selected from the catalog.

A pattern of immigrant commercial enterprise that had arisen in major immigrant neighborhoods after 1900 began to take on a defining role in the marketing and then in the production of American ethnic recordings. The Victor Company described such immigrant music entrepreneurs as doing 75 percent of their business "with [fellow] aliens":

> He is often the only one of his kind in the neighborhood and he lives right in the heart of the foreign neighborhood. He is the music maker of his district, and high priest, nabob, and ward leader among people who find music as essential to life as goulash and spaghetti.[53]

In Chicago, as Richard K. Spottswood has described this cultural phenomenon, the Polish-American musical entrepreneur Wladyslaw Sajewski opened a music store on the North Side in 1897 that sold sheet music, musical instruments, player piano rolls, records, and a large variety of nonmusical items that included form letters in Polish and postcards with preprinted messages appropriate to various holiday seasons. Chicago saw an immense increase in Polish immigration; that population nearly doubled in the 1890s, reaching about 150,000. Although Polish immigrants in Chicago quickly learned how to purchase nearly everything else they needed elsewhere, they still turned to Sajewski's "Polish 'general store'" for musical and cultural ties to Poland. Twelve to fifteen people were usually in the store on Saturday afternoons listening to records. Polish language newspapers were still very popular with these immigrants and Sajewski advertised in them.[54]

A very similar pattern arose in the 1920s in New York City's Upper East Side Italian neighborhood where G. Mazza and Son ran the European-American Opera Record Company. As Italian immigrants began flooding into the United States in the 1890s, nearly 250,000 settled in New York City. Most of the important Italian-American music stores opened on the Lower East Side in "Little Italy."[55] "Drawing trade from a large foreign settlement which embraces several nationalities," the Mazzas' store, located at an elevated train exit, played records over a loudspeaker right out onto the L stairs. Immigrants returning from work would hear Italian and other European music pouring forth and drop in to investigate further. As the proprietor put it to a trade reporter, "although they probably couldn't sell it on Fifth Avenue, "The Street Cleaner's Song" is a best seller, here."[56]

G. Mazza, who also sold postcards with preprinted messages in Italian, refused to reveal all the secrets of his success but did recommend that record salesmen interested in the foreign trade pay more attention to the schedule of European holidays that the immigrants had brought with them. "These holidays can fall on different days from our American holidays but they are even more productive of business." In fact, he felt that record sales personnel should emphasize both the immigrant and the American holidays: "We manage to cram the calendar full of red-letter days. Discover some little fad of the nationality . . . even cheese," he counseled.

Immigrant entrepreneurs like Mazza and Sajewski influenced recorded ethnic music through their association with the major record companies and worked to bring what they considered to be a greater cultural authenticity to the recording of their particular ethnic musical traditions. Responding in 1917 to complaints about their "foreign catalog," Victor solicited from its dealers suggestions for improvements. A.L. Maresh of Cleveland's Maresh Piano Company complained that "the artists chosen for the Hungarian records were not adapted to the work." Maresh pointed out that Victor's record of "The Rosary" by the Hungarian Quartette "was made by Scotch and Russian artists with an English leader." Maresh suggested that such personnel could not properly articulate the lyrics; he believed, furthermore, that "the proper pathos could only be given by native Hungarians or Bohemians." Maresh helpfully suggested "B. Sixta, a local [Cleveland] Hungarian singer . . . as a good man to make Hungarian song records" and "The Great Western Band of Cleveland" as appropriate for instrumental records. Victor promised to send a recording unit out to test these suggestions.[57]

Sometimes such musical and cultural businessmen went a step further by organizing ethnic recording companies of their own. For example, the Polonia Phonograph Company of Milwaukee specialized in making Polish records. One observer has called such small operations "genuinely ethnic record companies,"[58] and it is true that Polonia's officers were all of Polish birth or ancestry.[59] Similarly, the Gaelic Record Company that urged customers to "Bring the Breath of Ireland to Your Home" proudly claimed to be "the only all-Irish phonograph company."[60]

Similarly, the Victor Talking Machine Company relied upon Victoria Hernandez in New York City's El Barrio Puerto Rican neighborhood to recruit potential ethnic recording artists. Hernandez had organized her own independent "Hispano" label to produce recordings that mixed humor with patriotic music, often written by her brother Rafael. The Hernandezes' records used native instruments not found on many commercial recordings, as well as idiomatic lyrics and favorite local chord changes. Their discs "lovingly detailed Puerto Rican historical figures, towns, types of food, and slang expressions."[61]

Driven out of business by the Depression, Hernandez made her peace with Victor, a gigantic company that could outmarket her tiny operation, especially as Victor was then determined to develop local ethnic markets. She became an intermediary who scouted talent for Victor's Puerto Rican records, advancing the musicians money at the recording sessions and then taking a percentage of the musicians' pay checks when they eventually arrived. She may also have earned a commission from Victor for finding the talent. Such an arrangement was common in the race record business, as chapter 6 will explain. As with race records, Victor paid its ethnic recording artists bottom dollar and offered them no royalties, securing the mechanical rights before undertaking the session.

The Sajewskis of Chicago and the Mazzas and Hernandezes of New York City offer clear-cut examples of the marriage of ethnicity and capitalism involved in ethnic records. The small ethnic recording companies that sprang up after the worst of the Depression took this cultural synthesis in small business even further. A phonograph trade paper revealed how the great captains of American industry were able to use recorded ethnic music to promote their much larger industrial enterprises. In Pittsburgh in 1918, foreign records were "quite a flourishing business," as hundreds of records and an unspecified number of the cheaper record players were sold weekly "to the many foreigners employed in the large industrial establishments." *The Phonograph* also reported that steel mill employment offices had been located in working-class immigrant neighborhoods around Second and Third Avenues. These offices piped records of European musical traditions out over the avenues and "played on the love of music that is inherent in these aliens. Under the spell of a lovely song or a dreamy waltz of their native land, the men were listed for work in the mills."[62]

Whether working for the leading companies or local ethnic organizations, immigrant entrepreneurs played an essential role in a major shift in the evolution of "ethnic music" that began during World War I and continued through the 1920s. That war seriously interrupted American recording activities on the European continent and also cut off the export to the United States of records made by non-American companies.[63] Columbia admitted that it had relied largely upon "the company's laboratory in London, which has sent its recording experts into the countries of the Continent." The company had thus "furnished American-Europeans, if the term may be permitted, with remarkable records." The war had brought this practice to a halt, however. Anton Heindl, a company executive, had managed to secure 2,000 records in 12 languages in Europe early in 1914, but the war prevented their delivery to the United States.[64]

When the international political crisis interfered with the supply of foreign-made records, first Columbia and then Victor turned to the recording of ethnic music made by European immigrants to America. As Columbia put it: "Although failing to bring Europe to America in a musical sense at this time, . . . the Columbia Company is, so to speak, developing the Europe that is within us." In 1911, the company began recording in New York City "most of the 28 languages which comprise Columbia's 'foreign' offerings," but the war "systematized and intensified" an ongoing project into a national policy that extended well beyond New York.[65]

Near the end of the war, moreover, the major patents that had formed the basis for the all-important phonograph equipment patent pool began to expire. As a result, new companies could now enter the business and compete with Victor, Columbia, and Edison for the ethnic market. Smaller companies like Brunswick, Emerson, Gennett, Pathé, Plaza (Banner), Vocalion, and Okeh were obliged by their late entry into the business to develop new and future markets. When this policy was applied to ethnic records, a greater emphasis on popular ethnicity resulted.

The new American ethnic recording policy brought with it a mounting emphasis on vernacular music and entertainment. Company representatives "visited all the dealers in the foreign colonies of Chicago in March 1915, and went with them to cafes, dance halls and attended concerts and went every place where anything musical could be heard." Not long thereafter, a Columbia recording lab opened in the Atheneum Building at 59 East Van Buren Street in Chicago. There, under the direction of Anton Heindl, manager of the Columbia European Department, local German, Austrian, Bohemian, Polish, Spanish, and Italian talent began to make ethnic folk-music records. Needless to say, vernacular ethnic vocalists and musicians cost the company less in recording expenses than the old-time studio orchestras filled with professional musicians that had interpreted foreign music for Americans during the first decade of this century. "Although the company, of course, have an excellent list of operatic and classical records in other languages than English, the word 'foreign' as used here has a more specific meaning. It means largely the folk songs, the dances, and the religious hymns of the people."[66]

Heindl carried out the new Columbia policy that had been mandated by World War I, but he remained frustratingly obscure. The only trade journal reference identifies him as arriving in America in 1893 with his mother and sister, speaking not a word of English. To these all-too-brief facts was added the opaque comment that he subsequently achieved fame as "an intellectual bartender with an inventive turn toward the evolution of new varieties of mixed drinks."[67]

Clearly, World War I had created the necessary conditions for a systematic policy of recording music performed by members of immigrant groups in America. And once under way, this new brand of ethnic music had a profound and widespread democratizing impact on the recorded music of ethnicity. Company publications now emphasized that their foreign and ethnic records presented music "typical" of the particular countries involved and envisioned the market for this vernacular ethnic music as follows:

A customer enters and asks for Italian records and says, "I understand you have a special list of Italian records. You see, my wife is Italian, and I want to get her some records that are typically Italian—something that will remind her of home. These records by the big Italian artists, of course, are all right. We have many of them. But I want something a little closer to everyday life in Italy."[68]

Immigrants were now said to long for the "folk songs of their native land." Thousands, or even millions, still demanded "the popular things in their native tongue."[69] "Picturesque, haunting folk songs. Lullabies sung by faraway mothers under foreign skies. Lilting melodies of the old world—not merely the music, mind you but the atmosphere . . . records actually made in their native land."[70]

The companies were eager to supply more vernacular recordings. During the 1920s, sales grew by leaps and bounds, with hundreds of dealers carrying foreign records. As the immigrants prospered, they found themselves in a better position to buy phonographs and records. The Victor Company began marketing "actual sketches from life," 12-inch records retailing at $1.75 and $2.00 apiece. Records of Catholic peasant pilgrimage music with actual priests chanting prayers in Latin, the mighty pipe organ of Camden, N.J., and "humorous incidental talking" were sold to German, Hungarian, Polish, Ukranian, Slovak, and Slovenian markets in America.[71]

The shift in recording policies from records made in Europe to those made in the United States also introduced an Americanizing influence into imported musical traditions. This other dimension of the transformation from European concert hall music to more vernacular styles did not become apparent overnight, however, in great part because Victor, Columbia, and Edison executives did not have a detailed knowledge of local ethnic bands and singers. One of Heindl's first discoveries in Chicago, "Miss Elvira Leonora Galentine, a charming little Spanish girl from the North of Mexico," sang some of her Spanish dance, folk, and love songs in operatic style. So, too, the pièce de résistance of the new dispensation was said to be the singing of the Metropolitan Opera's Francesco Daddi, who recorded "some of the exquisite Neapolitan folk songs for the Columbia Italian catalog."[72]

Heindl is on record as having "discovered" on his path-breaking trip to Chicago in 1915 such immigrant musical groups as the "Filiarchi," a Polish-American vocal group that made records of Polish folk and patriotic songs, and the Polish Koledy or Christmas carols. He really got into the spirit with Solar's Concertina Club of 38 accordions led by Louis Solar. Historian Victor Greene, moreover, believes that Heindl discovered such subsequently important ethnic recording stars as Polish-American Frantisek Przybylski and Czech-American Anton Brousek.[73]

The experience with Louis Solar typified the new, more democratic orientation of ethnic recording policies. Solar was described as "a well-known music and talking machine dealer at 3558 West Twenty-Fifth Street." He therefore epitomized the new influence accorded local immigrant music dealers like Wladyslaw Sajewski in discovering and recommending talent and original materials. And as the 1920s spun on, ethnic records increasingly included American band instruments like the saxophone and trap drum kit as well as original numbers written in the States that commented upon immigrant experiences here.

The Americanization of recordings of European and Mexican music extended to European recording ventures as well as the domestic ones. The Italian Book Company of New York City distributed Phonotype records, an Italian label, to Italian-Americans, and early in the 1920s pressured Phonotype to "make records with an American color that will appeal to the record buyer in this country." The Italian-American company demanded more Italian recordings of Italian popular songs.[74]

While such policies ultimately stemmed from the market-driven desire to record music that American ethnic groups would recognize and buy, they also heightened the widespread fears that subversive internal European influences at work in the United States weakened the country's ability to make war against Germany. The Victor Company, for example, cited efforts begun in 1914 by the U.S. Bureau of Education, Division of Immigrant Education, to "acquaint the foreign-born with our language, customs, manners, laws, and ideals." The "Great War," Victor claimed, had "revealed a disgrace of ignorance, illiteracy, and unassimilation" among American immigrants. The war's end brought widespread social unrest. Foreign languages, which the record companies had been encouraging through their extensive marketing of European-made records, served to "slow assimilation to America."[75]

The Victor Talking Machine Company moved to meet these problems with a new emphasis on Americanized European folk music and dance. The company insisted that its Victrola and its new ethnic records could be used to "Americanize" immigrants by focusing attention on instrumental music, rather than songs with their troublesome foreign lyrics. Further, local leaders were urged to organize community singing of English translations of traditional foreign songs and to intermix them more thoroughly with American folk and patriotic songs, folk dances, and period music. Americanized ethnic music responded to the political climate of the country during the war and to the conservative 1920s when the door to immigration was closed, particularly to southern- and eastern Europeans.

This political dimension also influenced the folk dance movement sponsored before World War I by the reform-minded Playground Association of America. Led by Elizabeth Burchenal, Chairman of the Folk Dance Committee of the association, this effort to promote a greater appreciation of "the wealth of tradition in folk dances that belongs to us by inheritance from the many nationalities that make up our composite population" focused on inner-city playgrounds where supervised recreation helped to refine and civilize children raised in poverty. Burchenal also justified her patrician emphasis on proprietary rights to other people's dance traditions by reference to immigrant forgetfulness: "The rapidly increasing 'foreign' population is so quick in assimilating our mode of living, that in the sudden transition many of their old world customs fall into disuse, or are completely forgotten."[76] Burchenal supervised the making of records for use with folk dance exercises for children and not surprisingly chose military bands led by John Philip Sousa, Pryor, and the Victor Talking Machine Company's own Victor Military Band. Such efforts as these spread a greater appreciation of ethnic traditions to the population as a whole, but it is also safe to say that these same efforts served to direct ethnic culture into paths appropriate to an America at war.[77]

According to a prominent trade publication, Columbia, while less patrician than Victor in its public comments about itself and its recording policies, still took care to cast its recordings of immigrant musical traditions within overarching symbols of American patriotism. During World War I, the company decorated the large show window in downtown Pittsburgh's Kaufmann and Baer department store with "the colors of many nations, an American flag predominating, and in the background a large-sized replica of the Statue of Liberty."

> Strewn in front, around a large Graphonola, were records in all tongues. There were songs in Bohemian, Italian, Norwegian, Swedish, Roumanian, Russian, Ruthenian, Servian, Croatian, Swiss, and Spanish. Folk dance[r]s were also prettily arranged in the costumes of the various nations.[78]

After the war, a variety of different ethnic entertainers who worked in various European languages took over the vaudeville stereotypic humor that had earlier been the preserve of "the Coney Island Crowd." Immigrant entertainers molded it into an expression of an American immigrant point of view rather than that of the receiving culture. As described by historian Victor Greene, each of the major European ethnic groups produced vaudeville-style humorists: the Olson Sisters recorded the Norwegian variety; Hjalmar Peterson, an immigrant himself, recorded Swedish-American humor, especially the hit record "Nicolina;" Eduardo Migliaccio, known by the stage name of "Farfariello," may have cut more than 125 sides; Monroe Silver and Aaron Lebedeff became stars on numerous Hebrew-Yiddish records and played off European against American experiences in creating some of their laughs; Arthur Kylander, among others, starred on Finnish-American records.[79]

The cultural spectrum, from nativistic American humor about immigrants, through English-language immigrant humor about America, to foreign-language immigrant humor about the immigrant experience in America, emerges clearly in surveying records of Jewish ethnic humor. Non-Jewish Americans often recorded negative physical and moral stereotypes in their routines. For example, even such usually cheerful, often sweetly naive, comedians as Ada Jones and Len Spencer could turn ugly in their Hebrew-Yiddish imitations. On their recording of "Becky and Izzy" (Victor 5034), Jones and Spencer created a scenario in which the two Hebrew-Yiddish lovers first kiss and then banter and sing about each other. Becky wonders why Izzy turns his head to one side when kissing her and he replies that their noses prevent kissing in any other manner. Becky then launches into a song about some diamond earrings that Izzy has bought for her after burning down his father's clothing store for the insurance payments. Izzy asks Becky to call him by an endearing, intimate nickname, and the record concludes with Ada Jones singing "You Are My Fire Bug."

Not all Coney Island Crowd records communicated such blatant prejudice. In Jones and Spencer's "Original Cohens" (Victor 16110-A) Isaac and Rebecca sell second-hand clothing, hastily cutting off one trouser leg when a crippled customer asks for a suit, and devising a complicated "special price just for you." A coarse male customer with an Irish accent remarks that "All Cohens Look Alike to Me," and the rest of the humorous effects rely upon the way Isaac and Rebecca speak English ("Oie! Yoie!!"). No overtly physical caricatures or alleged criminal behavior emerges in the dialogue, even if the snickering joke is on the Hebrew-Yiddish "outsiders."

On the Hebrew-Yiddish records made by the American-born Monroe Silver, this category of ethnic humor brought a greater richness and consistency to the accent and a humorous pride in the alleged cultural characteristics of the characters. Silver (1875–1947) was a prolific recording artist for Victor and Edison from 1911, when he made "Abie, Take an Example from You Fader" (Victor 16841). In 1926, he cut "I Ate the Baloney!" (Victor 20096) with Billy Murray.[80] His ethnic humor encouraged group pride while joking about serious generational conflicts.

For example, in Monroe Silver's "Rebecca Came Back from Mecca" (Victor 18748-A), the humor emerges from the idea of a good Jewish girl going to live in an Arab Harem; but after dancing a belly dance that causes havoc in the tents and worrying her parents into a lather, Rebecca returns to the fold. Silver's "That's Yiddisha Love" (Victor 16846-B) portrays a young man who has fallen in love with an Irish girl ("Oie! Yoie! I'm in Love with Maggie"). Naturally, his parents strongly disapprove. Maggie then runs away with an Irish lad, and Silver sings about the older and wiser joys of "a Yiddisha woman who cooks, cleans, and helps at the store." Then, too, in "The Sheik of Avenue 'B'" (Vocalion A14371), Silver wrings the laughs from the intertwining of Arab and Jewish imagery in describing a young New York Yiddish lothario. "You should see his Hebrew Harem!" Silver's records, unlike those of Jones and Spencer, highlight the trials of an ethnic group trying to retain its colorful and often humorous ethnicity.

Recorded Hebrew-Yiddish humor played a significant role in the more than five thousand recordings made in the United States for a Jewish listening audience.[81] Three out of four of these discs featured secular material, and among those that took a humorous turn some developed the perspective of a non-English-speaking immigrant toward America while others adopted the English language.

The recurrent theme of generational conflict running through these ethnic records accurately reflected changing cultural patterns within

American ethnic communities. By the 1920s, the record companies began to realize that their categories "Ethnic," "Popular," and "American" were neither accurate descriptions of their markets nor were they mutually exclusive. Such marketing categories failed to describe overlapping and interwoven tastes among those classified as "immigrant" and the greater number known as "American." The policy of encouraging vernacular music and entertainment by and for American immigrant groups narrowed the musical and cultural gaps between groups of non-American and American origin and led to two major new developments: popular American hits translated and rerecorded for the immigrant markets and an intensified Americanization of ethnic music styles and lyrics.

Despite the name of their music store, the Mazzas' European-American Opera Record Company in New York City, for example, took a keen interest in the interplay of musical tastes in immigrant families. G. Mazza emphasized that even if the parents had been born abroad, "the children are embryonic presidents of the country." Because the parents loved their children and thought of them as better assimilated than themselves, they respected their musical tastes. If the children hummed the latest jazz, the parents would buy jazz records as well as "ethnic" ones. "The foreigner has great pride in his offspring and he is willing to learn through his children."[82]

As another report recognized, past policies, such as the marketing of records designed to stimulate nostalgia for the old country, failed to respect the complexity of the actual experiences of immigrants. Reminding them of life in Europe fell short of touching upon their experiences on the voyage to America and within its borders. "These people, through their constant association with native Americans are also interested in the popular music of America." Therefore, in 1928, the Victor Company began to "translate the big American hits into the various immigrant languages"; Victor's foreign versions of such popular American hits as "Ramona" and "Angela Mia" of that year sold in the thousands.[83]

Many "ethnic" records and the publicity generated to sell them represented nothing more than rerecordings of mainstream American popular records with appropriate translations of the lyrics. When in 1923 the Aeolian Company mounted an advertising campaign designed to sell its records to ethnic groups in the United States, foreign language ads were run in such New York City ethnic newspapers as Staats-Zeitung & New York Herold (German), Forward and the Day (Jewish), Il Progresso Italo-Americano, Carrière d'América, and Bolletino Della Sera (Italian) Amerikai Magyar Nepszava (Hungarian), and Novoye Russokoye Slovo (Russian). But the advertising used in each of these papers "was not drafted with the particular view of meeting the foreign idea, but simply represented a translation of corresponding copy used simultaneously in the regular American dailies."[84] Language carried a mighty cultural power, but the content of the commercial appeal and the music on the records knew no cultural diversity.

American "ethnic" records also stereotyped non-American cultures by imposing a form of ethnic nationalism upon the traditional regional and linguistic diversity within European nations. One scholar of immigration and ethnicity describes this as a cultural process of "ethnicization" in which American government, political machines, churches, and schools "created ethnic groups out of divided immigrants."[85] The phonograph companies played a dominant role in the musical dimensions of this process.

Following their primary concern with record sales, companies tried to create ethnic records that would appeal to as many immigrants as possible. They therefore avoided overtly dialectic performances of vocal works. As one trade writer put it: ". . . a Neapolitan Italian regards a Sicilian language record, if not with actual distaste, at least with complete indifference. He would not buy such a record under any circumstances." Sicilians, obviously, had had to overlook Enrico Caruso's Neapolitan accent when basking with "Italian" pride in his success. When, after the invention of electrically enhanced recording in 1924, instrumental music could be recorded with enhanced fidelity, lyrics were avoided altogether in making "ethnic" records of musical pieces so well known throughout Europe that people of many nationalities thought of them as their own.[86]

"Foreign" and "ethnic" records played a more ambiguous role in the construction of the American ethnic experience than most research on American ethnic history has recognized. One scholar has described patterns of ethnic response to new social experiences as "the new folklore," in which traditional genres expand to include new content, contract into a "quantitatively different output," and combine with modern cultural forms to form a qualitatively different configuration.[87] Foreign and American ethnic records clearly resulted from all of these patterns while creating, in themselves, a new kind of ethnic experience.

The timing of the record industry's active campaign to market foreign and ethnic discs therefore should not provoke our wonder.[88] Although it is true that this movement peaked during the culturally conservative 1920s, when further immigration from Europe had been drastically reduced to minimal legal quotas, and when, therefore, the politics of cultural assimilation more than those of cultural pluralism ruled America, "ethnic records" never presented any serious cultural subversion of American national identity. Before World War I, the marching band and the concert hall styles in which non-American music had been recorded safely cast what might have been more exotic musical experiences into familiar Euro-American cultural forms. World War I, moreover, set in motion the Americanization of recorded immigrant music traditions, a policy usually interpreted as a response to wartime conditions, but actually linked to the longer-term restriction of immigration.

The phonograph industry believed that its recordings of ethnic music played an important role in helping immigrants, their children, and their grandchildren to recognize their own ethnicity in a manner that joined ethnic group pride with American culture. The content of the recordings—the artists, orchestras, compositions—provided specific musical and cultural messages with which to document ethnic identities and traditions for people living far away from them. What it specifically meant musically to be of Italian, Hungarian, Polish, or Hebrew-Yiddish origins was stamped into the grooves of foreign and ethnic phonograph records.

Listening to the ethnicized music and narratives on these records, moreover, was said to stimulate powerful emotions of nostalgia, ethnic pride, and implicit emotional understanding—collective musical memories. Those who did not feel these emotions when listening to ethnic records were, by definition, not (or no longer) ethnic. Those who did, moreover, experienced their cultural and familial histories in that private, intimate, mystical way that people often receive recorded music. Emotional intensity experiences like those stimulated in playing phonograph records, moments of longing and yearning, formed a core ingredient in the definition of collective memories and demonstrated how readily memories shifted in content and form.

Buying and consuming foreign records conceivably could have intensified a sense of ethnic alienation and separation from mainstream culture in the United States; evidence discussed already indicates that some industry observers feared such reactions. But easily as much or more evidence from the same kinds of sources indicates that foreign and ethnic records served to help immigrants and their children psychologically adjust to life in the United States. For those who had actually made the trip to these shores, foreign records were said to provide a new form of solace. "Many a European immigrant has been made to feel more at home in this country through the fact that the talking machine brought to him the melodies of his homeland with words in his native tongue." The unhappy immigrant, "buffeted here and there on his journey to the 'land of the free,'" bought "happiness and a cure for homesickness." Foreign records served "the cause of Americanization."[89]

For those immigrants who became economically more secure in the United States, the phonograph and ethnic records served as tools in "a process of dissimilation" through which "the arts, life, and ideals of the nationality become central" and change from liabilities to distinctions,[90] a "library" of recordings of one's ethnic musical heritage, a distinguished domestic reflection of a new cultural consciousness and social autonomy.

If, therefore, the content of the records was obviously ethnic, the experience of the medium itself was not. Spring-driven turntables and 78 rpm discs were capitalistic commodities that one bought; the records could be played in one's home, used at parties, weddings, neighborhood gatherings, political rallies, and funerals, then put back on the shelf. But in themselves, without social and political contextualization, they offered only momentary, if often highly emotional, diversion and amusement.

Ethnic recordings, like the electronic media in general, severed "the link between physical and social space, diffusing ethnic music more widely throughout the United States, creating what Joshua Meyrowitz has called a "*placeless* culture."[91] The music of immigrant groups changed place in coming to the United States and then changed social place again in becoming an industrial commodity. Records played a major role in "ethnogenesis," the development and public presentation of a more self-conscious ethnic group identity. For second- and third-generation members of ethnic groups, ethnic phonograph records reconstituted musical traditions in a new form appropriate to living in twentieth-century America. While becoming assimilated in major ways into a different culture, members of ethnic groups could still keep their distinctive musical traditions on the shelves in their living rooms. Such cultural property could validate swiftly changing ethnic identities. Records functioned much like museums of ethnic musical culture.[92]

The success of the big three record companies in ethnic records suffered a serious interruption with the 1929 stockmarket crash and ensuing economic depression. At the same time, immigration restriction shrank the markets for traditional kinds of ethnic records, at the national level at least. Local ethnic-run recording companies continued to serve specific ethnic markets, however, and Decca Records, the most important new company spawned by the Great Depression, pioneered further crossovers of ethnic music into the mainstream popular music styles of the thirties, forties, and fifties. After the Depression, wartime conditions brought a widespread cultural intermixing of ethnic groups while particular conditions within the phonograph industry promoted further breakdowns of traditional music styles. According to Victor Greene, ethnic music became popular music, losing much of its compositional, instrumental, and linguistic distinctiveness.[93]

At the same time, ethnicity continued to encounter and absorb the influences of gender, race, and social class. It is time to turn to the first of these powerful countervailing forces within the phonograph industry.

5

THE GENDERED PHONOGRAPH

Women and Recorded Sound, 1890–1930

The talking machine trade naturally does most of its business
with *madame*.

—*The Phonograph*, 1916

Women Make Good Selling Phonographs.

—*The Phonograph*, 1916

She is entirely in her closed eyes, and quite alone with her soul,
in the bosom of the most intimate attention. . . . She feels in
herself that she is becoming some event.

—Paul Valéry,
"Dance and the Soul"

The public history of the early phonograph business echoes
with the sounds of its male inventors, entrepreneurs, and
recording artists. From the crusty phonograph patriarch, Thomas Edison
himself, all eyebrows and blunt curmudgeonly wisdom, to the rugged
globe-hopping of Frederick Gaisberg and the big game and fly rod hero-
ics of recorded sound tycoon Eldridge Johnson, the phonograph industry pulsed to male orders, so resoundingly engraved on the vocal recordings of Enrico Caruso.

This white-male domination reflected the nineteenth century's growing separation of the sexes into distinct domains. The industrial revolution, in which the mechanical phonograph played an important role,
relocated economic production away from the home, taking men into
the factories and urban commercial centers and leaving women at home
to raise the children, run the household, and provide their mates with

an oasis of psychological support. As Thomas Edison, Edward Easton of Columbia, and Eldridge Johnson invented their media empires, they also hoped to shape anew a modernized twentieth-century cult of musical domesticity for American women as "angels of the household."[1] Many women saw it differently.

The industry's growing involvement in music for domestic consumption made the phonograph into a medium for the expression of evolving female gender roles in America. Many American women's lives began to change in the early twentieth century and women, defined as the primary audience for recorded music, responded in unforeseen ways to the recorded sound industry's efforts to further shape their lives of domestic submission. Many women used the phonograph to give expression to a range of perspectives, sensibilities, and ambitions that males had not foreseen for them.[2]

On the one hand, the Victrola, Eldridge Johnson's domestic phonograph, like the piano before it, was intended to bring together women and music in the cause of civilization. The Victorian world's idealization of the proper wife's moral and spiritual purity, frequently noted in cultural history, closely paralleled its belief in the refining and uplifting power of art music.[3] Wives' "natural refinement and closeness to God" fitted them to create a joyful healing and rejuvenating refuge for their world-weary husbands. At the same time, music, at least of "the better sort," was thought to stimulate a sense of proportion, good taste, high moral sense, love, companionship, and familial affection.[4] No less a figure than symphony conductor Walter Damrosch believed that "mutual knowledge [of] and fondness for higher music by husband and wife will sooth domestic conflicts."[5] So too, properly uplifting music offered a spiritual antidote to mundane cares, filling flagging souls with the "power of beauty." At the turn of the century, many men thought themselves too masculine ever to become musicians; music had strong feminine characteristics and women dominated the cloistered world of the parlor piano in America, both as teachers and as students. Weary male white-collar workers would allow themselves to find comfort, solace, and a renewal of their sense of civilization through their wives' domestic musical offerings.[6]

On the other hand, however, nineteenth-century women were systematically excluded from the composition, public performance, direction, and production of concert music. Both single and married women were allowed to compose and perform mainly within their parents' or their husbands' homes. Short and narrow social paths did take womens' music outside the home and into the church, local women's social organizations, the PTA, and sororities. The introduction of recorded music into American society therefore altered the configuration of women's musical lives within the family and the community as some women turned their skills as record listeners into jobs.

The phonograph reinforced the process of musical reception (listening) over musical production (playing an instrument) within the middle-class American home. This new emphasis relieved middle-class married women of the burden of honing musical performance skills while simultaneously caring for their families. The selection, purchase, and playing of phonograph records supplemented and often replaced the playing of musical instruments by wives and daughters in the home. This technological modernization originally appeared to buttress the traditional social and aesthetic "inferiority" of women as subjective, emotional, and passive creatures who privately vibrated to recorded music while their more "objective" men publicly asserted musical authority and control.[7] The phrase "domestic musical colonization" might be used to suggest this aspect of the phonograph's intended impact on American women.[8]

In one sense, after all, phonographs were just domestic consumer products like vacuum cleaners and refrigerators. When sales dropped precipitously during the depression of the 1930s, some of the old "talking machine" trade publications turned to the marketing of washing machines and refrigerators as well as radios.[9] Since women had been assigned the responsibility of managing the household, they played a paradoxically powerful role in the nation's domestic retail buying.[10] Thus, not surprisingly, the advertising industry, upon which devolved the task of peddling consumer goods, including household appliances, believed that it spoke primarily to women. Since record companies watched sales figures carefully, record customers wielded more influence over the production of recorded sound than the terms "customer" and "audience" imply.

The phonograph trade certainly concurred in its own belief that, for several reasons, women were its best customers. One study found that 77.3 percent of the time, women made the final decision in purchases of phonographs.[11] According to this study, women dominated purchases in large and small cities, department and specialty music stores; and 95 to 100 percent of these female phonograph buyers bought machines for domestic use. Another study reported that in some cases the female phonograph purchaser brought her husband along when buying an expensive machine and, especially, to sign the sales contract.[12] Still, most dealers agreed that women played the dominant role in the consumption of recorded sound products.

Such widespread female involvement with the phonograph reached deeply into the Victorian era's assumptions about women's domestic lives. First, of course, as a trade journal put it, married women "were kept at home" taking care of the children and therefore felt "the need of music."[13] Recorded music was said to provide an antidote to domestic drudgery, by offering an intricate and stimulating world of musical sound within the world of the home. Recorded music could offer solace and "transcendence" to the overworked and lonely housewife and a burgeoning, exciting, and swiftly evolving world of recorded sounds into which women were encouraged to retreat.

Although they often stepped in to make the final transaction when buying the more expensive phonographs, most married men overwhelmingly deferred to their wives' phonograph suggestions. As one reporter put it, men tended to recognize the talking machine as "an article of furniture and the wife takes care of those things."[14] As "angels of the household," true women exercised control over interior decorating, often choosing the high-priced machines for their period-design cabinetry. One marketing study reported that the phonograph's appearance influenced female buyers 91 percent of the time but played only a minor role with male customers.

Women dominated the market for phonograph records even more completely than that for the machines that played them.[15] The amount of money involved in record purchases remained relatively small, at least when compared to the price of the record player, and middle-class housewives' budgets could usually absorb a record or two. The trade press believed that wives often bought records for their husbands, who were said to be too busy at the office to attend to such details, and for their children, whose tastes might be gently led into the proper grooves.

Actually, phonograph records were more likely to be played by women at home, particularly during the day when husbands and school-age children were away. The selection, purchase, and appreciation of recorded music offered the housewife a "psychological separation of the world associated with the arts and her world as wife, mother, and housekeeper . . . psychological space outside the domestic sphere."[16] Some women could gradually build a library of records, develop a trained musical ear, and read about the lives and careers of all those male musicians. As the leading phonograph trade journal bubbled: "[Women] develop more of a fan spirit, take greater interest in the various kinds of music, like to study the personalities of the recording artists and the musical historical surroundings of the different compositions."[17] The abjection implied in the word "fan" better described male perspectives then female plans.

The controversial notion of a special female sense of time, discussed more in French feminist literature than in that of this country, offers an intriguing explanation of the appeal of recorded music to housewives. This gender-specific time sense, closely associated with memory, has been said to involve a heightened awareness of repetition and eternity, "the return of the same, eternal recurrence, the return of the cycle that links it to cosmic time."[18] Whether this time sense is thought to be innate or culturally nurtured, phonograph records of "timeless" operatic and symphonic music would have brought to it auditory cues to memory and recollection. Recorded time, coming from some earlier period, interrupts the ongoing sense of public linear time. One is temporarily projected back in time to experience a technologically contrived performance of musical time. According to this line of thought, housewives, separated from the flow of public time, might the more readily project themselves into private experiences of recorded time.

In view of the strong appeals to gentility in phonograph advertising before World War I, talking machines like the Victrola also could help women enter worlds of musical taste and discernment, some of which extended into the community. No matter how limited the family income, "angels of the household" could create, through their purchases and subsequent attention to recorded music, powerful musical emblems of their own inner beauty and social refinement.[19] The trade encouraged heads-up talking machine dealers to seek out the women's clubs in their communities in order to present free phonograph demonstrations of the best music. Recitals held at afternoon teas in private homes could provide invaluable advertising if the salesman or saleswoman brought one of the best phonographs and only the "higher grade" records. At some point in the proceedings, volunteers from the club were invited to run the machine "to show that women can play them." Phonograph retailers pursued middle-class female customers wherever they gathered: at feminist conventions, P.T.A. meetings, and sorority gatherings.[20]

Regular attention to Victor Red Seal records was said to fit any housewife for refined social interaction as well as domestic management. Even if many females secretly preferred ragtime records, at teas and receptions where operatic and symphonic recordings were played, they could plaster "an air of polite attention" on their faces, while their minds became "a complete and comfortable vacuum."[21] In such very social surroundings, few women were willing to admit to ignorance of European concert hall music and most "claim[ed] some musical taste."

Strong turn-of-the-century social and political pressures in the best social circles encouraged a taste for European art music, particularly among the female Progressives who sought to reform America's cities and their wayward younger women and men. European concert music played an important role in the widely reported efforts at Jane Addams's Hull House settlement in Chicago and other urban settlement houses to uplift the laboring masses from the supposedly nefarious worlds of the penny arcade and the nickelodeon to higher levels of cultural refinement.[22] Jane Addams recognized an "ancient connection between music and morals and worked to channel musical tastes into "the realm of the higher imagination." She and her male counterparts in Progressive circles worried about the "expressive" function of the media in communicating sentiments and feelings through music.[23] Addams felt that emerging twentieth-century attitudes toward music were "typical of our carelessness towards all those things which made for common joy and for the restraints of higher civilization on the streets."[24] As I have described elsewhere, Jane Addams, Jessie Binford, and Louise de Koven Bowen worked assiduously to close down Chicago's cabarets and to regulate those of its dance halls where sensuous, undisciplined music was said to corrupt America's young women.[25]

The emphasis placed by the early phonograph industry on the sale of operatic and symphonic records convinced female reformers that the talking machine, when properly used in a domestic setting to play carefully selected kinds of music, could counteract the spread of musical vulgarity and sensuality. The Victor Talking Machine Company, of course, remained particularly sensitive to this understanding of the phonograph's role in social and cultural uplift and therefore organized its own educational department headed by Mrs. Frances E. Clark.[26] Mrs. Clark held yearly conventions of Victor sales personnel and educators at which she promoted the company's Red Seal recordings. She directed the efforts of a dozen female assistants who traveled about the country to promote the domestic and educational use of the better sort of records. Frances Clark and her educational assistants underlined the importance of extreme parental care in selecting what records their children could hear at home—"a good march, well performed, not flimsy trash":

> But let those records sound forth the trashy and worthless so-called "melodies," with their accompanying verses of vulgar slang and coarse innuendo and you set a standard of musical taste to your children that is as morally dangerous as it is musically misleading.[27]

Frances E. Clark linked the ideals of progressive urban reform to the Victor Talking Machine Company and the phonograph industry in general. In championing a none-too-well-defined idea of "the better sort" of recorded music, female urban reformers adopted a conservative musical stance that extended into middle-class homes the musical submission of women. As Susan McClary, Catherine Clement, and Ethan Mordden have demonstrated, nineteenth-century operatic libretti structured women's roles into the highly stylized prima donna syndrome in which ill-fated female characters involved themselves with men, only to meet violently punitive ends at their hands.[28] Nineteenth-century middle-class operas staged dramatic morality plays in which unconventional female behavior led to madness and suicide.

Recorded sound lifted female operatic singing out of its traditional context and focused public attention more on the singers and their vocal performances. Phonograph records fragmented the restrictions imposed by male librettists on female operatic roles. Since operatic music had always offered a small number of women a narrow but stimulating uphill path toward challenging national and international careers, the phonograph did a great deal to widen that path, making American opera singers like Geraldine Farrar and many others into touring show business stars.

Soprano Geraldine Farrar offers a particularly moving example of the way in which a few wonderfully gifted singers transformed operatic careers into independent public statements of female autonomy. Born in 1882 in Melrose, Massachusetts, to an eighteen-year-old mother and a father who played baseball professionally, Farrar went on to build an international career, making her debut in 1901 at the Royal Opera in Berlin and joining the Metropolitan Opera five years later. Her career and fame in America paralleled that of Enrico Caruso, with whom she often sang. A striking beauty and the first opera star to take the movie industry seriously, Geraldine Farrar starred in a dozen films, including Jesse

L. Lasky's *Carmen* (1915). She also recorded copiously and used her records and concert tours to build her popularity. She said that her recordings "went out over the country and served a wonderful purpose as advance réclame for later opera and concert tours, not to mention the generous royalties that accrued from their popular sales."[29] Geraldine Farrar became a media star whose fans, called "Gerryflappers," carried her through the streets of New York upon her retirement from the Met in 1922.[30]

Geraldine Farrar's own interpretation of her life, as published in her second autobiography *Such Sweet Compulsion*, suggests that she was unusually aware of the cultural status of music for women. The opera star organized her story into alternating sections subtitled "The Mother" and "The Daughter" both written in the first person in order better to convey the dominant influence that her mother had in turning her into an operatic singer. As "the Mother" explains, concerning her daughter:

> In her I soon began to formulate the dreams I never could realize for myself. Gently but surely she was brought to a conscious knowledge of a career that would demand the ultimate in perception, discipline, and work . . . I hoped to find [in my daughter] the complete expression of myself that had suffered a check in marriage and motherhood.[31]

The piano, voice, and dance became the potent symbols of "the flight toward freedom" which the often obstinate, individualistic, frank, and impulsive child craved when the local public school proved too boring.

Geraldine Farrar's vocal education flowered in female hands. With the sole exception of the Russian-Italian vocal teacher Graziani, she credited women with all of her important tuition—Mrs. J. H. Long in Boston, Emma Thursby in New York, and, most important, Lilli Lehmann in Berlin. Opera star Lillian Nordica, a native of the state of Maine, made the contact with Lehmann for Farrar, and Mrs. Annie Webb of Boston, a patroness of young female artists, paid the Farrar family's expenses in Paris while "the daughter" studied with Lehmann.[32]

The small Farrar family clung together throughout Geraldine's years of education and operatic fame. The "Sweet Compulsion" that had propelled Farrar into her fabulous operatic career made it psychologically imperative that she retire from it. Farrar had always planned to retire in order to find something of her own, a life not created by her mother. Shortly after the star's premature retreat from opera, her mother died; "a precious and inspiring tie to song had been broken. It was never to be the same again."[33] For five years Farrar lived in retirement but re-emerged in 1927 to begin years of national and international concert touring during which she exercised complete personal and professional control over her repertoire, scheduling, and reimbursement. Phonograph records became essential tools in building a middle-class audience for her concerts, whetting the public's appetite to see and hear in person the familiar recorded voice.

As Farrar knew, in decontextualizing operatically influenced singing from both the opera stage and operatic literature per se, the phonograph led those who heard it on their home machines to focus less on the libretto and more on the individual singing voices. Records lifted great voices out of their original dramatic context, and carried a disembodied vocal music into American living rooms, giving it a wide variety of different sorts of music to sing. In order to recreate some public awareness of the music's theatrical context, Victor regularly published its own *Victor Book of the Opera* through which record fans could learn about the plots of the operas from which Victor sold recorded excerpts.

Only a relatively few women could ever hope to pursue careers in operatic singing, but that was only one of several different levels upon which women interacted creatively with the phonograph and recorded music. Many middle- and lower middle-class American women involved themselves with the retail dimensions of the phonograph business. Phonograph records soon became an influential force in the emerging commercialized social worlds of turn-of-the-century American women. Although they would have preferred to market phonograph products exclusively through their own licensed outlets, phonograph companies recognized the large elegant urban department stores like Macy's in New York, Philadelphia's Wanamaker's, and Marshall Field in Chicago as appropriate retailers of their products. As a result, talking machines and records became part of the glamorous world of downtown shopping elaborately arranged to attract female customers into "dry goods palaces."[34] Large numbers of women circulated around and through these stores, creating a commercialized feminine consumer culture in which recorded music played a dramatic role.

The large urban department store had arisen during the nineteenth century and by about 1890, according to historian Susan Porter Benson, "a public and industrial consensus about the nature of the new beast had crystallized." Between 1880 and 1890, the number of department store saleswomen "jumped from under 8000 to over 58,000" and "selling was well established as a women's occupation, with a higher proportion of women in the nation's selling force than in the labor force as a whole."[35]

The rise of a female world of retail sales coincided with a major shift of younger single women away from their families. According to historian Joanne J. Meyerowitz, between 1880 and 1930 more and more Black women and white women began to live apart from their families and earn wages by working in the urban labor market. During these years, the female labor force grew from 2.6 million to 10.8 million.[36] Some of the more musically inclined of these younger women went into phonograph and record sales.

Phonograph trade papers reported that women also were most likely to do their record buying in the leading department store phonograph departments rather than the smaller "street-level" stores specializing in musical merchandise. Both sorts of retail outlets relied primarily upon female clerks and thus encouraged a women's culture of recorded music on both sides of the sales counter.[37]

The reasons for the high proportion of female clerks in America's retail sales force in general had to do with the tradition of women's cheap labor, their large supply and low cost. As men pursued greater opportunities as entrepreneurs and executives, females saw retail sales as preferable to factory labor and waitressing. In turn, women were seen as well fitted to low-pressure department store sales, more malleable than males trained in the hard sell, and likely to interact more smoothly with the department stores' predominantly female clientele.[38]

Department stores built elaborate phonograph and record departments of a sort that have generally disappeared. Typically, such merchandising departments included a series of three-sided phonograph demonstration "rooms" decorated with tasteful furniture and rugs in little domestic settings. Each of these privatized public spaces held a particular brand of phonograph placed in an idealized and romanticized domestic setting. Such demonstrations taught customers how to integrate a properly upscale phonograph into a pattern of coordinated domestic elegance.

Phonograph departments in large department stores also included as many as two dozen separate, sound-proof listening rooms where customers could sit comfortably in quasi-domestic surroundings, listen to records recommended to them by sales clerks, and select those that pleased them. Female clerks and their customers circulated through these phonograph and record departments and were often engaged in sales-related interactions.

The large urban department stores of the nineteen teens and twenties created small female recorded-music cultures. Many of them regularly organized free concerts of recorded music, often punctuated by personal appearances by great musical recording artists themselves. The combined impact of the glittering marble consumer palace, the elegantly arranged furniture, mysterious new playback technology, and soaring musical art must have carried great persuasive power and became an important aesthetic experience in women's consumer culture. Phonograph departments like Victor's retail outlet in Pittsburgh's Kaufmann's department store adjoined a Japanese Tea Room designed to appeal to female customers. Phonograph shopping often amounted to a total women's social experience.[39]

Phonograph retailers frequently employed women in their record departments and many of them rose to head those divisions. The reasons must have been quite similar to those that propelled the hiring of women in department stores in general, but the nineteenth-century Victorian cultural tradition of female domestic musicality lent socially prestigious cultural meaning to women's work in record sales. Both within the home and in the schools, musically inclined women had been expected to act as educators of their husbands, children, and communities. The phonograph's commodification of music propelled this tradition into the retailing of records. As one report put it:

The sale of talking machine records is to a very great extent in the hands of the fair sex and on the proficiency of those hands rests and has rested the musical education of the nation. She [the female sales clerk] has her reward at once in her success at thus spreading the gospel of good music, and, incidentally, she receives it later in her commission check.[40]

The rise of women to prominence in record sales slowly gathered momentum as the big three phonograph companies attempted to retail a broad and deep cross section of operatic, symphonic, ethnic, and popular music for their fine mechanical musical instruments. The yearly record catalogs of discs in print quickly became long and detailed, including so many different styles and recording artists as to require substantial study by both customers and sales personnel. Just handing such a thick catalog to buyers and expecting them to learn what was for sale presupposed more dedication and patience than most were likely to demonstrate.

Women were generally considered to know more about the literature of European art music than men; arranging for them to deal with the formidable record company catalogs and with the record-buying public brought the gender stereotype into commercial service. Before the depression of the 1930s, music stores and the record departments of downtown department stores stocked a large and expensive inventory of recordings. Wholesalers encouraged retailers to stock the entire catalog. Many complied, sometimes in the name of offering a representative sample of the fine arts musical tradition but often simply because they did not know how best to select from such copious lists of records that supposed an educated grasp of music history, performance stars, and stellar recordings. Record manufacturers repeatedly complained about the ignorance of record sales clerks, blaming them for the deeply disappointing sales of "high class" music, and searching for a well-informed female clerk.

World War I provided a further boost to the employment of women in retail record sales and certain other positions within the industry. With many men serving in the armed services, the trade replaced them with female employees. Trade publications reported that females had long worked in the educational and sales departments; such instances were "too numerous to mention." Some women, they acknowledged, had even become dealers themselves. The war, however, opened doors to female workers at the factory record presses, in packing departments, and on the assembly lines, too.[41] Citing an unnamed company, one report claimed that "male wages" were being paid "to over 1,600 wives and daughters of families whose husbands and sons are in military service."[42] The Victor Company instituted a program for training women to manufacture records.[43] By the time of the war's end, "so many women were engaged in the talking machine trade of the West Coast, that the men called it an "invasion." The prewar days of stag parties at dealers and jobbers conventions were over.[44]

A mixture of relatively older married women and younger single ones staffed the record divisions of department and musical specialty stores. Younger females tended to work on the sales staff; more mature females often headed the record departments, and sometimes managed the phonograph departments, but even they rarely managed or owned the music supply store.

Retail record sales likely earned younger women relatively small wages; many appear to have worked on commission. Companies like Victor and Aeolian that conducted highbrow record sales campaigns encouraged the employment of saleswomen "of culture and refinement, natural leaders who have held executive positions in clubs, societies, and churches." Such female retailers were "guardians of the hearth" and knew how the phonograph fit into the Victorian-influenced world of domestic music.[45] Younger working-class females with engaging personalities and musical knowledge could learn to become valuable sales personnel, selling either the concert or, more likely, the dance records.

Basic skill in social interaction with customers was one primary requirement for record saleswomen as it was for sales personnel in general. Lacking much formal authority either in the home or the workplace, women learned to use their influence (what one trade reporter called "the womanly talent of pleasing"[46]) and artfully persuade customers to buy more records than they had intended. Many women with relatively meager musical knowledge were still hired because of their winning personalities. Jean Moore Finley, who worked during the 1920s at Adams Music Shop in Fort Worth, Texas, was reported to have provided an excellent example of this application of "female psychology" to record sales. Finley, labeled "the record girl" in trade publications, tried to judge a customer's mood from his/her facial expression and to select records that would "intensify it rather than change it." She worked to "fall in with her customers' moods" and waxed enthusiastic "over what they profess to enjoy." Finley claimed to have made a study of psychology and "characterology," and was able to radiate sincerity and enthusiasm while adjusting her sales strategy to the customer's mood and perceived character.[47]

Such an approach must have been employed often because observers of the record-buying public reported that the average customer had no idea what she/he wanted. Jane Barth of the Eberhardt Music Company of Wichita, Kansas, "one of the most successful record merchandisers in the Middle West," claimed: "Quite a big proportion of those who come in to hear our records have in mind no particular numbers they want. They just say, 'What have you got that's new?'"[48] As we will see in chapter 8, Jack Kapp, the controversial "savior" of the record industry during the depression, fully concurred: "The majority who come into record stores have no idea as to what records to get and either say we want a dance record or a song leaving the rest to the dealer's judgment."[49]

Our contemporary world of record sales has changed remarkably over time. Between World War I and the stockmarket crash of 1929, record retailing often involved detailed recording of customers' past purchases, mailings to their homes that announced new phonograph products, including samples on approval, and door-to-door canvasing. Women were thought to be most effective in these sorts of sales activities because of their skill in socializing with other women. Mary Ellen Cross, a successful phonograph saleswoman, allegedly "cultivated the acquaintance and friendship of her [female] customers" and kept a list of 200 names and addresses. Cross telephoned and/or mailed information to these individuals when interesting new records arrived.[50] Mrs. A. L. Vance, manager of the record department of the San Antonio Record Store, employed females to do mailings of new record catalog supplements to her customers.[51] Adele V. Holtz similarly worked the telephone and her lists, sending out to some of her customers a package of six records that might be kept overnight. The salesperson who went around door to door the next day to collect either these records or payment for them was usually a woman, since many housewives would refuse to speak to a man they did not know.[52] Middle-aged female canvassers were thought to be particularly effective at getting into people's homes and gathering important information there regarding their musical instruments and musical tastes. Sales managers would later devise pitches to appeal to such tastes.[53]

The world of female merchandisers included much more than their so-called "female psychology." Some female record retailers took advantage of sharp musical memories to choose just the right records for their customers. Carrie Althauser, a longtime Columbia employee and manager of a Cincinnati record department, seemed to know every record in her large inventory "by heart."[54] Although this kind of control over the job was sometimes reported as if it was an innate female predisposition toward fandom,[55] it more likely came from study and hard work. Lucy T. Hackler of Rice and Company in Vicksburg, Mississippi, gained an enviable reputation as a successful salesperson of Victor Red Seal records. Hackler recommended that record sales personnel "learn about the composers by going to the library and reading and having anecdotes to relate as you put the record on."[56]

In objectifying and reorganizing musical culture in recorded form, phonograph records created a newly commodified musical world; knowledge of that intricate and swiftly changing new culture lent added interest to what was otherwise just another clerking job. Rosa Horn, manager of the Victor record department in Barker Brothers department store in Los Angeles, created a list of fourteen questions with which to interview job applicants in record sales. Her questions tested basic knowledge of European concert hall music and of Victor's efforts to market it in recorded form. Horn asked, among other things, that applicants create a "well-balanced" list of Victor Red Seal records, name five good records made by violinist Fritz Kreisler, name a representative work recorded for Victor by Igor Stravinsky, name the principal symphony orchestras and pianists found in the company's catalog, and identify the kind of voice possessed by Tito Schipa. Candidates who couldn't answer such questions didn't go to work for Rosa Horn.[57]

Not surprisingly, many of the leading music supply stores such as Chicago's Lyon and Healy employed music conservatory students, "women who are a real credit to our industry."[58] Those who were not conservatory-trained nevertheless often had considerable musical training.[59] Given the general exclusion of women from operatic and symphonic orchestras, record retailing must have provided women interested in music with one of a small number of practical public applications of a musical education that also included choral work.

Record merchandising represented a positive, active exception to the exclusion of women from most of the other professional worlds of instrumental music. Despite the continued dominance of Victorian domesticity in phonograph advertising, such work actually took a significant number of individuals out of the home, integrated them into the workplace, and gave them a richly complex body of phonographic and musical information to wield in improving their lives. The beauty of recorded arias and concertos must have done much to divert attention from their limited and usually subordinate role in the industry; it also may have been possible for them to ignore the grisly deaths that opera reserved for its female leads, who departed this life stabbed, disemboweled, terrified, anxious, poisoned, choked, burned, smashed onto the rocks below and even dead from, of all things, love.[60] Largely excluded from the composition, instrumental performance, and direction of symphonic music, women sold its recordings, most often to other women.

Some women shaped the business practices of the day in new ways. Helen Huggard, a singer who worked as a record saleswoman in Winnipeg, Canada, during the day, invented the "Record-a-Month Club." Taking the idea of telephone- and home-approval mailings a step further, Huggard devised a free record "club" membership that entitled the member to receive records by mail "without the nuisance of ordering." Payment must follow the receipt of any record for membership to continue. Huggard organized an advisory board of prominent musicians and music educators to choose the monthly selections and went on radio to play and talk about these recordings.[61]

The sweeping demographic changes that drew young American women away from their rural and small-town paternal families, drawing them into cities like Chicago and New York as garment workers and laundresses, saleswomen and clerks, cabaret dancers and day-working servants, teachers and nurses, brought new perspectives to popular female musical culture, vastly enhancing the influence of the phonograph. Removed from the direct influence of paternal musical expectations, young working women discovered in contemporary recorded sounds paths for the expression of a freshly independent, socially rebellious musical temperament. As Joanne J. Meyerowitz has put it: "Wage earning women who lived apart from family were a vanguard in the decline of Victorian culture."[62]

During the 1890s, the earliest phonograph entrepreneurs had established their industry on the streets of American cities, recording the songs and comedy routines of the Coney Island Crowd for replay on coin-op phonographs in public places. Although Ada Jones had been the only female recording star, the first era of popular records had included such female recording artists as Minnie Emmett, Marguerite Newton, Estelle L. Mann, Señorita Godoy, Elizabeth Spencer, May Kelso, and Corine Morgan.[63] In her own recordings and those with Len Spencer and Billy Murray, Ada Jones had provided the first recorded sounds of the independent female wage earner at play in the big city.

The movement of young single women to America's cities in search of work from 1890 to 1930 fueled a fast-accelerating "craze" for social dancing that has yet to slow down. Women and the phonograph played essential roles in this cultural phenomenon which at once freed young women from the musical and social restraints of their mothers' recreational values while providing the phonograph industry with a lucrative and influential product: social dance records.

The social dance craze began around 1910 at the grass roots levels of urban rooming house neighborhoods where young working women lived and socialized. The dangers to young women in unregulated dance halls and saloons began to attract the attention of female urban reformers in 1911 and, in Chicago, Jane Addams's colleague Louise de Koven Bowen published a series of pamphlets focusing upon the role of dance music and unsupervised social dancing in corrupting "Women Adrift." The upper middle-class female reformers used their considerable influence in municipal politics to counter that of the bootleggers and ward politicians in order to bring social dancing into line with traditional standards of Victorian social behavior.[64]

Although most scholars have followed the lead of the urban reformers in associating the dance craze with working-class saloons and dance halls, the phonograph industry actively promoted a domestic adaptation of the social dance craze. A 1914 advertisement for the culturally conservative Victor Company showed men in white tie and tails and women in floor-length gowns dancing to the sounds emanating from a custom-made hand-painted Victrola. The large print extolled the machine's volume, clarity, and perfect rhythm; the small print whispered that any Victor dealer would gladly play the latest dance records for such customers. In a 1920 Columbia advertisement, the tuxedos had been replaced by three-piece suits and the gowns' hemlines had moved to mid-calf. Most interestingly, the couples danced without touching one another. In this advertisement, in fact, the male and the female danced separately, the woman holding a phonograph record in one hand.[65]

Clearly, then, the middle and upper middle classes were dancing, too. The dance craze, regularly described as an inner-city working-class movement centered in cabarets and dance halls, actually appealed widely across social class lines, and the phonograph was largely responsible. As early as 1913, Victor issued records of turkey trots and tangos in response to the fast-mounting dance craze and urged dealers to "take advantage of the current desire for this type of dance to reap a profitable harvest."[66] Both of the major companies published booklets demonstrating how to do the latest steps.[67] As the industry bragged, "The dance craze may be the result of the talking machine bringing dance music into the home, club, cottage, seashore—the talking machine is convenient. Not everyone can have a five-piece band waiting to play for them."[68] Rolling up the rug (an imported oriental carpet, of course, in phonograph advertisements) kept social dancing at least near to and perhaps even under parental supervision. Dancing to a record rather than a live combo kept those half-crazed wastrel musicians out of the parlor and the kids out of the dance halls, creating a more controlled, socially sanitized environment.

When complaining about the dance craze, urban reformers talked mainly about the working classes because the phonograph industry was doing its part to domesticate the tough, sexually provocative dance steps of working-class dance halls. Victor hired first G. Hepburn Wilson "the greatest living authority on modern dancing" to supervise its dance recordings and then the more influential Vernon and Irene Castle. The Castles, according to historian Lewis A. Erenberg, were "the premier dancers" of the pre–World War I era. Irene became "one of the most written about women of the period, a model for dancers and a symbol of urbane fashion and the new woman." The Castles did much to reform dance steps in their New York City Castle House dance studio across from the Ritz Carlton Hotel. They endorsed both Columbia and Victor dance records that did much to refine and domesticate the "wild sexuality" in the urban popular dance craze.[69]

This same process of aesthetic and moral refinement influenced the records of the early 1920s' biggest popular vocal recording star—Marion Harris—who brought the sound of the female voice to popular records. Harris, "discovered" by Irene Castle, broke into vaudeville in 1916, touted as a new version of famous white coon shouters like Blossom Seeley, Nora Bayes, and Sophie Tucker, all of whom belted out their songs. The limitations of acoustic recording encouraged this style and between 1916 and 1924 Harris sold her recorded songs within an inch of their lives. Her vocal material remained close to the sound and spirit of African American cabaret and vaudeville as she recorded numbers like "I Ain't Got Nobody Much," closely associated with Bert Williams, Creamer and Layton's "After You've Gone," W. C. Handy's "St. Louis Blues," and Berton Overstreet's classic "A Good Man Is Hard To Find."

The introduction of electrically amplified recording in 1925 encouraged a simpler directness and greater intimacy of vocal style as Harris moved away from her earlier vaudeville sound and concentrated more on making best-selling popular records of a wide variety of show tunes written by George Gershwin, Cole Porter, and Hoagy Carmichael. Reviewers now categorized her voice as "roomy, tranquil, soothing, and effortless" and this approach to recording influenced Ruth Etting, whose career began in the mid-1920s and extended through the 1930s.

It also influenced Bing Crosby, to whom credit for "crooning" is usually given.[70]

As performers and customers, American women provided the focus of popular phonograph culture in the 1920s. Younger women particularly had attracted the gaze of close observers of the dance craze. The Progressive reformers had made the dance craze into a female concern, as older wealthy women focused on the dangers awaiting younger poorer women in unsupervised dance halls; the phonograph ads usually centered on the females; and the symbol of the dance craze in the 1920s was, of course, "the flapper." Phonograph industry publications unequivocally declared that young women bought the majority of social dance records.

Middle-class "women want[ed] dance music."[71] According to one trade journal, "If it were not for the flapper, the Victor people might as well go out of business. They buy ninety per cent of the records—mostly dance records." The teenaged female "flapper" rarely had enough of her own money to buy the phonograph, but she often pressured her parents into buying one in the first place. Elderly couples rarely purchased phonographs. The "flapper" usually had enough pocket money to purchase records, and in those cases where she came into the store with her mother, the mother "always allows her to make her own choice of records."[72]

The "flapper" stereotype of the 1920s symbolized a curiously ambivalent social and aesthetic rebellion of young women against the domestic roles and musical sensibilities that their mothers had prepared for them. The "flapper," named for the birdlike arm movements involved in dancing "the Charleston," carried a reputation for unconventional behavior. Sometimes known as "Jazz Babies" or "Gold Diggers," younger women defied the world of Victorian domestic propriety by throwing out the corsets, wearing short dresses, binding their chests to create a distinctly flat-chested, un-Victorian silhouette, cutting or bobbing their hair in short styles, smoking cigarettes and drinking prohibition alcohol in public, and generally challenging traditional white male expectations of them.

Much of this new female public image, pervasively touted by the newspapers, pulp magazines, movies, cabarets, and dance halls, took its stylistic cues from the urban social worlds of single working women who created subcultures copied by middle- and upper-class bohemian women as models of rebellion and freedom. Working-class women provided "blueprints of 'sexy' behavior" for young flappers who romanticized and imitated them. The lives of single working-class women might actually ache with loneliness and frustration, but appropriations of their social styles in the media emphasized "those Wild, Reckless Dare-Devils," dashing upon the world like a blazing meteor and insisting "Mother . . . I will *not* go home! I will not be good! I will not reform!"[73]

Vocalist Marion Harris gave voice to the young socially progressive female in many of her popular recordings: "I'm A Jazz Vampire" (Co

A3328) finds her reveling in her "wickedness" as she leads men astray; in "Sweet Papa (Your Mama's Gettin' Mad)" (Co A3300) Harris warns her man that she's got a razor and he's fooling with the undertaker; most obviously, however, in "I'm Gonna Do It If I Like It" (Co A3367), she's seventeen-year-old Mary who's "running wild" despite her mother's anger. Such songs, delivered in Harris's jaunty urbane manner captured for repeated listening new social possibilities awaiting single women working in the big cities.[74]

The teen-age female still living in her parents' home might mimic some of the tough personal style of Marion Harris and the chorus girls, waitresses, cabaret singers, and hash slingers they saw portrayed in the movies and pulp magazines, wearing the clothes and dancing the dance, but the phonograph lifted modern dance music out of the cabarets and dance halls, interlacing young women's social rebellions with a bourgeois domestic spirit. Trade publications reported that mothers of "flappers" hoped that the phonograph would keep their little jazz babies at home.[75]

Mr. Tipling of the Lauter Company in Easton, Pennsylvania, commented:

> The mother thinks if they have a talking machine or piano, it will keep the girl at home and the girl says she will stay at home if the folks will buy one. The largest percentage of our sales are made that way. I think the girl has a good deal more influence than she used to have.[76]

The phonograph both expressed and resolved some of the tensions over differences in social and musical style between mothers and their flapper daughters. When listening to the vocal and the dance records of their own choosing on either the family phonograph or one of the portables developed during the twenties to sell to young women (portables for young women were made to look like overnight bags), restless daughters might imaginatively recreate the brightly sassy, elegant world of the hotel or dance hall orchestra. When listening with their friends in a record department listening booth, or at someone's home, comparing reactions to the hottest new sounds, repeating media stories of handsome bandleaders and their savvy female vocalists, young women could begin to create through records a world of their own imagining. Even upper middle-class women responded to the wilder spirit of dance records in a St. Louis phonograph store where a worried salesman reported to his manager that a party of wealthy socialites who had gathered in a "well-secluded record demonstration room" were "acting plum nutty."[77]

The phonograph industry, after all, encouraged young people to roll up the rug and dance to phonograph records in their parents' homes. During the 1920s, doing the Charleston or the Black Bottom, or particularly the Shimmie, with a group of one's peers became an expression of generational social rebellion. These dances freed women from the embrace of men; to French writer Paul Valéry, they moved alone with the agitated music "tracing stars of movement, magic precincts, leaping from scarcely closed circles."

In a more analytical mode Valéry wrote that the dancer "is in another world . . . unaware of her surroundings . . . concerned only with herself and [the earth] from which she breaks free." The dancer loses the sense of her surroundings, according to Valéry, and "creates a special kind of time that is absolutely her own." The dance "has a kind of inner life . . . consisting entirely in sensations of time and energy which . . . form a kind of closed circle of resonance."[78] In twenties America, young women danced to all those swiftly spinning resonant discs, creating independent worlds of rhythm and movement.

As the needle swiftly hissed across the record's surface to the spiral's end, the dancers reentered the intense world of mating rituals. There, too, the phonograph and its discs provided industrialized support in discovering new commercialized worlds of companionate romance and married enchantment. F. W. Schnirring, Advertising Manager for the Sonora Company, fashioned appeals to young people, particularly "the marriageable young lady and her parents." Schnirring's advertisements for Sonora appealed broadly to small-town as well as big-city record jobbers.[79]

Sonora promised young women and their mothers that the phonograph and dance records would help them set irresistible romantic snares. Sonora presented its scenario through male eyes, creating a caricatured recent male college graduate who generally found women interesting but seemed to meet only "the dull quiet home girl" or beautiful but shallow theater-goers and night club hoppers. Female readers learned, no doubt to their relief, that "we men do not propose marriage in night clubs." Sonora Man had remained single . . . "And then 'she' came! Just a real girl, easy to look at, dressed nicely—She understood that: *it is in her home that he plans his*." Unlike the quiet girl, Sonora Girl "made every evening a cheerful one." The younger set gathered at her house, spending, thanks to recorded music, "enchanted hours together—subdued lights . . . music . . . beauty . . . romance!"

> Colorful harmonies steal upon the soul while they engender thoughts which find no speech. As the record plays, so, too, does their imagination and to the tune of its mystic music they build their air castles and plans for tomorrow.[80]

The phonograph therefore became a major promoter of middle-class dreams and fantasies of romance and companionate marriage and at the same time helped women to find their own private worlds of music and dance.

Trade papers encouraged dealers to promote records as Valentine's Day gifts, and Columbia developed sleeves with appropriate imagery.[81] A very short story reprinted from a British publication revealed that phonograph records helped to build and maintain romantic relationships. If pressing job responsibilities abruptly pulled the swain away from his betrothed, the gift of the right record, Mendelssohn's "Wedding March," for example, could communicate personal feelings too deep to verbalize, reestablishing emotional if not direct personal contact.[82]

The phonograph industry left it to its female African American "race record" vocalists to make a cleaner break with bourgeois morality. The so-called classic blues singers—Mamie Smith, Bessie Smith, Clara Smith, Trixie Smith, Alberta Hunter, Ethel Waters, Ma Rainey, Ida Cox, Rosa Henderson, Victoria Spivey, and Lucille Hegamin—finally got to record in the early 1920s, breaking down the racial barriers that had excluded most African Americans from the recording studios and introducing vocal blues there. Perhaps because they were considered by record promoters to be other than white, their records, designed by whites for sale to Blacks, made more daring breaks with conventional gender roles than did Marion Harris's discs, designed by whites for whites.

For example, the classic blues singers more frankly expressed a wider variety of female sensibilities made possible by the migration from rural and small-town paternal families to independent urban apartments. As Hazel C. Carby has put it, the "differing interests of women and men in the domestic sphere," "the rage of women against male infidelity," and the assertion of female sexual autonomy all found expression on classic blues records.[83] In a refreshingly honest, and far more radical, escape from gender straitjackets, the Black female blues singers of the 1920s offered their listeners strongly assertive role models for independent female thought and action, substantially widening the number of possibilities for living life. Ma Rainey and Ethel Waters sang openly of lesbian love's superiority to heterosexuality, and Bessie Smith left no doubts that her men had either to toe the line or move hastily out of her life. Smith, the best paid of these blues vocalists, achieved the greatest sales, her Columbia record of "Downhearted Blues" selling 780,000 copies in 1923.[84] When we recall that a single disc cost 20¢ to make and sold wholesale for about twice that, retailing at 75¢, Columbia grossed $156,000 in 1923 dollars on this hit record; all told, retailers grossed another $273,000. Columbia could well afford to pay Bessie Smith $250 per recording session.

The burgeoning sales of Classic Blues records, and particularly Bessie Smith's hits, therefore opened the door for the male country blues recording artists of the mid- to late 1920s, emphatically proving that a lucrative market existed for recordings of African American blues artists and rooting recorded blues in the American consciousness. According to Michael W. Harris, Smith's sales may have amounted to as much as 20 percent of all sales of race records in 1923, while by 1927, race records represented 5 percent of all record sales. Clearly, then, women had introduced race records, generated significant profits, and proved the existence of a market for a much wider variety of blues artists.

In many ways, therefore, a gendered experience of the phonograph found encouragement from an early date and women contributed in important ways to the history of the phonograph and recorded music. In order to get its product through the doors of middle-class homes, the industry promoted a phonographic adaptation of Victorian concepts of female musicality. American women quickly adopted the talking machine into their lives, as record consumers, often as retailers, and occasionally as vocal stars, turning the consumption of musical commodities into psychologically and sometimes economically useful activities.

The rise of the young record-consuming flapper signaled the birth of a pattern of female consumption of inexpensive phonographs and popular dance records that has become a familiar ingredient in American teenage culture as records of the latest vocalists and bands provide a sense of independence and distance from parents and school. Over the longer run, the industry has learned to systematically exploit this market in ways unknown to the 1920s.

Over the shorter run, the stockmarket crash and the ensuing economic depression destroyed the worlds of record retailing that had afforded many women a meaningful, if low-level, participation in shaping public musical tastes. The crash came so suddenly that most phonograph dealers were caught with large record inventories on hand. The industry had encouraged the sale of a broad, rich, representative cross section of musical styles, including but not limited to opera, symphonies, middlebrow popular music, and ethnic, race, and popular dance music. The very breadth and depth of that recorded sample had necessitated knowledgeable sales personnel. Since the Depression drastically reduced discretionary leisure-time income, retailers took a complete loss on their large inventories and closed down their elaborate and expensive record retailing departments, firing their female managers and clerks.[85]

Among resentful phonograph dealers, large unsold inventories that sat on the shelves or, at best, sold at a loss, became a silent argument for never going into that line of business again. Most turned to selling radios and washing machines in glorified hardware stores. Retailers could no longer afford to stock a large inventory of records in the name of cultural meliorism. As one trade journal put it: "Much of the 'Prestige' is gone from the business and dealers treat records like furniture or clothing."[86] Another one echoed: "High Class Prestige Music which didn't sell much has passed from the scene. Records are merchandise to be moved!"[87]

As chapter 7 will reveal in greater detail, the stockmarket crash and ensuing economic depression brought major changes in the way records were sold and in this process the female retailer agents disappeared. When records began to sell once more in 1933–34, there was no longer a large inventory to be memorized nor as broad a spectrum of highbrow and middlebrow recordings to sell. In a sense, the Depression killed off much of the lingering Victorianism in record merchandizing.

During the last years of the 1920s, moreover, the predominant style of popular female recording artists began to change in ways that anticipated the most popular 1930s recordings. Marion Harris, who had begun recording for the Victor Talking Machine Company in 1916, switched to Columbia in 1919 and made some of her best sides for Brunswick in 1929–

30. Harris's recording career moved to Great Britain, where she recorded for English Decca from 1931 to the end of her recording career in 1934.

The records Harris made for Brunswick under the direction of Jack Kapp, who was to play the key role in the revival of the popular music recording business in the mid-thirties, marked a new departure in her style, a clear break with her red hot mamma personna. Harris's recordings of "You Do Something To Me" (1930) and "Blue Again" (1930) feature a more sophisticated, intimate vocal interpretation of Broadway show tunes that she imbued with the rudiments of the "torch singer" style in which a beautiful but seasoned female performer ruefully expressed the complex workings of love in her life.

The Depression so powerfully interrupted the history of recorded sound in America that Marion Harris will forever remain the popular voice of the mass audience of the twenties. When the industry finally recovered, her voice, like those of the female record retailers, was replaced by Ruth Etting's and those of men like Rudy Vallee and Bing Crosby. The relatively brief interlude of the teens and twenties, during which many women made a bid to find meaningful economic and artistic activity in those areas of the world of recorded sound open to them, was not to be repeated. American society had shaped women's interactions with the phonograph in certain highly defined ways that served to open and then to close most paths toward greater opportunity. The interactions of women with recorded music from 1890 to 1945 had laid the groundwork for later moves into positions of leadership in the industry.

Ada Jones, the first female popular recording star. (Courtesy of the Ford Archives, Henry Ford Museum, Dearborn, Michigan)

Early male popular recording stars, from *Phonogram*; George Johnson in lower left-hand corner. (Reproduced from the Collections of the Library of Congress)

Eldridge Reeves Johnson, president of the Victor Talking Machine Company. (Reproduced from the Collections of the Library of Congress)

Emile Berliner's hand-driven Gramophone was the prototype from which Eldridge Johnson developed the Victor line of phonographs. (Reproduced from the Collections of the Library of Congress)

E. BERLINER'S

GRAMOPHONE.

THE GREAT **$18.** TALKING MACHINE

View with Horn Attached.

Will there be a Victrola in your home this Christmas?

The only instrument that brings you the world's greatest artists

A splendid surprise for your family—to have Caruso, Destinn, Farrar, Gluck, Hempel, Homer, McCormack, Melba, Ruffo, Schumann-Heink, Scotti, Tetrazzini and other famous artists sing for them; to have Elman, Kreisler, Paderewski, Powell, Zimbalist and other noted instrumentalists play for them; to hear Sousa's Band, Pryor's Band, Conway's Band, Vessella's Band, Victor Herbert's Orchestra; to enjoy Harry Lauder, Nora Bayes, DeWolf Hopper, Raymond Hitchcock and other celebrated comedians and entertainers.

Nothing else will bring so much pleasure to your family and friends all the year round.

There are Victors and Victrolas in great variety of styles from $10 to $400, and there are Victor dealers in every city in the world who will gladly demonstrate them and play any music you wish to hear.

Important warning. Victor Records can be safely and successfully played only with Victor Needles or Tungstone Styles on Victors or Victrolas. Victor Records cannot be safely played on machines with jeweled or other reproducing points.

To insure Victor quality, always look for the famous trademark "His Master's Voice." It is on every Victrola and every Victor Record. It is the identifying label on all genuine Victrola and Victor Records.

Victor
"HIS MASTER'S VOICE"

Victrola

The Victor Talking Machine Company's Victrola was publicized as having enough fidelity to convince listeners "of the best sort" that the opera stars were right there in the room with them. (Reproduced from the Collections of the Library of Congress)

Opera, recording, and film star Geraldine Farrar after her early retirement from the opera. (Courtesy of the Performing Arts Research Center, New York Public Library at Lincoln Center)

CARICATURE OF CARUSO MAKING A RECORD
Drawn by himself

Caricature of Caruso Making a Record. Drawn by himself. (Courtesy of the Performing Arts Research Center, New York Public Library at Lincoln Center)

Okeh race record star and vaudeville blues singer Mamie Smith with her Jazz Hounds. (Courtesy of the Institute of Jazz Studies)

Best-selling Columbia Classic blues recording star Bessie Smith.
(Courtesy of the Institute of Jazz Studies)

Columbia race records advertisement reproduced from *Talking Machine World.*

Cover from Okeh catalog of "Old Time Tunes," 1924. (Reproduced from the Collections of the Library of Congress)

Schoolchildren march around their classroom to recorded patriotic music during World War I. (Reproduced from the Collections of the Library of Congress)

Milt Gabler, proprietor of New York City's mecca for recorded jazz, the Commodore Music Shop. (Courtesy of the Institute for Jazz Studies)

John Henry Hammond, Jr., Columbia Records producer and leading mediator of big band swing. (Courtesy of the Institute of Jazz Studies)

Jack Kapp, president of Decca Records and savior of popular recorded music during the Depression. Reproduced from the Collections of the Library of Congress.

Ruth Etting and Bing Crosby, Jack Kapp's voices of reassurance during the Depression. (Courtesy of the Performing Arts Research Center, New York Public Library at Lincoln Center)

Two particularly active consumers of recorded sound—Marshall Stearns (*right*) and Sheldon Harris, author of the Blues *Who's Who*. (Courtesy of the Institute of Jazz Studies)

Dan Morgenstern, director of the Institute of Jazz Studies, Rutgers University, Newark, New Jersey, holds one of his many Grammys. (Courtesy of the Institute of Jazz Studies)

A 1945 photo of Capt. G. Robert Vincent, director of the V-Disc program. (Courtesy of Douglas Collar)

GIs in the Italian Alps
enjoy the sounds of
V-Discs during a
break in the fighting.
(Courtesy of
E. P. DiGiannantonio)

World War II sailors in
the Pacific theater
inspect a new ship-
ment of V-Discs. Each
shipment included 20
records and 100 new
needles. (Courtesy of
E. P. DiGiannantonio)

Caricature from the Jack Kapp
Collection showing United States
Marines listening to recorded
music just before the invasion of
Guam. (Reproduced from the
Collections of the Library of
Congress)

6

AFRICAN AMERICAN BLUES AND THE PHONOGRAPH

From Race Records to Rhythm and Blues

They don't care nothing about me. All they want is my voice . . .
If you colored and can make them some money, then you all
right with them.

> —Blues singer Gertrude "Ma" Rainey
> as portrayed in August Wilson,
> *Ma Rainey's Black Bottom*

I invented Louis Armstrong.

> —Ralph S. Peer, Okeh and
> Victor Record Producer

Commercial recordings of music made by African Americans, discs designed by record companies to sell to African Americans, finally emerged in the 1920s as a further extension of earlier ethnic music recording programs. The phonograph's mediation of the musical experience for both performers and listeners emerges clearly enough in ethnic records, but all the more so in those marketed to African Americans. The process whereby recordings of members of this particular group came to be made the way they were at a given period in time indicates how society helped to shape the uses of recording technology. As African Americans undertook a historic emigration from the rural South to northern industrial cities during this time period, their music tended to become more secular, individualized, and commercialized while retaining powerful elements of African and southern Black musical culture.[1] Those who sang and played the blues in recording studios recognized in their experiences with sound technology bright new possibilities in the musical entertainment business but also expressed a deep ambivalence about the ways that white people restricted their advancement within the record business.

Just as the record industry had created its spinning encapsulations of ethnicity, so too it now turned to making engravings of the sounds of race. Given the system of racial oppression in America, African Americans had either to gain a measure of control over the process of record production or be colonized in wax. From an early date, for example, they demonstrated a particularly lively interest in recorded music and actively pursued power and profit in the popular music business, often explicitly linking their efforts to the progress of the race. For a people so long kept in poverty, they consistently spent significant amounts of money on phonographs and records, largely shunning radio. Moreover, white Americans had long since opened a door to Black musical professionalization by crediting Blacks with possessing particularly distinctive musical traditions. Black jazz musicians in big-city cabarets had already provided the music industry with exciting new models for popular music. From 1890 to 1945, however, the best they could maneuver was a tension-filled alliance with sharp-dealing white recording entrepreneurs. This arrangement created a special category of phonograph recordings that came, in 1922, to be called race records (the companies adopted the more euphemistic phrase "rhythm and blues" at the end of World War II). Under these conditions, to be so ruthlessly marginalized in the record business alienated many African Americans from their studio employers. In the post–World War II era, for the first time, increasing numbers of records by and for Blacks consistently reflected the production decisions of African American phonograph entrepreneurs.[2]

Race records therefore present a dilemma: widely celebrated for preserving and spreading a taste for the blues and gospel music, we can never know how different they might have sounded if Blacks had been able to control their production. Surely race records contained far less of the overt and single-minded racist stereotyping routinely broadcast over radio throughout the period.[3] But race records might be of the race and for the race, but not fully by the race, and several Black musicians and singers, as we shall see below, claimed that despite the rich eclectic variety of Black popular music they were allowed to record only blues.

Between 1920 and 1945 (with time out for the stockmarket crash, the worst of the Depression, and the recording ban of World War II), a robust business in recording Black musicians and vocalists developed within the recording industry, one which led to a far broader national and international appreciation of racially and commercially mediated African American popular music. An estimated 5,500 blues and 1,250 gospel recordings by about 1,200 artists were issued between 1920 and 1942. Recording provided some revenue and publicity to strengthen the careers of a relatively small number of African American performers who would otherwise have reached a much smaller audience. Providing a real, if quite limited, source of income—usually a flat payment per recording issued—studio work also made it possible for a variety of jazz and blues musicians from Joseph "King" Oliver and Louis Armstrong to Bessie Smith and Big Bill Broonzy, to exert a major influence in the subsequent history of blues and jazz.

From 1920 to 1945, the race record era, many different companies made recordings of African American music, but four major labels—Okeh, Paramount, Brunswick/Vocalion, and Columbia took control of the field. The Victor Talking Machine Company was slow to involve itself in the African American market,[4] while Decca, along with Victor's inexpensive Bluebird label, dominated it from 1934 to the end of World War II. A few small independent Black companies challenged white hegemony during the 1920s but swiftly bowed from the field—the Pace Phonograph Corporation, the Spikes Brothers' Sunshine label, Chappelle and Stinnette's C & S Records, Winston Holmes's Merrit Records, J. Mayo Williams's Black Patti label (named after the nineteenth-century African American soprano Siserietta Jones, who was often compared to Adelina Patti) and the mysterious Echo Records. All of the major companies that dominated the field were of course owned and run by whites. Not until Berry Gordy, Jr. founded Motown Records in 1959 did a Black-owned record company seriously challenge white hegemony.[5]

During the leanest years before the start of race records, a small number of Blacks still did manage to get recorded. As explained in chapter 1, George W. Johnson's 1892 recordings were the first by an African American. Vaudeville star Bert Williams made cylinders for Universal Phonograph Company in New York in 1897 and Victor issued fifteen of his titles beginning in 1901. Clarinetist Wilbur Sweatman cut a cylinder of Scott Joplin's "Maple Leaf Rag" for a Minneapolis music store in 1903–1904 and recorded many titles in 1916 and 1917.[6] But even a large company like Columbia was still excluding Black performers from its studios into the 1920s.[7]

Even as all but a few Black musical entertainers were denied access to the recording studios, the companies developed their catalogs of African American-inspired music recorded by white artists. Sophie Tucker, Marion Harris, Billy Golden, and Billy Murray poured out the minstrel show-inspired coon songs, some of them written and published by African Americans.

The pre–blues era breakthrough of African Americans as recording artists slowly accelerated as the industry began to recognize a potentially lucrative market for records among Blacks. The Black emigration from the South into northern industrial cities had not escaped the attention of white record executives. The industry trade papers first mentioned the possibility of an African American market in September 1913, when *Talking Machine World* reported that an unidentified black salesman working for an unidentified record wholesaler had convinced his boss that "the black man is greatly misunderstood. He is not nearly so ignorant and unappreciative as the world in general would have us believe." The salesman was proving his point by amassing "a really good trade among these people." The publication enjoined its retailers to go out and get that Black business.[8] This short article, with its important claim that northern urban Blacks wanted phonographs and records, was accompanied by a photo of an African American baby holding an Edison Blue Amberola Cylinder package over the clichéd caption "the Black and Blue—Baby Wants It." The article makes it appear that by 1913 the phonograph industry was already trying to associate things "blue" with Blacks.

The year 1913 was, of course, seven years before the phonograph industry embraced the blues; a nationwide grass roots social dance craze had gotten under way in 1910 and was assiduously encouraged by the recording industry beginning in 1913. In that latter year, the pioneering African American orchestra leader James Reese Europe, who provided the accompaniment for the nationally popular ballroom dance instructors Vernon and Irene Castle, began his recording career on the Victor label. Europe's Victor contract, the first ever offered to an African American musician by a major recording company, and therefore an important breakthrough for Blacks in the recording business, was made possible by his association with the Castles.[9] Europe's Society Orchestra presented a variety of the dance music of the day—one steps, tangos, maxixes, waltzes, and rags. Even if these records could not have appeared without the support of the Castles, their wonderful sales helped awaken an industry interest in selling records of African Americans making music.

By the end of the same year, the industry had begun to respond to what was becoming a fairly well anticipated African American market. The Chicago *Defender* reported that "the record companies" were interested in knowing how many phonographs were owned "by members of the Race." The paper requested that readers who owned machines send in their names and addresses; once some statistics had been compiled, the *Defender*, which, significantly, made no mention of any specific stylistic preferences, felt sure that "records of the Race's great artists will be placed on the market."[10]

By the end of that same year, the Emerson Company issued some sides by Wilbur Sweatman, a clarinetist and vaudeville entertainer known for playing three clarinets at once. Sweatman recorded a variety of Hawaiian music and ragtime for Emerson in 1916 and 1917 and went on to cut ragtime, blues, and ballads for Pathé.

The pioneering songwriter and music publisher W. C. Handy with "Handy's Orchestra of Memphis" got into Columbia's New York recording studio in September 1917 for a series of productive sessions. Handy, in those days a struggling bandleader and booking agent, periodically improved his income through royalty checks from companies that employed white artists to interpret his tunes.[11]

But two forces continued to limit the development of recordings for and by African Americans: first, the firmly established tradition of cover versions by white minstrel entertainers who acted out the role of the racial "other" for whites fascinated with Black culture; and second, a corresponding marketing dilemma linked to outdated assumptions about dispersed rural Black settlement patterns and restrictive patent law.

Racial prejudice imbedded itself in the phonograph industry's social ambitions to become a vital part of middle- and upper middle-class musical culture. As Perry Bradford, who later broke through some race barriers in the popular music recording industry, put it: "Victor [Talking Machine Company] just couldn't afford to lower their prestige" by issuing records by Black artists.[12] W. C. Handy had to listen to one record company executive tell him that he had "made ten times too much money [in royalties] from their phonograph company."[13] Ralph Peer, the white record executive who was to play such an important role in developing race records, casually referred to music by African Americans as "the n_____ stuff."[14]

As chapter 2 indicated, several of the early stars of popular entertainment records, Len Spencer, Cal Stewart, and Arthur Collins, for example, transferred the sounds of minstrelsy to records, leaving little room for George W. Johnson and Bert Williams to establish an African American interpretation of recorded African American music and culture. The lack of faces that the average record listener could put with the voices he heard permitted a record fan to imagine that recorded minstrel routines actually reflected African American culture.

Also, the Victor and Columbia companies, which dominated the production and distribution of phonographs and records, jointly owned patent rights on the "lateral" process of recording, one designed so that the needle moved from side to side in a groove of uniform depth. Records of this sort could be made only by Columbia and Victor and could be played only on their machines. Therefore, the vertical-cut "hill-and-dale" recordings of Wilbur Sweatman by Emerson and Pathé Frères, in which vibration patterns were cut vertically into the recording medium, were manufactured to be played only on machines made by any of a handful of much smaller companies using the hill-and-dale method. The chances of any family, not only an African American one, owning a turntable that could play an Emerson or Pathé record were slight; most were more likely to own a Victor or Columbia machine. Patent-protected technology reflected the special privileges enjoyed by the phonograph pioneers, but it held back at an early and significant date the distribution and appreciation of music recorded by and for African Americans.

From 1914 to 1916, several small new companies entered the phonograph field and began to challenge Victor's and Columbia's exclusive patent rights over lateral-cut recording. By 1919, two of them, the General Phonograph Company and New York Recording Laboratories, Inc., had begun issuing lateral-cut records, but the judicial appeals process on lateral-cut patent rights did not end until the summer of 1920. The first lateral-cut Okeh record of an African American popular female vocalist, a record that could be played on any machine, was issued in August of 1920.[15]

The Okeh label, manufactured by the General Phonograph Company, presented a serious challenge to the dominance of the record business established by Victor and Columbia and ultimately forced those two giants to become more active in the African American and, by extension, the popular, market. Otto Heinemann, a German phonograph and record industry pioneer who founded the Okeh record label in 1918, therefore played a key role in the history of recorded African American music. Heinemann intended his label to cater to popular tastes and promoted it as "the Most Popular of Popular Records."[16] He had designed his vertical-cut records so that they could be played on any kind of phonograph with minimal adjustments. The German businessman also led the attack on the lateral-cut patents. In 1920, thanks to his business ambitions, Mamie Smith, a Black vaudeville artist, became the first female African American to record a popular record, Perry Bradford's "That Thing Called Love" backed by "You Can't Keep a Good Man Down." Court appeals were pending on the lateral-cut patents in February when the disc was made; Bradford called these sides a company "feeler." Marketed in August, the disc sold 10,000 copies, twice the number needed to cover expenses. The Pace & Handy Publishing Company had printed the sheet music of these two Bradford originals; Okeh paid both Handy and Bradford their royalties in promissory IOUs that could be "discounted" at some banks.

Given the success of that record and of General Phonograph's challenge to restrictive lateral-cut patents, Okeh quickly recorded Smith again on August 10, 1920, singing "Crazy Blues" (Okeh 4169) accompanied by Mamie Smith's Jazz Hounds, an all-Black group. This blues number, entitled "Harlem Blues" in Smith and Bradford's current theatrical production "Made in Harlem" and renamed to avoid copyright infringement, sold so well that Okeh soon gave Bradford, according to his own testimony, a royalty check, not a promissory note, for $53,000. A series of other companies like the Pace Phonograph Company, Paramount, and Vocalion swiftly began recording African American vocalists as well.

The groundwork for the breakthrough of Black Americans into the blues and jazz recording business had been carried out not in the United States but in Germany, where, in 1902, Otto Heinemann, Max Straus, and H. Zunz had pooled the equivalent of $500 in capital and opened a small talking machine store in Berlin. The partners then had scraped together $4,000 and bought the nascent gramophone company of Carl Lindstrom A. G. of Berlin. Heinemann dominated the group, and Lindstrom swiftly grew to be one of the largest and most influential companies in the European phonograph trades. Zunz, who became Heinemann's brother-in-law, died in 1906 and from that year to 1914, Heinemann was managing director of Lindstrom.[17]

Heinemann soon became an experienced, savvy record man. Lindstrom companies produced 700,000 phonographs and 40 million records per year.[18] He served as director of the Fonotipia, Odeon, Favorite, Dacapo, and Lyrophone labels and built recording studios and pressing plants around the world, including five in Germany and one apiece in Switzerland, England, France, Poland, Austria, Spain, and Brazil. As a result, he was able to sell successfully symphonic and operatic music recorded in Europe on the Odeon label and offer "foreign" and "ethnic" music in most known languages of the world.[19]

In 1914, the pioneer German Jewish phonograph executive brought with him to the United States invaluable European patents on crucial phonograph parts, record labels, matrices, and, significantly, in view of the legal expenses involved in challenging American patents, working capital from Germany. Heinemann established, along with his brother Adolph, the Otto Heinemann Phonograph Supply Company at 45 Broadway in New York City. In 1915, the company was incorporated, renamed the General Phonograph Company, and moved to 25 West 45th Street.[20]

The timing of Heinemann's American venture reflected the outbreak of World War I but also some of the inner workings of the industry. By moving his phonograph empire out of the European battle zone, Heinemann protected his investment, but crucial American recording patents, good for seventeen years after being issued, were set to expire before the end of the decade, opening the record business to new initiatives.[21] In 1916, two other new record companies that would challenge Heinemann—the Aeolian Company and the New York Recording Laboratories, Inc.—created the Vocalion and Paramount labels, respectively.[22]

Heinemann appears to have been a clever businessman and carefully timed his entry into the recording end of the business. At first, he avoided direct competition with Victor, Columbia, and Edison by becoming a supplier of phonograph parts rather than an omnibus phonograph-producing company. Yet, part by part, he steadily built his own American empire. He began in 1915 by manufacturing spring-driven turntable motors under an agreement with A. G. Bean of Elyria, Ohio, to make "The Motor of Quality" according to his own specifications. He bought out important competition through his purchase of the A. F. Meisselbach Company of Newark N.J., and he subsequently bought the John M. Dean phonograph needle factory of Putnam, Connecticut, as well.

Only later, in 1918, did he move into the hill-and-dale record business too, by buying a record pressing plant in Springfield, Massachusetts, and a New York City recording laboratory then controlled by Charles Hibbard, technical director, and Fred Hager musical director. Hager and his assistant Ralph S. Peer were to play particularly influential roles in recording black musicians and vocalists. In that same year Heinemann marketed for the first time his Okeh records.[23] Priced at the then standard retail price of 75¢ per record, the label presented an uninspired cross section of the day's popular vaudeville headliners and a very wide variety of ethnic music; Okeh's success in great part stemmed from its being the first record placed on the market that could be played, with relatively minor adjustments, on any brand of phonograph. Heinemann had so cleverly timed his entry into the recording business that he was ready when the patents on lateral-cut recording finally crumbled. As John Cromelin put it at the time, Okeh was "the first good record which had been offered to dealers . . . without [their] being obliged to carry a corresponding line of machines."[24]

Heinemann's Okeh label followed its founder's conviction that a vast and swiftly growing potential market for popular music records awaited development in America. "America is the marketplace for the best ideas of the world," he was quoted as having said.[25] His general manager, John Cromelin, explained that the United States government had not really closed down the record business during World War I, even though many of the industry's raw materials and its technology had been reserved for the war effort. The laboring classes, he said, had made "unprecedented wages" during the war and had spent them on phonographs and records.[26] General Phonograph Company believed that postwar prosperity would continue while wartime restrictions on manufacturing supplies would cease. Demand for records seemed "unlimited."

But only if Okeh could find some hot-selling new sounds. For the most part, since 1918 Okeh had recorded the same older, established white entertainers doing traditional nineteenth-century material, resulting in records much like those that Victor and Columbia had long since placed on the market.[27] Moreover, the largely unexpected 1921 entry of radio on the market for home musical entertainment machines drove down the sale of phonographs and records. Columbia went bankrupt even though it continued to make records. Victor's sales dropped by half.[28] Otto Heinemann had excellent reasons to take a chance on recording African American music.

For their own part, Black musicians, entertainers, and song writers like W. C. Handy, Joseph "King" Oliver, Bert Williams, Chris Smith, Wilbur Sweatman, Jim Europe, Rosemond Johnson, Bill "Bojangles" Robinson, and, of course, Perry Bradford felt keenly the limited role of Black musical entertainers, songwriters, and music publishers in the phonograph business. Recognizing the convergence of favorable legal and economic conditions, they undertook a concerted drive to break the barriers around the recording business; destruction of the lateral-cut patents and competition mounted by radio had provided new opportunities in the phonograph business.

Three musical entrepreneurs—songwriter Perry Bradford, phonograph company founder Harry Pace, and record producer J. Mayo Williams—reveal several important facets of the African American experience in the recording business before World War II.[29] The career of Bradford, who broke through resistance in 1920 by producing, with the cooperation of Okeh's Ralph Peer and Fred Hager, recordings of Mamie Smith that sold more than enough to impress white executives throughout the industry, reveals the extremely narrow margin for maneuver that opened to African Americans before World War II.

Bradford's ambitions hinged on access to Fred Hager, a violinist and studio concert band director retained as Okeh's musical director of the New York studio purchased by Otto Heinemann in 1918. Hager, with the assistance of Ralph S. Peer, had decided to expand the production of "popular" records in general without publically signaling anything in particular about developing the African American market. Hager already had direct business contacts with Bradford's songwriter colleagues Chris Smith and Bill Tracy in connection with his Helf and Hager Music Publishing Company. Bradford used Tracy's name to get by Hager's secretary. Bradford found Hager more receptive than any other white executive in New York City.

Why Bradford touted the idea of recording African American female vocalists can only be inferred from the context of his effort, for he would only say that "that was what I was trying to sell." By 1920, all of those Blacks who had managed to record—George Johnson, James Reese Europe, W. C. Handy, Bert Williams, and Wilbur Sweatman—had been men. In a business that throve on novelty, the promotion of a woman gave both Bradford and his white counterparts something new to put on the market. When Mamie Smith's records sold well, other companies contributed to the classic blues phenomenon when they rushed to cover Okeh's success with their own female "blues" vocalists.

The most startling, and therefore revealing, ingredient in Bradford's potential breakthrough was his success in making Hager think in more positive terms about the potential for both a Black urban and a white southern market for "blues" records by Black female vaudevillians. Bradford did not specifically mention what later proved to be an extremely lucrative southern African American market. Perhaps adjusting to the industry's apprehensions about selling to African Americans and to the strong disapproval among established northern Black urbanites of jazz and blues, he waffled, predicting that the 14 million African Americans would buy records by "one of their own" and "not to expect any fast sales up here in the North . . . but the Southern *whites* will buy them like nobody's business."[30] This latter opinion, based, he claimed, on prior white southern exposure to "blind men on street corners in the South playing guitars and singing 'em for nickels and dimes," came as a surprise to Hager and other northerners, according to Bradford. Bradford's testimony suggests that he thought of what came to be called classic blues records, made by Black female entertainers, as designed at least in part for whites.

At that time, about 85.2 percent of the nation's black population lived in the South, 74.7 percent of them in rural areas.[31] Phonograph industry perceptions about the potential market for records by African Americans seem to have reflected an amalgam of ignorance and wishful thinking. In 1920, all aspects of the business were still overwhelmingly northern and urban. Few precedents existed for doing business with African Americans since custom dictated that one work the middle-class white market. Judging by the nature of their first race records, Okeh seems to have decided on a limited testing of the northern urban crossover market, recording cabaret vocalists and jazz musicians from the commercialized bright light districts of cities like Chicago and New York where whites and Blacks had long shared the black-and-tan trade.

This cautious vision left northern Black urban music entrepreneurs largely on the margins of the business and excluded rural southern Blacks nearly completely from the process of making records. In the northern cities, for example, being paid for making records was merely one part of the business; selling them was another, more profitable one. Black entrepreneurs like Handy and Clarence Williams in Harlem and Chicago had "applied to Okeh for local agencies to sell records, but, until the company was convinced of the northern urban Black market, they had been 'begging . . . in vain.'" The Spikes brothers were forced to buy 500 of Mamie Smith's "Crazy Blues" at retail price in order to sell them at above retail price in Los Angeles.

As a result, northern urban African American music entrepreneurs organized a sales campaign that would provide overwhelming evidence of the eager market for race records that they believed, from their experiences in cabaret show business, could be developed. They found willing allies among the editors of the major urban Black newspapers who were themselves eager for more advertising money from the record companies.[32] The Chicago *Defender*, for example, urged that Blacks buy Okeh records out of race pride.[33] So, too, Pullman porters "bought Mamie Smith's 'Crazy Blues' by the dozens" and sold them at stops along the lines down South.[34] More than 70,000 copies sold during the first month,[35] impressive evidence of the money to be made in making race records.[36]

But a bitter debate has raged over how that money might have been most equitably divided. From 1909 onward, one vital source of revenue in the record business had been carefully squirreled away by record company executives. According to the 1909 Copyright Act, the record companies had been obliged to pay 2¢ per recording to the copyright holder of each tune they recorded. To get this law passed, writers and publishers had accepted a "compulsory licensing provision" that allowed any other record company, provided it paid the required 2¢ per side to the copyright holder, also to record the same song after it had been granted a license to do so. This defined the practice of "covering," by which other labels marketed their own versions of a new recording that had demonstrated promising sales potential. Fearful of losing sales of their own original race recordings when other companies "covered" them to get in on the profits, record producers for the small race labels pressured their performers and songwriters to sign over their copyrights. Even if another company's version eventually sold better than the original record, the company that had first recorded the number and secured to itself legal control of copyright would be sure at least to get royalty payments from the second label.[37] In those cases where a given recorded selection sold well for a relatively long period of time, copyright could produce significant long-term revenues. Moreover, the rights to reproduce strong-selling recorded selections on cheaper dime store labels could earn the record company even more.

Clearly, the record companies would have preferred not to pay copyright holders at all and had opposed the 1909 Copyright Law by insisting that a recording, an aural document, was completely different from visual documents like sheet music and therefore should not be seen in the same light. Since the more powerful sheet music publishing firms remained in a position to force the recording companies to pay at least some royalties to copyright holders, many recording executives created their own music publishing companies to copyright tunes brought to them by recording artists. For the vocalist or bandleader, the price of making a record was to settle for some travel expenses, a flat, one-time payment from the record company, and to sign over composer's royalty rights to the record company or, more often, a subsidiary publishing company.

Perry Bradford, not one to minimize his own contributions, claimed to have fought all efforts to make him waive (sign away) his royalty rights as the copyright holder of material engraved on record (reportedly telling one executive "The only thing Perry Bradford WAIVES is the American Flag.").[38] He consequently reported having received a check for a sum in five figures. But the purchase of copyright by the recording company was still to be a widespread procedure in the race record business, and it continues to provide a basic factual reference point for African American accusations of musical exploitation in the United States. As chapter 7 reveals, the record companies, contrary to their practice with African American musicians and vocalists, did pay at least a small percentage of copyright royalties to their best-selling white country music artists.

Blues singer Bessie Smith's financial dealings with the Columbia Graphophone Company have been better documented than those of the other race recording stars with the various record companies. There are at least one or two statistical statements with which to work. Bessie Smith's 1923 recording of "Downhearted Blues," made under the direction of Frank Walker of Columbia records, sold better than any other blues recording, a reported 800,000 copies in the first six months after its release and over 2 million copies by the end of the first year. Many of her other 159 sides also sold extremely well, becoming the most popular race recordings of the 1920s. Bessie Smith's estimated total sales of around 6.5 million discs kept the perennially floundering Columbia label afloat during the Twenties.[39]

Frank B. Walker, in charge of rural southern recording at Columbia in the 1920s, is generally credited with having been more enlightened about race in the phonograph business than most of the white record producers. Born in 1889, Walker, who went on to make a major contribution to hillbilly recording and later to the "Nashville sound" in white country music, in addition to originating the movie sound track album,[40] had gone to work for the Columbia Graphophone Company. His business dealings with Bessie Smith have been clouded by questions of royalty rights.[41] At first, Smith's problem at Columbia involved as much the African American pianist, composer, and show business entrepreneur Clarence Williams as it did Frank Walker. In 1923, Smith had allowed Williams to negotiate her first recording contract; he had taken for himself a percentage of the royalty payments on her original copyrighted numbers plus one-half of the $125 flat payment per selection issued. Upon learning of her mistake, Smith and her husband Jack Gee fired Williams in no uncertain terms and negotiated successfully with Walker for rights to all of her $125 payment per issuable side (raised to $200 less than a year later) and received from Columbia a guarantee of a flat payment of at least $1,500 per year (later raised to $2,400) in exchange for her copyrights that now belonged partly to Walker's own publishing firms—Frank Music Company and later Empress Music Company—and partly to Columbia Records. Her biographer asserts that she actually earned "more than double" the contract guarantee.[42]

These arrangements, more generous than most, due as much to the impressive popularity of Bessie Smith's records as to the fatherly generosity of Frank Walker, reflected customarily sharp but legal practices in the industry. The question of whether they were ultimately fair to Bessie Smith is a complex one. Just how much anyone earned in copyright royalties on her records was known, after all, only by the record company which then and thereafter exercised caution in making public any evidence of their sales figures. In response to a question about Smith's record sales, Columbia Records producer John Hammond later stated that her original 78 rpm records had sold at least 6.5 million copies between 1923 and 1928.[43] Of the 160 different tunes she recorded, 38 were copyrighted in her name.[44] If we assume that the recordings of her 38 numbers sold at least as well as those copyrighted by others, those copyrighted in her name earned approximately $30,875 in copyright royalties. Smith, of course, had signed away her copyright royalties when signing her recording contracts, but Frank Walker nevertheless supposedly "put aside upwards of $20,000" to cover her royalties."[45]

However, $20,000 is not $30,875. On the other hand, Smith had voluntarily surrendered her right to any and all copyright royalties. But the plot further thickens! John Hammond spoke ambiguously of "between six and seven million *records*," not "sides" or "recordings," and we are forced to take him at his word. He therefore indicated between 12 million and 14 million sides, and copyright amounted to 2¢ per side. Seen in this light, Smith was given less than half of what her copyrights would have earned, had she not signed them away. By way of comparison, in the 1920s record companies paid to a few of their best-selling white hillbilly recording artists a maximum of 25 percent of the copyright royalties. According to industry spokesmen, Bessie Smith appears to have earned about the same amount.

The great popularity of Bessie Smith's earthy records, so evocative of the South from which she had moved in order to record, led the popular labels into several years of recording male country blues singers. Although some of them—Blind Lemon Jefferson, Big Bill Broonzy, Charlie Patton, and Papa Charlie Jackson—enjoyed significant sales, many of the others failed to sell the 5,000 copies per disc needed by the company to pay back production costs. According to Russell Sanjek,[46] these singers preferred to accept a flat fee rather than count on royalty.

But more African Americans found ways to make money in the business as race records continued to evolve. Otto Heinemann's General Phonograph Company and his jobbers such as the Chicago Talking Machine Company pioneered bulk sales of race records to African American retailers. Such arrangements extended for the first time to African Americans the usual discounting by wholesale jobbers to retailers. After 1922, the General Phonograph Company took the lead in selling "agencies" to African Americans on the south side of Chicago, in Harlem, and in the largest cities throughout the country. This solidified a second form of alliance between Blacks and whites: both would profit from retail record and phonograph sales over the long run, not just when a given disc "hit." Even if franchised record company retail outlets were soon a thing of the past, as nearly all records became lateral-cut and thus interchangeable on the vast majority of turntables, African American retailers now paid somewhere between the 20¢ it cost to produce one double-sided record and the 75¢ retail price aggressively promoted by Otto Heinemann.[47]

The two circus-style promotions of Okeh records in 1926 in Chicago, so often celebrated in the histories of early jazz, announced through their marketing ballyhoo an unprecedented market outreach to African Americans and the announcement of a new northern urban era of black enterprise in the record business. On February 27, the Consolidated Talking Machine Company of Chicago, Okeh's principle "jobber" in the midwest, staged a star-studded program called the Okeh Race Record Artists Night at the Chicago Coliseum, only the second time that Blacks had gathered in the main auditorium. Guitarist Lonnie Johnson and cornet sensation Louis Armstrong and his Hot Five made a record in front of the crowd "to demonstrate how its done." After the record was played back to the crowd, Clarence Williams, Bennie Moton, King Oliver, and Richard M. Jones also entertained; ex-Mayor William Hale Thompson made a speech and the whole program was broadcast over WGN radio.

The second major Okeh publicity stunt, the Okeh Cabaret and Style Show of June 12, 1926, organized by E. A. Fearn, President of the Okeh label's Chicago wholesaler, Consolidated Talking Machine Company, took shape in a two-day meeting of midwestern Okeh wholesalers during the Okeh Race Record Artists Night in February.[48] According to the trade papers, "the sole purpose of the entire affair was to popularize and sell Okeh records."[49] A thirty-day newspaper advertising campaign in the Black newspapers preceded this event, for which 65,000 flyers and posters circulated through the South Side; movie theaters ran slides announcing the event and Black-owned taxis carried stickers announcing that they were the "official" transportation for the show. During the week before the affair, parades with floats and bandwagons circulated through the streets, led by members of the Black musicians' union.

Most important, tickets were discounted with the purchase of at least one Okeh record at any one of the thirty-three music stores handling Okeh products in both the southern and the western ghettoes of Chicago. Franchised dealers usually paid a good deal less than retail price for records. Okeh records retailed at 75¢ apiece; but customers who bought both a ticket and a record got a reduction of 25¢ on the ticket, no reduction of price on the record, and a special $1.60 combination price for both. The sale of tickets to the Okeh Cabaret and Style Show, therefore, acted as publicity for Okeh records. Fearn further allied the self-interest of Black retailers and white record entrepreneurs by naming five South Side retail clothing outlets for women as official judges for a contest that was to name the forty best-dressed ladies at the show. The stores displayed large "beautifully-prepared" show cards advertising Fearn's promotion in their windows for two weeks before the Coliseum extravaganza. A 3:00 a.m. Charleston dance contest among dancers winnowed by the South Side dancing schools was decided by applause.

E. A. Fearn's Okeh Cabaret & Style Show of June 12–13, 1926, presented ten bands, two blues vocalists, and the comedy team of Butterbeans and Suzie. Just as important for the history of more democratic racial relations in the record business, it channeled at least some proceeds into the hands of African Americans: specifically, funds derived from the sale of advertising space in the evening's program, check room privileges, and the sale of beverages and food were donated to Local 208 of the Musicians' Union. However, Fearn pocketed the proceeds from ticket sales, the single largest sum of money involved. An estimated 18,000 persons were said to have attended the Coliseum event; at 85¢ a ticket that would have placed $15,300 into his coffers. With these proceeds, he paid $1,000 for rental of the Coliseum and unspecified amounts to print the tickets, programs, and advertising, have a special stage built, rent a state-of-the-art sound system for $600, and pay the 400 people who helped manage the affair.[50]

In the name of its own greater profits, therefore, the Okeh record company opened a narrow door of economic opportunity—exclusive company franchises, a retailing category that quickly disappeared. Thanks in large part to Okeh, African American entrepreneurs as well as the singers, musicians, songwriters, music publishers, and record promoters had initiated more extensive and lucrative business dealings with the industry. But the Okeh Race Records Artists Night was symbolic in more ways than one: the company's "demonstration" of how a record was made had been presented in the form of a theatrical performance. Okeh did not set about training African American recording technicians, and left to Fred Hager decisions about which African Americans to record.

Cornettist and entertainer Louis Armstrong played the starring role in the Okeh record promotions, but his own experiences with representatives of Okeh were typical of the ambivalent relations between Black artists and the race record companies. Armstrong's Hot Five and Hot Seven records for Okeh were some of the best-selling instrumental sides of the decade and they have continued to sell during the following seventy years. But according to Ralph S. Peer, who signed off on the production of these sides without being personally present at the recording sessions, these opportunities to record came as a backhanded "favor" to the jazz artist.

> I invented Louis Armstrong. I used to go frequently to Chicago for Okeh on sales trips. I would go out late at night to the "Royal something Gardens," a Negro dance hall. A lot of white musicians would go there to hear the orchestra. I got acquainted with Armstrong and his wife [Lil Hardin]. She was an awfully nice 'ol n_____ girl and she came to me and said "Louis has an offer to come to New York—Henderson's Orchestra—could you give us recording work there?" Well, we had already used Louis Armstrong [long silence on the tape] so we formed a pickup band with Louis Armstrong on trumpet. He was our house man on trumpet; when we wanted a jazz band he would be our first choice.
>
> Later the girl came to see me again and said Louis wanted to go back to Chicago, so I created an Armstrong Orchestra for them so that they could get some work, make it, you know, and we sent a recording unit out there . . . Louis Armstrong and His Hot Five . . . I got the best musicians you could get cause I liked Louis Armstrong. Of course, they were all from Oliver's band. The funny thing was, I wasn't even present when those records were made. I ok'd the musicians, all of whom I knew, and as long as Louis and the girl were there, I knew it would go alright since they'd worked in our studio. I set up the date around Armstrong. I really did it to give him enough money to get out there. That's how Louis Armstrong got started.[51]

Peer stopped short of stating that he had not given away any money but had rather advanced it to Hardin and Armstrong against future recording session payments. The trumpet virtuoso, always prudent and elusive when dealing with white authority figures, took what was for him a typical approach toward dealing with Peer. He sent Hardin to talk to him and, as Peer admitted many years later: "You know, the fella has almost forgotten me. I ran into him in Germany. I think he takes dope. "Mr. Peer . . . I can't remember." We've had a a tenuous connection over the years." Given the exceptional long-term sales of the Hot Fives, Armstrong may have deeply resented Peer's condescension.

In 1921, Harry H. Pace (1884–1943), partner with W. C. Handy in the Pace & Handy Music Company, tried to overcome the economic barriers to African American musical enterprise in the record business by founding the Pace Phonograph Corporation.[52] The efforts of Perry Bradford, Mamie Smith, and Fred Hager had demonstrated the existence of a potentially valuable northern, urban African American market for blues records. But Pace proposed his Black Swan label, named after the nineteenth-century soprano Elizabeth Taylor Greenfield, in order to appeal to middle-class Black listeners who often deplored both earthy blues and raucous jazz.[53]

Pace's phonograph company, the first owned and directed by African Americans to produce a substantial number of records, included W. E. B. Du Bois and William Grant Still among its directors. The company opened offices at 257 W. 138th St. and later moved to 2289 Seventh Ave. in the Harlem ghetto of New York City. In the face of the powerful race record fad for blues records made by white-owned companies, Pace determined to record a cross section of musical styles by Black artists, refusing to specialize in ethnic-sounding musical stereotypes. He even rejected Bessie Smith because of her "unmistakable nitty-grittiness."[54] His policy reflected hopes of appealing to the established Black middle class with what Robert Vann of the Pittsburgh *Courier* called "Negro music in the Negro home,"[55] as well as a desire to fight racial musical stereotyping. Back in 1916, the Chicago *Defender*, a major Black newspaper with both a local and national edition, had documented a Black middle class market for phonograph products, writing that Blacks had been buying records by white opera stars. The newspaper had urged them to pressure the record companies into making records by Black operatic singers: "How many of our race ever asked for a record of Mme. Anita Patti Brown, Mr. Roland Hayes, Miss Hazel Harrison, Miss Maude J. Roberts, Mr. Joseph Douglas . . . ?"[56] As Pace put it: "We ask and get the support of colored people because our products compare favorably in merit and price with the products of other companies of the same kind." This approach also would open opportunity to struggling Black artists in various nonblues and nonjazz musical genres. Black Swan recorded several sides of operatic singers Antoinette Garnes and Florence Cole-Talbert, for example.[57]

Nevertheless, the company's best-selling recording was Ethel Waters's "Oh, Daddy" backed by her version of Wilbur Sweatman's "Down Home Blues" (BS2010), recorded in May 1921. It was said to have sold 500,000 copies in six months. Waters recalled that although Pace wanted Black Swan to promote Black artists and African American music he had not wanted his product to appear "too colored."[58] Black Swan was soon issuing twelve records a month and bought three new presses to keep up with demand.[59]

But the arrival of radio broadcasting in 1922–23 sent the entire record business reeling and quickly toppled Pace's struggling new concern. Moreover, Pace's well-known association with Handy in the music publishing business led to a coordinated boycott of Pace & Handy copyrighted tunes in the white recording studios. Pace interpreted these moves as racist, proudly announcing to the press:

> The opposition of the white companies to the entry of a race organization into the phonograph record producing field makes me all the more determined to give the race representation in an entirely new field of business endeavor, and convinces me of the necessity of preserving our race music and preserving for our children the wonderful voices and musical talent we have in the race. The public wants the kind of records I shall put out and they will have them no matter who objects.[60]

He withdrew from his position as president of Pace & Handy Music Company, nevertheless, and Handy, his old partner, later insisted that whites did not know that Handy "had no stake in the Black Swan record company." "Other recording companies must have felt that by doing business with me as a publisher they were helping a rival recording outfit, fattening frogs for snakes, as it were."[61] No one appears to have registered any objections to Fred Hager, Okeh's musical director, co-owning the Helf & Hager music company that copyrighted songs released on the Okeh label. Despite Handy and Pace's separation of the recording and publishing companies, the Handy Music Company's copyright royalties swiftly declined; W. C. Handy had a nervous breakdown and lost his eyesight.

But without substantial capitalization and/or a string of best-selling records, the survival of Harry Pace's pioneering record company always would have remained in doubt.[62] Pace, a highly educated banker and insurance salesman, surely knew enough to make a go of his venture, although one of his competitors, Mayo Williams, claimed that he was more interested in banking and insurance than the record business.[63] Pace did have a couple of hit records, after all, but he lacked the kind of financial resources that had allowed Otto Heinemann to purchase record pressing factories. Even Heinemann had had to pay his artists in promissory notes before landing a hit record. When the established companies refused to press records for him, Pace entered into a partnership with the fledgling New York Recording Laboratories in Port Washington, Wisconsin—a geographically strained arrangement that inevitably led to problems of record distribution—and then joined John Fletcher in the Fletcher Record Company at 156 Meadow Street, Long Island City, N.Y. This company declared bankruptcy in December 1923, and was purchased in April 1924 by Paramount.

Thus died Harry Pace's effort to break into the production and marketing of records of African American singers and musicians. At least one industry executive believed that the failure of Black Swan turned wealthy Blacks away from investing in independent record companies, since it had been the only company that had wanted to record a wider spectrum of music by African Americans. And certainly it is true that the Black bourgeoisie living in northern cities at the time of the Great Migration firmly opposed the new commercialized leisure cultures that young African American immigrants from the South found so attractive.[64] Until the end of World War II, therefore, African Americans would continue to record and listen to race records listed by white recording companies in special race catalogs.

The middle years of the 1920s saw the rise of the Paramount label owned by the Wisconsin Chair Company of Grafton, Wisconsin, a small town north of Chicago. Wisconsin Chair, it is important to note, hoped to sell phonographs and other furniture to African Americans living in Detroit and Chicago. A line of records appeared necessary to selling phonographs, and recently arrived immigrants with regular pay checks were ready to enjoy the recorded sounds of the city and of Paramount's newly minted memories of the rural South they had left behind.[65]

Wisconsin Chair took little direct interest in the record business, but, thanks in large part to its Black record producer J. Mayo Williams, its Paramount label still managed to issue between 1,147 and 1,155 blues records before its demise in 1932, often pressing as many as 100,000 a day for the African American market,[66] including the vocals of Gertrude "Ma" Rainey, the classic blues of Ida Cox, Alberta Hunter, and Charlie Patton, and the country blues of Blind Lemon Jefferson, "Papa Charlie" Jackson, Big Bill Broonzy, and Charlie Spand, as well as the piano blues of Cow Davenport, Will Ezell, Jimmy Blythe, and Blind Leroy Garnett. Paramount thereby used its recording equipment to frame both urban and rural blues by African Americans.

Mayo Williams, the first Black executive in a white record company,[67] built the longest-running and most productive career of any African American in the phonograph business before World War II. The Paramount executive, brought up in Monmouth, Illinois,[68] believed that the blues were an important ingredient in the African American heritage. After graduation from college, Williams turned his hand to this and that before moving to Chicago where he sold bathtub gin to the important jazz club called the Grand Terrace, wrote articles on sports for the Chicago *Whip*, and played professional football for the Hammond, Ind. Pros. A Brown University fraternity brother who worked as Harry Pace's executive treasurer hired Williams as a collection agent and this experience whetted Williams's appetite for a career in the phonograph business.

The sad history of the Pace Phonograph Company might have discouraged a lesser man, but Mayo Williams devised an intelligent and creative strategy of invisibility for dealing with his unprecedented position in the record business. The industry had decided to sell to African Americans, all the while insisting that white companies, not Black ones, do the work. None of the record companies wanted to associate openly with either the African Americans who bought or those who made race records. This left them in need of someone who was willing to associate with such African Americans in the name of company profits.

Mayo Williams wanted to be that man. Learning of Paramount's purchase of the Black Swan masters, he traveled north to the company's headquarters to apply for a job. Given its far deeper involvement in the furniture business, Paramount certainly needed someone knowledgeable about the popular musical tastes of Black communities. In a strictly verbal agreement, Paramount named Mayo Williams to run its Chicago recording program, but refused to make him a salaried employee and bestowed no official title upon him. Company directors gave one of their own—M. A. Supper—a salaried position as recording director. Rather, Paramount gave their invisible, unsalaried recording director permission to extract a "talent" or "sales royalty" from the artists he decided to record. This was a common practice among the European, Latin American, and Asian immigrant intermediaries who recruited talent for the ethnic record lists produced by the largest record companies.[69]

In order to get and hold his ambiguous position with Paramount, Mayo Williams silently accepted what he considered to be the racially demeaning retailing category of race records. In so doing, he agreed never to scout out or record white talent: "They didn't want me to be identified with the white records, or the white side of the situation at all," he said. Williams also fully cooperated with the company's assumption that Blacks could not sing "white material." Despite the bitter recriminations of some of his best artists, Williams steadfastly refused to let them record anything other than blues.

For his willingness to work within these constraints, Paramount gave Williams the right to involve himself in copyrighting the music that he recorded on their label. Paramount had created Chicago Music as a satellite music publishing company that could buy, own, sell, and issue licenses for the mechanical rights to the musical selections that Paramount recorded. Paramount made Williams manager of Chicago Music, in which capacity he used various stratagems to wrest copyright or mechanical rights from the performer/composers, and arranged to have songs scored for publication and lead sheets registered for copyright with the Library of Congress. He earned one-half of the 2¢ royalty per recording that went from the record company to whoever owned copyright on the material recorded.[70]

Mayo Williams frequented the clubs and vaudeville theaters of the South Side, measuring popularity. He proved particularly adept at gauging the tastes of the vast southern African American market for blues, the one musical genre that the company believed would sell. But many of his recording artists later complained about him. Some, like jazzman Danny Barker, criticized his refusal to record anything but blues. Williams replied that he personally believed that ballads recorded by Black vocalists would be a commercially successful but that the company disagreed. Others condemned his "performance royalty" or recording fee before the session took place. Alberta Hunter accused him of pocketing money owed to her by negotiating with other record companies for rights to record her material. He also encouraged "cut-ins," the insertion of the names of famous people into what should have been exclusively her own composer credits and failed to send royalties to any of them.[71] Using a loaded signifier, Williams allowed that "I've got a good bit of Shylock in me." Indeed, a standard artist recording contract, written by Paramount, not Williams, provided for a 1¢ royalty for each "net" record sale, leaving plenty of doubt over the definition of terms. His creative bookkeeping assured that the vast majority of all artists saw no sales royalties at all, realizing only however much might be left of their flat recording payment after Williams's "fee" had been subtracted.

In order to prosper in his covert recording empire, Williams vowed to remain invisible by adopting the tactics he had learned in the United States Army's officers' training school: delegate authority to as few people as possible, trust no one, tell no one anything he/she doesn't need to know. He applied these rules alike to his employees and to his bosses at Paramount. The latter, after all, never revealed to him that he played the single largest role in producing their race records, which were, moreover, their sole line of recordings.

Williams had little choice about dunning the vocalists and musicians; if he had not worked in this way, it is hard to see how he could have made any money at all. And one could argue, at least, that the company's insistence on recording only blues merely reflected a desire to record what had proven to sell. August Wilson's play, quoted at the head of this chapter, portrays white studio executives exploiting Ma Rainey for profit. In reality, of course, African Americans like Mayo Williams, Clarence Williams, and Perry Bradford also exploited them for their own and the company's profit.

Recording companies together had refused to allow Pace & Handy to do openly what the established companies were already doing covertly: linking a recording company to a music publishing company. That mechanism ensured that the company made money at least twice and often three or more times on each record sold—once upon sale of the record and again by earning royalties from other record companies that subsequently recorded copyrighted music. If other companies were to "cover" a Paramount record by issuing their own version by some other performer, they would have to pay Paramount royalties. In the long run, of course, more money could be earned by selling the rights to reproduce records to a cheap dime store label like Champion, Banner, or Oriole.

Williams's work for Paramount also provided a product with which to begin to develop the African American market in the South. His records also would have appealed to the emotions of a recently urbanized people. Certainly a pervasive tension between city and country infused what were called "country blues" recordings. Both Black musicians and their audiences were moving about the South and, of course, migrating north. The Country Blues recordings made by male vocalist/guitarists from 1923 to 1941 actually were made in major urban areas of the Piedmont South, such as Atlanta, Ga., Greenville and Spartanburg, S.C., Charlotte and Durham, N.C., and Lynchburg and Richmond, Va. Whether or not the bluesmen actually lived in the countryside or had moved to more urban areas is still unclear. After the Civil War, large numbers of southern African Americans had migrated into such cities from the rural areas of the southern Piedmont and the Coastal Plains.[72]

Paramount pioneered distribution of Williams's records through its mail order campaign in the Chicago *Defender* and by initiating a system of jobbers and retailers in southern cities. The mail order idea could appeal only to the literate and was favored by white southern retailers who feared that the sale of race records would bring "a hoard of Blacks" into their stores. Mail order also fit into Paramount's low-overhead approach by allowing them greater profit margins than would have been possible had they sold to wholesale intermediaries.[73]

Paramount began with no wholesale or retail distributors in the South and landed the E. E. Forbes Piano Company of Birmingham, Alabama, as its first wholesaler. Harry Charles, Forbes's music department supervisor, became Paramount's first jobber, selling through thirteen states between Tennessee and Alabama. Charles also operated a string of retail outlets, usually in department stores, in various southern towns and cities throughout the region. Paramount, moreover, reached an agreement with the St. Louis Music Company to distribute Paramount blues records in Memphis, Dallas, Kansas City, and New Orleans. The Artophone Talking Machine's $13.85 suitcase model was the phonograph of choice among many southern African Americans.[74]

Southern African Americans in the late 1920s eagerly welcomed phonograph products, swiftly demonstrating that they would provide an important market. Both writer Zora Neale Hurston and gospel singer Mahalia Jackson insisted that an overwhelming majority of southern Blacks were buying phonos and records.[75] A 1927 study of the homes of both whites and Blacks in Greene County and Macon County, Georgia, revealed that none contained a radio, a very significant finding in an era said to have fallen under its influence. Practically no blues or other African American programming got on radio in the 1920s.[76] Because of the relatively greater dedication of the record industry to developing a market among African Americans, 19 percent had purchased phonographs, and a high percentage of these were found in sharecropper homes. Another 1930 study of economically depressed homes in Macon County, Alabama, revealed that one in eight families owned a phonograph.[77] One white southern retailer noted that African Americans "outbought whites in record consumption 50 to 1." On Saturdays, H. C. Speir frequently did $500 worth of retail record business with Blacks.[78] An important summary report on the industry emphasized the lengths to which economically strapped Black southerners went to have their own phonograph.[79] Writing in 1925, ethnomusicologists Howard Odum and Guy B. Johnson estimated that blacks were buying 5 to 6 million records per year, an estimate that Jeff Todd Titon raised to 10 million.[80]

Aside from the exceptional number of records they bought, patterns of purchase and use among southern African Americans differed little from other groups. According to Jeff Todd Titon, most Black customers bought their blues records in a town near their home and many of them bought records that the store owner had demonstrated on his store machine. Few informants could explain why one record pleased them more than another and most tended to buy the latest release of favored artists.

Titon found that record buyers played blues records on three kinds of occasions: alone at home, when listening and dancing at home with neighbors, and at outdoor picnics and barbecues. Following the national pattern, African American women and children did most of the listening alone at home since they tended to spend the most time there. Blues records permitted women who would never enter a "juke joint" to listen to country blues in the more proper surroundings of their own homes. Anticipating more contemporary patterns, many phonograph owners took their machines and records out of the home to whatever other locations they thought appropriate.[81]

Although more than one scholar argues that the record companies imposed their own segregation upon Piedmont music,[82] Columbia's Frank Walker claimed that a combination of company racial policy and southern segregation laws created and preserved the separate worlds of race and hillbilly records. Walker discovered that on the outskirts of cities like Atlanta in the 1920s poor whites and Blacks tended to live in proximity.

> They would pass each other every day. And a little of the spiritualistic singing of the colored people worked over into the white hillbilly and a little of the white hillbilly worked over into what the colored people did, so you got a little combination of the two things there. But they were very easily distinguished, you could tell them.[83]

Walker, who tended to list artists and records by type of music rather than the racial identification of the artist, recorded two young whites from Chattanooga, Tennessee, called the Allen Brothers, who had learned what he called "a colored song" entitled "Salty Dog Blues," but the vocalists sued for breach of Tennessee law when Walker included their record on his race record list.

At the same time, however, companies like Columbia did segregate African American music, recordings, and musicians by creating the category of "Race Records," "in order to have a differentiation between that and normal phonograph records," as Frank Walker put it. As will be seen in the following chapter, Columbia initially called white country music "Old Familiar Tunes." Separate racial categories for recorded music also endured through the separate and special numbering series for race records. Furthermore, auditions and recording sessions were scheduled separately for white and Black artists.[84]

In encouraging a segregated market among African Americans, Paramount's pioneering efforts to make and sell racially denoted recordings in the South created a new class of white middlemen, entrepreneurs of recorded sound who not only sold phonograph products but scouted for new race talent in the South. Among those who played influential roles in this way during the 1920s were H. C. Speir, who scouted Mississippi and Louisiana for several different companies; Atlanta's Polk Brockman, who worked for Okeh; Okeh and Victor's Ralph Peer; Columbia's Frank Walker and Dan Hornsby; Paramount's Art Satherley; A.R.C.'s James Baxter Long; Lester Melrose of the Bluebird label; and Decca's Kapp brothers. Such men acted as musical and cultural mediators, selecting the artists and the recordings that would be issued, encouraging Black artists to record certain kinds of music, watching their sales closely, and deciding whose sales justified further recordings.[85]

In general, these white record men showed little interest in soliciting the opinions of their Black customers when deciding which singers to record. H. C. Speir trusted his own ear and never even considered whether or not singers had a reputation in the Black community.[86] Speir did not hire African Americans as talent scouts either. He claimed that any given discovery might sound fine in person but record poorly, so that in the final analysis the recording studio personnel had to judge the value of the "talent." Thereafter, of course, record sales determined who became a recording artist.

Speir, who owned a music store at 225 N. Farish Street in the Black business district of Jackson, Mississippi, became a major force in the country blues recording business from 1925 to 1935: he "discovered" (a verb defined from the white record company's point-of-view) Charlie Patton, Son House, William Harris, Tommy Johnson, Skip James, and Ishmon Bracey. Speir had installed a recording machine on the second floor of his store and demanded $5 per side from the hopefuls who walked in to record. He himself claimed to have usually earned only a flat payment, instead of the more lucrative royalties, for the recording activities of those artists he brought to the company studios.

Other company talent scouts, like Victor's Ralph Peer, who did not live in the South, planned yearly or biyearly recording trips into the region. Notices were placed in the local newspapers alerting readers to the time and place of auditions, usually in a store or in a hotel in the various southern cities. Peer would search for new talent in the theaters of the racially segregated Theater Owners' Booking Association, but Victor and most of the other companies also worked the rural areas and favored periods of relative inactivity in the agricultural cycle in order to attract as many vocalists as possible from the surrounding towns and farms. Once the newspapers carried a story on a future recording session, many aspiring artists began calling in and appearing in person. Local furniture merchants who carried a line of phonograph products could be counted on to announce all new recording programs.[87]

Columbia's Frank Walker supervised two yearly trips south to record both race and white "old-time" music. The company had determined to amass as large a collection of master recordings as possible, and recorded nearly anyone who applied, sifting through them later to decide what to issue. The anticipation of getting on records drew a large number of aspiring regional musicians and vocalists into the city. Walker concluded that making a phonograph record "was the next thing to being President of the United States in their mind." Some got so nervous that they were unable to perform. Others fainted or burst into tears upon hearing their voices for the first time.[88] H. C. Speir believed that whites became more nervous than Blacks in the recording studio.[89] Most managed to get through the experience, often with the help of alcohol supplied by the record producers, and, before learning about the intricate and lucrative matter of royalties, left content with between $5 and $25 and sometimes some inexpensive gifts from the company.[90]

None of the white cultural mediators of the race record business knew enough about the musical dimensions of blues performance to interfere with their artists' vocal and instrumental interpretations in the studio. Lawrence Levine correctly states that the businessmen were forced to extend "a great deal of freedom to the singers they were recording."[91] But white recording entrepreneurs did shape the musical repertoire of the records they supervised in ways not mentioned by Levine. Ultimately, their influence had legal and economic roots. From the time of Mamie Smith's 1920 blues recording, white record entrepreneurs wanted African Americans to sing the blues. They insisted on that genre to the nearly total exclusion of the popular songs that appealed to large numbers of whites and at least some Blacks.

Within that admittedly flexible and varied musical genre, whites urged Blacks to record blues based on new-sounding lyrics encapsuled in a new title. Due to the nature of copyright law in the record business, Speir, Peer, Art Laibly, and the others insisted that aspiring African American blues and gospel singers record titles, melodic lines, and lyrics that had not been recorded before, so that the company would not have to pay 2¢ per side in royalties to a competitor and, in addition, might well reap its own windfall in future royalties. This requirement encouraged a creative, commercial, and ultimately entrepreneurial attitude toward folk music traditions and resulted in records that sounded both familiar and different to those who liked blues.

All of the companies for whom Speir worked, for example, required that each singer have "at least four different songs of his own composition."[92] Many artists with extensive repertoires sang a lot of traditional material and their own versions of the popular songs of the day. If they didn't have enough of the more original-sounding blues numbers, the white talent scout would either send the aspiring artist away or help him to flesh out melodic fragments and/or lyrics and tune titles.[93] This kind of "original" material might actually sound very traditional in its general musical contours but still avoid any direct repetition of copyrighted material. Ralph Peer echoed Speir's observation that the companies insisted on "original material"; "if they sang some old pop tune, I'd say, 'do you have any material of your own?' If they said 'no, but I can get some,' I just sent 'em away. They didn't have a chance." Peer also revealed that he and the artists routinely decked out old tunes with new lyrics and titles and recorded them as "original" material. Only one was ever challenged for its "originality" in court.[94]

This pattern, stimulated by the Copyright Act of 1909, amounted to an important white influence on what record buyers did not hear when they listened to new blues records: they did not hear old traditional folk songs, copyrighted blues, or any popular songs that had already been recorded. Elements of tradition and of popular music found their way into blues recordings, but the record company executives, in the name of their own profits, set the parameters of the recorded blues.

The race record business survived the stockmarket crash and the Depression better than many other record lines. Production and sales certainly declined for all companies, and Okeh's founder, Otto Heinemann, who had sold his company to Columbia in 1926, retired from the business in 1931. The Okeh label barely survived the Depression and Columbia staggered along under a series of new owners. Paramount and Gennett succumbed to hard times, but race record issues continued right through the worst years from 1929 to 1935, although the average order to the pressing plants declined, as well.[95] But the far greater size and stability of the RCA Victor Company permitted it to survive the worst of the Depression and even lead a revival of blues recording on its inexpensive Bluebird label beginning in 1932.

Once more, Chicago led the renaissance in blues recording, attracting, as it had just after World War I, an impressive number of African American blues singers such as William Lee Conley ("Big Bill") Broonzy, Minnie Douglas ("Memphis Minnie"), Thomas A. Dorsey ("Georgia Tom"), Robert Brown ("Washboard Sam"), John Lee ("Sonny Boy") Williamson, Hudson Whittaker ("Tampa Red"), Amos Easton ("Bumble Bee Slim"), and William McKinley Gillum ("Jazz Gillum"). Themselves migrants from the Southeast, these Depression-era recording artists led in a further urbanization of the country blues style of the 1920s and laid the groundwork for such post–World War II developments as rhythm and blues, and, by extension, rock and roll.

But it would take the decade of the 1940s to shake up the recording industry enough so that African Americans could begin to assert control over blues recording. During the Depression, the same pattern of white mediation of African American music endured. As the industry emerged from the Depression, Victor came up with an influential white mediator named Lester Melrose. Born in Illinois in 1891, Melrose, more than any other single record promoter, led the revival in blues recording during and after the Depression. One of the two Melrose brothers who entered music retailing and publishing in Chicago during the 1920s, Lester became a powerful man on the blues scene as an artists' manager, record producer, and talent scout—just the sort of music entrepreneur to understand copyright law and the economics of the record business. Melrose found himself on Chicago's marvelously creative blues scene just at a time when musical, social, economic, and technological trends converged to make a fresh recorded blues sound possible. He moved swiftly to shape a new school of urban blues.

From the mid-thirties to well after World War II, Lester Melrose took charge of blues recording for the Bluebird label, RCA Victor's race and jazz subsidiary. He erased many of the rustic characteristics of the country blues by selecting singers without strong deep southern accents who could sing in even, moderated, and standardized melodic and rhythmic patterns. Further, Melrose mixed in a new, jazz-influenced and regularized rhythmic pattern played on the string bass, piano, and drums. The white blues entrepreneur thereby guided the emergence of "the Bluebird beat," produced by a stable of Bluebird label musicians who acted as a blues studio orchestra.[96]

Despite the wide variety of musical forms that had been performed by late nineteenth-century Black "songsters," record producers pursued a structurally limited form of blues, usually the twelve-bar AAB form that banished admixtures of blues with elements of other popular music styles.[97] As bluesman Willie Dixon observed of Lester Melrose: "Most of Melrose's things was 12 bar blues music . . . a straight 12 bar pattern with a punchline and I couldn't get any of them to use introductions or melodic lines for their music. Melrose wanted all those things to sound alike."[98] The Bluebird beat took recorded rhythm and blues into the postwar years when African Americans were to gain a greater measure of control over the recording process.

Within the period of time covered in this study, African Americans, despite their exceptional efforts, could play but a limited role in the business of making and selling records. Although there is no direct evidence for it, perhaps some of them agreed that recorded Black blues music ought to remain a highly stylized, distinctive style reflective of a segregated society. Plenty of evidence does exist, however, to indicate that whites also shaped the creation of blues records, and they created a distinctive, structurally rigid recorded style, one that they distinguished in many ways from the rural white hillbilly records they made. It is time to turn to the early history of that other category of records produced in the same southeastern region of the United States among people of different skin color.

7

ECONOMICS AND THE
INVENTION OF HILLBILLY
RECORDS IN THE SOUTH

In the early history of the phonograph and recorded music, if not in the minds and performance practices of all vernacular musicians, blues and hillbilly music must receive separate consideration; the industry rigidly distinguished between rural white and rural Black recorded music by creating and maintaining segregated recording and marketing categories. In the process, much of the richness and variety of cross-cultural assimilations disappeared from the records as musicians worked, seemingly without undue effort, to fit their music into their employers' categories. Even in jazz, interracial recording sessions remained extremely rare until the 1930s. As the preceding chapter argued, what may have begun as marketing categories also created consequences for the recorded music itself. Very few Black string bands ever got to make "race" records; some Black musicians found company definitions of "blues" too restrictive. Companies likewise misshaped white rural music by avoiding old ballads as well as certain instruments like the banjo, dulcimer, and Autoharp.

Making and replaying sound reproductions of what record producers first called "old familiar tunes," "hill country tunes," "old time music," and, beginning in 1925, "hillbilly" music, swiftly intertwined supposedly rustic white southeastern American musicians with complex patterns of northern urban industrial commerce. Producing, recording, and consuming records of what passed for white rural southern music primarily served the economic interests of the northern record companies that discovered remarkably little difficulty in harnessing southern entrepreneurial ambitions to their own corporate ends.[1]

In what might even be seen as a colonial economy, southerners readily offered their raw materials—musical talent and entrepreneurship—to northern record producers and engineers in exchange for a major leap forward in the professionalization of their careers and also for what seemed to the musicians to be generous piecework payments and unprecedented regional and national publicity. Northerners remained firmly in control of the recording technology, secured legal control of the musical materials recorded, directed the actual production of records, designed their marketing and sales, and made the vital calculations of royalty payments.

This economic pattern, according to historian Edward L. Ayers, typified the post–Reconstruction South where "federal banking policy, railroad freight rates, absentee ownership, reliance on outside expertise, high interest rates, cautious state governments, and lack of industrial experience . . . hindered the growth of Southern industry."[2] Although the cigarette, textile, and furniture industries made strides, the region's economic development remained heavily dependent upon the extraction of raw materials from forests and mines.[3] Recording "hillbilly" music, the term itself expressive of northern urban attitudes toward the rural mountain South, extracted musical performances from white southern musicians and sold them back as industrial commodities.

Southern white musicians, like their Black counterparts, eagerly cooperated in this highly unequal regional partnership with northern recording companies. Despite their reputed rural backwardness, most of those who became successful hillbilly recording artists were already moving swiftly toward commercialized interpretations of rural musical traditions when the recording machines began to arrive in 1923. Moreover, even if the region's industrial development had failed to match that of either the North or other western nations, hillbilly records often reflected the attitudes and tastes not of actual mountain dwellers but of transplanted rural workers in the factories and mill towns of the North and South and, of course, of record producers and phonograph company executives who eagerly catered to the popular modern fascination with "backward" rustics.

In the South, as in the nation as a whole, slightly more than one-half of the population lived on farms.[4] By the 1920s, despite over thirty years of commercial expansion, the phonograph industry had still to seriously penetrate rural America. Like the rural Midwest, the South therefore had lagged behind the more urbanized North in developing phonograph culture. In 1927 across the nation, the larger the city, the higher the percentage of homes that owned a phonograph. Of the homes in cities with a population of 100,000 or more 60.3 percent had phonographs in them. In towns of 100,000 or less, however, only 29 percent of the homes contained phonographs.[5] Part of the problem stemmed from the relatively fewer rural homes with electricity.[6] This provided an ongoing market for spring-driven record players long after the industry electrified them.

Phonograph trade papers claimed that rural dwellers would make excellent potential customers for turntables and records, if one could only get the products into their hands. According to industry publications, the psychological mind-set of people living on isolated farms made them excellent candidates for assimilation into phonograph culture. Their "isolation, lack of amusements, long winter evenings with little or nothing to do, the need for something that will influence the children to remain on the farm . . ."[7] stirred the northern industry's anticipation. Moreover, industry writers felt sure that people in country towns would be attracted to the coin-op: "the sooner it can be put to work successfully in gathering in the nickels of the untraveled countryman and villager, the better it will be for us all."[8]

At the same time, as we saw in the previous chapter, the extension of Rural Free Delivery of the mail throughout rural America in the late nineteenth and early twentieth centuries offered the record industry another way of reaching rural and small-town customers. The inauguration in 1913 of parcel post further solidified the relations between the recorded sound industry and the national government, making it possible to get phonographic products more easily into rural homes through the postal system.[9]

As improved road systems penetrated the South in the 1920s, more and more urban phonograph and record salesmen from country towns and smaller cities drove their panel trucks out to canvas the surrounding countryside, consulting phone books to address mailings and placing advertisements in local newspapers. The industry believed that the farmers wanted to be able to listen to "jigs, reels and old time songs." It was also thought that they would make excellent customers for the other sorts of records that the industry already made: trade publications indicated that if 50 percent of farm families wanted music associated with their own culture, a large minority—40 percent of the rural market— would buy popular dance records and another 10 percent would buy "classical" ones.[10]

By the time that the phonograph companies finally got around to the South, many southerners had been forced off their farms and lived in the new industrial towns spawned by the railroads and southern textile manufacturing. Given unacceptably low prices for raw cotton, and the depredations of the boll weevil, many southern farmers were prepared to abandon their acres for the factory towns. This made the retailing of records to southerners that much easier.

Even if industrialization and especially urbanization had lagged behind the optimistic predictions in New South newspaper editorials, industrialization in the Southeast also had progressed much further in selected areas than over the region as a whole.[11] Thus, paradoxically perhaps, industrialization contributed to the creation of more compact, easily reached southern markets where many felt cut off from their country culture and drawn to commercialized "country" and "old-time" musical memories recorded for them by northern industrialists and ambitious southern musicians. As an Okeh company catalog put it, southerners wanted "melodies [which] will quicken the memory of the tunes of yesterday."[12]

In addition to adverse conditions in cotton production and marketing, the rise of rayon production drew many southeastern farmers off their farms and into the mill and mining towns of the Piedmont industrial crescent that stretched along the mountainous back country of four southern states from its southern tip at Birmingham, Alabama, to a northern end near Danville, Virginia. The Piedmont industrial crescent, in which the phonograph industry also concentrated its rural country blues recording programs,[13] passed through such southern cities as Little Rock, Montgomery, Atlanta, Columbus, Macon, Raleigh, Charlotte, Winston-Salem, and Richmond, following the fall line of the southeastern coastal rivers. It represented the driving wedge of the North into the South.[14]

More than any other factor, the availability of cheap labor had attracted industrialists into the Piedmont crescent. By the 1930s, the region's rural areas had not begun to be depleted of their manpower. Textile manufacturing required an unusually large number of workers, for the most part unskilled, who toiled at largely perfunctory tasks. Piedmont workers earned low wages, about 66 percent of wages earned elsewhere. This relative deprivation increased as one moved further south into Georgia and Alabama, and farmers who had struggled unsuccessfully with tobacco, cotton, and the boll weevil had little alternative but to look for low-paying drudgery in the coal mines and textile mills.

The bleakness of the lives of transplanted southern mountain people in the cotton mill villages of the 1920s—declining wages, the stretch-out system, lay-offs—must have made it easy for poor southern workers to dream and reminisce about the rural mountain past. One perceptive historian has written about "the noise, congestion, and filth of industrial communities,"[15] and this picture contrasted vividly with widely spread national memories of idealized and romanticized country mornings of quiet natural purity. Life in company towns brought disease, dietary deficiencies, divorce, delinquency, and desertion. Not all aspects of preindustrial life disappeared, however, and old-time music, for one thing, lived on in collective memory where record producers could mix it with aspects of contemporary musical culture.

In moving into the South, phonograph executives sought out the more industrialized areas that most closely resembled their northern markets. Once in those areas, they enjoyed the eager entrepreneurial cooperation of ambitious local musicians seeking paying gigs and wider audiences. Most histories of the first hillbilly records stress the prime importance of Ralph Sylvester Peer of New York City's General Phonograph Company in a Northern urban invasion of the rural American South, and his influence on the evolution of recorded hillbilly and country music if not unalloyed did cut deeply. Peer, with the indispensable help of Polk C. Brockman, "discovered" for his employers Fiddlin' John Carson, the first commercially successful hillbilly recording artist from the South; but Carson, we must recall, was eager to be "discovered."[16] Peer was also the first to record such commercially successful and musically influential stars as the Carter Family and Jimmie Rodgers, the leading country recording artists before World War II, but we have every reason to assume that these ambitious vernacular musicians saw professional advantage in associating with a record producer, and that they had their own ideas about how to deal with him. After doing so much to create a lucrative new market for phonograph products, Peer went on to develop important music publishing markets in Latin America and around the world.[17]

His retrospective attitudes toward creating hillbilly recordings emerge with special clarity in the lengthy 1959 interview he granted in Hollywood, California, to Lillian Borgeson. Speaking in a soft, slowly drawling bass voice, the ringing of his telephone interrupting frequently as subalterns sought his laconic instructions, Peer insisted that, with all due respect to his interviewer, who seemed to consider them to contain sparkling examples of American music, his records were to him but industrial product in a far more dramatic and exciting world of making money in the phonograph business.

Peer, who became a pioneering and much underappreciated record executive and music publisher, was born on May 22, 1892, in Independence, Missouri, the son of Abram Peer, who sold sewing machines, phonographs, and Columbia records. By 1902, the younger Peer had gone to work on weekends in his father's store, and, like Decca's Jack Kapp, had quickly memorized the release numbers of every title in the Columbia catalog. Even before his teens, the young man had been granted the responsibility of ordering records and phonograph parts for his father's store.[18]

After graduation from high school in 1910, Peer began working full time in the credit department of Columbia's Kansas City affiliate and he soon rose to credit manager, showing his aptitude for the financial dimensions of the recording business by working his way swiftly through credit and retailing. In 1915, he transferred to the Columbia office in Chicago where he participated in a historic midwestern expansion of the recording industry that did much to stimulate the national musical fads of the 1920s.

Upon mustering out of the navy after World War I, Peer followed his old Columbia boss, W. S. Furhi, over to the General Phonograph Company's Okeh label. Peer started at Okeh as assistant to Fred Hager, the label's director of production, and followed the latter through his historic moves into the production of African American race records.

Having positioned himself on the cutting edge of the popularization of the recording industry, Peer became one of the first in the industry to grasp the significant amounts of money that could be made in owning copyrights or legal control of mechanical royalties on recorded music. He swiftly mastered the business implications of the Copyright Law of 1909, a national law, first suggested by President Theodore Roosevelt, that defined a composer's rights in the mechanical reproduction of his work on phonograph records. As explained previously, the so-called mechanical clause of this law, which remained in effect from 1909 to

1976, allowed to the author of a musical composition, *or to whoever legally possessed the rights to its mechanical reproduction*, royalty payments of 2¢ per reproduction.[19]

This law, heavily structured in favor of the recording companies and those successful popular recording artists such as Rudy Vallee and Marion Harris who could demand advantageous recording contracts, placed composers at a legal disadvantage, particularly under the 1909 Copyright Law's "compulsory license provision": once the composer allowed one firm to make a reproduction of his work, any other firm might do so in a similar manner provided they filed in the copyright office a notice of intent and paid to the copyright holder the 2¢ royalty. This allowed anyone to record a song after the first permission had been granted. Under this law, the composers' rights in their recorded music ended with the record company's sale of the record. They had no control over any commercial uses to which records were subsequently put. Recording studio musicians retained no property rights in the records they had such an important hand in making.[20]

The law obliged the recording companies to furnish to the composer or his licensee a sworn monthly report on the 20th of each month on the number of records manufactured during the preceding month. In practice, however, companies sent quarterly statements of the number of records sold, rather than manufactured. Needless to say, the companies guarded their sales figures carefully and the more unscrupulous labels invented a number of ways to avoid paying royalties, either in part or at all. Only civil, not criminal, action could be taken against a company that paid no royalties. In these cases, a temporary injunction might be obtained to prevent the company from manufacturing any more records until the composer had been paid what was owed him. Once restitution had been made and the injunction lifted, the company in question could resume its recording of the same composer's work.[21]

The position of northern urban Tin Pan Alley songwriters and music publishers remained stronger than that of southern composer/performers of hillbilly and blues music. The American Society of Composers, Authors, and Publishers (ASCAP) had formed in 1914 to collect performance royalties for member songwriters and sheet music publishers. Along with the Music Publishers Protective Association, a sister organization, ASCAP had succeeded in collecting mechanical royalties from companies making recorded transcriptions of radio broadcasts.[22] But southern blues and hillbilly artist-composers lacked the invaluable protection of such organizations because ASCAP refused them membership. Influential ASCAP members felt that hillbilly songs and blues were not really compositions in the formal, written, and printed sense, and the organization discriminated against race and hillbilly music and actively promoted selected Tin Pan Alley music publishers.[23]

The lack of any protection of their performance rights made the mechanical rights all the more financially important to southern songwriters. But the recording entrepreneurs of blues and hillbilly, be they white or black—Ralph Peer, H. C. Speir, Perry Bradford, Frank B. Walker, Clarence Williams, Fred Hager, Polk C. Brockman, Art Satherly, Dave Kapp, H. C. Calaway, Arthur Laibly, and Mayo Williams—did not rush to educate their recording artists. Peer, for one, left no doubt that a crucial element in the successful pursuit of his recording business involved a disciplined marshalling of essential information about copyright law as well as about the sales figures on records made by his discoveries.[24]

Peer told his recording artists as little as possible about how much he and the companies he worked for needed them. Despite the fact that he had sought them out, coming all the way from New York City—first to Atlanta, Georgia, and thereafter southwestern Virginia—Peer bet that rural entertainers would conclude that they needed him more than he needed them, that they would prove so eager to record that the majority would, if that were the only alternative, eagerly do it for free. After all, Peer's modern technological mediation of their musical efforts appeared seductive: the northern record executive offered them from $25 to $50 for each recording of their "original compositions" even though he privately believed that it was "absolutely unnecessary as most of them expected to record for absolutely nothing."[25] He had "those that were worth anything" also sign a couple of contracts, each of which appeared to promise an ongoing relationship with the record company; that was, of course, just what the entertainers had hoped for.

Once he had decided that any given musical act would be able to produce a significant stream of fresh-sounding materials, Peer insisted that the leader sign a recording contract. He claimed to have been primarily concerned with the competition, fearing that Columbia, Victor, and Paramount would move in after his departure and make records with the same artists. While still working for Otto Heinemann's General Phonograph Company, Peer signed his rural white southern artists to contracts that prohibited their recording for any other label. As he put it, "they were all employed exclusively by Okeh records. I had them under control enough so that they would sign contracts."

To the aspiring recording artists, a long-term legal connection with a recording company looked beguilingly attractive, at least until they discovered that Okeh would stop recording their music if their initial efforts failed to sell as well as the company had hoped. For a brief honeymoon, the city and the country enjoyed a blissful and exciting marriage; but all those musical avatars of America's rural past soon learned who was in charge of their exciting new relationships with northern urban industrial life.

Then too, Peer was ready to offer white "hillbilly" artists what he carefully called "royalty," not "their copyright royalties" but "royalty," up to 25 percent of the amount that the record company owed to the new owner(s) of all rights to the mechanicals. Peer claimed that the musicians were thrilled to get even one-quarter of what had been rightfully theirs before they signed his contracts: "On top of this $50.00 [per marketable side], I gave 'em royalty on their selection. They thought it was manna from heaven! I did it from the start."

This payment of 25 percent of copyright royalties, later to rise to 50 percent after World War II, separated the recording of white rural southern musicians and vocalists from Black rural southern musicians and vocalists. Peer would have preferred to pay whites no royalties at all, of course; he would happily have treated them as he treated his African American artists, but, in looking over his shoulder at Columbia and the smaller labels, feared that if he didn't, others would offer "royalty" in order to lure Peer's disgruntled white hillbilly artists away from Okeh. Clearly, then, whether or not a recording artist got even a percentage of his or her copyright royalties depended upon the color of his or her skin.

Pioneer record producers like Peer liked to call their work in the South "recording expeditions," leaving a false impression of camping through the mountains in search of pure-hearted rustic musicmakers. In only one sense, and that one was crucial, was this implied claim to superior sophistication justified: no one in the South had ever invented the recording technology that Peer brought down from New York City. The Okeh label's portable recording equipment had been very recently designed by Charles Hibbard, a recording engineer ". . . who'd been trained by Thomas Edison and had a lot of diverse experience, experimental work with Edison." Up until 1923, Okeh had never recorded successfully outside of its urban studio, but Hibbard told General's President Otto Heinemann "That wouldn't be any trouble to record anywhere." As Peer recalled:

> He arranged the machine, that he could put into a trunk, and everything was designed in New York. The field recording machines were practically hand-made. They ran with weights. You had to have a tower six feet off the ground made of wood so you could fold it up and put it in a trunk. There were these large weights like a cuckoo clock that ran the mechanism with a big governor on it to keep the regulated speed. You had a ½ inch thick wax on the turntable and the sound was cut right into it.

To back-country singers and musicians all this equipment must have seemed much more sophisticated than it actually was at that time or than it might now appear to have been. The rural American's awe before urban technology was encouraged by the carefully insulated, soundproofed (and searingly hot) rooms in which the recording activity took place: Peer and his engineers sought out small unused warehouses and other retail spaces available for rent, and Hibbard "had a lot of heavy blankets that he would hang around on the walls," to muffle intrusive street noise and deaden interior echoes. All of that, not to mention the mutely staring recording horn that had already terrified so many foreign concert, ethnic, and popular singers, must have made Peer's traveling studio a humbling experience for its rural initiates.

Unbeknownst to the recording artists, however, Charles Hibbard's portable recording equipment could not match the levels of technological sophistication installed in Okeh's New York City recording studio. Portable equipment had been sent out to record the San Francisco Symphony with unacceptable results. As Peer put it, ". . . acoustically the thing wasn't really very good. . . . I had to put over the thought [at Okeh] that a hillbilly recording didn't need to have the same quality as a Caruso."

Actually, the recording machines had major difficulties even capturing hillbilly music. Peer is often said to have found the first recordings of his first hillbilly star, Fiddlin' John Carson ("The Little Old Log Cabin in the Lane" and "The Old Hen Cackled and the Rooster's Going to Crow"), so "terrible" that he refused to include them in the Okeh catalog,[26] but he later added that he had referred not to his own personal distaste for Carson's mountain warbling but rather to the technological limitations of his own equipment. As he explained it, Carson sang and simultaneously accompanied himself on the fiddle. "With only one [recording] horn in the studio, there was no way to balance the voice and the violin so these recordings were really bad. We really needed two [recording] horns." In addition, Charles Hibbard's heavy rugs failed to silence the room echo, further distorting the sound on Fiddlin' John Carson's first Okeh records.

Thanks to the eager cooperation of a variety of southern businessmen, Peer easily constructed a business network in southern Piedmont towns and cities before actually recording any rural southern talent. His networks served to protect him and his record companies from any financial losses and may even have helped guarantee a modicum of success. Peer selected his recording sites according to prior research on the talent pool that they held or could attract, but his plans depended upon the research of others.

Peer had invaluable help from southern radio stations, for example, in finding talent for his hillbilly series. Despite his evident pride in having "discover[ed] these musics . . . ," southern radio stations had gotten the drop on the record industry in the southern vernacular music business, broadcasting programs of country music as early as 1922 when WSB, "The Voice of the South" in Atlanta, Georgia, beamed to the surrounding countryside and the mill and mining towns music by Fiddlin' John Carson, a seasoned country music performer,[27] and the Rev. Andrew Jenkins, a prolific song writer and gospel singer; both were to record extensively for Ralph Peer's hillbilly series on the Okeh label. Radio had featured live musical performances from the start, and most stations refused to pay the musicians, insisting that the publicity they received was payment enough. The influence of the American Federation of Musicians as well as ASCAP had forced northern broadcasters to pay radio musicians, but southern vernacular musicians worked for free.[28]

The Okeh record label set up at one time or another "field recording studios" in Atlanta, Ga., Asheville, N.C., Bristol and Johnson City, Tenn.,

St. Louis, Mo., and Dallas, Tex.[29] Two of Ralph Peer's recording expeditions proved particularly fruitful: his 1923 efforts for Okeh in Atlanta and his 1927 work for the Victor Talking Machine Company in Bristol, Tennessee. On both of these particularly productive trips, the cultural process that produced hillbilly records very much involved an active southern effort to get involved in the business of northern recording companies. Peer's trips south resulted from many prior jaunts north by southerners. His efforts depended more heavily than he cared to admit, in his later interview, on native Atlantan Polk C. Brockman, an enterprising young furniture merchant in the well-established firm of James K. Polk, Inc., a company originally founded by Brockman's grandfather. Bored with the furniture business and intrigued with the potential of phonographs, Brockman convinced his father to take on a retail line of General Phonograph Co. products. By 1921, Polk, Inc. had become Okeh label's largest wholesale record jobber, serving hundreds of retail outlets over the Southeast and opening branches in Richmond, Cincinnati, New Orleans, Memphis, and Dallas. Beginning in 1926, Polk, Inc. focused solely on wholesaling phonographic products.

Even back in 1921, Brockman traveled frequently to New York City, making contact with Peer's bosses, Otto Heinemann and W. S. Furhi, and convincing them to grant him a wholesale Okeh distributorship.[30] Furhi had relatives in Macon, Georgia, and "knew Southern material." Soon thereafter, Heinemann and Furhi introduced Brockman to Peer, their young race record producer.

Hillbilly records were born, therefore, when northern and southern entrepreneurs began to envision how professionalized southern vernacular musicians would appeal when recorded and packaged as untutored rural southern mountaineers. The general idea of making records of local and regional southern vernacular music was hatched in New York City as record executives sought to fix upon a recording program that would stimulate a badly lagging record market. By 1923, according to Henry D. Shapiro, the North was heir to well-developed and persuasive tropes that explained mountaineers as technologically "primitive," socially isolated, and culturally "backward" people who either lived in or had once lived in a land called Appalachia. On the eve of hillbilly recording, these stereotypes had been accepted as describing "a distinct element in the American population."[31] Here was another media market to develop, particularly those so-called Appalachians who had conveniently emigrated and gathered in southern cities like Atlanta ("the Chicago of the South") and Northern industrial ones like Detroit.

The phonograph industry drew the personnel for its hillbilly phonograph records from radio broadcasts. Since one of Atlanta's three major newspapers, the *Journal*, owned the city's WSB radio station, Peer went to meet its editor.[32] Meetings like these produced a greater mutual understanding of how radio, the phonograph, and the newspaper mutually reinforced one another and led to newspaper articles that touted Peer's activities, in turn attracting still more eager recording artists to his travelling studio. Peer clearly selected recording sites that had already received modern commercial development from radio.[33]

The specific idea of recording Fiddlin' John Carson, who had performed on WSB, took hold of Polk Brockman as he watched a Hollywood documentary film report on southern rural music: the urban southern record retailer got his historic idea while sitting in New York City's Palace Theater on Broadway and contemplating a newsreel about a Virginia fiddlers' convention. He had been well aware that since 1913 the fiddling contests held in Atlanta's City Auditorium routinely attracted as many as 6,000 people from all over the surrounding area and states. Brockman suddenly imagined recording Fiddlin' John Carson and wrote the idea down in a memo book, turning his back to the screen to direct its light onto the page.[34]

Brockman had no need to backpack into the mountains to find Carson, whose place of birth is none too well documented; since at least 1900, he had lived in Cabbagetown, a working-class factory suburb of Atlanta. Brockman had known him since his own childhood days on Decatur Street in Atlanta. Carson had been entertaining at dances, circuses, and political rallies (those of the Ku Klux Klan included)[35] all over Georgia for many years, while competing in fiddling contests in the Atlanta Auditorium at least seven times since 1913. Carson's own version of his origins stressed his birth in the Blue Ridge Mountains of northern Georgia on March 23, 1868.[36] Whatever the actual date, two facts about Carson stand out: one, he was at least fifty years old when he made his first records; two, he had long supported himself by factory work while also becoming an experienced, ambitious musical entertainer who knew how to take advantage of sentimentality about the lost woodlands of the past. Like so many of those who were to buy his records, Carson had abandoned the farm in 1900, entertaining along Decatur Street in Atlanta's tenderloin. His hillbilly music, in passing from a transplanted mountaineer to an audience of migrants from country farms to city factories, formed an important southern collective memory.

Well-established southern musical entrepreneurs and professionalized working musicians like John Carson had eagerly participated in contests, fairs, and July 4th celebrations in Atlanta. The big-city newspapers began in the nineteen teens to play up the musicians' supposed rusticity, according to Carson's biographer, Gene Wiggins.[37] Long before Polk Brockman found him, Carson had involved himself in the urban commercialization of collective country memories.[38]

Any experienced phonograph man would have recognized Carson as an ideal candidate for recording: his raucous, raw, and rasping voice, just the sort to cut through the sound-dulling limitations of acoustical recording, had gained an edge during years of out-of-doors singing to large crowds. Carson had routinely entertained up to 6,000 paying customers in Atlanta's Civic Auditorium, which had no sound-amplification system. He had that sharp vocal "ping" heard in the recorded voices of Billy Murray, Ada Jones, Eddie Cantor, Al Jolson, and many opera singers.

In recording Carson, Peer and Brockman also chose a performer with a large, well-established audience of Atlanta factory workers with rural roots; they had been migrating back and forth to Atlanta from the surrounding countryside since the end of Reconstruction.[39] Compared to the residents of other American cities, Atlantans were more likely to be white, Protestant, female, native born, wage earners. Most revealing, Atlanta's population did not reproduce itself and therefore depended upon continued immigration from the surrounding countryside.[40] An ideal market profile for records of hillbilly music. A writer from the Atlanta *Journal* had long since pinpointed the way these old-time fiddling contests had come to trigger the memories of emigrants from the southern countryside then living and working in industrial Atlanta:

> In these russet festivals, the melodies of the Old South are awakened, and the spirit of folklore comes back to flesh and blood. The life of mountain and meadow, of world-forgotten hamlets, of cabin firesides aglow with hickory logs, the life of a thousand elemental things grows vivid and tuneful.[41]

Working-class white Atlantans had long been associated with the idea of "wool hats," reference to the coarse woolen hats worn by the poor white people living in the mountains, piney woods, and coastal plain outside of Atlanta. Largely farmers or those in the small towns who served farmers, the "Wool Hat Boy" tradition taught that they were honest, thrifty, and industrious, people of Protestant faith who lived by the sweat of their brows.[42] Their nickname went back to colonial times; a term of opprobrium at the start, by the nineteenth century, thanks to the political influence of Andrew Jackson, the grass roots "democratic" political rebels like the Farmers' Alliances, Georgia Populists, and die-hard supporters of Georgia's agrarian rebel politician Tom Watson, Wool Hats had adopted their nickname with pride.[43]

Carson's close and enduring ties to Georgia politicians Tom Watson and Eugene Tallmadge reveal much about the cultural significance of those who would so enthusiastically buy his records. The fiery, brilliant Watson, a major leader of the Populist movement of the 1890s, had tapped the deep vein of rebellion in debt-ridden farmers and mill hands who lived in what they believed to be peonage to northern financiers and manufacturers. His career had paralleled the rise of the Farmers' Alliances throughout the rural South, organizations headed by Leonidas L. Polk and seething with bitterness and violence. Tom Watson campaigned against the Wool Hats' old nemesis "the Silk Hats," city slickers who lived by exploiting the poor and manipulating government and business.

Carson had attached himself first to Tom Watson and then to Georgia Governor Eugene Tallmadge, warming up the electorate for them with his raw, gamey, jarring voice and fiddle. Carson, playing the role of a "corny, redneck character, a little down and out but happy,"[44] evoked high-spirited devilment but also fanned that lingering spirit of rural southern rebellion, still a potent collective memory at the time of his Atlanta fiddling championships, recalling for people who had been defeated on the farm their lingering rural pride and frustrations with recordings like "The Farmer is the Man that Feeds Them All," "Honest Farmer," "Tom Watson Special," and "Dixie Boll Weevil."

Carson even recorded three songs—"Little Mary Phagan," "The Grave of Little Mary Phagan," and "Dear Old Oak in Georgia"—that resurrected the murderous campaign of Tom Watson in 1913–1915 for the execution of Leo Frank, a Jewish factory supervisor accused of the murder of young Mary Phagan, a worker in the same factory. Watson, obsessed with Frank, encouraged his followers to defy the court system that had consistently questioned the evidence in the case. When finally, on August 16, 1915, Frank was spirited out of jail by a group of masked men and hung by the neck until dead in Marietta, Georgia, Fiddlin' John, who knew members of her family, is said to have played and sung about Mary Phagan throughout the day from the courthouse steps.[45]

Carson's ties to Eugene Tallmadge, candidate for Governor of Georgia in 1932, again allied him with a leader of rural Georgia. Tallmadge bragged that he never expected to carry a county that had a streetcar in it, but he made more democratic transportation his major issue by supporting cheaper automobile license plate fees. When Tallmadge proved unable to convince the state legislature to go along with his $3 license tag, he took over the automobile registration office by force and registered cars at $3 anyway, endearing himself to the rural electorate.[46] The better to advertise Carson's record "The Three Dollar Tag" on the Bluebird label, Polk Brockman sent the fiddle player and a photographer over to present the governor with a copy. The resulting photograph, sent to Victor, became part of Victor window displays.

Southern workers could no more escape their industrial present than they could their country past. The hillbilly records they made and bought contained commercialized sound wave engravings that could be made to elicit memories of a golden mountain past, repeatedly reviving recollections of the past in the present.

The association of Carson's hillbilly music with southern economic protest did nothing to change the eagerness with which southern hillbilly musicians involved themselves with representatives of the northern urban recording companies. The Atlanta *Journal* eerily reported that records were being "manufactured" in the city, but really meant that imported machines made wax master discs there. The waxes, packed in ice, were sent to New York City to be transferred onto copper matrices and placed on hydraulic presses there that stamped out the records, which were then sent back down south. Neither Atlanta nor the South manufactured phonograph records in the 1920s.

But Polk C. Brockman, the urban southern businessman, epitomized the enthusiasm with which the region's musical and furniture entrepreneurs involved themselves in the copyright side of the recording business.

Brockman wrested legal control of recorded hillbilly songs from musicians who signed contracts with him, either buying outright the copyrights to Carson's recorded materials or leaving the copyright in the hands of the composer whilst gaining control of the rights to mechanical reproduction. He then profited even further when James K. Polk, Inc. subsequently published hillbilly tunes in sheet music form. To manage the latter, Brockman hired a musician adept at "taking songs off records" and writing them out, for $1 to $3 apiece, so that he could publish them or sell them to other music publishing houses.[47]

The cultural interventions of record producers contrasted sharply with those of the Progressive Era mixture of writers, song collectors, art music composers, and New England cultural missionaries who invaded the mountains of the Southeast in the years immediately preceding the phonograph's arrival. Song collectors like Cecil Sharp and Olive Dame Campbell sought a pure "authentic" English-influenced ballad tradition.[48] The record producers sought what would sell. Becoming an entrepreneur of the recording studio required that they suspend their own personal musical tastes. Brockman did not personally care for Carson's music, while Peer found it "pluperfect awful." But as Brockman explained: "I don't ever look at a thing as to what I think about it. I always try to look at it through the eyes of the people I expect to buy it. My personal opinion never comes into anything I ever have anything to do with when it comes to merchandizing."[49] Peer had not wanted to put Carson's first recording into the Okeh catalog but had been perfectly willing to make a pressing of 500 copies to be sold locally in Atlanta. Brockman easily sold those by promoting Carson in a concert onstage at Cable Hall on Broad Street; after performing two numbers for a group of visiting Elks, Carson put his record on a large German machine with a morning glory horn and slyly announced "I decided to stop makin' liquor and go to makin' phonograph records." They played his record on "a big horn phonograph" and swiftly sold out the entire order. When Peer saw that Brockman ordered more of Carson's disc, he decided that his own opinion had been wrong.[50]

Further insight into the cultural process of creating hillbilly records, starting with John Carson, results from Robert Cantwell's acute observation that stylistically they were "*already old-fashioned when they were recorded.*"[51] Cantwell attributes this important fact to the record producers' northern urban stereotypes about southern mountaineers, but cultural pressures exerted by the transplanted musical composers, folk music collectors, and academics also had targeted the supposedly nefarious influences of urbanization and industrialization on southern lives and on traditional vernacular music. Finally, the unhappiness of southern workers, whether in Atlanta, Detroit, Chicago, or the small mill and mining towns of the Piedmont, trapped in lives of industrial drudgery, cannot be eliminated as another possible factor that created a demand for recorded music capable of evoking sentimental recollections of a preindustrial era.

The process that produced the records that elicited the sentimental responses included plenty of calculation and media manipulations. Polk Brockman employed Irene Spain Roberts Futrelle, the stepdaughter of Atlanta's Rev. Andrew Jenkins, "the blind newsboy evangelist" of WSB, as amanuensis to her stepfather, who was the most prolific of the hill-billy composers in the 1920s. With her "father," as she preferred to call him, and her younger sister, Mary Lee Eskew Bowen, she had performed with the Jenkins Family, singing on WSB. As she later explained to Archie Green, that group involved itself with radio at such an early date that the airways offered WSB little competition and they received fan mail from Canada, Mexico, and both coasts of the United States.

Jenkins's story reveals the influence of the phonograph on rural south-ern music, the eager cooperation of southern musicians with northern companies, and the essential fallacy of portraying the southern musicians and songwriters as the naive rural victims of big-city northern corporate businessmen. Andrew Jenkins composed in assembly-line fashion more than 800 songs, most of them sacred, and included moral lessons in the secular ones as well. He played the French harp, banjo, mandolin, and guitar, and specialized in religious songs, tragic event songs, and ballads. The vast majority he sold outright for $25 to Polk Brockman and with 800 of them to sell made a living that he supplemented with frequent radio broadcasts and personal appearances.

Jenkins's best-selling numbers included "The Death of Floyd Collins," "Ben Dewberry's Final Run," and "God Put a Rainbow in the Clouds," and according to his stepdaughter, who wrote them out for him, Jenkins "made songs like similarly to the mill grinding out [flour]."[52] Once he had a concept in mind, Jenkins needed only a few minutes to work out his song at the piano, although it might then take his stepdaughter longer than that to get the composition in proper shape.

Jenkins immersed himself in the twentieth-century world of the com-munications media much as had Polk Brockman back in that Broadway movie theater. He created many of his best-known numbers by listening to the news on the radio, noting down colorful details of various dramatic and/or tragic events such as fleeing outlaws, airplane crashes, floods, train wrecks, the kidnapping of the Lindbergh baby, the trial of Bruno Hauptman, and so on. He often wrote several different songs about a particular event whenever record sales jumped on the first one. Jenkins used the twentieth century's first great media event to construct one of his greatest hits. In response to the dramatic death of Floyd Collins, de-spite all efforts to rescue him from an underground cave, Jenkins took inspiration from several days of radio and newspaper coverage of the event to turn out his best-seller "The Death of Floyd Collins," and then followed it up with "Memories of Floyd Collins" and "Floyd Collins' Dream in the Sand Cave." The whole Jenkins family had been listening intently to the broadcasts about Floyd Collins, "living it with the crowd that was trying to get Floyd out," when Brockman wired them that the incident should make the subject of a new Jenkins song.[53] Many other Jenkins songs developed the pathos and proper didactic reactions to the broken lives of drunkards and their children, dying hoboes, cowboys, and orphans, and nostalgic recollections of rural romance and familial bliss. Nearly all included overt moral lessons.

Southern musical entrepreneurs were rarely assimilated into the core of the record business; as performers and songwriters they relied on piecework payments. In addition to the region's failure to produce its own recording technology, the crucial imperatives of copyright law also remained a mystery to many of those southerners most closely involved with them. Irene Futrelle described in detail her stepfather's efforts to evoke old country songs without overtly repeating them:

> Most of the tunes . . . had the off-color of the original hillbilly tunes, without making a repetition of them and having them so far from any original tune that they were brand new lyrics, yet they were so much kin to the original . . . I think that was the real secret of Daddy's lyrics of the hillbilly songs. . . . He never copied another man's song tune . . . yet, all tunes are some kin in some way.

But her recollections veered away from any direct recognition of the laws of copyright. She attributed to her stepfather the knack of writing familiar-sounding songs that were original enough to be copyrighted—by Polk Brockman. Had Jenkins copyrighted them himself, he would have better provided for his stepchildren, since copyright endured for twenty-eight years from the time of issue. On this subject, an uncomprehending frustration frequently broke through Irene Futrelle's abiding Christian faith. While repeatedly denying any personal bitterness, she did go so far as to say that Brockman had "cheated" her stepfather, and she took comfort in thoughts that the Lord was also the God of vengeance. She attributed what she seemed to consider her stepfather's victimization to the avarice of those who cheated him, to his inability to see, and to the Christian faith that led him to deal charitably with everyone—the "innocent southern victim" hypothesis.

Futrelle never admitted to having any concrete knowledge of copyright law, despite the fact that she herself worked for Brockman, copying down melodies from recordings of Jenkins's songs that had escaped copyright! But her manner of expressing her attitudes betrayed a sense of guilt: "That was a job and one I was never quite proud of . . . however, I did that kind of work for Mr. Brockman for years and for different artists." Perhaps it would have appeared unseemly for a musical mountaineer in her position to discuss the finer points of the hillbilly music industry as *industry* with folk music scholars.

However much or little Futrelle understood, Polk Brockman's sagacity in copyright law left him the owner of Andrew Jenkins's work. He knew what Futrelle appeared not to fully grasp: that Ralph S. Peer would not record hillbilly or country artists who had primarily traditional or popular songs to sing. He couldn't copyright such materials and copyrighting the music on his records was Peer's business. Consequently, Peer pushed country music, as he had blues music, in the direction of melodic and lyric innovation within a generally familiar-sounding style. As he put it:

> I was asked by a fellow, 'How do you go about getting a hillbilly recording artist established? I've got a wonderful fellow. . . .' I said, 'well, he's either got to write his own music or you've got to get it for him, and then you take him to a record company. Which is essentially the method I invented and I take credit for.

Columbia's Frank B. Walker, who in 1925 moved into the South to compete with Peer and produced by 1931 a rich variety of 750 southern string-band records, similarly commented that ". . . many of the acts he recorded had limited repertoires of 'eight or ten things,' and recalled that when one found an artist who had an expandable repertoire, who could learn new material readily, 'you hung on to him.'"[54] While the 70 percent of the first 100 records of southeastern mountain music in Columbia's 15000–D series recorded from 1926 to 1931 sounded traditional to music historian Norm Cohen, only 10 percent of the last 100 records in that series did.[55]

With the triumph of Fiddlin' John Carson records, Brockman, acting in a role typical of dealers in records of other sorts, aggressively scouted local musicians by listening to his far-flung network of southern urban retailers, often themselves musicians. As he described the process, he would ask the record dealers to find talent for recording and set a date for them to be interviewed by Brockman, who got space in a hotel or vacant store. There Brockman listened and made his judgments, using his intuition and the advice of his retailers to select potential recording artists. Brockman often worked for three or four months in this fashion before Okeh actually held a recording session.[56]

From 1923 to 1926, Okeh, Columbia, and Victor continued to record primarily in Atlanta, usually bringing only their most successful artists up to New York to the company studios.[57] By 1927, however, they moved on to Bristol and Memphis, Tennessee, and Charlotte, N.C. Ralph Peer's second historic recording expedition, this time to Bristol in 1927, turned up the Carter Family and the great crossover hit artist Jimmie Rodgers.

By the time he arrived in Bristol, Peer had left the General Phonograph Company to produce records for the Victor Talking Machine Company, under revealing conditions. According to country music historian Charles K. Wolfe, the average hillbilly record issued during the 1920s sold between 5,000 and 10,000 copies, with a "hit" record selling around 100,000.[58] During the Depression 1,000 copies amounted to a major sale. But even with such reduced sales, record companies owned rights to the mechanicals on hundreds of records, each Depression-era disc bringing in between $20 and $40, when they owned the rights to the musical materials on each side of each record.

Sometime after his success with Carson and Jenkins, Ralph Peer had decided that he, personally, and not General Phonograph Company should be earning the royalties on hillbilly records. The company, after all, already earned its money on sales. According to Peer, the record companies, and Victor in particular, did not seem to realize how much money could be made from owning copyrights to the materials on hillbilly records. The royalties and profits in sales were so immense on mainstream popular records that the lesser-selling hillbilly discs appeared secondary. According to Peer, any popular record on the Victor label sold 40,000 copies simply because of the company's name, nationwide distribution, and effective advertising.

Unable to convince Heinemann, Peer was able to strike a brilliant deal with Victor. He would work for them free of charge if they would allow him to own the mechanical rights on all country music he recorded. Armed with this innocuous-looking agreement, Ralph Peer insisted that promising hillbilly recording artists sign two contracts with him personally: one by which they signed over to him rather than the record company 75 percent of their mechanicals or copyright royalties for 28 years; the other legal agreement, called an artist management contract, made the record producer into their exclusive manager. Peer never did much of any active artist managing and preferred to delegate to others. He did want legal control over the artists: under the artist management contract, if the artist or his representatives should wish to take over legal control of their mechanicals after 28 years had passed, Peer could produce evidence that they had been in his employ when the records were made.

As in Atlanta, Peer had plenty of eager cooperation from western Virginia and Tennessee businessmen. The local Victor dealer in Bristol, Tennessee, took Peer to meet the local newspaper editor "who seemed to me to be a quite intelligent man." Making the most from his insider information, Peer "gave him a tip . . ." that the Radio Corporation of America was about to purchase The Victor Talking Machine Company; ". . . so he bought some Victor stock and in a few days made quite a bit of money." "I can't say that was the reason but he ran an article in the left hand column, front page Victor to Establish Recording Studio in Bristol! He gave the name of my hotel and I got mail, including a letter from Jimmie Rodgers."

Newspaper articles and scuttlebutt from the radio stations stimulated a rash of applications from ambitious country musicians and vocalists. Many of them, like the young Jimmie Rodgers, wrote to Peer, who returned to New York to work up a recording schedule and prepare some recording contracts. He then returned to the South and began systematically recording.[59]

Peer's first Bristol discovery—the Carter Family, made up of songwriter and arranger A. P. Carter, his wife, Sara, who was the group's lead vocalist, and his sister-in-law, guitarist Maybelle Addington Carter—is generally considered to have originated commercial "mountain music," the principal forerunner of the "bluegrass style." They sang in traditional high nasal harmonies and accompanied themselves on a variety of stringed instruments, creating a repertoire strongly colored by religious sentiments. While they had no one enormous hit record, their discs sold well over many years. "My Cinch Mountain Home," "Wildwood Flower," "Single Girl, Married Girl," "Coal Miner's Blues," and "Wabash Cannonball" figured among their more popular recordings, and their music strongly influenced Woody Guthrie, Joan Baez, and Bob Dylan.[60]

The Carters negotiated a comfortable relationship with Ralph Peer and the record business, one built upon a healthy respect for themselves, a pragmatic adaptability to the imperatives of the industry, and an uncanny ability to protect and manipulate their music's relationship to the shifting social context of the Piedmont. A. P. Carter, Sara, and Maybelle and her husband, Ezra J. Carter, all lived in the tiny community of Maces Springs, Scott County, Virginia, a Piedmont town a far cry from urban Atlanta, where most recorded hillbilly music had originated. Yet even in this secluded corner, modern influences of urban, industrial America had deeply penetrated the musicians' lives.

The railroad, for example, had come to the region before the Civil War, and by the 1880s the tristate region where Virginia, North Carolina, and Tennessee meet had entered the throes of industrialization. Lumber companies built logging towns and began to clear-cut the forests. At the turn of the century, furniture and textile plants moved in. Influences of urban-industrial life had long since transformed the lives of those living in Scott County, Virginia, of which Bristol was the country seat.[61]

And in like manner it had often taken the Carter males out of the region. A. P. had traveled to and worked in Detroit and Indiana as a young man. E. J. worked as a railway mail clerk between Bristol and Washington, D.C., where he lived and worked for a year. During the years of their recording career, they traveled frequently throughout the region and well beyond.

Modern influences appeared in many guises. First, all three traditional musicians had already listened to records and radio before entering Victor's studio. At the time of her marriage to "E. J." Carter, Maybelle Addington found that he owned "a victrola and a gang of records" that included sides by Vernon Dalhart, Riley Puckett, and many pop recordings. He had bought most of these in Bristol, just over the border in Tennessee. The young couple also had a radio and listened to "country and old time music" on it.[62]

The modernist drive in the Carter Family's hillbilly music careers expressed itself most powerfully through A. P. "Doc" Carter, the group's leader and business manager. In live and studio performance, his musical contributions to the group were limited to his unpredictable "bassing-in," in which he suddenly punctuated the vocal harmonies with his bass voice, and he was likely to wander around the stage during numbers.

More important, A. P. clearly understood the economic importance of copyright. Sometime in 1926, A. P. and Sara had auditioned for a representative of Brunswick records in Kingsport, Tennessee. While Brunswick had liked what they performed and predicted great sales of their records, they had urged A. P. to play the fiddle so that they could bill him as "Fiddlin' Doc Carter." The company also refused to pay any copyright royalties, "and A. P. wouldn't do it." One year later, Victor offered the group a long-term contract that included .045¢ per side issued on "original" material that Ralph Peer copyrighted for them. As usual, "Peer didn't want them to put on anything that had been used or copyrighted or anything. At least not songs that people had the copyright on." Having been intelligently prepared for their Victor recording session, the Carters waited until the first royalty check arrived in the mail. After seeing that check (they did not divulge its amount) ". . . they really went into the music business as much as they could."[63] Obviously, A. P. had believed in their potential for economically significant record sales from the start, the first royalty check merely confirming what he had insisted. Now, he was the one to systematically create for the group a substantial repertoire of uncopyrighted "original" tunes and songs that would allow Ralph Peer and, to a lesser extent, the Carters to make royalty money.

A. P. cleverly insisted on booking the Carter Family's live performances. All members of the group referred to their stage shows as "personals," and the majority of these presentations took place in small-town churches, schools, town halls, and private homes. These affairs appeared extremely folksy: admission charges were modest, and the Carters mingled with the audience both before and after the show. They opened their performances by singing "How do you do, everybody? . . . How are you? . . . We are here, we must confess, just to bring you happiness. . . ."

The group had carefully rehearsed their material, however, and insisted on strictly professional comportment on stage. Moreover, as A. P. circulated through these small gatherings before and afterward, the subject of music and old songs naturally arose and he habitually chatted up individuals who knew old songs that the Carters had not yet heard. Often the Carters boarded in the homes of people like Kate O'Neil Peters of West Norton, Virginia, and Big Tom Carter, a Methodist preacher in Mt. Vernon who knew old songs. Estley Riddle, a crippled African American from Kingsport, Tennessee, would come to visit them in Maces Springs and teach them his numbers, like "Motherless Children" and "Sunshine in the Shadow."[64]

A. P. Carter became a modern commercializer of the songs and lyrics he gathered. He wanted old material but felt a limited obligation to it. Rather, he lifted out of songs whatever particular part he personally liked best, highlighting it by combining it with music and lyrics of his own choosing. In this modern synthesis of time's musical scraps, he aimed to please a northern urban record producer, collect the recording fees, and await the quarterly royalty checks. If Ralph Peer took 75 percent of the Carter Family's royalties, the Carter Family took as great a part from those country people who eagerly helped them.

On August 4, 1927, Jimmie Rodgers, the country performer of Peer's dreams, came into Peer's makeshift Bristol recording studio for his scheduled RCA Victor audition.[65] Unlike Fiddlin' John and the Carters, Rodgers was no mountaineer but rather a vagabond southern vocalist full of the latest popular songs from vaudeville—a railroad worker who had come to Asheville, North Carolina, for his health and to advance his career on the town's powerful new radio station, WWNC.

Rodgers, suffering from the tuberculosis that would kill him in 1933, plunged headlong into a search for fame and riches in show business, eagerly pursuing crossover audiences with his hauntingly personal blend of popular songs, African American blues, and rural white Southern inflections. He had shown little interest in the music of the early hillbilly greats and routinely entertained his audiences with the latest pop songs put over with his own version of the twenties hot-shot style: sharp city clothes, sparkling eyes, jaunty poise, and heavy on the personality.

Ralph Peer had been looking for just such an artist from the time he had first realized that his was the business of controling copyright royalties. Obviously, the hillbilly record sales could never match those of the larger popular market and therefore royalties on hillbilly records would never equal those on successful pop records. But Jimmie Rodgers represented several record markets in one: hillbilly, popular, and a little race and jazz thrown in. As such, Rodgers's blend most faithfully represented the swiftly modernizing world of Piedmont record fans. According to his best biographer, all of Rodgers's record releases up to about 1930 sold at least 350,000 copies. His first nine issues may have sold as many as 4 million copies. Ralph Peer's royalties for the second quarter of 1927 ran to $250,000, and in 1928 Rodgers's royalties, one-quarter of Peer's, averaged $1,000 per month.[66]

The record producer's influence on hillbilly repertoire emerges particularly clearly in Rodgers's brief recording career. The Singing Brakeman, as he was billed, did not create his own material; he was more of a vocal and guitar stylist and show business personality. Peer often found materials for him and had no difficulty convincing Rodgers to learn popular-style country songs. The vocalist wanted to reach the largest audience possible.

And the continued appeal of Jimmie Rodgers's records proved the wisdom of Ralph Peer's early insistence on having his artists sign performance management contracts with him. In the late 1950s, after the twenty-eight years of enjoying the partial ownership of the mechanicals on Rodgers's best-selling early sides, his widow Carrie tried to wrest all mechanical rights on them from Ralph Peer. Peer brandished his original employment contract with Rodgers, however, saying: "No use Carrie! If you force me to do so I will use that contract to say that at the time of renewal I would replace Rodgers. That's the legal situation under copyright law. There's no doubt he did work for me." Legally, therefore, Rodgers had been working for Peer when he had made his famous records and the record executive's control of the mechanicals was renewed. Reflecting on his legal control of Rodgers's recorded legacy, Peer drove the nail just a bit deeper:

> That would cut her out completely. I don't want to do that. She eventually settled for $15,000 over 28 years which doesn't really amount to much. You don't want to figure out how much these people might earn and then give it to them because then they would have no incentive to keep working. With Carrie [Rodgers], we fed her the money in small bits—$1,500 every six months—that way she propagandizes the Jimmie Rodgers myth. She's working to keep Jimmie Rodgers famous.

As various of his artistic discoveries began to produce significant record sales, Ralph Peer began to amass a fortune. Many years later, he minimized the amount of money involved in hillbilly music: on the one hand, he readily admitted that ". . . to have a royalty statement of $250,000 for 3 months and keep 75% of it, well that was wonderful;" but on the other hand, he also felt that "if you take 75% of the mechanical royalties, it doesn't amount to anything. If you've got a record that sells 1,000,000, the total legal royalty is $20,000, set by law. It's unfair."

Peer still got to a point at which he had to worry that Victor would learn of the actual sums he was making in collecting copyrights. An unidentified friend noticed that in the second quarter of 1928, Peer had earned close to $250,000 and advised the hillbilly record producer not to have such sums paid directly to himself. "Why don't you incorporate or do something?" he counseled.

Peer quickly saw the point and organized Ralph S. Peer, Inc., Southern Music Publishing Company, Inc. and United Publishing Company, and split the royalty statements four ways. "I would divide these copyrights among these four names on the recording sheets, which was just a device, not to cover up exactly but at least not to make it so obvious that I was taking out large sums of money [from Victor's business]."

As record producer in a specialized minority market with the potential of a much wider appeal, Peer had looked enviously upon the larger worlds of popular music recording and sheet music publishing. Those at Victor who had been placed in charge of pop records defended their turf, so Peer used his knowledge of copyright to move further into the popular music publishing business by making sheet music out of recorded music. His Southern Music Publishing Company put out Hoagy Carmichael's "Rockin' Chair" (1930) and "Lazy Bones" (1931), while Benny Goodman opened his concerts with "Let's Dance" and closed them with "Goodbye," both Southern copyrights. Such copyrights brought him enough money to begin opening offices in Britain, Spain, Italy, France, Mexico, and many other Latin American countries. He hoped to exploit the music from these countries in the United States and elsewhere.[67] He organized the American Performing Rights Society to license Latin American music in the United States, and signed contracts with all the respective groups "south of the border." In this way, Southern Music gained copyright control of such international hit records as Agustin Lara's "Grenada" (1932), Ary Barroso's "Baia" (1938) and "Brazil" (1939), and Alberto Dominguez's "Perfidia" (1939) and "Frenesi" (1941), as well as "Amor" (1941), "Besame Mucho" of the same year, and many others.[68] In this "empire of sound," the "hillbillies" of the southern United States had been but the colonial prototype.

8

A RENEWED FLOW OF MEMORIES

The Depression and the Struggle over "Hit Records"

The economic depression of the 1930s decimated the record business; hard times so undermined the phonograph companies that many never recovered, and Decca, the emergent leader of the popular record business during the thirties, arose only through investments from abroad. Victor and Columbia survived by merging with other media corporations. In this process of corporate consolidation, the booming ethnic and race record production of the 1920s shrank to a trickle during the 1930s, and the greater musical diversity introduced by the upstart labels of the 1920s—Okeh, Gennett, Black Swan, and Paramount—was renewed mainly by dedicated members of jazz's left-wing subculture who founded independent labels modeled after Milt Gabler's Commodore, as well as jazz and blues record stores, and magazines of criticism.[1] Despite such independent efforts to use recording technology to create an "aesthetics of social significance," the Depression's long-term economic effects, combined with the development of new communication technologies, served to accelerate the expansion of a few leading recording companies into what A. J. Millard has called "empires of sound": business conglomerates that supplied recorded music for the movies, radio, and jukeboxes. These multimedia consolidations led to the simultaneous playing of a limited number of popular songs on movie sound tracks, radio broadcasts, and jukeboxes, saturating the media with hit songs, overwhelming young and musically unformed Americans, and absorbing ethnic and race music traditions into popular music formulas.[2]

The hit record phenomenon, so often exaggerated by phonograph critics, does highlight a fundamental process in popular recorded music in the United States and a phonographic paradox: the power of a particular musical performance diminishes with repeated listening.[3] The beauty of treasured musical performances tends to be exhausted by the sort of repeated attention that the phonograph made possible. Consequently, people are often ready to put on a record that sounds new to them without being so novel as to defy the basic structures of musical memory. This inherent phonograph contradiction in which the memory machines were capable of destroying the power of the musical memories, led to an increasing emphasis on novelty.[4]

A mysterious art arose of combining fresh recording talent, novel materials, and clever arrangements into a large number of new-sounding popular recordings from which the public chose hits. A relatively small number of individuals struggled to dominate it. Men like Jack and Dave Kapp of Decca Records and John Hammond of Columbia somehow, and in different ways, seemed to have their fingers on the public pulse. Working in what was largely uncharted territory, they exerted unprecedented influence by taking charge of those musical ingredients that they deemed essential to putting records in touch with Depression-era sensibilities. In the process, each of these "record men" devised new commercialized musical memories, fantasies, and dreams for record buyers who needed them more than ever.

Jack Kapp and John Hammond made major contributions to the popularization of musical memory in the United States. Thanks to Hammond's unusual combination of patrician breeding and left-wing politics and Kapp's modest origins and public political silence, their influences on recorded music are usually contrasted, but both of these record men fashioned discs for the 1930s in part by reaching back into the 1920s and drawing into the Depression years familiar instrumental and vocal sounds, which they repackaged in ways appropriate to a new era.

Differences of social background and aesthetics did separate these two popular music talent scouts and record producers: Kapp, founder in 1934 of Decca Records, Inc. and its president until his death in 1949, did much to resurrect the record industry by recording a reassuring brand of popular vocal music that calmed the anxiety of a large part of the general public; John Hammond used the same technology to record what he considered to be more artistically significant instrumental jazz and dance music that appealed to those who liked jazz and hot dance records, sometimes hearing in them heralds of a greater racial and social equality.

Of the two, Kapp's roots went deeper into the history of the recording industry; he mastered more of the many different dimensions of the business, and wielded his understanding of the underlying economic and social forces at work on the old talking machine culture to generate impressive corporate profits at a time when the future of the industry depended on them. Jack Kapp, who became the champion of recorded music for people with few definite musical tastes, was born June 15, 1901, on Chicago's North Side, to Meyer and Minnie (Leader) Kapp. He graduated from high school in Chicago in 1918, and began to mature just as the recording industry, long an East Coast fixture, started to establish itself in the midwestern metropolis. The Okeh label set up a temporary Chicago recording studio in 1923 and Columbia followed one year later. Soon most of the important companies had begun to record in Chicago and used Kapp's hometown as a base of operations for extensive field recording trips through the South. Kapp emerged as a power in the industry at the same time as Jules Stein, another Chicagoan who became director of MCA.

Meyer Kapp had worked in Chicago as a door-to-door record salesman and then opened his own retail outlet, the Imperial Talking Machine Store, a franchised Columbia dealership from which he drove a horse-drawn buggy to take and deliver orders.[5] The elder Kapp, known in Chicago as a "hit forecaster," brought home popular records of the day and lectured Jack and his younger brother David on public taste in recorded musical entertainment. Jack and David Kapp obviously profited enormously from their father's knowledge and example; Jack began working part time for Columbia as a shipping clerk when he was only fourteen years old.[6]

In 1921, Jack and David opened a Columbia store of their own in a multicultural neighborhood on Chicago's West Side, a few blocks from the second largest African American section in the city. Here, for eleven years, they sold race and country records; they also developed a record mail order business and distributed discs to other dealers.[7]

During the 1920s Kapp's connection to race-music retailing temporarily led him into the production and promotion of records by African American cabaret musicians. In 1924, the Brunswick-Balke-Collender Company of Dubuque, Iowa, added the Vocalion record label to its Chicago phonograph and record business and turned it from a purveyor of concert hall music into a dance, jazz, blues, spirituals, and hillbilly music label.[8] In 1926 Kapp was named head of the Vocalion race record division of Brunswick Records after eleven years with Columbia.

Kapp entered a complex field pioneered in 1920 by Otto Heinemann's Okeh label.[9] After six years of outstanding success, Heinemann, a German immigrant, sold his Odeon and Okeh divisions in 1926 to Columbia, and in that same year, Kapp moved from Columbia to Vocalion. Vocalion claimed, among other things, to provide middle-class African Americans with recorded musical entertainment appropriate for home consumption.[10] Under the advertising slogan "Better and Cleaner Race Records" Vocalion sought to sell "the colored people records made by artists of their own race which are absolutely above reproach in so far as the theme and manner of presentation are concerned." Columbia replaced Kapp with T. G. "Tommy" Rockwell, who went on to fame by recording and promoting the career of Louis Armstrong.[11]

Kapp's first two years as race record producer created a relatively undistinguished list of discs. His major contribution to the genre came in creating a new kind of religious record by recording itinerant guitar-playing evangelists like Blind Joe Taggert and Edward W. Clayborn.[12] This mixture of sacred music with secular, blues-style performance would not be forgotten when Kapp got his chance to tap the popular market in 1934. In the meantime, he hired J. Mayo Williams as Vocalion talent scout. Jack Kapp learned during the 1920s much of what he would need to know to successfully produce popular records in the 1930s. He rose in rank to a full-time position in the order department of Columbia upon his graduation from high school and in 1925 became head of record sales for Columbia's Chicago office. In the latter position, Kapp covered a considerable portion of the middle west and worked closely with Columbia dealers.[13] Moreover, the young entrepreneur showed an unwavering admiration for effective performers of popular music who worked in Chicago's bright-light districts.

One important secret to Kapp's subsequent success lay in this close attention to the talent. He haunted the clubs, theaters, and dance halls, listening carefully to sounds that could be engraved into best-selling records. He came to focus his attention on the crucial dimensions of that obscure territory between the art of live musical performance and that of recording sound, and worked to turn a variety of vaudevillians, dance hall performers, and cabaret singers into recording stars. In 1921, while still working for Columbia, Kapp even reversed the process and used popular recordings to teach vaudeville singers "the clever business that will ensure success."[14]

Also, Kapp combined his extensive knowledge of Chicago's popular music scene with his father's concern with record sales. He became the prototype within the record industry of the popular record producer, who, to quote Antoine Hennion, ". . . has the task of introducing into the recording studio the ear of the public" and to "'draw out' of the singer what the public wants."[15] Dave Kapp described the record producer's job as "being able to hear and being able to translate these things into terms of what people will like because—as has been said 9 million times—they're the ones that decide. I think I have some kind of an idea of what they like. And I try to anticipate it."[16]

Jack Kapp's approach to predicting popular tastes reveals another fundamental fact about music in America. According to his own testimony, he learned to base his recording and sales policies on his belief in the general public's musical ignorance and malleability; the majority of those who came into his Chicago record store, he was convinced, had "no idea as to what records to get and either say we want a dance record or a song, leaving the rest to the dealer's judgment."[17] Those who were not fans and who asked for a specific number, he believed, had been influenced by song publishers who worked closely with dance band leaders, movie house organists, and leading actors in order to get their tunes played and sung in places of public entertainment. Kapp believed that once the average person got to the stage of whistling traces of a widely promoted melody, he or she was likely to want to buy a recorded copy of it. Kapp therefore specialized in creating recorded musical memories for people who had little or no musical education nor established musical taste.

Kapp's major breakthrough in the recording business involved him in the blackface minstrel tradition. In 1928, he produced for the mainstream Brunswick label a double hit record of Al Jolson's "Sonny Boy" backed by "There's a Rainbow 'Round My Shoulder" said to have sold 2 million copies.[18] This success with the traditions of minstrelsy earned him a promotion to sales and recording director of Brunswick's Vocalion subsidiary. In announcing the move, Vocalion bragged that Kapp "has a full knowledge of music so that he is able to direct and arrange the routine for an orchestra in a manner that will appeal to his trade."[19] They did not necessarily mean that he possessed a ready grasp of music theory; rather, that he understood what he had to get musicians and orchestra leaders to do in order for a record to appeal to the vast numbers of people who knew little about music per se.

While the core talent in producing hit records may have been exercised in the recording studio, massive sales also depended on new merchandizing and marketing techniques. As director of sales and recording for Brunswick Records, a position he was to retain until the stockmarket crash of 1929, Jack Kapp introduced a new and more specialized approach to merchandising by dividing the company's records into "Popular," "Old Time Tunes," and "Race Records" so that record retailers could focus their sales efforts on the kind of music their customers most demanded. This system removed African American and hillbilly vocalists and instrumentalists from the Popular record category, an important harbinger of Kapp's influence in this regard during the Depression as well.

Kapp's merchandising dealt a blow to old-time phonograph culture and simultaneously helped to lay the groundwork for a new popular culture of hit records. His plans contradicted the old industry policy of recording and marketing the widest possible variety of military march music, opera, folk song performances by operatic singers, vaudeville acts, minstrelsy, ethnic music, and increasingly symphonic music as well. For at least twenty years, the largest recording companies had issued catalogs that became more and more lengthy and elaborate, listing all of the records available. Retailers had been urged to buy as broad a cross section of them as possible in order to offer their customers a representative sample of musical styles.

As explained in chapter 4, many of the larger retail outlets had hired young female sales personnel who could memorize long lists of record numbers, titles, and artists. Such female employees were said to represent the revered blending of idealized feminine virtue and high musical culture; they worked at the cutting edge of the phonograph industry's determination to interpret itself as an "active agent in the spread of civilization."[20]

This self-proclaimed "high culture" approach to the phonograph provided a veneer that hid the talking machine's roots in turn-of-the-century popular culture. Some retail dealers in wealthy neighborhoods or those located in the best urban department stores had carried an impressive number and variety of records, but many more modest ones struggled to adapt to jobbers' entreaties to buy so many different records. Turnover on some of the record stock could be painfully slow; retailers experienced conflict between their idealized visions of their cultural responsibilities and the economic obligation to "move the merchandise."[21] The dilemma of dust-gathering discs had played the crucial role in bringing down the Victor Talking Machine Company's price-fixing arrangements, and the persistent chorus of complaints from retailers had led manufacturers into periodic buyback plans. The much heralded record album sets resulted in part from schemes for unloading discs that were poor sellers by combining them with the better sellers. World War I had offered a God-sent opportunity to get rid of "dead records" by sending them free to the troops as a patriotic gesture.[22]

The crash of 1929 and the enduring economic depression brought home to the entire industry the need for change in the marketing and retailing of records. By that time, Jack Kapp had worked in most of the vital areas of the popular record business and had gained invaluable experience in working with talent scouting, recording, marketing, and sales. He knew how to spot performers who possessed something that could be made into an interesting-sounding record and how to work with them in getting their individual recorded sound skillfully accompanied and effectively engraved on records. Perhaps most important, he had become a seasoned record man whose taste, however "corny" to people with definite musical tastes, appealed to the general public.[23]

For nearly three years after the stockmarket crash, the record business lay shattered, its sales figures plummeting and many recording firms sliding into bankruptcy. Only 6 million records were sold in the United States in 1932, about 6 percent of total record sales for 1927.[24] The production of phonographs dropped from 987,000 to 40,000, or 96 percent. As A. J. Millard notes, RCA Victor issued no catalog at all in 1931 and limited all recording to one take per selection.[25] Thomas A. Edison, Inc. dissolved completely and Columbia went through several new owners before being acquired by the American Record Corporation at the ridiculously low figure of $70,000.

Brunswick, which had entered the radio business in 1928, survived the Depression longer than many other recording companies but was purchased in 1930 by Warner Brothers and resold to the American Record Corporation late in 1931. That year marked the nadir in Jack Kapp's life; he foresaw a fast-approaching time when the American public would be buying no records at all. Kapp took that moment to enroll in a correspondence school specializing in business courses. He graduated two years later.[26]

Brunswick, however, survived, and once the company moved to New York City from Chicago, the label led the revival of the recording industry in 1933–1934,[27] thanks to its aggressive embrace of electronic recording, electronic playback machines, high-quality radio-phono combinations, recordings of the latest vocal and instrumental stars, particularly Bing Crosby, and swift and efficient delivery of records to retailers.

Some of the recording and business techniques for which Kapp made Decca famous starting in 1934 had already been developed by Brunswick. During the latter half of the 1920s, for example, Brunswick had gradually improved its ability to get its latest recordings to retailers swiftly by issuing them weekly and sending them out through a system of regional wholesale distribution warehouses.[28] Similarly, Brunswick had played an active role in "tie-ups," the accelerating industrywide efforts to link record promotions to radio play, and vocalists, instrumentalists, and popular tunes to performances in the movies.[29] The impressive sales of Jolson's "Sonny Boy," for example, were generated in part by the release of the film *The Singing Fool* whose sound track, provided by 16-inch, one-sided synchronous Vitaphone sound discs, included the number."[30]

Kapp worked for Brunswick from 1926 to 1934. In 1931, during a trip to England, he and Joe Bishop sold rights to the British manufacture of Brunswick records to Edward R. Lewis, head of Decca Record Company, Ltd. The American Brunswick records proved to be the English company's "biggest potential source of profit."[31] In the process, Kapp and Lewis became friends and the British businessman was to become Kapp's patron. Significantly, the English company had featured the cheaply priced records that had been much used on the portable phonographs prized by British troops during World War I.[32] Kapp would become known as the American champion of the 35¢ record.

In 1933, after a second trip to England, Kapp approached Brunswick about naming him director of a new line of cheaply priced popular records. When Brunswick rejected his offer, he turned to E. R. Lewis. Lewis, eager to take a hand in reorganizing the vast potential American market, despite the dire economic straits of English Decca, agreed to make an initial $250,000 investment in a new American Decca company. He opposed the idea of Kapp as president but finally agreed to give him that title without the corresponding power by making himself chairman of the board. E. F. Stevens, Jr. was placed in charge of record sales and Milton Rackmil made treasurer and production supervisor; along with Kapp, both reported to Lewis until new arrangements were made in 1937.[33] With repeated injections of capital from Lewis, Kapp led American Decca in the popularization of the record industry by specializing in cheaply priced popular records that featured the latest efforts of the top radio, dance hall, and movie stars. By 1939, Decca had become the second largest producer of phonograph records in the country, and 18 to 19 million of the 30 to 50 million records made that year were Decca's.[34]

Kapp's success with Decca Records is widely attributed to his introduction of the 35¢ 78 rpm record. While it is true that he did market his popular records at 35¢ or three for $1, at a time when Victor and Brunswick charged more than twice that amount, the recording industry's proud attachment to the 75¢ popular record had long camouflaged widespread retail discount pricing in certain retail outlets, particularly on records that seemed not to sell at 75¢. Just as industry trade papers had publicized the more expensive phonographs, the trade had always produced and sold cheaper models; it just preferred to talk publically about the more expensive ones.

Jack Kapp did more than simply make records that people with little leisure-time income could more readily afford. He championed a reorientation of an economically prostrate industry away from the relatively long-term preservation of "immortal" and "timeless" recorded concert hall music that would surely sell eventually (but not necessarily soon), and toward short-run profits from the quick sale of the latest recordings of popular music. In thus redefining the role of the phonograph as a popular music memory machine, Decca Records successfully adapted business practices in the record industry to better reflect both hard times and new trends in the public's demand for engravings of itself singing and playing musical instruments.

For his efforts, Kapp, who was as responsible as any single individual for pulling the record industry out of the Depression, has been buried in a mixture of highbrow snobbery and left-wing condemnation as the man who catered to America's lowest common musical denominators. Guardians of America's cultural hierarchy and journalists condescended to him. In 1940, the *New Yorker* in a profile entitled "Pulse on the People," portrayed him as a typical uneducated, self-made businessman given to the kind of malapropisms carried in the article's title. Seven years later, *Colliers* elaborated on this image and portrayed him as a kind of vaudeville vulgarian, a one-man whirlwind driven by the propellers of persiflage, full of hilarious malapropisms and, before bowing to Manhattan's "Oxford-gray suits and navy blue ties," given to wearing Chicago-style "suede shoes and checkered suits under a flapping polo coat" as he "half walked and half ran" to his next destination.[35]

On the other hand, upon his untimely death from a cerebral hemorrhage in 1949 when he was only 48 years old, Jack Kapp was memorialized in Congress by Representative Arthur G. Klein of New York as "the boy Horatio Alger wrote about."[36] Henry Luce, referring to Kapp's humble origins, editorialized that the record man "is living proof [sic] that no man in America is destined by circumstances to spend his life behind a large and immovable eight ball."[37] No one thought to thank him for designing soothing musical memories with which Americans could carry the buoyancy of their 1920s prosperity through economic disaster into an exciting but still musically familiar future in the 1930s.

The key to Kapp eluded most commentators who invariably stumbled into mysticism when describing the secret to his success. The *New Yorker* called it his "eerie spiritual contact with the Multitude."[38] Other popular magazines credited his marketing skills. But most observers have not been able to accept the meaning of Kapp's success because to do so would have been to question the beneficent effects of capitalism and democracy on music. Kapp, after all, only worked on the principle that Thomas A. Edison had established as a basic point of departure in the record business: most Americans knew nothing about music and therefore could be sold simple, clear melodies played, but especially sung, by talented and glamorous individuals with musically untrained voices.

Moreover, Kapp worked effectively at several different levels of the business. Thanks to Edward Lewis, at Decca Kapp got the power to tackle the industry's long-standing problem of burdening its retailers with too much record inventory. In the 1930s, neither the average customer nor the retailer nor even the recording company had the money for substantial investments in phonograph records. But at the same time, savvy observers had long seen records as "feeders" for the sale of phonographs and needles. Customers who came into a phonograph supply store to make a 35¢ purchase often ended up buying more than one record and at least casting an eye over the latest playback equipment as well. While unimpressive in amount, the money in these kinds of record transactions came in cash, and, significantly, the percentage of profit was substantial. A 35¢ record had cost the retailer no more than 21¢ and, for the operators of jukeboxes, often much less.

Decca therefore made it as easy as possible for the various radio, refrigerator, and washing machine stores that had specialized in phonographs and records before the Depression to return to them gradually. Most had room for a small display of records that had been designed to sell quickly. The company sold its popular records in much smaller lots to jobbers and to retailers, offering thereby a much reduced investment risk. In 1934, dealers began to fill customer demand successfully with much smaller record inventories.[39] The new popular plan hinged on the swift turnover of a strictly limited retail stock. A complete turnover of retail record stock had been rare in the twenties, but under the new Depression-generated policy, a dealer could turn over his record investment twenty-four to thirty times a year.[40] Such rapid sales, of course, depended upon the retailer's disciplined analysis of market demands leading him to buy just enough, and not too many, of the new discs at just the right moment in order to meet his customers' rapidly changing demands. Record producers and their jobbers now had to quickly deliver whatever quantity of the latest records might be desired to replace those that had sold out. Timing and inventory counted most.

The 1933 Repeal of Prohibition also played an essential role in Decca's resurrection of the phonograph industry. Repeal created four to five taverns for every speakeasy that had flourished under Prohibition. Folk and popular music had traditionally accompanied the consumption of alcoholic beverages. New "automatic phonographs"—the word "jukebox" came into popular usage only in the late thirties[41]—were developed by Homer E. Capehart and marketed by the Rudolph Wurlitzer Company, the J. P. Seeburg Company, the Capehart Company, Rock-Ola, and AMI, all of whom began, in the mid-thirties, providing recorded music for beer gardens, restaurants, clubs, hotels, poolrooms, roadhouses, soda fountains, ballrooms, and public parks.[42] By 1935, Wurlitzer manufactured 300 automatics a week.[43] Trade publications claimed that each of the approximately 150,000 coin-operated automatics sold between 1933 and 1937 "consumed" two records a week or 100 per year, vastly increasing record sales, particularly quick sales of a limited number of popular records of the kind made by Jack Kapp. By 1936, at least 40 percent of all records produced in the United States went into automatics; by 1939, jukes were consuming 30 million records (60 percent of all manufactured) and Decca made 19 million of them.[44]

The "operators," the independent entrepreneurs who bought and then leased and serviced automatics in public drinking places, wanted only the latest "hit" records, the larger operations buying individual discs in lots of several hundred.[45] In general, a relatively small number of the sides available on jukeboxes actually attracted the nickels that allowed repeated play. Having tied up their capital in the automatic phonographs, juke operators avoided investing much in record inventory. Rather, operators of automatics tailored their record purchasing and distribution carefully to please the different kinds of clientele to which the various drinking establishments catered. The jukebox provided a new way for record dealers to estimate the probable demand for popular records without relying upon the guesswork of sales representatives. During the thirties, show-business trade papers began citing the most popular records played on the automatics.[46] Kapp successfully tailored Decca's record business to the jukeboxes, undercutting RCA Victor and Brunswick by selling his records at 21¢ each, less than what the other companies could afford. Under Kapp's direction, Decca, according to Russell Sanjek, took a profit of only .0075 per record and still prospered by cutting the costs of production and selling more records than their competition.[47]

But the Copyright Law of 1909, as Jack Kapp was in a position to know, exempted the owner-operators of more than one jukebox from the payment of any performance royalties to those holding copyright on the recorded music.[48] Copyright owners or their licensees had the right not only to royalties from the recording of their music but also from its public performance. Under the 1909 law, however, "public performance for profit" applied only to places that charged an admission fee. Even though the public inserted coins in the jukeboxes in order to listen to a public performance of someone's copyrighted music, this was not defined as public performance for profit. As one legal commentator put it:

> If no coin were deposited, the copyright holder under this very Act would be entitled to compensation for such a public performance for profit. Paradoxically, in the very situation where the deposit of money itself proves that the performance is for profit, the copyright proprietor is deprived of any remuneration.[49]

This large legal loophole, made the jukebox business more profitable and jukebox owner-operators that much more able to buy Jack Kapp's Decca records.

Kapp also selected the recording artists who attracted a significant percentage of the nickels that Americans pumped into the jukeboxes. According to his patron E. R. Lewis, Kapp "stood head and shoulders above all others" when it came to finding and shaping the recording artists.[50] Kapp created a 1930s popular sound at Decca. His choices reflected his ability to manipulate proven musical entertainers successfully into musically expressing the dreams and sensibilities of the white middle-class public with pocket money to spend on records. Kapp recorded them with the latest wonders of technology, and sold them to the public with the latest marketing techniques.

When in 1933, industry publications began trumpeting signs of revival in record sales, Brunswick had featured Ruth Etting, Guy Lombardo, and Bing Crosby, all of whom worked with Kapp either at Brunswick or Decca. These popular artists carefully emphasized melody and delivered it and the lyrics in a soft, soothing, carefree but relaxed style, called "crooning" as it applied to Crosby's vocalizing. Their musical skills owed more to informal musical apprenticeships than conservatory training. The vocalists had performed extensively on radio and each made movies whose production was minutely coordinated with the appearance of their recordings.

As Victor Greene describes it, Guy Lombardo's dance band found its distinctive sound and greatest success performing and recording "highly melodic, danceable pieces played with staccato phrasing and a rich vibrato from the saxophone section."[51] Lombardo, a Canadian, had established this style in Chicago's Grenada Cafe during the waning years of the Roaring Twenties and subsequently took it to New York's Roosevelt and Waldorf Astoria hotels. Jack Kapp trailed the Lombardo band so doggedly that Jules Stein, Lombardo's agent and president of the Music Corporation of America, took pity on him and allowed his bandleader to sign with Brunswick Records. Lombardo had brought his new dance band sound to Columbia records in 1927–1932 but signed with Brunswick in 1932 and followed Kapp to Decca, from 1934 to 1935, when he temporarily abdicated to RCA Victor.

This successful sound in a democracy still beset by a terrifying economic depression asked as little of its middle-class public as possible, challenging them neither emotionally nor musically. Guy Lombardo, for example, attributed his band's enormous success to musical reductionism: "Simple arrangements, simple beat, everything goes so easy."[52] The band, led by its nucleus of Lebert Lombardo on trumpet, Carmen Lombardo on saxophone, and Guy, a sometime violinist, refused to complicate the basic melody "with fancy embellishments." Despite the intimidating array of gifted jazz and then swing musicians who turned out to listen to the band, the Lombardos insisted that they were not playing for musicians; they "were playing for the people who demanded the melody of their favorite songs and the beat that encouraged them to dance."

Most revealingly, the band cherished its hallmark vibrato in both the saxophones and the brasses. When brother Lebe got complexes about his unorthodox technique and started to take lessons in legitimate trumpet tone and style, Guy lectured him sternly:

You dope, if you had a legitimate tone, you'd be like every other trumpet player looking for a job in a pit band. You've got your own tone and it's one of the big reasons your band and mine is the hottest outfit in Chicago. If I ever catch you fooling around with that teacher again, I'll wrap the horn around your neck.[53]

The band learned to retain what one fan called its very basic "bump-bah, bump-bah" rhythm, its heavy vibrato, and its completely unadorned melodies.

The qualities that propelled Bing Crosby to success as a Decca recording star were similar to those of the Lombardos. Crosby offered a vocal parallel to the sound of the Guy Lombardo dance band. Both stayed close to the melody, rarely improvised, and thereby fulfilled perhaps the major requirement for one of Jack Kapp's recording artists. Kapp is said to have decorated the Brunswick recording studio with a doctored enlargement of a family snapshot of the Pocahontas statue at Jamestown, Virginia, which, according to Kapp's interventions, was seen to be pleading "Where is the melody?" in a comic-strip style bubble.[54]

In this, Kapp merely resurrected, as a response to the Depression, Thomas A. Edison's earlier determination to sell records by offering musically uneducated people clearly articulated, relatively unadorned, and ultimately reassuring melodies. But, like any other record producer, Kapp also looked for a special "new" vocal quality or instrumental sound, and in this domain no white performer surpassed Bing Crosby, who gradually developed his soothingly soft, rounded "crooning" recording style while working with Jack Kapp for the Brunswick and Decca labels. When singing with Paul Whiteman's Rhythm Boys, Crosby had produced a hotter, "twenties" type of rhythmic vocal style, never as intense and sharp-edged as his hero Al Jolson's but still energetically animated. Jack Kapp's microphones brought out a more warmly intimate, romantic side of Crosby's musical sensibilities.

Among the likely influences on Crosby's work, recording star Ruth Etting is usually overlooked. The similarities in style and repertoire between Etting and Crosby include the former's blithe melodic accuracy and clear diction, which, when combined with her pretty blond good looks, earned her the title of "America's Sweetheart of Song" when she performed on radio.[55] Actually, Etting had come up the hard way as a singer and dancer in Chicago night clubs where she met and married Martin "Moe the Gimp" Snyder, who possessively followed her everywhere staring balefully at the males in her life. Although Etting signed with Columbia in 1926, recording flapper-type numbers such as "The Varsity Drag" and "Shakin' the Blues Away," she subsequently moved to Brunswick and recorded a less agitated repertoire under Kapp's direction.

An entire Etting and Crosby performance on Brunswick came packaged in a soft tone and a gentle warmth worthy of the Lombardo sax section. Crosby smoothly glissed his rich baritone voice up to his melodic notes in a subdued, nearly conversational style, as if, as Martin Williams put it,[56] he had been overheard by the microphone. Crosby subdivided his vocals into musical phrases by, as he put it in his autobiography, "slurring the words until they're mashed together in a hot mush in the mouth."[57] This kind of singing would have been difficult to capture on records cut in the days of acoustic recording: Crosby and Kapp took advantage of the new electronic microphone's sensitivity to create a new sound designed for the 1930s.[58]

In his memoirs, Bing Crosby understandably claimed his vocal technique as his own invention but did give Jack Kapp full credit for having conceived of and then produced all of his early hit records. Kapp, Crosby made clear, "formulated my recording plans. He even selected the numbers I sang." The clever matching of the intimate but relaxed crooning style with an extremely varied repertoire that would, as Gary Giddens puts it, "please all of the people at one time or another," accounted for a major portion of the appeal of Crosby's Brunswick records.[59] But Kapp did not merely cover all the familiar bases; his most famous genre mixtures paired Crosby's soothingly popular democratic style with middle-class religious memories like "Adeste Fideles," "Silent Night," and, of course, the nostalgic "White Christmas."

In the history of recorded vocal music, Kapp reversed the older formula that had applied classically trained voices to folk songs. Opera star Alma Gluck's million-copy Victor recording of James G. Bland's "Carry Me Back to Old Virginny," as well as other songs written by Stephen Foster, provides an instructive counterpoint to Crosby's "Adeste Fideles." In the former case, the interesting mixture of high and low music genres is achieved by bringing an operatic voice to bear on old parlor songs, while in the latter, an untrained common man's voice, one with none of the characteristics of formal musical training in pitch, enunciation, and attack, delivers a sacred song in Latin.

One insightful scholar, Jean-Pierre Vignolle, argues that popular songs become such by constructing "the unity of a new object out of loans from diverse sources. Seen in this way, the act of creation consists in rejecting the 'laws of the object.'"[60] Ample evidence documents Kapp's awareness of the appeal to be generated in mixing elements of contrasting genres and musical traditions in unexpected ways: when, for example, in 1935 Crosby performed on the Kraft Music Hall radio program, Kapp often paired him with opera stars, and radio audiences loved this "humanizing" of the "longhairs." While taking care to avoid making Crosby's "guests" seem "tawdry or cheap," the show had Lotte Lehmann, Feodor Chaliapin, and Risë Stevens, among many others, sing scat songs and talk with Crosby about things like baseball and horse racing.[61] While Gluck had cast her folk material in the self-proclaimed high culture mold of a Victor Red Seal record, Kapp and Crosby cast high (or perhaps middling) culture material within the popular mold of radio and the 35¢ Decca record.

But Kapp also spent a good deal of time designing a kind of lush, violin-filled orchestral setting that contrasted sharply with, for example, the solitary guitar accompaniments of the country blues records. On many of Crosby's Brunswick recordings of 1933–34, such as "Two Cigarettes in the Dark" and the aptly titled "It's Easy to Remember," the orchestral backing was carefully calculated so that different sounds—now a tinkling piano, next a harp, then a xylophone, then strings—filled in between vocal phrases. As a savvy observer of recordings puts it, these gimmicks, while usually unnoticed by the listener, stick in his mind and bring a smile when they pass by.[62] They also brought the sounds of democratic opulence into the lives of struggling Americans.

In promoting Decca recordings of Guy Lombardo and Bing Crosby, Kapp had successfully read important cultural trends of the early Depression years. As described by historian Lawrence Levine, large segments of the population found relief from their economic anxieties and faltering sense of self-worth by basking in the reassuring glow of their favorite "idols of consumption" whose casual, stylish nonchalance provided models for surviving hard times. Taking time to live life fully, to relax, and to live for the day provided an avenue of hope for people struggling through troubled times.[63] Kapp and Crosby provided gentle musical reminders of the past as antidotes for deep Depression anxieties about the present and future. Bing confronted the Depression directly only on "Brother, Can You Spare a Dime?" (Brunswick 6414) where his interpretation of the lyrics suggested plenty of bitter humiliation. But his Decca recordings of "Oh, Come, All Ye Faithful" and "Silent Night" (Decca white Label specials) skirted realism into Christian assurance. In his many ballads and popular recordings from 1931–1936 Crosby pleads, moans, groans, and wails of his love for various women.[64]

When Crosby and Lombardo are compared to Kapp's other 1930s Decca recording stars, a Kapp sound emerges. The smooth and relaxed vocal quartet of the Mills Brothers similarly offered melodies with few sharp edges. They and the Boswell Sisters produced a gentle, slowly but jauntily swinging melodic sound reminiscent of the old barbershop style. Even the famous Tommy Dorsey Orchestra became known for recordings on which the bandsmen sang in unison. Tommy Dorsey's silken muted trombone sound similarly replaced the raucous tailgate rhythmics of the twenties. Ethel Waters sang with a refinement and restraint unknown to Sophie Tucker or Bessie Smith's bawdy style or to that of most of the other classic blues singers of the twenties. Kapp also smoothed out the percussive banjo-bred jazz rhythms of 1920s recordings, substituting, thanks to more sensitive electrical microphones, the guitar; this soothing sound, so appropriate to the depths of the Depression, characterized most of the records Decca made in the mid-thirties.

The record that put the company into the black once and for all, Decca's "monster hit" of late 1935, "The Music Goes Round and Round," whose sales were reported to have reached 650,000 by mid-1936,[65] suggested that a clientele with younger, more energetic, rowdy tastes had yet to be fully served. Kapp's hit had been created from a song by Red Hodgson, a relatively obscure West Coast trumpet player, and performed in the Onyx Club on New York's 52nd Street by Ed Farley, another trumpeter, and Mike Riley, a trombonist; both musicians had been added to Red McKenzie's Mound City Blue Blowers.[66] This catchy novelty number, whose lyrics about the progress of sound through a trumpet could also be taken to refer to its progress from the spinning grooves of a record through the innards of a phonograph, combined comedy, melody, and good-natured, easygoing swing, performed in a rowdy, very nearly sloppy, manner.

"The Music Goes Round and Round" capitalized on a second major musical sensibility and market category with which Kapp had done relatively little. If many people of all ages needed to be gently soothed and reassured, many others began looking for livelier and more original forms of recorded music, reassuring in their beauty, as the country slowly emerged from its darkest hours. Swing featured the vigorous, exciting beat and flashily instrumental sounds that had been eliminated from Kapp's more staid popular formula. With his rich, detailed memory for the recorded jazz of the 1920s, John Hammond did more than any other record producer to repackage jazz as "swing" by helping Benny Goodman, Teddy Wilson, William "Count" Basie, and Harry James to combine the well-entrenched tradition of dance hall and ballroom orchestras with important elements of African American jazz and blues traditions.

Although swing became a major force in popular recorded music, it is possible to overestimate, as has Theodor Adorno, its dominance. In 1939, four years into the swing era, *Time* magazine reported that "*aficionados* of swing" accounted for 25 percent of record sales in the popular field.[67] White and black youth—high schoolers as much as, or more than, collegians—formed the primary market for more overtly hybrid records that combined elements of the race record musical traditions with white dance band music. Bing Crosby seems to have appealed to young white adults while a wealthier crowd enjoyed Guy Lombardo's dance music. High schoolers wanted to dance to a more exuberant music. During the 1920s, a market for hot dance music had been served by a wealth of jazz-influenced dance band records. By 1933, these bands, which had performed mostly in expensive hotels and the leading dance halls, were no longer in touch with Depression-era youth.

At the same time, college students had demonstrated a continuing interest in race records. Recorded primarily for sale to southern rural Blacks, race records sold well in white college towns where some students collected them. Decca reported to the trade papers that "the popular music of blacks sells to [white] record collectors as 'primitive.'" But college record collectors also called race record music "hot music," a term that carried a wealth of more socially daring potential.[68] After nearly five years during which few if any records had been made for young people, Decca, for example, felt that "the generation raised on the phonograph is not as important to increased sales as the younger one now converting to the phonograph from radio."[69] When sales began to increase in

1934, Decca announced that "new customers" were responsible, naming "school youths" impressed with screen and radio stars.[70]

In 1928, industry publications had begun to awake to untapped demands among white collegians who found themselves trapped in the smaller towns and cities and forced to entertain themselves with, among other things, records. The industry quoted the U.S. census that 508,714 male and 312,338 female collegians were potential customers. The number of high schoolers far exceeded these collegiate numbers. College student newspapers became an important advertising medium for race, jazz, and blues records.[71] The Yale *News Pictorial* became the first to carry industry ads.

John Henry Hammond, Jr., who had spent one year at Yale, turned his attention to developing and shaping the dance band market, devising a new, explosively powerful popular music called "big band swing" that could appeal to the aural memories of jazz and hot dance music that had been established before the Depression. Kapp's hit records had caught the calmer, sweeter, more tranquil and nostalgic side of Depression sensibilities; Hammond worked with jazz's proven appeal to an energetic and more adventurous sensibility.

More important, however, the tension between Kapp and Hammond also encapsuled the struggle over the significance of the phonograph in American life: could it only be expected to mass-produce flashy and formulaic musical diversions for those with no fixed musical taste, or could it be used to disseminate a creative and democratically "authentic" music that would remind Americans of something forgotten and, in the process, raise the artistic level of American popular music?

That Hammond and not Jack Kapp became the champion of jazz and swing as original forms of American popular art music in the recovering recording industry can be partly explained by the two men's different socio-economic backgrounds. Kapp, child of the record business, thought first in terms of popular record sales. Hammond, born on December 15, 1910, into the Vanderbilt family, was raised in a Fifth Avenue mansion that featured, among other things, sixteen bathrooms, two elevators, and a private ballroom. He qualified as a full member of the American aristocracy and retained elements of the old Victorian belief that the phonograph should propagate examples of musical art. Although Kapp offered no public opinions about Hammond, the latter made no bones about his boredom with what he called Kapp's "commercial junk."

Hammond had been raised in a genteel home and at Hotchkiss, an Anglo-Saxon boys' college-preparatory school in the Berkshire mountains of western Connecticut. His mother, the granddaughter of William H. Vanderbilt, played an active role in the moral reform movement led by upper middle-class ladies like Chicago's Jane Addams, and was also deeply involved in the world of concert hall music, regularly performing at the piano for her friends, sometimes with her only son playing violin. Her exceedingly demanding moral and social standards may have contributed to her son's rebellious interest in popular culture. He brought to popular music, however, his mother's commitment to social meliorism through musical art and combined it with his own discovery of left-wing Popular Front politics.[72]

As a musically inclined youngster, Hammond understandably turned early to recorded music, taking a particular interest in jazz and blues. According to the *Saturday Review of Literature* music columnist Irving Kolodin, Hammond, thanks to a liberal allowance, had been an avid record collector as a youngster, one who memorized labels, numbers, and names of recording artists.[73] In 1939 his collection numbered only about 6,000 records since he had thrown away most of the estimated 20,000 that he had bought.[74] Hammond's exceptional musical memory provided the continuity necessary in order for the general public to recognize the jazz in swing.

These jazz records so spurred his curiosity that the teenaged Hammond, allowed to travel alone from Hotchkiss to New York City, ostensibly to take violin lessons, snuck up to Harlem to listen to his favorite jazz instrumentalists in person. As he later explained it, these musical and social experiences, when combined with the religious teaching of William Sloan Coffin and the liberal philosophy of George Van Santvoord, set him upon a left-wing quest for social justice.

From Hotchkiss, Hammond graduated to Yale, where health problems and his fascination with the record business produced a short, one-year career. He celebrated his twenty-first birthday in 1931 by moving out of the family mansion and into a bohemian Greenwich Village apartment. There he found the right artistic and political environment to encourage his unique combination of politics and recorded music.

Hammond's career as a record producer would reflect the precarious position of a professional with social democratic, Popular Front ideas trying to produce musical culture in a business dominated by a small number of large corporations. As described by George Lipsitz and Michael Denning, private corporations like Columbia and RCA Victor Records that manufactured culture responded to Franklin D. Roosevelt's New Deal through the ideology of "corporate liberalism" which, whatever its token recognition of unions, left some contested space for left-wing populist and anti-Fascist employees eager to explore ways in which one could turn corporate professionalism to the goals of social democracy.[75]

Hammond's independent wealth and the precarious fortunes of Columbia Records during the 1930s permitted him much more room for maneuver than most corporate leftists. He produced some of his most acclaimed discs while working as an independent; he signed on with Columbia in 1939 but resigned in 1941 when Columbia objected to his becoming president of a small independent label, Keynote Records, that had been established a year earlier by Eric Bernay, former publisher of the *New Masses*.

From 1931–1934, during the worst of the Depression, Hammond pursued the record business and was also involved in promoting the legal defense of the Scottsboro Nine, a group of African American youngsters accused in Alabama of having raped two young white women on a train. The Communist Party and a wide variety of other leftists organized the legal defense of "the Scottsboro Boys," and Hammond, in addition to covering the trials for the *Nation*, combined his family's wealth and connections and his own contacts with politically active Black musicians like Duke Ellington and Benny Carter to organize swinging benefits for the cause.

The Scottsboro trials wore on nearly interminably, so Hammond had plenty of time to organize recording sessions for the English and the American Columbia labels while doing his best to expose exploitative practices in the industry. He had used his wealth intelligently, buying his way into the recording business in 1931. Having decided that a cabaret pianist named Garland Wilson deserved to be recorded, he went to the Columbia Phonograph Company studio, at that time controlled by the English Columbia company, and paid "a stiff price" for the right to make four 12-inch sides.[76]

Beginning in 1933, Hammond, on the strength of these earlier recordings and articles he wrote for British magazines *Gramophone* and *Melody Maker*, was contracted by Sir Louis Sterling, head of the British Columbia company, to direct jazz recordings for sale on the English and continental markets. Coming at a time when most jazz musicians, even those like Benny Goodman who had risen to prominence in the latter years of Chicago's cabaret and studio scene, needed the work desperately, Hammond gained invaluable influence among jazz musicians and went on to use it to promote racial integration and swing in the recording studios.[77] During the fall of 1933, he produced pioneering jazz records that featured among others clarinetist Benny Goodman with vocalist Billie Holiday and trumpeter Shirley Clay from the Don Redman band. Many other racially integrated sessions followed, several of them acclaimed for their exceptional musical achievements.

The scholarly discussion of John Hammond and the swing era overemphasizes the big bands at the expense of the small groups that Hammond gathered to record with vocalist Billie Holiday on the Brunswick label from 1935 through 1937. These unprecedented records of what he called the Teddy Wilson-Billie Holiday Orchestra featured the Basie swing rhythm section of Walter Page on string bass, Freddie Green on rhythm guitar, and Jo Jones on drums, in addition to Wilson's piano and a shifting group of wind instrumentalists that included tenor saxophonist Lester Young, clarinetist Edmond Hall, and, of course, Holiday. Hammond put Black musicians in the majority but usually included individual white jazzmen from the Goodman camp.

The booming big-bands got the attention of the crowds, but this other chamber swing sound—very much the creation of Hammond, who chose the musicians—engraved in wax the intimate, elegant sounds of Cafe Society's new world of greater racial equality. Harking back to Harry Pace's desire to record Ethel Waters doing something other than Bessie

Smith's rough-timbred blues, Hammond made a subdued but emphatic aesthetic and political statement: Black musicians could bring to the jazz tradition in swing an unequaled finesse of sensibility and instrumental technique.

These records seem to have expressed Hammond's personal sensibilities by bringing together the refinement of his mother's "soirées musicales," his quest for racial equality and integration through the nightclubs and cabarets of Harlem, and his search for an "original" musical formulation. When shaping the first Goodman band, Hammond did his job in pulling the industry out of the Depression. When making the Wilson-Holiday sides, he, more than any other individual, demonstrated how creative the record producer could be, setting new standards of jazz recording not matched until the bebop revolution of the 1950s. From his earliest appearance in the record business, the content of Hammond's criticisms of popular music records, those of Jack and Dave Kapp in particular, eerily paralleled the broadsides against jazz and swing by the left-wing German critic Theodor Adorno. Both complained of the transformation of popular music into a standardized, musically sterile commercial commodity. Hammond felt certain that he could wield the commodity technology to make an artistically arranged and performed popular music, a claim that Adorno appeared to dismiss.

Soon after establishing his credentials as a record man, Hammond began to promote hot dance music in live performance. By 1935, no one was supplying fresh dance music for the commercialized public spaces— dance halls, hotel ballrooms, movie theaters—that were still featuring the dance bands of the 1920s. Hammond worked closely with another Ivy Leaguer, Willard Alexander, a dance band booker who had begun his career while still enrolled at the University of Pennsylvania and who went on to work for the powerful Music Corporation of America (MCA) organized by Chicagoan Jules Stein. Alexander was looking for a new dance band sound to appeal to the teenage and college markets. He was able to get Goodman's new band booked on a cross-country tour that, along with regular live radio broadcasts, created the big break needed.[78]

With other promoters working on the Goodman band's radio exposure and publicity, Hammond helped to shape the band's personnel in ways that would appeal to the mass youth market. Hammond influenced the buoyancy and power of the Goodman band's rhythm section. First he got Goodman to replace his rather tame drummer with Gene Krupa. Young, darkly handsome, athletic, flamboyant, charismatic, and a powerful, heavy-handed and heavy-footed drummer, Krupa was more likely to mesmerize the mass market than anyone other than his fellow Chicagoan Davey Tough, whose personal habits made him unreliable. Second, he got Goodman to replace his competent but rhythmically erratic pianist with Jess Stacy, known for the steady buoyancy of his rhythm. According to Goodman, Hammond was "almost entirely" responsible for getting the clarinetist to adopt what musicologist Gunther Schuller has called the "riff cum call-and-response formulas of the Henderson brothers."

Again, Hammond brought Fletcher Henderson's arrangements to Goodman's attention, injecting an African American antiphonal call-and-response pattern into the structure of Swing.[79]

Hammond later used his influence on Goodman to seize control of recording of the Goodman band in 1938–39. After his early work with Hammond on English Columbia, Goodman had signed with RCA Victor, the best deal for the clarinetist since American Columbia had declared bankruptcy in 1933. But, under the urging of Emmanuel "Ted" Wallerstein, William Paley's CBS network bought the Columbia label and Hammond went to work there in 1939.[80]

Hammond believed that the influential Victor record producer Eli Oberstein had increasingly encouraged a "stylistic stultification" of Goodman's recorded music, repeatedly producing an uninspired formula of pop standards, overdoing the antiphonal brass and wind instrument choirs, and leaving only the solos to enliven the band's Victor records. At Columbia under Hammond's direction, Goodman recorded some sixty numbers arranged by Eddie Sauter who gave the big band a new harmonic and timbral quality based not on the Henderson call and response of brass and reed sections but, as Gunther Schuller put it, on "a *blending* of brass and reeds into new warmer timbral combinations and textures."[81] The gist of the new dispensation amounted to a perceptibly greater harmonic and compositional sophistication. Hammond convinced Goodman to include Black guitarist Charlie Christian, then considered avant garde, in his sextet and occasionally in his big band, too. The precursors of bebop began to color Goodman's popular swing sounds.

While establishing himself within the business as a record producer, Hammond regularly stepped outside of the corporate walls to mount vigorous attacks in the press on the Kapp brothers and Decca Records for blatantly exploiting its African American musicians. In articles written under the pseudonym Henry Johnson for the Communist publication *The New Masses*, Hammond, who insisted that he was not a Communist sympathizer, exposed the kind of practices that had become habitual in the race record business since the Okeh label had introduced the idea in 1920. Decca, Hammond wrote, had recorded forty titles played by Andy Kirk, more than half of which were originals created by various members of the band who "either received a minute percentage of the profits or a small outright payment." By contrast, a Decca official received one-third of a cent per side.[82] Hammond also condemned the Kapps' practice of creating their own company to buy up copyrights at a flat rate, even copyrighting the term "boogie-woogie" so that any song title using it would have to pay him a fee.[83]

The weight of established business practices from the 1920s, for example, had shaped the Kapps' work in race records. Jack's younger brother Dave, who took the traditional race records approach, one that Hammond rejected, signed Count Basie's Band to a Decca recording contract in 1935. Dave Kapp worked out of Chicago where he directed the recording of race and hillbilly music. Kapp read Hammond's *Down Beat* articles praising the Basie outfit and went west to Kansas City to sign Basie to a contract. Hammond had not hustled out to make contact with Basie, preferring to suggest in his *Down Beat* columns that Basie get in touch with him![84]

Kapp, according to Hammond, at any rate, passed himself off as a friend of Hammond's, and suggested to the musicians that he would pay for a Pullman car to take the entire band to Chicago, and got Basie to sign a contract to make twelve records (twenty-four sides) a year for a flat payment of $750. Such small outright one-time payments left the recording company in possession of copyright on the music and lyrics, the standard procedure in the race record business for more than ten years.

Hammond has been criticized for his patriarchal attitudes toward the musicians he promoted and recorded, but he did oppose the traditional kind of race record business practices while issuing racially integrated small-group recordings on the old Vocalion label. According to his own testimony, for example, he hit the roof when told of Basie's Decca contract. He couldn't get Basie out of the deal; however, he did see to it that the musicians' pay was raised to union scale. In his autobiography, published fifty years later, Basie mixed his praise of Hammond with an allusion to the record producer's sense of entitlement, taking care to recall how the patrician New Yorker had walked into the Reno Club, come right up on the bandstand, and sat down next to Basie on the piano bench! Yet Basie sincerely thanked Hammond for his help in getting the influential band booker Willard Alexander to send the band eastward to a prominent opening at the Roseland Ballroom in New York City. He also credited Hammond with recording small Basie groups for Vocalion, in order to get around the infamous Decca contract, and for booking the band into 52nd Street's Famous Door in 1938, complete with a radio wire and coast-to-coast hookup. Basie's praise documents Hammond's historical importance in racially integrating the recording of popular music and promoting African American bands:

> Some people have their differences with him too. But as far as I'm concerned, John Hammond was the one who made the big difference in my life as a bandleader, no question about it. Without him I probably would still be in Kansas City, if I still happened to be alive.[85]

The record producer also attacked as exploitative the piecework system at Decca and elsewhere in the industry. Lest he be accused of picking on Decca, Hammond also criticized work conditions at the American Record Company factory where tremendous heat, the powerful odor of hot shellac, the constant tension of placing master plates onto the presses absolutely correctly, correct labeling, and taking the record from the press at exactly the right temperature created oppressive conditions for the poorly paid workers who turned out Columbia records.[86]

Hammond, for example, took the position that recording technology could be used in a less blatantly nostalgic and less racially exploitative manner. In the 1930s on the other side of the Atlantic, Theodor Adorno roundly condemned the popular jazz and swing music he heard on records and radio in Germany, bludgeoning their false claims to an association with African American music while, as far as he was concerned, actually manipulating racial images in order to titillate the white public. Hammond's musical politics departed from much this same point of view, but he took several steps in another direction that Adorno never recognized: the American turned to producing what he believed to be artistically significant popular music by blending into the white dance band tradition more African American musicians and arrangements, thus linking racial integration to improved musical quality in the popular recording business.

While Adorno condemned all jazz and swing, Hammond, and later critics such as Gunther Schuller, condemned only part of them. Neither Hammond nor Schuller denied that jazz and swing often degenerated into commercial formulas. Schuller has even argued that Hammond's influence on the Count Basie Orchestra helped turn it into a cliché-ridden outfit. But Schuller credits Hammond for exercising a dominant influence in saving the Goodman band from a similar fate. Hammond's promotion of musicians like Goodman, Basie, Teddy Wilson, Billie Holiday, Red Norvo, and so many others immeasurably raised the quality of popular recorded music without sacrificing its public appeal.

At the same time, however, Hammond's mediation of big band swing did largely justify Adorno's accusations of aristocratic control of what was billed as democratic popular music. Whatever its claims to populist spontaneity, both big band and small band swing were heavily mediated. Within the record business, Hammond's genteel social background was most unusual, but the American-style aristocrat did exercise power over many of the swing bands. During the thirties, four major dance bands—those of Benny Goodman, Count Basie, Teddy Wilson, and Harry James—owed much of their prominence to Hammond.[87] Hammond played the determinative role in selecting the talent for Café Society and the Famous Door, two leading jazz clubs in Manhattan. His views on jazz and swing influenced most jazz periodicals. And, of course, he played a crucial role in shaping the sound of the Benny Goodman Orchestra, a dance band with no fixed stylistic identity when he first heard it, into a major force for hot dance music in the world of hotel ballrooms and big-city dance halls. Hammond, moreover, made big band swing records whose appeal stemmed from their artfully conceived and performed reformulations of the traditions of jazz and dance band traditions. In the process, he wielded the power to make and break recording careers, bestowing his godlike favor or disapproval on this or that poor, aspiring, often African American, musician. He made an undisputed claim having "discovered" and thus having been responsible for launching the recording careers of

Benny Goodman, William "Count" Basie, Billie Holiday, Teddy Wilson, Lionel Hampton, Jess Stacy, Charlie Christian, and Helen Humes, not to speak of Aretha Franklin, George Benson, Bob Dylan, and Bruce Springsteen, whose careers he guided after 1945. The concept of "discovery," defined from the point of view of the white record executive, fully expressed the conflict in swing, an arranged and spontaneous music played by poor whites and Blacks at the bidding of a few powerful white mediators.

Whatever the final verdict on the degree of musical art in jazz and swing, Theodor Adorno, apparently basing his judgments on the records and radio broadcasts available in Berlin, vastly exaggerated the ubiquity of popular records by the big bands from 1935 to 1941. Even though 75 percent of hit records featured swing bands during that period,[88] at the time that swing caught on with the public, *Time* magazine reported that only 25 percent of all record purchases fit that style category. Similarly, in assessing the relative markets for different sorts of recordings for the period 1939 to 1967, Columbia Records executive and record producer George Avakian estimated that 35 percent of all sales were of the popular "hit parade" sort that certainly would have included swing without excluding other styles—15–20 percent race, 20 percent hillbilly, 25 percent classical, and 5 percent a miscellany of children's records, imports, and ethnic.[89] Two studies that have tried to assess the dominance of pop music in America since World War II have offered very similar conclusions: James K. Skipper[90] finds that about one-third of record buyers choose pop records, while Hall and Blau[91] underline the diversity of musical preferences among American youth.

The impression of a national uniformity of taste for swing came not from market saturation of hit dance band records but rather from a multimedia promotion in which records played only one part. Although associated strongly with the jukebox, swing's apparent ubiquity was deeply indebted to the popularity of radio broadcasts and movie sound tracks. Beginning in 1929, radio networks had adopted 16-inch, 33 1/3 rpm electrical transcriptions, a larger, more slowly turning form of record that contained a total of 30 minutes of music, patter, and comedy. The same big bands whose music filled the 3-minute, 78 rpm records for sale to the general public dominated electrical transcriptions. Swing's ubiquity derived as much from radio networks as the home phonograph. Beginning in 1926 when the National Broadcasting Company was formed, chains of radio stations across the country broadcast the same music at the same time.[92]

Popular recorded music before World War II expressed a far more varied and diverse set of influences than critics like Adorno have claimed. Adorno, who didn't care for popular music recordings, didn't listen to them and instead took the easier route of overgeneralization and blanket condemnation. His articles offer no examples at all. As this book shows, the record industry recorded many different kinds of music: ethnic, race, jazz, opera, classical, and so on. Moreover, these terms are merely marketing labels and they conceal a diversity of musical styles.[93] That is why jazz writers have had so much trouble defining the term *jazz*. Swing, a promotional term used in defining dance music aimed at the youth market, actually encompassed the "sweet bands" of Guy Lombardo, Jan Garber, and Sammy Kaye, as well as the "hot" ones, and a typical electrical transcription program included plenty of slow ballads and vocal numbers.

But the fad for swing during the thirties must be seen as having emerged from the economic circumstances of the Depression that forced the record companies into corporate mergers with radio and the movies while changing the industry's marketing emphasis to the intense promotion of a limited number of popular records. The combined impact of the media, of which phonograph records were but one ingredient, created musical fads of greater intensity and increased breadth of appeal than had ever been known before. A series of crucial events in the late 1930s and early 1940s began to spell the end of the swing era and the creation of yet another new world for the phonograph.

9

POPULAR RECORDED MUSIC
WITHIN THE CONTEXT
OF NATIONAL LIFE

More than we used to realize, the phonograph and recorded music served to stimulate collective memories among Americans of different social and ethnic backgrounds, who were, like the few large recording companies that survived the Depression, caught up in the swiftly changing patterns and politics of national life. Among the social forces that led many Americans to welcome recorded music, none were more powerful than the wrenching historical changes of urbanization, domestic and international migrations, and social dislocations that resulted from World War II. The personal changes brought on by life itself provided ample stimulus for seeking solace in musical memories, but the additional burdens of national economic adversity and war, which drew workers into urban factories and GIs onto lonely battlefields, led many in both groups to long for the music they had left behind.[1]

Throughout the first half of the twentieth century, many Americans felt that they had been torn from the social and cultural worlds in which they once had sunk roots. Many had to move from county to county, from country to city, from other countries to the United States, or from the South to the North, and, for a goodly number, movement became a way of life. Many moved down the social ladder during the depression. In all of these cases, the specific content of popular musical memories varied with, among other things, the experience of ethnic, racial, gender, and regional identities in American life. But, whether consciously or not, almost all citizens found in recorded music a vehicle for carrying musical memories through time and into the present.

Because the people of the United States were enmeshed in sweeping twentieth century developments, they also looked for and shared experiences of recorded music that crossed ethnic, racial, and gender boundaries. If one were to fully accept the assumptions of the phonograph trade papers concerning marketing categories for records, one might assume that record producers had predicted audience tastes so exactly that few

Americans ever listened to records other than those that had been designed for their particular group.

And it is true that domestic musical memory machines did not require that one listen to unfamiliar music: industry leaders gloated that their technology allowed people more control over the music of their lives than did radio. Many Americans, like some of Edison's customers, took advantage of their ownership of records and turntables to refuse to listen to records of newer popular styles of their day. They preferred to play and replay records of music in a style with which they were already familiar, constructing and reconstructing reassuring memories of the America they had known. So too, southern Black migrants to the northern cities and transplanted rural white southern factory workers listened to the records prepared for them as part of a process of recognizing their groups' identities as they moved through time and space.

In reality, however, recorded music also stimulated as well as reflected shared national sensibilities that shaped the lives of many different groups in similar ways. From 1890 to the end of World War II, the phonograph industry, more than radio, did produce musical entertainment by people who were not white or Anglo-Saxon or Protestant; but with the exception of Billie Holiday's recording of "Strange Fruit" on the Commodore label, the voices on these discs rarely articulated minority group political attacks on the nation's attitudes toward race, class, and ethnicity. Records of women, African Americans, and members of various ethnic groups making music might have been created in order to stimulate disrupting musical and emotional experiences among those who had not heard such music before—alternative patterns of music, language, and sensibility with overt political messages—but, given the web of national laws and politics within which the phonograph industry worked, as well as unprecedented global threats to American sovereignty, musical memories in the twentieth century generally conformed to the boundaries of prevailing national values. Even race records, after all, had stopped short of directly confronting racial oppression.

Moreover, various groups of Americans were at least exposed to and sometimes actively and consciously listened to recorded music from traditions other than their own, experiences in sound that broadened their awareness of other musical sensibilities. As the eclectic recordings of such popular stars as Jimmie Rodgers, Ethel Waters, Bing Crosby, Benny Goodman, and the Andrews Sisters clearly show, in order to produce records that would sell to as broad a cross section of customers as possible, record producers often mixed stylistic genres and, less creatively, simply issued ethnic cover versions of hit records. Such processes of cultural and musical assimilation created another basis for shared popular musical memories.

This growing mutual awareness of what had been presented as separate traditions in recorded music emerged particularly among left-wing artists, professionals and intellectuals during the Depression, as we have seen in the previous chapter. The Culture Front of that time had advocated a dynamic brand of Americanism that emphasized the cultural vitality of various ethnic groups within the broad spectrum of American popular culture. Working with a rich amalgam of second-generation immigrant musicians, the left-wing record producer John Hammond had shaped a racially integrated and self-consciously American popular culture that highlighted the important musical traditions of African Americans in particular.

But this culturally assimilative, integrative approach that blended elements of the multiple musical traditions of the country into popular music recordings aimed at the mass audience also stemmed in part from the economic impact of the Great Depression on the recording industry. Hard times largely destroyed the ethnic record business and undercut the small independent companies that had been making race records as well. By stimulating a wave of media consolidations, the number of different companies that made records for highly defined markets declined, and the country was given fewer opportunities to listen to the kind of ethnic musical separatism that specialty companies had promoted.

The coming of World War II served to strengthen nationalist pressures within the culture industries while bringing Americans of different backgrounds together in northern industrial areas. In Detroit, Chicago, and Cleveland, for example, white and Black workers listened during World War II for musical reminders of their rural past played and delivered in an appropriate urban mode. Black popular musicians like Louis Jordan, Ray Charles, and Muddy Waters forged a new urban crossover blues style influenced by country music sounds. white country singer Bob Wills blended elements of country fiddle tunes, Dixieland, Mexican mariachi music, big-band sounds, and the blues.

But in the broader perspective of the national government's responses to the economic depression and the looming prospect of a second world war, the decline of the separate ethnic labels coincided with the rise of corporate liberalism in the United States. As government leaders increasingly emphasized national economic stability and placed limitations on economic competition, they worked in partnership with the large corporations to make just enough concessions to potentially dissident groups to give them reason to support the system.[2] The record companies, in the midst of difficult times, got into line. No longer promoting ethnic musical separatism, they invented big-band swing into which they blended Black and ethnic musical traditions.

By the late 1930s and early 1940s, the recording industry's participation in a network of national institutions and values became more significant than ever. Four national developments strongly influenced the companies during this period. First, the two leaders were bought out by radio corporations. The Victor Talking Machine Company, the most powerful of all the record companies, was taken over by the Radio Corporation of America in 1929; the Columbia Phonograph Company was swallowed up by the Columbia Broadcasting System in 1938. Two of the top three record companies were thereby absorbed into corporate conglomerates. By 1940, of the leading record companies only Decca retained its independence of radio. President Jack Kapp proved to be the last of the old-time record men to oppose the growing dependence on radio play to stimulate record sales.

Then the increasingly powerful radio broadcast networks decided to exert more authority over the kinds of music they beamed across the country. In the process, the record companies were obliged to move away from established sources of popular music and pioneer some new ones, most notably vocal styles like hillbilly and blues that allowed them to avoid high production costs in wages and copyright royalties. In addition, the American Federation of Musicians mounted a debilitating two-year strike against the record companies, an experience that also led these subsidiaries of the radio networks into a strategic turn toward vocal renditions of popular songs by nonunion musicians. Finally, the recording industry, responding to wartime necessities, turned its laboratories over to military research and its recording studios to the V-Disc program. These four developments muted the independence of the popular record business as the leading companies discovered that they were no longer the only nor even the primary players in the rapidly evolving national struggle for control of the country's popular musical life.

A major shift in the direction of popular music occurred during the 1930s as the result of a struggle between radio broadcasters and the American Society of Composers, Authors, and Publishers (ASCAP). Radio interests, represented by the National Association of Broadcasters (NAB) faced off against ASCAP over the latter's demands for royalty payments for the broadcast of copyrighted musical works. ASCAP was formed in 1914 as a response by established songwriters and music publishers to the logistical problems of enforcing the payment of both performance and "mechanical" royalties on copyrighted music by the huge number and variety of organizations and institutions that regularly and copiously used that commodity. A group of copyright lawyers, music composers, and politicians had combined in order to fashion ways to collect royalties due by law to copyright holders on the live performance and recording of their music.

Because of the swift centralization of radio programming that gathered force during the 1920s, ASCAP's interest in collecting licensing fees focused primarily on radio. In 1926, the Radio Corporation of America formed a subsidiary, the National Broadcasting Company, to transmit radio programs on a growing network of affiliated stations across the country.[3] This first broadcast network was followed in 1927 by William S. Paley's Columbia Broadcasting System; and in 1934 by a third major network, the Mutual Broadcasting System; and in the early 1940s, by the American Broadcasting Company. These networks attracted enormous sums of money from advertisers eager to reach national audiences, and ASCAP insisted that network and unaffiliated radio stations pay for licenses to broadcast copyrighted music under its control.

Beginning in 1923, the organization managed to sell licenses to an increasing number of radio stations, and most resistance to its demands had disappeared by 1926. Throughout most of the 1930s, ASCAP and the National Association of Broadcasters signed contracts that annually sent millions of dollars to ASCAP, whose board of directors redistributed the funds to its members according to a complex formula that favored the established music publishing houses and older composers with many published songs to their credit.

Relations between ASCAP and NAB remained difficult, however, for two reasons: first, ASCAP self-consciously discriminated in favor of what it considered to be the musically artistic popular compositions of such songwriters as Victor Herbert, one of its principal founders, and Irving Berlin. The group's formula for redistributing the money collected from selling performance rights licenses favored older, established composers, and music publishing houses and ASCAP looked down upon radio for indiscriminately broadcasting so much hillbilly music in such programs as the WLS "National Barn Dance" and Nashville's "Grand Ole Opry."

The licensing organization's music publishers also complained that radio, by playing tunes so frequently, wore them out more quickly, thus lessening the sales life of its hit numbers from a year or more to as little as six weeks. In 1928, NBC, then a chain of 69 affiliated stations that could be tuned in on more than 80 percent of all the radio receivers in America, inaugurated a successful series of popular music broadcasts sponsored by Lucky Strike cigarettes. These prime-time network shows featured "Your Hit Parade," which music business historian Russell Sanjek called "a bland homogenization of Hollywood songs and those in the familiar Tin Pan Alley hit pattern" as well as older music.[4] From the point of view of the more powerful ASCAP music publishers, newer songs broadcast over radio gained and lost their popularity before the sheet music publishers could take advantage. In playing and replaying a limited number of popular songs in order to turn them into hits, radio also created a new highly successful group of younger songwriters who did not receive royalty payments from ASCAP as large as those of the established writers and publishers, despite the radio play that their tunes attracted.[5]

Radio broadcasters resented their obligation to do business with ASCAP. In 1939, NAB invested half of the money it had gathered to pay for ASCAP licenses in its own music licensing agency, Broadcast Music, Incorporated. When NAB's contract with ASCAP expired on the last day of the year 1940, NAB defied ASCAP's new contract demands completely and focused on building up its BMI catalog so that it could go on about its business and ignore the established ASCAP composers and music publishing houses altogether.

Broadcast Music, Incorporated (BMI) turned to copyrighting and publishing music in the public domain like the parlor songs of Stephen Foster, and to race and hillbilly music, the latter two having long been refused recognition by ASCAP as even being composed musical forms.

Joe Davis's Georgia Music Corporation, which specialized in race music, joined BMI, while Ralph Peer moved his country music publishing subsidiary, Peer International Corporation, to NAB's licensing body in 1941. The transformation of American popular music was not immediate, for ASCAP adjusted its tastes and its distribution formulas to meet changing times. But BMI did provide unprecedented commercial encouragement and copyright protection to rural white southern (hillbilly) and African American (race) music.[6]

The recording industry had long tried to play both sides of this conflict. On the one hand, the phonograph industry pioneers had publicly celebrated their devotion to recording European operatic, symphonic, and chamber music. On the other hand, however, when forced, the industry had always admitted that profits from sales of its far more numerous popular music records sustained the relatively more limited sales of opera singers, chamber music groups, and symphonies.

Ralph Peer's career epitomized the recording industry's dilemma in the face of radio's preference for more vernacular musical styles. His first employer, the General Phonograph Company, had encouraged him to make race and hillbilly records and had taken for itself not only the profits from record sales but also at least part of the copyright royalties. Okeh President Otto Heinemann had openly embraced popular and ethnic music and would have applauded his producer Ralph Peer's ultimate defiance of ASCAP and his embrace of BMI.

Peer's second employers, however, the Victor and then RCA Victor companies, had decided to make and issue records of vernacular race and hillbilly music but preferred to keep their distance from too intimate an embrace of the resultant mass markets. This tendency to look the other way had allowed Peer to amass what he later claimed to have been a small fortune in mechanical rights. He then branched out into music publishing, and pulled vernacular music into the mainstream of the music business.

During the 1930s, the National Association of Broadcasters transformed itself into one of the most powerful lobbies in Washington, using the political clout from its phenomenal sales of network advertising time and its ever increasing control of the airwaves to secure passage of the Communications Act of 1934 that irrevocably turned the airwaves over to commercial broadcasting.[7] At about the same time, of course, the radio networks also took control of most of the major record companies, and this greatly reduced the latter's independent power to set the tone of American musical life. When Peer recorded Jimmie Rodgers, for example, he had worked for the still independent Victor Talking Machine Company. If RCA Victor, which was no longer in competition with radio, wanted its affiliated stations to broadcast prepackaged programs of hillbilly and race music and had decided to pay for it into its own BMI licensing agency, there was little that the old-line record men could do about it, and some of them actually had pioneered the recording of that sort of music.

At the same time the record companies' product absorbed even more of the influence of radio as the latter turned, slowly at first and then very dramatically, from live recorded performance to prerecorded programs. A special 16-inch 33⅓ rpm disc euphemistically called an "electrical transcription," invented by Harold J. Smith of the Vitaphone Company, made inroads into live radio broadcasting. Created as a method of providing synchronized sound for movies and quickly overshadowed by the optical sound track, electrical transcriptions were first broadcast on radio by station WOR in New York in 1929. They could provide fifteen minutes of programming on each side with reduced surface noise compared to that available on the standard three-minute 78 rpm commercial records. Produced by several companies that included World Broadcasting Service, Standard Radio Library, and RCA-Thesaurus, electrical transcriptions gave advertisers greater efficiency in targeting specific areas of the country with carefully prepared recorded messages. Electrical transcriptions allowed local radio stations to broadcast independently of the networks and, for that reason, the major radio broadcasting companies did not get into the business until 1934.[8]

In the early 1930s, as many as 600 independent radio stations began turning to commercial records manufactured by the major record companies for their programming. On February 3, 1935, Martin Block, an announcer for WNEW in New York City, started broadcasting his own version of a West Coast show that relied upon recorded music. He called it "Make Believe Ballroom" and quickly established an audience of 4 million listeners in the New York City area.[9] This show set the national pattern for the influential "disk jockeys" who made hit records by bringing new popular recordings to the public's attention.

Despite the benefits of radio advertising in increased record sales, the relations between radio and record men were muddied by a major economic, political, and legal struggle over the definition of a phonograph record. Jack Kapp remained adamantly opposed to radio's use of his records. His primary reason stemmed from what the Copyright Law of 1909 had not said. In granting a copyright claim in phonograph records to composers and music publishers, the government had only indirectly granted any copyright claim to the record companies or to the musicians. Both of those groups believed that their creative contributions to the making of any given record merited copyright protection: the record companies claimed that the taste and skill of their record producers and engineers had done much to shape the final product; musicians insisted that their arrangements and instrumental interpretations helped to make records what they were. The law, however, had directly granted rights to the composers and publishers of the music.

Unionized musicians brought their claims to public attention in a way that the record companies never did. Bandleaders of the stature of Fred Waring and Paul Whiteman, who might have been expected to welcome airplay as leading inevitably to increased sales of their records, nevertheless opposed it. Such bandleaders had contracted with record companies, not radio stations or networks, when making their records. By simply buying records at the local record store and playing them over the air, radio stations attracted substantial sums of money from advertising companies without in any way compensating the musicians and vocalists who had performed the music on the records.[10]

This placed the musicians who had performed on the records broadcast by radio in competition with themselves, since network-affiliated radio stations and independent stations broadcast fewer live musical performances as they came to rely upon the cheaper form of recorded music. Musicians sometimes even heard on radio music that they had performed earlier for live radio broadcasts but which had been surreptitiously recorded and then rebroadcast.

In the late 1930s and early 1940s, musicians mounted a three-pronged attack on what they perceived as unfair reuse of their recordings for public performance for profit. First, a small number of leading musicians went to court to seek further definition and protection of their property rights in phonograph records. Second, the American Federation of Musicians took increasingly militant stands in its dealings with the National Association of Broadcasters until the Justice Department advised that its militancy might well amount to a restraint of trade and thus a potential violation of the Sherman Antitrust Act. Third, having been warned away from striking radio, the musicians' union struck the recording companies.

Several dimensions of these developments reveal that legal and political interpretations of recording technology, rather than the technology itself, had come to determine the fate of recorded sound in the United States. In turning to the state and national courts, musicians explicitly asked that the legal system determine who, if anyone besides the holder of copyright on the recorded musical material, possessed any property rights in phonograph records. The Copyright Law of 1909 had affirmed that songwriters, music publishers, and record companies could retain rights to musical property in records, but what about the musicians who had interpreted the music? Did not making records entitle them to any subsequent right to influence or profit from their use?

Musicians tested the courts on this issue and received a mixed, but generally negative, response. The first case—*Frank Crumit, Plaintiff, v. Marcus Loew Booking Agency and Others, Defendants* (1936)—found Crumit, with the support of Jack Kapp of Decca, seeking from the Supreme Court of New York an injunction against the broadcast of one of his Decca records by the defendants. Crumit and Kapp claimed that their recording contract specified that Decca had formally hired Crumit's "services as a performer so that commercial sound records could be manufactured in a form suitable for use upon home talking machines." To this end, Decca had specified on the label "Not to be used for Radio Broadcasting." The court denied the injunction and explained that the plaintiffs had not presented a copy of the recording contract and therefore could not prove what they claimed about their initial understanding. The defendants, the court said, had no way of knowing anything about the terms under which Decca and Crumit had made their record. Furthermore, the statement stamped on the record was not explicit enough nor linked to any formal licensing restriction. The court carefully pointed out, however, that its decision left open "the fundamental and novel question of law" as to the "general rights of a purchaser of a phonographic record of a performer to use this record for broadcasting purposes without special permission." The rights of Decca or its jobbers and retailers to restrain the broadcasting of their records also remained moot.[11]

One year later, however, in *Waring v. WDAS Broadcasting Station, Inc.,* the Supreme Court of Pennsylvania ruled that the plaintiff, bandleader Fred Waring, did retain rights of property in commercial recordings due to the "novel and artistic creation" with which he and his musicians "consummated" the "incomplete work" of written musical compositions that had merely provided the structure for music, but not music itself. Under this ruling, any bandleader who participated in a commercial recording was said to have "participated in the creation of a product in which he is entitled to a right of property." That being the case, although the court decision did not so specify, bandleaders had a legal right to restrain radio broadcasters from using their recordings in public performances for profit.

But the Federal Courts did not uphold the application of this decision outside the state of Pennsylvania. In *RCA Mfg. Co., Inc., v. Whiteman et al.* (1940), the United States Court of Appeals for the Second Circuit, Justice Learned Hand presiding, ruled that bandleaders like Paul Whiteman, who recorded under contract with record companies, retained no musical property at common law in their commercial recordings; common-law musical property ended with the sale of the records. The court further declared that a radio broadcaster did not in any way duplicate copyrighted work when it played a record of it over the air: a broadcaster like WBO merely "used those copies which he and the RCA Manufacturing Company, Inc. made and distributed."

RCA v. Whiteman ended national efforts by leading musicians to gain judicial protection of the property rights in records that they believed their studio work had earned them. The federal circuit court alluded to the need for new congressional legislation if musicians were to get what they demanded. That legislation did not come until 1976, and it then brought minimal change in the common-law property rights of musicians in records.

Even though the federal courts refused to reinterpret the Copyright Law of 1909 in a way that would serve the interests of studio musicians, the issue of radio broadcasting of recorded music would not go away. On June 8, 1942, James C. Petrillo, president of the American Federation of Musicians (AFM), mounting a campaign against the ways that jukeboxes and radio threatened the livelihood of professional musicians, declared a union ban against any further recording activities by its members. In April of 1942, the U.S. War Production Board had already placed strict limitations on such activity by imposing a 70 percent cut in the amount of shellac, mostly imported from India, that might be devoted to non-military uses.[12] Taking advantage of the weakened position imposed upon the record companies by these wartime restrictions, Petrillo set out to restrict the commercial use of recordings on radio and thus preserve and even expand upon the existing jobs held by his members at radio stations.[13]

AFM's strategic decision to strike the record companies, who made and sold the recordings, and not the radio networks, who bought and broadcast them, had been forced upon the union by the government of the United States. Petrillo had wanted to force radio stations to hire fixed numbers of musicians to protect the profession of music against complete capitulation to "canned" music in the marketplace.[14]

The national government, however, prevented the union from directly confronting radio. In 1939, Thurmond Arnold, head of the Antitrust Division of the Department of Justice, had let it be known that compelling companies to employ "useless" or "unnecessary" workers constituted an unreasonable restraint of trade and a violation of the Sherman Antitrust Act. As Petrillo was trying to force the National Association of Broadcasters to hire more of his musicians in order to keep them working, he might well have been creating what the government called a "secondary boycott," "an action designed to pressure a third party to force employers to comply with union demands." Indeed, the Federal Communications Commission informed Petrillo that the Justice Department would act against any AFM effort to force broadcasters to employ musicians.[15]

AFM's real aim was to limit the broadcasting of recorded music. To achieve this goal, the union might have confronted either the radio broadcasters, as it had in the late 1930s, or the record companies, or both. The first tactic had been precluded by the government, so the union pursued the second one. Here its announced aim was to deny the record companies the ability to sell records to radio broadcasters. If the union could prevent the companies from making records, so the thinking went, it thereby prevented them from selling them to broadcasters.

Several anomalies clouded the union's vision: first, two of the big three record companies—RCA Victor and Columbia—were owned by radio corporations. The Victor Division of RCA Victor and the Columbia Phonograph Corporation of the Columbia Broadcasting System both had been purchased in the first place precisely to furnish their parent companies with a product to use in broadcasting. Decca, the smallest of the big three record makers, remained the last of the traditionally independent major record companies. The AFM demanded that corporate subsidiaries refuse to do the job for which they had been created.

Moreover, the record-producing subsidiaries of the major radio networks had themselves created further subsidiaries that made electrical transcriptions for use on radio. RCA Victor owned RCA-Thesaurus, for example and in 1942, Decca had bought World Transcription Service.

Phonograph companies had compensated for their inability to control radio's use of their commercial records by going into the electrical transcription business themselves.

That musicians deserved some compensation for the use of their recorded music on radio seems, in retrospect, not unreasonable. By the same token, the record companies also possessed a claim to compensation from broadcasters for the use of their records on the air. Unfortunately, however, no laws existed that declared that those who recorded the platter, and thereby made a major contribution to its final content, deserved legal protection of a continuing property right in the record once it had been sold. The record companies therefore could not place any conditions on how record buyers used their purchases. Back in 1917, after all, the Supreme Court had declared that the Victor Talking Machine Company might not control what was done with its phonographs after they had been sold.[16]

Decca, RCA Victor, and Columbia needed a new national law granting to record companies a copyright that would allow them to collect a fee from radio for the use of their records. But that idea also ran into the 1909 Copyright Law's grant of exclusive rights to all "arrangements" used on a recording to the person or company holding copyright on the song or tune. To grant to record companies a copyright over any aspect of the material's interpretation might amount to granting a copyright on something that was already copyrighted.[17]

The AFM ban on recording held remarkably firm for over a year, but, on September 30, 1943, Decca, the one major corporation that had remained independent of radio, signed a four-year agreement with the AFM to pay into an AFM record and transcription fund a fixed schedule of fees on records sold. Based on common retail prices for different types of records, Decca would pay .25¢ for records selling for up to 35¢; .50¢ per 50¢ disc; .75¢ per 75¢ platter; 1¢ for a $1.00 record; 2.5¢ for one selling at $1.50; and 5¢ per record sold at up to $2.00. Decca also agreed to pay to the union 3 percent of the gross sales and rentals of its World Transcription subsidiary.[18] This fund would support free live concerts by union musicians, thus devoting some of the profits from records to support working musicians.

The agreement that ended the recording ban did nothing to prevent radio from broadcasting phonograph records for profit, although Decca and eventually the other companies would continue to pay a schedule of fees to the musicians' union. If the musicians were appeased, the NAB must have been ecstatic. But what about Decca? Columbia and RCA Victor had adamantly refused to go along with the plan. Why were Kapp and his right-hand man, attorney Milton Diamond, willing to cut into profits when the other companies were not?

First, Kapp and Diamond must have seen short-term advantage in signing with Petrillo. The longer the other companies held out, the more Decca could corner markets, not only for popular records, the company's traditional strength, but even "classical" and jazz records, fields usually associated with RCA Victor and Columbia, respectively. Decca's short-term advantage implied impending disaster for RCA and Columbia, both of which held out until November 1944, a full fourteen months after Decca's settlement. According to their spokesperson, the two giants believed that they finally had to sign with Petrillo or "go out of business." Decca's big three popular baritones—Frank Sinatra, Dick Haymes, and Perry Como—had produced many hits during the strike. Once it ended, Kapp happily wooed big-band and symphonic stars away from his idle competition.

Second, not long before settling the dispute with the AFM, Decca had purchased World Transcription Services, a leader in electrical transcriptions, and thereby doubled its combined government allotment of shellac. Kapp immediately recruited many of his Decca stars over to World in order to keep them busy and increase World's share of the unaffiliated radio station market. The longer Columbia and RCA Victor held out against Petrillo, the greater the advantage to Decca's transcription subsidiary.

The AFM recording ban revealed how deeply the phonograph was enmeshed in a web of national institutions and politics. Although the union was said to be striking against canned music, a national system of law and politics had set the parameters of the struggle's social and cultural definitions. Interpretations of technology were just as influential in the record ban as the technology itself, and record producers, musicians, and studio personnel had to find a way to either live with or change those interpretations.

The recording industry actively promoted national values whenever the United States went to war. As the country moved to enter World War I, for example, the industry tended to wring its hands about the end of business as usual but then swung into a more optimistic and opportunistic consideration of new profit opportunities. When fighting broke out in Europe, for example, the leading trade publication announced that the disruption of European industrial patterns and business organizations would throw Americans upon their own resources, compelling this country's recording companies to find new sources of raw materials like shellac, that had come through Europe to America in peacetime.[19] That problem had remained unsolved. The U.S. government had rationed the use of shellac on the home front. In addition, the business had been further hampered by a 3 percent excise tax placed upon phonographs and records in the War Revenue Act.[20]

As long as the United States remained only indirectly involved in the war, the phonograph industry publications encouraged its readers to think about how the European conflict could be made profitable to Americans.[21] For example, the war could be turned to advertising advantage by sending office boys back and forth to the newspapers to collect war news which could then be recorded and played back into the street to attract crowds to talking machine stores.[22] Germany had played a major role in supplying phonographs and records to other European countries, and Americans reveled at the thought of moving into German markets throughout the world.[23]

When the United States finally did join its forces to the war effort, retail dealers were urged to dig out of their inventories "the glorious songs of faith and inspiration that nerved our forefathers"—war songs, and military marches—as well as to design jingoistic window displays featuring war themes, presidential speeches, and representations of the healing power of music for those who had been wounded.[24] Most important, America's involvement in World War I fully convinced a wide range of government officials that recorded music of some sort was a necessity and not just a secondary or tertiary diversion.[25]

The deeper the American involvement in World War I, the more the prospects seemed to brighten. Wartime conditions seemed to stimulate the industry. Industry publications assured retailers that whether at home or abroad, a "war-ridden people crave[d] entertainment and diversion,"[26] particularly the soldiers.[27] The military had come to agree that "song makes a good soldier, a better soldier; a tired soldier, a rested soldier; a depressed soldier, a cheery soldier."[28] Industry lobbyists took their case all the way to President Woodrow Wilson himself. As had William Howard Taft, the president let it be known that he kept a phonograph in the White House, and Wilson publically acknowledged his daughter's work as a recording artist.

In World War I, the government pursued a largely voluntaristic approach to bringing recorded music to the troops, as the industry agreed to sell at cost large, specially constructed phonographs for use in military camps. Thomas A. Edison invented a very stoutly constructed army-navy floor model, while Victor offered its special school model. General Phonograph Company contributed talking machines to the Marine Corps in the Caribbean.[29] The Knights of Columbus and the Young Men's Christian Association, placed by the war department in charge of entertaining the troops, distributed the phonographs to camps, ships, entrenchments, and hospitals where military chaplains were supposed to oversee their use.[30]

Because of the rationing of shellac, supplying records to go with the military talking machines remained problematic throughout the war. As it was not possible to press many new records, the industry entreated its jobbers, retail dealers, and customers to collect unsold and used records for shipment to the troops.[31] This helped to give a decidedly traditional and patriotic note to the recorded music of World War I. Victor sent recordings of "America," "The Star Spangled Banner," "Dixie," "We'll Never Let the Old Flag Fall," "The Old Flag Never Comes Down," "My Own United States," "Battle Hymn of the Republic," "Tenting Tonight on the Old Camp Ground," the "Marseillaise," and "Answer I Love You."[32]

But the record industry learned something during World War I about the kind of music that young soldiers preferred. Having sent them patriotic music, it was finally discovered that they preferred records of popular music. "Rag is the Rage . . . a rag or at least a song with some syncopation. That is what the boys always ask for."[33] For those in the business who embraced the talker's dissemination of "music of the better sort," this came as an unpleasant surprise. "So great is their longing for music" . . . the phonos rarely stopped in the YMCA huts. "Sometimes the boys comfort themselves with what most of us would consider pretty depressing music and are satisfied to play the same records over and over again."[34]

The efforts of the United States to win World War II provided the occasion for massive movements of troops and supporting personnel and an explicit nationalization of the phonograph, recorded music, and collective memories. In those perilous times, the talking machine's involvement in an intricate web of national values, institutions, and laws emerged in bolder relief. Record industry leaders dedicated their factories and laboratories to the war effort while doing what they could to further the cause despite wartime restrictions on the domestic consumption of the raw materials needed to make records.[35]

World War I had convinced the industry that recorded popular music could play an important role in sustaining troop morale;[36] World War II provided the occasion for the export to the various theaters of the war of a militarized multimedia complex that included phonographs and records, radios, movies, and big bands.[37] American GIs encountered for the first time, or renewed through phonograph records and electrical transcriptions broadcast over radio, commercialized collective memories of "home," and in the process further defined their emotional reasons for risking their lives. The phonograph replayed for many of those in harm's way a variety of musical sounds that evoked friends, hopes, schools, dance halls, and soda shops that they had left behind.[38]

The conjunction of World War II with the AFM's recording ban presented the record companies, the union, and the U.S. government with unprecedented circumstances when, in 1943, the Pentagon decided to supply phonographs and records to American troops. As they had in the First World War, the record companies, shackled by shellac shortages and therefore already in a partnership with the government, saw a governmental recording program as an attractive possibility. The AFM's James Petrillo, faced with hostile publicity in the press and media, looked for a way to demonstrate his own and the union's patriotism by allowing his musicians to record for the government. The government, with the temporary exception of the Navy, accepted the morale value of recorded music to the war effort.

With so much at stake and so many good reasons to proceed, the nationalization of the business of recorded music moved swiftly ahead. Copyright royalties, the infamous and largely camouflaged tradition of the phonograph business were removed from the emerging equation in a series of agreements between the AFM, Music Publisher's Protective Association, and the American Federation of Radio Artists by which those groups waived all fees and royalties on V-Disc recordings, provided that government money alone paid for the recordings and that they would be circulated to the troops only and never exploited commercially.[39]

In July 1943 Lieutenant George Robert Vincent of the Radio Section of the Army's Special Services Division (which expanded to become the Armed Forces Radio Network) lobbied hard at the Pentagon for support of an active recording program. Vincent hoped to offer to the troops the phonograph's tradition of individual selection in their choices of records. Up until that time they had been offered only electrical transcriptions on radio. He secured a pledge of $1 million in unencumbered funds, a promotion to Captain, and complete authority over what was to be a government financed and controlled popular music recording program.[40]

G. Robert Vincent's life and career epitomized several important dimensions of the cultural history of the phonograph in America. Born in Boston, Massachusetts, in 1898, the son of a medical doctor, whom he never really knew, and an Austrian Jewish émigrée, Vincent grew up on the fringes of upper middle-class society, searching for money, status, and father figures.[41] He felt powerfully drawn to Theodore Roosevelt, Thomas Alva Edison, and John Rockefeller, Sr. In 1916 on the eve of America's entry into World War I, when he was only 15 years old, Vincent had combined T. R.'s audacity and Edison's inventiveness to take passage to Europe with the idea of recording voice tracks on wax cylinders. He tried unsuccessfully to enlist in the British army and then served as a dispatch rider for the French infantry before getting sent back to the United States for being underage. Vincent enlisted in the U.S. army in 1918 and graduated from officer candidate school when he was just 17 years old. He returned to France and continued to make voice recordings.

Back in civilian life, Vincent took his time finding a direction to take, finally making himself into one of the best recording engineers in New York City. His life blended recorded sound with a strong patriotic spirit. His road to World War II and V-Discs ran from childhood contacts with the first President Roosevelt straight through Edison—in whose laboratories he is said to have worked in 1927—and on if not to Rockefeller himself at least to New York City's Radio City, where in 1935 he ran a voice recording company that he called the National Vocarium.

Vincent made his story as fabulous as Roland Gelatt's phonograph: as a teenager, he managed to record Theodore Roosevelt's voice with a cylinder machine borrowed from Edison's son Charles; he then ran away to World War I where he did his best to emulate Teddy's derring-do. As the phonograph industry had commercially designed "authentic" recordings, so Vincent recorded his own persona, claiming to have graduated from Yale (he never attended the institution) and to have worked for the great Edison himself (the evidence to support this connection seems particularly thin) and turning just before the Depression to a career in restoring Edison's old voice recordings. His own record productions resurrected Edison's original belief in the Talking Machine's destiny. Moving with the flow toward radio, Vincent produced transcribed radio shows, such as "Voices of History," that featured his own word portraits of famous Americans, capped by a replaying of their voices on old recordings and Vincent's analysis of their vocal qualities.[42]

The Japanese attack on Pearl Harbor found Vincent in his Radio City office suite feverishly recording air checks of the breaking news. Sensing opportunity in crisis, he undertook a tour for the USO of military installations along the Atlantic coast, where he recorded the sounds of the young army "at work and at play" as war preparations advanced. In keeping with his Edisonian outlook, Vincent made a series of voice mail recordings on paper discs of the GIs' messages to their families as they prepared to ship out. Vincent enlisted in the Army in July 1942 and was invited to the White House by Eleanor Roosevelt to dine and play some of his USO recordings for the other guests. Much to his disappointment, the president excused himself immediately after dinner.

After taking his unorthodox route to a new rank and military posting, he directed the army's production of newly recorded V-Discs, a series of 12-inch, 78 rpm double-faced records manufactured from October 1943 through May 1949. Special waterproof containers went out monthly and contained 20 V-Discs manufactured in new, more durable plastics, 100 tone arm needles, and detailed GI audience questionnaires asking what discs they liked best and what they would like to hear in the future. More than 8 million V-Discs were distributed and used to entertain overseas military personnel by stimulating powerful memories of life in the United States.[43]

The V-Disc program included both popular records designed for use on 125,000 spring-driven portable phonographs sent around the world and also electrical transcriptions intended for broadcast by the Armed Forces Radio Network. At the start, the record and transcription companies had supplied material from their libraries, what had been called "practical patriotism" when done in World War I. But the GIs asked for "current songs." Because of the AFM ban on recording, the army asked for a meeting with James C. Petrillo, who gave his permission for his musicians to record for V-Disc free of charge. All V-Disc expenses went into production, processing, and pressing.

In addition to company libraries, V-Disc materials came from recording sessions held specifically for that purpose, from broadcast rehearsals, and from movie sound tracks. Given the larger format of V-Discs, nearly 6.5 minutes per side, Vincent inserted spoken introductions reminiscent of those in which Len Spencer had excelled, and the jazz V-Discs allowed the soloists more time to stretch out than the old three-minute limit had permitted. By 1944, fully 85 percent of V-Discs were new recordings, all of them by vocalists and musicians who had performed free.

In 1944, 70 percent of V-Discs carried popular music, more than double that genre's domestic market share in peacetime. Responding to popular demand among the fighting men, the majority of the popular records featured big band swing. America fought World War II to the accompaniment of the big name bands: the hot dance bands of Benny

Goodman, Count Basie, Woody Herman, Duke Ellington, Harry James, and Artie Shaw, all led in popularity among the GIs by the "sweet swing" of the Glenn Miller American Armed Forces Orchestra.[44]

Thirty percent of V-Discs presented hillbilly, blues, classical, and other minority tastes. Vincent delegated music selection to his staff, which included Sgt. Morty "Perfect Pitch" Palitz, former recording director at Columbia and Decca; Walter Heebner of the RCA sales promotion staff, who worked out the details of the V-Disc agreement with the AFM; Steve Sholes of RCA's recording department, who together with Tony Janak, a recording engineer for Columbia, coordinated the procurement of musical talent; George Simon, formerly a big-band musician and *Metronome* editor who replaced Palitz in 1944; and songwriter Frank Loesser. These men tried to issue V-Discs that would respond to the swiftly shifting theaters of the war and the calendar of holidays in the United States. During the invasion of Italy, Arturo Toscanini and the NBC Orchestra recorded the Garibaldi hymn combined with a personal message to the Italian people from the conductor. For the Christmas holidays, Bing Crosby's "White Christmas" tore at the hearts of lonely GIs. Most of the top popular musical talent (640 artists in all) contributed their services to V-Discs, including Frank Sinatra, Glenn Miller, Artie Shaw, Bing Crosby, Fats Waller, Jo Stafford, the Three Suns, Lionel Hampton, and many others.[45]

V-Discs represented a fundamental change in the government's official understanding of the role of music in making war. The traditional attitude, represented by Captain Howard Bronson, who had been an arranger, composer, and bandleader for John Philip Sousa, emphasized the secondary role of music in war and harnessed all of it toward instilling a martial spirit in the fighting men with military band recordings.[46] Vincent, on the other hand, had no career in music. His USO tour had given him a good sense of the distinctly nonmilitary spirit of the young soldiers who had grown up with films, magazines, and jukeboxes.[47] As he later put it, "To the kids, the musicians were like baseball players. They knew every one of them, who they were, see. And here they were over there fighting away for them and they couldn't get the music of America, which was a greater morale builder."[48] Let the U.S. Armed Forces motivate the young men to fight; V-Discs would remind them of home and what they were fighting for.

Bandleader Capt. Glenn Miller best caught the difference between the approaches to recording music for the soldiers. When Major Bronson grumbled about the need for march music, not dance music, Miller promised him a march record and directed the 418th Army Air Force Training Command Band in his own arrangement of "The St. Louis Blues March." Drawing upon the memory of James Reese Europe's Hell Fighters Marching Band that had never had the chance to record the syncopated marches that had attracted so much comment in France during World War I, Miller played humorously with the traditional march beat, gradually injecting it with increasing suggestions of W. C. Handy's classic blues until it became a swinging big-band strut, all flashing antiphonal trumpet and trombone choirs.

V-Discs provided GIs with highly charged emotional links to the sorely missed, if economically depressed, America that they had left behind. In 1944, the big bands led the way, and Miller's aggregation led the big bands with 28 V-Disc releases (followed by Harry James's 27, and Tommy Dorsey's 26). Among the vocalists, Bing Crosby had the largest number of V-Disc recordings with 17, followed by Dinah Shore and Frank Sinatra.[49]

Miller's big band drew GI memories to the recorded sounds of their country's segregated white dance halls and movie theaters, and, in place of hot rhythmic excitement, they poured on nostalgic, romantic sentiment. As Miller, himself, put it: "we play only the old tunes. . . . [The GIs] know and appreciate only the tunes that were popular before they left the states." Since they were facing death, Miller reminded them of many feelings that they hoped to be allowed to feel again if they survived: "Chattanooga Choo Choo," for example, reminded GI Joe of the excitement of entering Penn Station, ticket in hand for a trip home, getting a shine, hopping aboard and barely having time to read the latest magazine before arriving in Baltimore. He could swing into the dining car and eat and drink while watching the Carolina countryside flash by, and step out of the train in old Tennessee, looking sharp and feeling fine.[50]

So, too, the Hal Kemp band with hip vocalist Skinnay Ennis introduced the record "Got A Date With An Angel" with the humble hope that the soldiers would like "our little offering," and took listeners into an eerie double world, part blissful anticipation of a hometown Saturday night date and part wartime hope that if they had a date with destiny they were headed somewhere they'd like. Woody Herman's storming band sent the guys a steaming "Woodchopper's Ball," letting them feel again the exhilaration and remember just how hot Saturday night could be back home.

The big-band vocalists gave them what must have been painfully powerful memories of lost love. Among them, Jo Stafford rose to the occasion, giving a new meaning to the old-time "Baby, Won't You Please Come Home." To those who didn't know why they were fighting and had good reason to doubt that they would ever live through it, she recorded, with the Paul Weston (her husband) band, a V-Disc of "I'll Be Seeing You," a very timely, commercialized memory, in which she sang to those listening that she was remembering them as she waited in a small cafe across from a little park—you know, one of those old familiar places—and that she thought of them as she noticed the sunshine, the trees, the children's carousel, and all the other things bright and gay that fill a lovely summer's day. For that matter, she'd be seeing them as she looked at the moon that night, too.

Popular recorded music from home carried an exceptional power for those who heard it in such dire circumstances. Colonel Leonard E. Pratt, who flew sixteen missions for the Army Air Force before being shot down over Germany, recalled in a letter to historian Lewis Erenberg that YMCA International managed to get a phonograph and a few records into his POW camp. Pratt's manner of emotional recollection through recorded music makes the point:

> I shall never forget the first time I heard one of the records. It was Lena Horne singing "Embraceable You." This was followed by Frankie Carle's theme "Sunrise Serenade" with Miller's "Moonlight Serenade" on the flip side. One of the most stirring records which brought tears to my eyes was "I'll Be Home for Christmas." We played the records for hours at every opportunity permitted by the German guards.[51]

Moreover, Pratt's active mode of using these records demonstrates how the phonograph encouraged musical as well as emotional participation. Pratt's POW camp had a piano as well as a record player, so the American prisoner played songs from the records, bringing big-band numbers to many who crowded into the room with him and stood outside the door. Occasionally, even the guards would shout through the window "Ein der Mood!"

Probably only a minority of GIs got off on the jazz V-Discs, although it would have taken an effort to remain unmoved by Lionel Hampton's joyous "Flyin' Home on a V-Disc." It must have felt something like the emotions in that recording to realize that you were heading home—and not in a pine box. Some GIs must have experienced a longing for freshly recorded V-Discs of the wonderful sounds of the Duke Ellington Orchestra. But the history of V-Disc had reiterated the national pattern in which the U.S. government had granted to minority groups only enough consideration to secure their cooperation. Although V-Disc reissues featuring Ellington band prewar recorded performances were sent out to the troops during the war, George Simon, G. Robert Vincent's liaison to the big bands, had trouble getting the Ellington musicians to cooperate in any new V-Disc recording sessions. Simon recalled that Harry Carney and Lawrence Brown, whom he had known for years, said to him, "George, if you are asking us to do this for free as a personal favor for you, of course we'll do it. But if you are asking us to do it for the Army, forget it—not when you consider the way they have been treating our people." That significant silence in the sounds of V-Disc caused a blank spot in collective memories of the nation, and it remains an absence of recorded music worth remembering.[52]

And here at the juncture of race and nationalism, V-Disc discovered the price that the industry paid for weaving ingredients of ethnic music into its own synthesis of popular mass-marketed music. Like the army, the leading record companies had created a brand of supposedly democratic American popular music, one that depended upon the contributions of minority groups, particularly African Americans, without allowing room for them to wield power over record production, not even over records intended for their own consumption.

This was as much the case for the Kapp brothers as for John Hammond, and applied, furthermore, to the so-called independent record labels like Milt Gabler's Commodore founded in 1938; Savoy, owned by Herman Lubinsky; Blue Note, established in 1939 by Alfred Lion and Frank Wolfe; Keynote Records, run by Eric Bernay; and Bob Thiele's Signature label that began issuing sides in the mid-1940s. These smaller companies, run by whites, specialized in smaller group jazz performed by Blacks. Commodore and Keynote, moreover, were known to be connected to left-wing Popular Front circles. Even those like Lubinsky's Savoy label, which limited itself to the business of making and selling records, basked in the reflected glow of the avant garde prebebop sounds pioneered by its Black "talent."[53]

No matter how closely associated with the spirit of an unconventional new style of Black music, the independent labels of the late Depression era were still run by white, often Jewish, businessmen who saw economic opportunity as well as social commentary in a Black jazz style that the major labels had overlooked. Wartime rationing of shellac and the profits of hit records had forced the majors to concentrate on sure-fire hits. Particularly after the end of the AFM recording ban, with the public hungry for new sides, the independents stood to make money on all of their issues. The same old game in which the record companies copyrighted the new bebop melodies that the musicians had improvised in place of those on registered compositions complicated the brotherhood of recording studio leftists.

And so, with bebop, as with 1920s jazz, blues, hillbilly, and big band swing of the 1930s and 1940s, the recording industry mediated cultural and musical diversity in the United States, fashioning cross-cultural musical formulations in which records of and for minority groups were *by* those same groups only in a limited sense. Those old 78 rpm sides certainly did present the sounds of the country's ethnic groups—but only in ways that reflected the companies' economic and political motives. The Americans who wielded the power in recording technology played as much of a role as did the machines in determining what music the country might replay, while those who bought and played their discs fashioned around and through them their own consuming worlds of popular phonographic art and sensibility. The conservative function of recording technology forever reintroduced the sounds of modern America's past into its present; record buyers made what they wished of those sound tracings, filling their lives with a creative flow of memories that helped to define how it felt to be American.

NOTES

Introduction

1. In America, "phonograph," a trademark term referring to Edison's cylinder, came to describe all sound-recording and playback machines. In England, the preferred term came to be "gramophone," Emil Berliner's trade name for his disc invention.

2. Roland Gelatt, *The Fabulous Phonograph: From Edison to Stereo*, rev. ed. (N.Y.: Appleton Century, 1965), 151, 189, 305; Andre Millard, *America on Record: A History of Recorded Sound* (Cambridge: Cambridge University Press, 1995), 5. The publication of this book brings yet further attention to the industrial and technological dimensions of phonograph studies. Michael Chanan, *Repeated Takes: A Short History of Recording and Its Effects on Music* (London: Verso, 1995) ably summarizes the technological impact.

3. Philip H. Ennis, *The Seventh Stream: The Emergence of Rocknroll in American Popular Music* (Hanover, N.H.: Wesleyan University Press, 1992), the best scholarly analysis of the "rocknroll" revolution.

4. Carlton Mabee, *The American Leonardo: A Life of Samuel F. B. Morse* (N.Y.: Knopf, 1943); Steven Lubar, *Infoculture: The Smithsonian Book of Information Age Inventions* (Boston: Houghton Mifflin, 1993), 73–117.

5. Claude S. Fischer, *America Calling: A Social History of the Telephone to 1940* (Berkeley: University of California Press, 1992).

6. J. Fred MacDonald, *Don't Touch that Dial: Radio Programming in American Life from 1920 to 1960* (Chicago: Nelson-Hall, 1979). Daniel J. Czitrom, *Media and the American Mind from Morse to McLuhan* (Chapel Hill: University of North Carolina Press, 1982) analyzes both movies and radio but omits the phonograph. Susan Douglas, *Inventing American Broadcasting, 1899–1922* (Baltimore: Johns Hopkins University Press, 1987).

7. Lary May, *Screening Out the Past: The Birth of Mass Culture and the Motion Picture Industry* (New York: Oxford University Press, 1980).

8. John B. Rae, *The American Automobile* (Chicago: University of Chicago Press, 1965); James Flink, *The Car Culture* (Cambridge: MIT Press, 1975).

9. Millard, *America on Record*, ch. 8.

10. See, for example, Oliver Read and Walter L. Welch, *From Tin Foil to Stereo: The Evolution of the Phonograph* (Indianapolis: Howard Sams, 1977) and its drastically revised edition, Walter L. Welch and Leah Brodbeck

Stenzel Burt, *From Tin Foil to Stereo: The Acoustic Years of the Recording In-dustry* (Gainesville: University of Florida Press, 1994).

11. Lubar, *Infoculture*, 178.

12. Wilber Schramm, as quoted in James S. Ettema and D. Charles Whitney, "The Money Arrow: An Introduction to Audiencemaking," in Ettema and Whitney, eds., *Audiencemaking: How the Media Create the Audi-ence* (Thousand Oaks, Cal.: Sage Publications, 1994).

13. Gelatt, *The Fabulous Phonograph*, 11.

14. Herbert Gans, *Popular Culture and High Culture* (New York: Basic Books, 1974).

15. "A Sociology of Popular Music: A Review," in Serge Denisoff, ed., *Sing a Song of Social Significance* (Bowling Green, Ohio: Bowling Green State University Press, 1983) and Denisoff, "Massification and Popular Music," *Journal of Popular Culture* 9 (Spring 1976): 881–88.

16. Lawrence Levine, *High Brow/Low Brow: The Emergence of Cultural Hierarchy in America* (Cambridge: Harvard University Press, 1988), and Levine, ed., *The Unpredictable Past: Explorations in American Cultural History* (New York: Oxford University Press, 1993).

17. M. Gottdeiner, "Hegemony and Mass Culture: A Semiotic Ap-proach," *American Journal of Sociology* 90, 5 (1985): 979–1001.

18. D. Hebner, *Subculture: The Meaning of Style* (London: Methuen, 1979).

19. Allen Bloom, *The Closing of the American Mind* (N.Y.: Simon & Schuster, 1987), ch. 3.

20. "Perennial Fashion—Jazz," in *Prisms*, trans. Samuel and Sherry Weber (Cambridge: MIT Press, 1981), 119–32; *Introduction to the Sociology of Music* (N.Y.: Continuum, 1988); "On the Fetish-Character in Music and the Regression of Listening," in *The Frankfurt School Reader*. Jamie Owen Daniel, "Introduction to Adorno's 'On Jazz,'" *Discourse* 12, 1 (1989–1990): 39–69.

21. Millard, *America on Record*, passim. Much of my argument here evolved from thinking about the phonograph while reading John Fiske, *Understanding Popular Culture* (Boston: Urwin Hyman, 1989).

22. Daniel J. Boorstin, *The Americans: The Democratic Experience* (N.Y.: Vintage Books, 1974), ch. 41, and Boorstin, "Welcoming Remarks," in Judith McCullough, ed., *Ethnic Recording in America: A Neglected Heritage* (Washington, D.C.: American Folklife Center, 1982), xi–xii.

23. Boorstin, *The Democratic Experience*, 89–90.

24. I have borrowed this wonderful phrase from French poet Paul Valéry, who applied it to the dance. It is unclear whether or not Valéry had in mind, as do I, phonograph records as well: Paul Valéry, "Philosophy of the Dance," in *What Is Dance: Readings in Theory and Criticism*, ed. Roger Copeland and Marshall Cohen (N.Y.: Oxford University Press, 1983), 60–62. I would like to thank Victor Greene for bringing this book to my attention.

25. Douglas Kellner, "Cultural Studies, Multiculturalism and Media Culture," in Gail Dines and Jean M. Humez, eds., *Gender, Race and Class in Media* (Thousand Oaks, Ca.: Sage Publications, 1995), 5–17 and glossary.

26. Leonard B. Meyer, *Emotion and Meaning in Music* (Chicago: University of Chicago Press, 1956), 34.

27. Meyer, *Emotion and Meaning in Music*.

28. Charles Keil & Steven Feld, *Music Grooves: Essays and Dialogues* (Chicago: University of Chicago Press, 1994).

29. Jefferson A. Singer & Peter Salovey, *The Remembered Self: Emotion and Memory in Personality* (N.Y.: The Free Press, 1993), 29–30.

30. On collective memory, see Maurice Halbwachs, *The Collective Memory*, trans. Francis J. Ditter, Jr. and Vida Yazdi Ditter (reprint N.Y.: Harper & Row, 1980); David Lowenthal, *The Past Is a Foreign Country* (Cambridge: Cambridge University Press, 1985); and David Thelen, ed., *Memory and American History* (Bloomington: Indiana University Press, 1990). The literature on music and collective memory is more limited, but see John Mowitt, "The Sound of Music in the Era of Its Electronic Reproducibility," in *Music and Society: The Politics of Composition, Performance & Reception*, ed. Richard Leppert and Susan McClary (Cambridge: Cambridge University Press, 1987), 180–85; and George Lipsitz, *Time Passages: Collective Memory and American Popular Culture* (Minneapolis: University of Minnesota Press, 1990).

31. Halbwachs, *The Collective Memory*, ch. 5.

32. E. A. Shils, *Tradition* (Chicago: University of Chicago Press, 1981), as quoted in Bruce M. Ross, *Remembering the Personal Past: Descriptions of Autobiographical Memory* (N.Y.: Oxford University Press, 1991), 157–58.

33. Walter Ong, *Orality and Literacy: The Technologizing of the Word* (London: Routledge, 1982), ch. 3.

34. This approach finds its fullest development in David C. Rubin, *Memory in Oral Traditions: The Cognitive Psychology of Epic, Ballads and Counting-out Rhymes* (N.Y.: Oxford University Press, 1995) and *Remembering Our Past: Studies in Autobiographical Memory*, ed. David C. Rubin (N.Y.: Cambridge University Press, 1996), and Wanda T. Wallace and David C. Rubin, "'The Wreck of the Old 97': A Real Event Remembered in Song," in *Remembering Reconsidered: Ecological and Traditional Approaches to the Study of Memory* (Cambridge: Cambridge University Press, 1988), 283–310.

35. J. Nerone and E. Wartella, "'Introduction,' Special Issue on 'Social Memory,'" *Communication* 11 (1989): 85–88.

36. "Between Memory and History: *Les Lieux de Memoire*," *Representations* 26 (1989): 7–25.

Chapter One

1. Evan Eisenberg, *The Recording Angel: Explorations in Phonography* (N.Y.: McGraw Hill, 1987), 25–46.

2. Warren L. Susman, *Culture as History: The Transformation of American Society in the Twentieth Century* (N.Y.: Pantheon Books, 1984), xxvii; William E. Hall and Judith R. Blau, "The Taste for Popular Music: An Analysis of Class and Cultural Demand," *Popular Music and Society* XI, 1 (1987): 31–49.

3. Pierre Nora, "Entre Mémoire et Histoire: La Problematique des Lieux," in *Les Lieux de Mémoire* (Paris: Quatro Gallimard, 1997), 23–43; also see "Between Memory and History: *Les Lieux de Mémoire*," *Representations* 26 (1989): 7–25.

4. Ibid., 20.

5. Keya Ganguly, "Migrant Identities: Personal Memory and the Construction of Selfhood," *Cultural Studies* 6 (Jan. 1992): 27–50. I would like to thank Jonathan Crewe of the Dartmouth Humanities Institute for sending me this citation.

6. Ong, *Orality & Literacy*, 34–35.

7. The School of Music Library at the University of Michigan at Ann Arbor holds 2,644 returns from an alleged 20,000 surveys that Edison, Inc. claimed to have sent out. I am indebted to Professor Mark Tucker of the Music Department, Columbia University, for alerting me to these unparalleled primary sources and to Calvin Elliker, head of the School of Music Li-

brary for making them available to me. My description of this collection is based on reading returns that included narrative comments by respondents.

8. *Rethinking Popular Culture: Contemporary Perspectives in Cultural Studies*, ed. Chandra Mukerji and Michael Schudson (Berkeley: University of California Press, 1991), 29–37; Paul M. Hirsch, "Processing Fads and Fashions: An Organization-set Analysis of Cultural Industry Systems," ibid., 313–34. My thanks to Professor Victor Greene, University of Wisconsin-Milwaukee for suggesting that I read this book.

9. Mark Tucker, "Report on Edison Company 1921 Market Survey," 7p., ts., photocopy, August 24, 1981 kindly furnished by its author.

10. Thomas A. Edison, *Mood Music: A Compilation of 112 Edison Re-Creations According to "What They Will Do for You"* (Orange, N.J.: Edison, 1921); Harvith and Harvith, *Edison, Musicians, and the Phonograph*, 13–15. Photoduplicates of letter carbons from William Maxwell to Bingham dated Feb. 11, 1922 and Feb. 27, 1922 in the Edison National Historic Site, West Orange, N.J., indicate that this project, pursued by Charles Edison, was abandoned when Thomas A. Edison opposed it. Telephone conversation with Doug Tarr, Assistant Archivist, Edison Nat. Hist. Site, Aug. 7, 1995.

11. W. V. Bingham, "Research on Moods and Music," in Edison, *Mood Music*, 28–31.

12. Meyer, *Emotion and Meaning in Music*, 38–39.

13. Fischer, *America Calling*, 5. The same point about the meanings of music is made in Susan D. Crafts, Daniel Cavicchi, and Charles Keil, eds., *My Music* (Hanover, N.H.: Wesleyan University Press, 1993).

14. Charles Hamm, *Yesterdays: Popular Song in America* (New York: W.W. Norton, 1979), ch. 12.

15. Nicholas E. Tawa, *A Music for the Millions: Antebellum Democratic Attitudes and the Birth of American Popular Music* (N.Y.: Pendragon, 1984), 22; Susan Key, "Sound and Sentimentality: Nostalgia in the Songs of Stephen Foster," *American Music* (Summer 1995): 145–66. Key (p. 165, n30) notes that recordings of pre–Tin Pan Alley minstrel songs communicated "an aura of purity and idealism even into the twentieth century."

16. Key, "Sound and Sentimentality," 145.

17. Singer and Salovey, *The Remembered Self*, 30–37.

18. Edison, *Mood Music*, 24.

19. Fred Davis, "Nostalgia, Identity and the Current Nostalgia Wave," *Journal of Popular Culture* XI (Fall 1977): 418, should be compared with Nass, "Psychoanalytic Interpretation of Music."

20. Singer and Salovey, *The Remembered Self*, 51–53.

21. *New Grove Dictionary of American Music*, ed. H. Wiley Hitchcock and Stanley Sadie, II (London: Macmillan, 1986), 156–57.

22. Fiske, *Understanding Popular Culture*, 49.

23. Barbara Welter, "The Cult of True Womanhood," *American Quarterly* 18 (Summer 1966): 151–74; Daniel Walker Howe, "American Victorianism as Culture," ibid. 27 (1975): 507–32.

24. Craig Roell, *The Piano in America, 1890–1940* (Chapel Hill: University of North Carolina Press, 1989), 20; Joseph A. Mussulman, *Music in the Cultured Generation: A Social History of Music in America, 1870–1900* (Evanston, Il.: Northwestern University Press, 1971), chs. 1–4.

25. *The Phonograph* II, 8 (Dec. 6, 1916): 10; "Do Men or Women Prove the Bigger Purchasers of Talking Machine and Record Outfits?," *Talking Machine World* XV, 2 (Feb. 1919): 67–69, 71, 107; "Those Who Buy Talking

Machines and Records—and Why—An Analysis of the Field," ibid., XV, 10 (Oct. 1919): 25.

26. *Edison Phonograph Monthly* VII, 7 (July 1909): 14; ibid. VI, 2 (Feb. 1910): 34.

27. Ibid., 7 (Aug. 1909): 24.

28. *Making a New Deal: Industrial Workers in Chicago, 1919–1939* (Cambridge: Cambridge University Press, 1990), 68.

29. Ganguly, "Migrant Identities," 37.

30. "Turning Foreign Records into Real Cash," *Talking Machine World* (hereafter *TMW*) XXI, 9 (Sept. 1925): 14; also see "Advertising for Foreign Trade at Home," ibid., XIX, 7 (July 1923): 45.

31. Jonathan Sarna, "From Immigrants to Ethnics: Toward a New Theory of 'Ethnicization,'" *Ethnicity* 5 (1978): 370–78. Sarna emphasizes the active creation of ethnicity in a way that allows for popular participation in defining culture.

32. The diversity of products varies with the amount of competition between culture-producing industries. See Ettema and Whitney, *Audience-making*, 12; P. DiMaggio, "Market Structure, the Creative Process and Popular Culture: Toward an Organizational Reinterpretation of Mass Culture Theory," *Journal of Popular Culture* 11 (1977): 436–52; D. G. Berger and R. A. Peterson, "Cycles in Symbol Production: The Case of Popular Music," *American Sociological Review* 40 (1975): 158–73.

33. John Fiske, "The Cultural Economy of Fandom," in *The Adoring Audience: Fan Culture and Popular Media*, ed. Lisa A. Lewis (N.Y.: Routledge, 1992), ch. 2.

34. James P. Kraft, *Stage to Studio: Musicians and the Sound Revolution, 1890–1950* (Baltimore: Johns Hopkins University Press, 1996), 61.

35. Richard M. Sudhalter and Philip R. Evens with William Dean-Myatt, *Bix: Man & Legend* (New Rochelle, N.Y.: Arlington House, 1974), chs. 1–2.

36. Stearns Vertical File, Institute of Jazz Studies, Rutgers University.

37. "Country's Hot Clubs Founded by 'Swing' Devotees at Yale," IJS Vertical File, Rutgers University.

38. Neil Leonard, *Jazz, Myth and Religion* (N.Y.: Oxford University Press, 1987), 136–50.

39. "Critiquing Jazz: The Politics of Race and Culture in American Jazz Discourse, 1935–1995," forthcoming, University of Chicago Press. My thanks to Professor Gennari for making chapters of his manuscript available to me.

40. Interview with Dan Morgenstern, Newark, N.J., June 24, 1996.

41. Jerry Wexler and David Ritz, *Rhythm and Blues: A Life in American Music* (N.Y.: Alfred Knopf, 1993), 23.

42. Interview with Walter Schaap in Ronald G. Welburn, "American Jazz Criticism, 1914–1940," Ph.D. diss., New York University, 1983, 261–64.

43. Leonard Feather, *The Jazz Years: Earwitness to an Era* (N.Y.: Da Capo, 1987), 5–7.

44. Ibid., 6–7.

45. Gennari, "Critiquing Jazz," ch 1; Gary Giddins, "Setting the Standard: Martin Williams, 1924–1992," *Village Voice* April 28, 1992, 91; "Talk of the Town," *New Yorker*, April 1950.

46. Bob Thiele, *What A Wonderful World: A Lifetime of Recording* (N.Y.: Oxford University Press, 1995), 10.

47. Hugues Panassié, *Monsieur Jazz: Entretiens avec Pierre Casalta* (Paris: Editions Stock, 1975), 13.

48. Ibid., ch. 18.

49. Paul F. Berliner, *Thinking in Jazz: The Infinite Art of Improvisation* (Chicago: University of Chicago Press, 1994), 1–35.

Chapter Two

1. Edison as quoted in the leading history of the phonograph by Roland Gelatt, *The Fabulous Phonograph: From Tin Foil to High Fidelity* (Philadelphia: J. B. Lippincott, 1955).

2. Evan Eisenberg, *The Recording Angel: Explorations in Phonography* (New York: McGraw-Hill, 1987), 65, interprets the impact of earphones in this manner.

3. *Proceedings of the 1890 Convention of Local Phonograph Companies* (Nashville, Tenn.: Country Music Foundation Press, 1974), 163–65. Oliver Read and Walter Welch, *From Tin Foil to Stereo: Evolution of the Phonograph* (Indianapolis, Ind.: Bobbs-Merrill, 1976), 50–57.

4. Guy A. Marco, ed., *Encyclopedia of Recorded Sound in the United States* (New York: Garland Publishing, 1993) 20, 125–26.

5. As quoted in Read and Welsh, *From Tin Foil to Stereo*, 302.

6. *Phonogram* 1 (1891): 86–87, 139, 143; *Talking Machine World* (hereafter *TMW*) 2, 7 (July 1906): 43–44; Tim Brooks, "Columbia Records in the 1890s: Founding the Record Industry," *Association for Recorded Sound Collectors Journal* 10 (1978): 9–10. For shopping districts, see *Edison Phonograph Monthly* 3 (Oct. 1905): 10.

7. *TMW* 3 (Dec. 1907), 73–74; *TMW* 5 (April 1909): 6. Russell Sanjek, *American Popular Music and Its Business: The First Four Hundred Years*, II (New York: Oxford University Press, 1988), 383.

8. F. W. Gaisberg, *The Music Goes Round* (New York: Macmillan, 1942), 6.

9. On phonograph parlors in general, see Marco, ed., *Encyclopedia of Recorded Sound* for popular spending habits, National Phonograph Company, *Edison Coin-Slot Phonographs* (Orange, N.J.: Nat. Phono. Co., 1906, R&HARS).

10. I have taken the phrase "Cheap Amusements" from Kathy Peiss, *Cheap Amusements: Working Women and Leisure in Turn-of-the-Century New York* (Philadelphia: Temple University Press, 1986).

11. *Edison Coin-Slot Phonographs*, R&HARS. The company announces its entry into the business and its desire to keep its distance from the market in *Edison Phonograph Monthly* 2 (Aug. 1904): 10.

12. Frank Dorian, "Along the Memory Trail," *Music Lovers Guide* (Feb. 1934): 167–68 as quoted in Brooks, "Columbia Records in the 1890s," 17–18.

13. *Edison Coin-Slot Phonographs*. Luc Sante, *Low Life: Lures and Snares of Old New York* (New York: Vintage Books, 1991), 102–3, and photos facing. *Edison Phonograph Monthly* 3 (Oct. 1905): 10.

14. For Vitascope Hall, see Oliver Read and Walter L. Welch, *From Tin Foil to Stereo: Evolution of the Phonograph* (Indianapolis, Ind.: Bobbs-Merrill, 1976), 115. *TMW* 5 (Jan. 1909), special "Side Line Section."

15. *TMW* 5 (April 1909), 6.

16. Sherman C. Kingsley, "The Penny Arcade and the Cheap Theater," *Charities and Commons: A Weekly Journal of Philanthropy and Social Advance* (June 8, 1907): 295–97. I am indebted to Kathy Peiss, *Cheap Amusements*: 223 for this source.

17. "Penny Arcades," *Moving Picture World* (June 8, 1907), 214. I am indebted to Kathy Peiss, *Cheap Amusements*, 223 for this source.

18. Gelatt, *The Fabulous Phonograph*, 45.

19. Ibid., 70.

20. The best collection of record company catalogs in the U.S.A. is housed in the Division of Recorded Sound, Library of Congress.

21. "The Reorientation of American Culture in the 1890s," in *Writing American History: Essays on Modern Scholarship* (Bloomington: Indiana University Press, 1970), ch. 4.

22. Charles Fremont Church, Jr., "The Life and Influence of John Philip Sousa," (Ph.D. diss., Ohio State University, 1942), 309, as quoted by Pauline Norton, "Nineteenth-century American March Music and John Philip Sousa," in *Perspectives on John Philip Sousa*, ed. Jon Newsom (Washington, D.C.: Library of Congress, 1983), 49.

23. 1911 advertisement of Victor Talking Machine Company in "Pioneer Phonograph Advertising"—Walsh Collection, DRS,LC.

24. *The Phonogram* 1 (June–July 1891): 143.

25. Neil Harris, "John Philip Sousa and the Culture of Reassurance," in *Perspectives on John Philip Sousa*, ed. Jon Newsom (Washington, D.C.: Library of Congress, 1983), 29.

26. Harris, "Culture of Reassurance," 28–29.

27. On the nineteenth-century traditions in military march music, see Pauline Norton, "Nineteenth-century American March Music and John Philip Sousa," 43–52.

28. Frederick P. Williams, "The Times as Reflected in the Victor Black Label Military Band Recordings from 1900 to 1927," *Association for Recorded Sound Collections Journal* 4 (1972): 37.

29. "The Work of Art in the Age of Mechanical Reproduction," in Walter Benjamin, *Illuminations* (New York: Harcourt, Brace & World, 1955), 219–53.

30. Eisenberg, *The Recording Angel*, esp. 25–33.

31. *TMW* 2 (June 1906): 21; "An Act to Ammend and Consolidate the Acts Respecting Copyright" [1909], in Alfred M. Shafter, *Musical Copyright* (Chicago: Callaghan & Co., 1932), 328–53. Composer Victor Herbert, a champion of greater legal rights for composers, was similarly deprived of his royalties by the 1909 law.

32. *TMW* 2 (Sept. 1906): 21. John Philip Sousa, "The Menace of Mechanical Music," *Appleton's Magazine* 8 (Sept. 1906) and "Sousa's Protest Against Canned Music," *Current Literature* 41 (Oct. 1906), as cited in Craig Roell, *The Piano in America, 1890–1940* (Chapel Hill: University of North Carolina Press, 1989), 54.

33. Gaisberg, *The Music Goes Round*, 5.

34. Ulysses (Jim) Walsh, "Favorite Pioneer Recording Artists: Arthur Collins," *Hobbies* (Nov. 1942): 12.

35. *The Phonogram* (March 1900), 14–15; Marco, ed., *Encyclopedia of Recorded Sound*, 356.

36. Ulysses (Jim) Walsh, "The Coney Island Crowd—Billy Murray," *Hobbies* (April 1942): 15; (June 1942): 21, 23.

37. On Len Spencer see: Ulysses (Jim) Walsh, "Favorite Pioneer Recording Artists—Len Spencer," *Hobbies* (May 1947): 18–19; Brooks, "Columbia Recording Artists," 123; F. Gaisberg, *Music Goes Round*, 3–4, 8, opens his description of the world of cylinder recording with a contrast of "smug" bureaucratic, middle-class Washington, D.C., with the adjoining tenderloin and ghetto areas.

38. Marco, ed., *Encyclopedia of Recorded Sound*, 61. *TMW* 9 (Dec. 1913): 23.

39. "Reminiscences of Early Talking Machine Days," *TMW* 10 (April 1914): 38; 9 (Dec. 1913): 23.

40. Ibid.

41. I have been able to listen to early disc recordings through the Rigler and Deutsch Index of 78 rpm records held by Syracuse University, Stamford University, Yale University, the New York Public Library, and the Library of Congress. At present, cylinder recordings are unavailable to the public.

42. *The Columbia Record* 2 (May 1904): n.p.; 5 (April 1907): n.p.; *Phonoscope* 3 (Feb. 1899): 6; Marco, ed., *Encyclopedia of Recorded Sound*, 692.

43. Sante, *Low Life: Lures and Snares of Old New York* (New York: Vintage Books, 1992), 12–13.

44. "Mose the Far-Famed and World-Renowned," *American Literature* 15 (1943), 288.

45. Sante, *Low Life*, 131.

46. Peiss, *Cheap Amusements*, 101–104.

47. Eric Lott, *Love and Theft: Blackface Minstrelsy and the American Working Class* (New York: Oxford University Press, 1993), 81.

48. Ulysses (Jim) Walsh, "Favorite Pioneer Recording Artists: Steve Porter, I" *Hobbies* (July 1943): 21.

49. "Favorite Pioneer Recording Artists: Ada Jones," *Hobbies* (June 1946), 18–19.

50. Sante, *Low Life*, 131. Kathy Peiss, *Cheap Amusements*, 66, 98 paints a parallel portrait of young urban working-class females.

51. Tim Gracyk, *The Encyclopedia of Popular American Recording Pioneers, 1895–1925*.

52. Ulysses (Jim) Walsh, "Favorite Pioneer Recording Artists: Ada Jones," *Hobbies* (June 1946): 18–19; (July 1946): 17–18; (August 1946): 18–19; (Sept. 1946): 24; (Oct. 1946): 26; (Nov. 1946): 26–27; (Dec. 1946): 25–26; (Jan. 1947): 22; (June 1972): 37–38, 52, 110–13.

53. Joanne J. Meyerowitz, *Women Adrift: Independent Wage Earners in Chicago, 1880–1930* (Chicago: University of Chicago Press, 1988), xv-xxiii, 111–18.

54. Sante, *Low Life*, 129–133, describes the balls in detail.

55. Ada Jones, "Singing to the World," *Edison Amberola Monthly* (Feb. 1917) as quoted by Ulysses (Jim) Walsh, "Favorite Pioneer Recording Artists: Ada Jones, II" *Hobbies* (July 1946): 17–18; also excerpted in *TMW*.

56. *The Columbia Record* 3 (May 1905), n.p.

57. "F.P.R.A.: Arthur Collins," *Hobbies* (Nov. 1942), 11–12; (Dec. 1942), 18–19; Marco, ed., *Encyclopedia of Recorded Sound*, 124.

58. *The Phonogram* (Nov. 1900): 14–15; *Phonoscope* 2 (July 1898): 12; Marco, ed., *Encyclopedia of Recorded Sound*, 356.

59. Gaisberg, The *Music Goes Round*, 8.

60. I am indebted to Lott's *Love and Theft*, 43, for insights into black performers in minstrelsy. His own quotation is from jazz musician Herbie Hancock.

61. Here I follow the persuasive argument of James H. Dorman, "Shaping the Popular Image of Post-Reconstruction American Blacks: The 'Coon Song' Phenomenon of the Gilded Age," *American Quarterly* 40 (1988): 450–71.

62. Lott, *Love and Theft*, 85.

63. Walsh, "F.P.R.A.: Ada Jones, II," *Hobbies* (July 1946), 17–18.

64. Walsh, "The Coney Island Crowd," *Hobbies* (April 1942), 15.

65. Walsh, "Coney Island Crowd," *Hobbies* (May 1942), 15.

66. *The Phonogram* 2 (Dec. 1892), 278; Giasberg, *Music Goes Round*, 6.

67. As quoted in *TMW* 12 (April 1916), 30b.

68. *TMW* 3 (Jan. 1907), 42.

69. See Interview with Ernest L. Stevens, Thomas Alva Edison's per-

sonal pianist-arrangers, in *Edison, Musicians, and the Phonograph: A Century in Retrospect*, ed. John and Susan Edwards Harvith (Westport, Conn.: Greenwood Press, 1987), 24–35.

70. Stevens, in John and Susan Harvith, eds., Edison, Musicians . . . , 33.

71. As quoted in *TMW* 3 (Nov. 1907): 20.

72. *The Phonogram Monthly* 2 (Nov. 1900): 6.

73. *TMW* 2 (Feb. 1907): 46.

74. *The Phonogram* 2 (Dec. 1892): 278.

75. *TMW* 3 (Nov. 1907): 20.

76. *TMW* 2 (Feb. 1907): 46.

77. Walsh, *Hobbies* (July 1946): 17–18.

78. *TMW* 3 (Nov. 1907), 20.

79. Gaisberg, *Music Goes Round*, 7, 17; Marco, ed., *Encyclopedia of Recorded Sound*, 163.

80. Yvonne de Treville, "Making a Phonograph Record," *The Musician* XXI, 5 (1916): 658.

Chapter Three

1. Roland Gelatt, *The Fabulous Phonograph: From Tin Foil to High Fidelity* (Philadelphia: J. B. Lippincott, 1955).

2. I remain indebted to Dr. Richard Berrong for sharing his ample documentation of this special sort of opera record.

3. *TMW* 2 (July 15, 1906), 5.

4. Michael Broyles, *"Music of the Highest Class": Elitism and Populism in Antebellum Boston* (New Haven: Yale University Press, 1992). My thanks go to my Kent State colleague Richard Berrong for bringing this book to my attention.

5. Craig H. Roell, *The Piano in America, 1890–1940* (Chapel Hill: University of North Carolina Press, 1989), 3–27. *Talking Machine World* (hereafter *TMW*) V (Feb. 15, 1909): 10, quotes Walter Damrosch's belief that the phonograph could "soothe domestic conflicts."

6. Guy A. Marco, ed., *Encyclopedia of Recorded Sound in the United States* (New York: Garland Publishing, 1993), 355; Gelatt, *Fabulous Phonograph: From Tin Foil to High Fidelity*, 130–57; Read and Welch, *From Tin Foil to Stereo*, xx.

7. E. R. Fenimore Johnson, *His Master's Voice was Eldridge R. Johnson: A Biography* 2d. ed. (Milford, Del.: E. R. Fenimore Johnson, 1975), 7–24.

8. Fenimore Johnson, *His Master's Voice*, 26.

9. Ibid., 26–27.

10. Ibid., 27–36.

11. As quoted in Fenimore Johnson, *His Master's Voice*, 40.

12. *Talking Machine Journal* XXII, 1 (June 1927): 26, hereafter referred to as *TMJ*.

13. Fenimore Johnson, *His Master's Voice*, 107. On worker contentment with wages, see *TMW* XV, 11 (Nov. 1919): 128.

14. Fenimore Johnson, *"His Master's Voice*, 71–72; Marco, ed., *Encyclopedia of Recorded Sound*, 127, 740–41. Raymond Wile, "The Seventeen-Year Itch: The Phonograph and the Patent System," in *The Phonograph and the Patent System, 1877–1912*, comp. and ed. Allen Koenigsberg (Brooklyn, N.Y.: APM Press, 190), xii–xvi.

15. *The Phonograph* III, 16 (April 18, 1917): 3; Wile, "Seventeen Year Itch," xiii–xvi.

16. *The Phonograph* III, 1 (Jan. 3, 1917), 4.

17. Information on price-fixing lies scattered through the pages of the three longest-lasting trade publications upon which so much of this study is based: *TMW*, *TMJ*, and *The Phonograph*. The quote is taken from *The Phonograph* III, 5 (Jan. 31, 1917): 1. Also see "Victor Loses Macy Case," ibid. III, 15 (April 11, 1917): 3, "Opinion of Supreme Court of the United States in the Victor-Macy Case," ibid., III, 16 (April 18, 1917): 10–11, 14; "Victor Renounces License before the F.T.C.," ibid., IV, 6 (Aug. 8, 1917): 3.

18. Eldridge Johnson, "A Bad Name," *The Phonograph* I, 23 (Sept. 20, 1916): 16.

19. *The Phonograph* I, 9 (June 14, 1916): 5.

20. *TMW* XV, 3 (March 1919): 4;

21. *TMW* XIII, 7 (July 1917): 37.

22. *The Phonograph* I, 5 (May 24, 1916): 4.

23. *TMW* III, 7 (July 1907): 9.

24. *TMW* XV, 6 (June 1919): 4.

25. List of nonoperatic recordings by opera stars prepared by Richard Berrong, ts., n.d.

26. Fenimore Johnson, "*His Master's Voice*," 65.

27. *TMW* II, 10 (Oct. 1906): 34.

28. Roell, *The Piano in America*.

29. For example, *The Phonograph* I, 12 (July 5, 1916): 3.

30. *TMW* III, 10 (Oct. 1907): 39; ibid. VIII, 11 (Nov. 1912): 8.

31. *TMW* II, 8 (Aug. 1906): 55.

32. *TMW* II, 10 (Oct. 1906): 19.

33. *TMW* VI (Jan. 15, 1910): 5.

34. *TMW* II (Oct. 15, 1906): 34; IV (April 15, 1908): 15.

35. *TMW* XVIII, 11 (Nov. 1922): 4.

36. "The Record Cabinet as a Business Developer," *TMW* IV, 4 (April 1908): 15.

37. *TMW* IV, 12 (Dec. 1908): 59.

38. Gelatt, *Fabulous Phonograph: From Tin Foil to High Fidelity*, 190–92.

39. Ibid., 142.

40. Johnson, "A Bad Name," *The Phonograph* I, 23 (Sept. 20, 1916), 16.

41. Ibid. I, 23 (Sept. 20, 1916), 16.

42. Victor advertising 1907–1921 from the collection of Jerry Madsen, reproduced in Arnold Schwartzman, ed., *Phonographics: The Visual Paraphernalia of the Talking Machine* (San Francisco: Chronicle Books, 1993), 48. I would like to thank Phil Cartwright for kindly giving me a copy of this elegant little book.

43. "At Home with the World's Greatest Artists," *Ladies Home Companion* (Sept. 1916): 7, in "Pioneer Phonograph Advertising," Walsh Collection, L.C.

44. *TMJ* XVIII, 4 (April 1925): 53.

45. *McClures*, Sept. 1906, Walsh Collection, L.C.

46. Harry M. Kassowitz, "The Wonder Story of Records," *TMJ* XIII, 3 (Sept. 1922): 16–17.

47. *TMW* II, 12 (Dec. 1906): 28.

48. Ad in *Ladies' Home Journal*, May 1918, Walsh Collection, L.C.

49. Martin W. Laforse and James A. Drake, *Popular Culture and American Life: Selected Topics on the Study of American Popular Culture* (Chicago: Nelson-Hall, 1981), 36–37.

50. *Cosmopolitan*, July 1912, "Pioneer Phonograph Advertising," Walsh Collection, L.C.

51. "Aesthetics, Technology, and the Capitalization of Culture: How the Talking Machine Became a Musical Instrument," *Science in Context* 8 (1995), 417–49.

52. Stephen Struthers, "Recording Music: Technology in the Art of Recording," in *Lost in Music: Culture, Style and the Musical Event*, ed. Aaron Levine White (London: Routledge & Kegan Paul, 1987), 241.

53. *The Story of "Nipper" and the "His Master's Voice" Picture Painted by Francis Barraud*, comp. Leonard Petts (Bournemouth, Eng.: Ernie Bayly for the T.M. Review International, 1973).

54. Roland Marchand, *Advertising the American Dream: Making Way for Modernity, 1920–1940* (Berkeley: University of California Press, 1985), 349–52. In his efforts to explain why the playback mode triumphed over the recording mode in the evolution of the phonograph, Dave Laing, "A Voice without a Face: Popular Music and the Phonograph in the 1890s," *Popular Music* X, 1 (1991): 1–9, curiously ignores the economic power gained thereby by phonograph entrepreneurs.

55. In his discussion of the politics of Gilded Age culture, Alan Trachtenberg refers to "a view of aesthetic experience as merely receptive, passive, spectatorial" in *The Incorporation of America: Culture and Society in the Gilded Age* (New York: Hill & Wang, 1982), 146.

56. These two examples are reproduced in Schwartzman, ed., *Phono-Graphics*, 26.

57. *The Edison Phonograph Monthly* VI, 8 (August 1908): 1.

58. Ibid., VI, 5 (May 1908): 20.

59. Trachtenberg, *The Incorporation of America*. In generously sharing drafts of her work on Scott Joplin, historian Susan Curtis was the first to demonstrate to me the links between Trachtenberg's idea of incorporation and music.

60. *The Phonograph* III, 12 (Mar. 21, 1917): 3.

61. Fenimore Johnson, *His Master's Voice*, 91.

62. Trachtenberg, *Incorporation of America*, 147.

63. *Phonogram* II, 8–9 (Aug.–Sept. 1892): 180–88.

64. T. J. Jackson Lears, "From Salvation to Self-Realization: Advertising and the Therapeutic Roots of Consumer Culture, 1880–1930," in *The Culture of Consumption: Critical Essays in American History, 1880–1980* (New York: Pantheon Books, 1983), 3–38. Lears more fully develops his description of these bourgeois sensibilities in *No Place of Grace: Antimodernism and the Transformation of American Culture, 1880–1920* (New York: Pantheon Books, 1981).

65. Roell, *The Piano in America*, 3–27.

66. "Faults of the Talking Machine," *Musical America* XXIV, 14 (1916): 31.

67. "Do Men or Women Prove the Bigger Purchasers of Talking Machines and Record Outfits?" *TMW* XV, 2 (Feb 1919), 67–71.

68. *TMW* V, 2 (Feb. 1909): 10.

69. "John Philip Sousa Still Alarmed," *TMW* II, 9 (Sept. 1906): 21; "Sousa's Protest Against 'Canned' Music," *Current Literature* 41 (Oct. 1906): 426–28.

70. *TMW* II, 5 (June 1906): 30.

71. Fenimore Johnson, *His Master's Voice*.

72. *TMW* XII, 8 (Aug. 1916): 8.

73. *TMW* XIV, 7 (July 1918): 34–35.

74. Schwartzman, *PhonoGraphics*, 51, includes an excellent photo of one of these Victor educational phonographs.

75. *TMW* XIV, 7 (July 1918): 34–35.

76. *The Victrola in Rural Schools* (Camden, N.J.: Educ. Dept. of Victor Talking Machine Co., 1916), 7, 10–14, 17. This publication reappeared yearly.

77. Gelatt, *The Fabulous Phonograph: From Tin Foil to High Fidelity*, ch. 10.

78. *TMW* II, 11 (Nov. 1906): 19.

79. *TMW* VIII, 10 (Oct. 1912): 14.

80. Howard Greenfeld, *Caruso* (New York: G. P. Putnam's Sons, 1983), 111–12.

81. Rust, *Record Label Book*, 75; Marco, ed., *Encyclopedia of Recorded Sound*, 182–83, 615–16, 618–19.

82. Robert H. Schauffler, "Canned Music—the Phonograph Fan," *TMW* XVII, 5 (May 1921): 26.

83. *Voice of Victor* II, 6 (Nov. 1907): 6.

84. *TMW* XIV, 2 (Feb. 1918): 67.

85. *TMW* XI, 5 (May 1915): 9.

86. *TMW* XIII, 4 (Apr. 1917): 62.

87. *TMW* XII, 5 (May 1916): 8.

88. Robert Grau, "Grand Opera of the Talking Machine," *Voice of Victor* VIII, 12 (Dec. 1913): 18. See also, *TMW* VI, 6 (June 1910): 27.

89. John Dizikes, *Opera in America: A Cultural History* (New Haven: Yale University Press, 1993), 284–86.

90. Evan Eisenberg, The *Recording Angel: Explorations in Phonography* (New York: McGraw-Hill, 1987), 29.

91. These are the words used by T. J. Jackson Lears to describe emerging theories of advertising in the early twentieth century. "From Salvation to Self-Realization," 19.

92. As quoted in Gelatt, *Fabulous Phonograph: From Tin Foil to High Fidelity*, 142. Ulysses (Jim) Walsh claims that Eldridge Johnson thanked the Black Label artists whose sales in the millions made it possible to issue Red Seal records "because the profits we make from them more than absorb our Red Seal losses," in "Favorite Pioneer Recording Artists: Arthur Collins, I," *Hobbies* (Nov. 1942): 11–12. Mr. Walsh did not document this comment and I have been unable to find it.

93. *TMW* XIV, 6 (June 1919): 141.

94. Ibid. VII, 1 (Jan. 1911): 42.

95. Ibid. XIII, 9 (Sept. 1917): 9.

96. Ibid. XIII, 11 (Nov. 1917): 49.

97. Ibid. VII, 11 (Nov. 1911): 22.

98. Ibid. VI, 11 (Nov. 1910): 3.

99. Ibid. XV, 6 (June 1919): 4.

100. Ibid. IX, 3 (Mar. 1913): 48.

101. Ibid. XII, 4 (April 1916): 49.

102. Ibid. VII, 5 (May 1911): 33.

103. On the dance craze see Lewis A. Erenberg, *Steppin' Out: New York Nightlife and the Transformation of American Culture, 1890–1930* (Chicago: University of Chicago Press, 1981), 158–59, 164–70.

104. Brian Rust, *The Record Label Book*, 309–12.

105. *TMW* XV, 8 (Aug. 1919): 120–21.

106. Marco, ed., *Encyclopedia of Recorded Sound*, 146–53.

107. Rust, *Record Label Book*, 309; Marco, ed., *Encyclopedia of Recorded Sound*, 764.

108. See my own discussion of the Whiteman band's reception by

Chicago's dancing crowd, in: *Chicago Jazz: A Cultural History, 1904–1930* (New York: Oxford University Press, 1993), 78–79.

109. *Variety* (Aug. 6, 1924): 37.

Chapter Four

1. Throughout this chapter, I intend the word "ethnic" to refer to a group of people sharing cultural characteristics that may include language, religion, folklife, customs, and\or history. Such a definition fits the historical experience of immigrants to the United States but implies that dominant groups such as "Yankees" in New England may not be "ethnic." See Werner Sollors, *Beyond Ethnicity: Consent and Descent in American Culture* (New York: Oxford University Press, 1986), 25, and Thomas K. Fitzgerald, "Media, ethnicity and identity," in *Culture and Power: A Media, Culture and Society Reader*, ed. Paddy Scannell, Philip Schlesinger and Colin Sparks (London: Sage Publications, 1992), 112–33. *Harvard Encyclopedia of American Ethnic Groups*, ed., Stephan Thernstrom (Cambridge: Harvard University Press, 1980), v–vi, 234–42.

2. *Talking Machine World* (hereafter *TMW*) XXII, 1 (Jan. 1926): 6.

3. Guy Marco, ed., *Encyclopedia of Recorded Sound in the United States* (New York: Garland, 1993), 295.

4. Stephen Stern, "Ethnic Folklore and the Folklore of Ethnicity," *Western Folklore* XXXVI, 1 (1977): 7–32. My thinking about the interactions of the phonograph and ethnicity has been strongly influenced by Werner Sollors, *Beyond Ethnicity*, and Joshua Meyrowitz, *No Sense of Place: The Impact of Electronic Media on Social Behavior* (New York: Oxford University Press, 1985).

5. Victor Greene, *A Passion for Polka: Old-Time Ethnic Music in America* (Berkeley: University of California Press, 1992), 71. I am deeply indebted to Dr. Greene's book for its many insights into the cultural significance of ethnic records. I have come, however, to a different interpretation of the cultural functions of ethnic records.

6. Greene, *Passion for Polka*, 32–33.

7. Richard K. Spottswood, "The Sajewski Story: Eighty Years of Polish Music in Chicago," in *Ethnic Recordings in America: A Neglected Heritage*, ed. Judith McCullogh (Washington, D.C.: American Folklife Center, 1982), 141.

8. *Edison Phonograph Monthly* II, 12 (Feb. 1905): n.p.; III, 5 (July 1905): 3.

9. Pekka Gronow, "Ethnic Recordings: An Introduction," in *Ethnic Recordings in America: A Neglected Heritage*, ed. Judith McCullogh (Washington, D.C.: American Folklife Center, 1982), 5, 12; estimates of the potential size of the market for non-American music in the United States appear in *Talking Machine Journal* XXX.

10. Frederick W. Gaisberg, *The Music Goes Round* (New York: Macmillan, 1942), 25–26; Marco, ed., *Encyclopedia of Recorded Sound*, 56–57, 382–83.

11. Joseph A. Mussulman, *Music in the Cultured Generation: A Social History of Music in America, 1870–1900* (Evanston, Il.: Northwestern University Press, 1971), chs 1–6.

12. *Edison Phonograph Monthly* 6 (Mar. 1908): 10.

13. Ibid., 7 (Aug. 1909): 24.

14. *Talking Machine World* II, 8 (August 1906): 10.

15. *The Columbia Record* II, 2 (Feb. 1904), n.p.

16. Ibid.

17. Gronow, "Ethnic Recordings," 16.

18. *Edison Phonograph Monthly* VII, 7 (July 1909): 14.

19. Ibid. VI, 2 (Feb. 15, 1910): 34.

20. *TMW* VIII, 11 (Nov. 1912): 6.

21. Ibid., 29.

22. *Edison Phonograph Monthly* III, 7 (Sept. 1905), 5.

23. *TMW* X, 2 (Feb. 1914): 6.

24. *The Columbia Record* II, 1 (Jan. 1904), n.p.

25. Ibid. III, 5 (May 1905), 135.

26. Gaisberg, *The Music Goes Round*, 54.

27. Gaisberg, *Music Goes Round*, 56–58.

28. "Recording Artists of All Castes in India," *TMW* IX, 4 (April 1913): 32.

29. Gaisberg, *Music Goes Round*, 56, 58.

30. *TMW* XVII, 1 (Jan. 1921): 3.

31. "Naniwabushi best seller along the Ginza," *TMJ* XVIII, 4 (April 1930): 38.

32. Gaisberg, *Music Goes Round*, 64.

33. *Talking Machine Journal* [hereafter *TMJ*] (March 1928): 48.

34. *TMW* VIII, 3 (Mar. 1912): 36.

35. Gronow, "Ethnic Recordings," 15.

36. *TMW* IX, 3 (March 1913): 11.

37. *TMW* IX, 4 (Apr. 1913): 6.

38. *TMJ* XX, 4 (April 1926): 16.

39. Gronow, "Ethnic Recordings: An Introduction," 5.

40. As quoted in Spottswood, "Commercial Ethnic Recordings," 55.

41. As quoted in Spottswood, "Commercial Ethnic Recordings," 54.

42. *TMW* II, 8 (Aug. 1906): 10.

43. *Edison Phonograph Monthly* VI, 3 (Mar. 1908): 10.

44. *Voice of Victor* XII, 9 (Sept. 1917): 173.

45. *Edison Phonograph Monthly* VI, 7 (July 1908): 12; *TMW* XIX, 8 (Aug. 1923): 22; *TMW* XX, 2 (Feb. 1924): 8.

46. "The Buyer of Foreign Records," *Voice of Victor* XIII, 4 (May 1918): 87.

47. *TMW* XVII, 6 (June 1921): 11.

48. *Voice of Victor* XII, 10 (Oct. 1917): 183.

49. John Marion Schlachter, "30% of Your Population are Prospects for Foreign Records . . . ," *TMJ* XVI, 1 (Jan. 1924): 23.

50. *TMW* II, 8 (August 1906): 10.

51. *Talking Machine Journal* (hereafter *TMJ*) XI, 1 (July 1921): 37. On the market for foreign records in factory towns, see also *TMW* IX, 3 (March 1913): 36.

52. *Voice of Victor*, 10 (Oct. 1918), n.p. Also see: *TMW* V, 9 (Sept. 1909): 6.

53. *Voice of Victor* XII, 9 (Sept. 1917): 173.

54. "The Sajewski Story," 134–40.

55. See Greene's lucid account of these developments in *Passion for Polka*, ch. 3.

56. A. W. Calder, "Changing Thousands of Foreign Records into Good U.S. Dollars," *TMJ* XX, 4 (April 1926): 16.

57. "Victor Solicits Suggestions," *The Phonograph* IV, 10 (Sept. 5, 1917): 3, 18.

58. Kathleen Monahan, "The Role of Ethnic Record Companies in Cultural Maintenance: A Look at Greyko," *John Edwards Memorial Foundation Quarterly* 14 (1978): 145–56.

59. *TMW* XVII, 3 (Mar. 1921): 170.

60. *TMW* XVIII, 2 (Feb. 1922): 149.

61. Ruth Glasser, *Music Is My Flag: Puerto Rican Musicians and Their New York Communities, 1917–1940* (Berkeley: University of California Press, 1995), 143–44.

62. "Talker Speaks Many Tongues: Aid to Employers," *The Phonograph* VI, 3 (July 17, 1918), 10, 14.

63. Gaisberg, *Music Goes Round*, xx. *TMW* X, 9 (Sept. 1914): 14.

64. *TMW* XI, 8 (August 1915): 67.

65. Ibid.

66. *TMW* XI, 8 (Aug. 1915).

67. *The Columbia Record* XI, 4 (1913), n.p.

68. *Voice of Victor* XII, 9 (Sept. 1917): 173.

69. *TMW* XIV, 4 (April 1918): 13.

70. *TMW* XIII, 7 (July 1917): 24–25.

71. Dan Des Foldes, "Revolutionizing the Domestic-Foreign Record Field," *TMJ* XXV, 5 (Nov. 1928): 32.

72. *TMW* XI, 8 (August 1915): 67.

73. *TMJ* XI, 8 (August 1915): 67; xi, 9 (Sept. 1915): 52. Greene, *Passion for Polka*, 75–76.

74. *TMW* XVIII, 8 (August 1922): 50.

75. Education Department, Victor Talking Machine Company, *The Victrola in Americanization* (Camden, N.J.: Victor Talking Machine Company, 1920), 5–6.

76. *The Victor in Physical Education, Recreation and Play* (Camden, N.J.: Educational Department of the Victor Talking Machine Company, 1916), 7–10.

77. Greene, *Passion for Polka*, 116–18, emphasizes the role that Progressive reformers played in spreading a multicultural appreciation of immigrant traditions, but the methods by which this appreciation was encouraged served also to remove much that was ethnic from folk dancing.

78. *The Phonograph* VI, 3 (July 17, 1918): 10, 14.

79. Greene, *Passion for Polka*, ch. 5.

80. Marco, ed., *Encyclopedia of Recorded Sound*, 624–25.

81. Henry Sapoznik, "Mysteries of the Sabbath: Classic Cantorial Recordings, 1907–1947," notes to Yazoo c.d. 7002, 7.

82. *TMJ* XX, 4 (April 1926), 16.

83. *TMJ* XXV, 5 (Nov. 1928): 32. Gronow, "Ethnic Recordings," 13.

84. "Advertising for Foreign Trade at Home," *TMW* XIX, 7 (July 1923): 45.

85. Jonathan D. Sarna, "From Immigrants to Ethnics: Toward a New Theory of 'Ethnicization,'" *Ethnicity* 5 (1978), 370–78.

86. "Turning Foreign Records into Real Cash," *TMW* XXI, 9 (Sept. 1925), 14.

87. Stern, "Ethnic Folklore," 25–26.

88. Greene, *Passion for Polka*, 77, argues that "to make money, Anglo-American [phonograph] entrepreneurs were flying in the face of assimilation pressures" during the 1920s, but they were also pioneering a musical synthesis of immigrant with popular American musical elements, interweaving exotic European musical traditions with elements of music more familiar to the native-born.

89. "Some Thoughts on the Foreign Record Trade," *TMW* XIX, 11 (Nov. 1923): 80.

90. Richard Weiss, "Ethnicity and Reform: Minorities and the Ambience of the Depression Years," *Journal of American History* 66 (1979): 577.

91. As quoted in Fitzgerald, "Media, ethnicity and identity," 112. See Joshua Meyrowitz, *No Sense of Place*, chs. 7–8.

92. Ibid., 121–23.

93. Greene, *Passion for Polka*, ch. 10.

Chapter Five

1. Barbara Welter, "The Cult of True Womanhood," *American Quarterly* 18 (Summer 1966): 151–74; Daniel Walker Howe, "American Victorianism as Culture," ibid., 27 (1975): 507–32.

2. For analysis of the literary dimensions of women's lives in late nineteenth-century America, see Ann Douglas, *The Feminization of American Culture* (New York: Knopf, 1977) and Kathryn Kish Sklar, *Catherine Beecher: A Study in American Domesticity* (New Haven: Yale University Press, 1973). Michele Mattelart, "Women and the Culture Industries," in *Media, Culture and Society: A Critical Reader*, ed. Richard Collins et al. (London: Sage Publications, 1986), 63–81, analyzes radio programming from a feminist perspective.

3. Joseph A. Mussulman, *Music in the Cultured Generation: A Social History of Music in America, 1870–1900* (Evanston, Il.: Northwestern University Press, 1971), chs. 1–4. Evan Eisenberg, *The Recording Angel: Explorations in Phonography* (New York: McGraw-Hill, 1987), 14–17.

4. Craig H. Roell, *The Piano in America, 1890–1940* (Chapel Hill: University of North Carolina Press, 1989), 20.

5. *Talking Machine World (TMW)* V, 2 (Feb. 1909): 27.

6. Neil Leonard, *Jazz and the White Americans: The Acceptance of a New Art Form* (Chicago: University of Chicago Press, 1962), 21–23, discusses women in music education. Richard Leppert, "Music, Domestic Life and Cultural Chauvinism: British Subjects at Home in India," in *Music and Society: the Politics of Composition, Performance, and Reception*, ed. Leppert and Susan McClary (Cambridge: Cambridge University Press, 1987), 63–104, analyzes the cultural significance of female domestic music making among Anglo-Indians in eighteenth-century India. Roell, *The Piano in America*, 5–16.

7. Andreas Huyssen, "Mass Culture as Woman: Modernism's Other," in *Studies in Entertainment: Critical Approaches to Mass Culture*, ed. Tania Modleski (Bloomington: Indiana University Press, 1986), 189–90.

8. Joshua Meyrowitz, *No Sense of Place: The Impact of Electronic Media on Social Behavior* (New York: Oxford University Press, 1985), 222, suggests the phrase "interior colonization" to describe the possible impact on women of restricting literacy to men.

9. In 1931, *Talking Machine Journal*, for example, took on the title *Radio and Electric Appliance Journal*.

10. Roland Marchand, *Advertising the American Dream: Making Way for Modernity, 1920–1940* (Berkeley: University of California Press, 1985), 66.

11. "Those Who Buy Talking Machines and Records—and Why—An Analysis of the Field," *Talking Machine World* (hereafter *TMW*) XV, 10 (Oct. 1919): 25–26.

12. "Do Men or Women Prove the Bigger Purchasers of Talking Machines and Record Outfits? *TMW* XV, 2 (Feb. 1919): 67–69, 71, 107.

13. "Do Men or Women Prove the Bigger Purchasers of Talking Machine and Record Outfits?" *TMW* XV, 2 (Feb. 1919), 67–69, 71, 107.

14. Ibid., 69.

15. *TMW* XV, 2 (Feb. 1919): 67–69, 71, 107; ibid, XIX, 3 (Mar. 1923):

10. "The Importance of Age Factor in Selling Talking Machines and Records," *Talking Machine Journal* (hereafter *TMJ*) XIV, 4 (Apr. 1923): 32.

16. Susan Kippax, "Women as Audience: The Experience of Unwaged Women of the Performance Arts," in *Culture and Power: A Media, Culture and Society Reader*, ed. Paddy Scannell et al. (London: Sage Publications, 1992), 247.

17. *TMW* XIII, 12 (Dec. 1917): 11.

18. Michele Mattelart, "Women and the Culture Industries," in *Media, Culture and Society: A Critical Reader* (London: Sage Pub., 1986), 72.

19. Pierre Bourdieu, "The Aristocracy of Culture," trans. Richard Nice, in Richard Collins et al., eds., *Media, Culture and Society: A Critical Reader* (London: Sage Pub., 1986), 164–93; Kippax, "Women as Audience, 239–55.

20. "Catering to the Women," *TMW* IX, 3 (Mar. 1913): 12; *The Phonograph* I, 8 (June 7, 1916): 3.

21. Alice Clark Cook, "Faults of the Talking Machine," *Musical America* XXIV, 14 (1916): 31.

22. Susan Estabrook Kennedy, *If All We Did Was to Weep at Home: A History of White Working-Class Women in America* (Bloomington: Indiana University Press, 1979), ch. 7. Allen F. Davis, *American Heroine: The Life and Legend of Jane Addams* (New York: Oxford University Press, 1973), 150–56.

23. Daniel J. Czitrom, *Media and the American Mind from Morse to McLuhan* (Chapel Hill: University of North Carolina Press, 1982), 45, 51–59.

24. Jane Addams, *The Spirit of Youth and the City Streets* (New York: Macmillan, 1909), 19.

25. Kenney, *Chicago Jazz: A Cultural History, 1904–1930* (New York: Oxford University Press, 1993), 23, 31, 64–65, 72.

26. *The Phonograph* VIII, 12 (Sept. 17, 1919): 3; *TMW* XIII, 12 (Dec. 1917): 11; ibid. XVII, 4 (April 1921): 87.

27. *TMW* III, 11 (Nov. 1907): 40.

28. Susan McClary, "Sexual Politics in Classical Music," in McClary, *Feminine Endings: Music, Gender, and Sexuality* (Minneapolis: University of Minnesota Press, 1991), ch. 3; Catherine Clement, with a foreword by Susan McClary, *Opera, or the Undoing of Women*, trans. Betsy Wing (Minneapolis: University of Minnesota Press, 1988); Ethan Mordden, *Demented: The World of the Opera Diva* (New York: Franklin Watts, 1984). Also see, "John Shepherd, "Music and Male Hegemony," in *Music and Society: the Politics of Composition, Performance and Reception*, ed. Richard Leppert and Susan McClary (Cambridge: Cambridge University Press, 1987), 151–63.

29. As quoted in Francis Robinson, "'Such Sweet Compulsion': Geraldine Farrar's Autobiography," *American Music Lover* IV 7 (1938), 241.

30. *New Grove Dictionary of Music and Musicians*, ed. Stanley Sadie, VI (London: Macmillan, 1980), 407; John Dizikes, *Opera in America: A Cultural History* (New Haven: Yale University Press, 1993), 402–6; Geraldine Farrar, *Such Sweet Compulsion: The Autobiography of Geraldine Farrar* (New York: Greystone Press, 1938).

31. Farrar, *Such Sweet Compulsion*, 5, 11.

32. *Such Sweet Compulsion*, 26–34.

33. Ibid., 189–91, 193.

34. As quoted in Gunther Barth, *City People: The Rise of Modern City Culture in Nineteenth-Century America* (New York: Oxford University Press, 1980), 111.

35. Susan Porter Benson, *Counter Cultures: Saleswomen, Managers, and Customers in American Department Stores, 1890–1940* (Urbana: University of Illinois Press, 1986).

36. Joanne J. Meyerowitz, *Women Adrift: Independent Wage Earners in Chicago, 1880–1930* (Chicago: University of Chicago Press, 1988), xv–xxiii.

37. On the rise of a female retailing culture, see: Barth, *City People*, 135–38 and Benson, *Counter Cultures*, 23.

38. Benson, *Counter Cultures*, 23–24; Barth, *City People*, 134–37.

39. "Kaufmann's Enlarges Victor Department," *The Phonograph* VIII, 1 (July 2, 1919): 32.

40. "Selecting Efficient Record Sales Women," *TMW* XXI, 12 (Dec. 1925): 62.

41. Will Saleswomen Replace the Men Serving the Colors on the Business Firing Line?" *TMW* XIII, 12 (Dec. 15, 1917): 11; "Employment of Women in Talking Machine Factories . . . of the British Trade," ibid.: 101.

42. "The Practical Patriotism of the Talking Machine Business," *The Phonograph* IV, 22 (Nov. 28, 1917): 4.

43. *The Phonograph* VI, 3 (Sept. 25, 1918): 3.

44. "Fair Sex Prominent at Dinner of San Francisco Talking Machine Association," *The Phonograph* VII, 9 (Feb. 26, 1919): 12.

45. *TMW* XXI, 12 (Dec. 1925): 62.

46. *TMW* XIII, 12 (Dec. 1917): 11.

47. *TMW* XXIII, 12 (Dec. 1927): 40.

48. "Blends Selling and Art—Wins Success," *TMW* XXIV, 4 (Apr. 1927): 16.

49. "Jack Kapp, Reasons for Popularity of Certain Selections and Their Effect on Sales," *TMW* XIX, 3 (Mar. 1923): 162b.

50. *TMW* XXI, 3 (Mar. 1925): 8.

51. *TMJ* XIX, 3 (Sept. 1925): 36.

52. *TMJ* XIX, 5 (Nov. 1925): 56.

53. "Women Canvassers Bring Home the Bacon," *TMW* XXI, 2 (Feb. 1925): 8.

54. *The Phonograph* VII, 10 (Mar. 5, 1919): 23.

55. *TMW* XIII, 12 (Dec. 15, 1917): 11.

56. *TMW* XXIV, 4 (Apr. 1928): 32.

57. "Selecting Efficient Record Sales Women," *TMW* XXI, 12 (Dec. 1925): 62.

58. *TMW* XIII, 12 (Dec. 1917): 11.

59. *TMW* XXIV, 4 (April 1927): 16.

60. Clement, *Opera*, 47.

61. *TMJ* XXVIII, 3 (Mar. 1930): 32.

62. Meyerowitz, *Women Adrift*, xxiii.

63. Ulysses (Jim) Walsh, "Favorite Pioneer Recording Artists: Ada Jones, I," *Hobbies* (June 1946): 18–19.

64. On the dance craze, see my own analysis in *Chicago Jazz*, 62–66, and Lewis A. Erenberg, *Steppin' Out: New York Nightlife and the Transformation of American Culture, 1890–1930* (Chicago: University of Chicago Press, 1981), 158–59, 164–70.

65. Arnold Schwartzman, *Phono-Graphics: The Visual Paraphernalia of the Talking Machine* (San Francisco: Chronicle Books, 1993), 50, 61.

66. *TMW* IX, 3 (Mar. 1913): 48.

67. *TMW* X, 5 (May 1914): 35, 48; ibid. X, 6 (June 1914): 30–31.

68. *TMW* XV, 3 (Mar. 1919): 3.

69. Erenberg, *Steppin' Out*, 158–71.

70. *The Artistry of Marion Harris* (Los Angeles: Take Two Records TT 217, 1984), liner notes by Bill Tynes.

71. *TMW* XV, 2 (Feb. 1919): 67, 69, 71.

72. "The Importance of the Age Factor in Selling Talking Machines and Records," *TMJ* XIV, 4 (Apr. 1923): 7.

73. Meyerowitz, *Women Adrift*, xvi, xxiii, 117.

74. I would like to thank Rob Bamberger of the Library of Congress who alerted me to the British Neovox reissue collection of Harris's entire recording career.

75. "Interesting Analysis of the Age Factor in the Merchandising of Talking Machines, *TMW* XIX, 3 (Mar. 1923): 10; *TMJ* XIV, 4 (Apr. 1923): 7.

76. "Importance of Age Factor," *TMJ* XIV, 4 (Apr. 1923): 7.

77. *TMW* X, 3 (Mar. 1914): 38.

78. As quoted in Victor Greene, "Friendly Entertainers: Dance Bandleaders and Singers in the Depression, 1929–1935," ts. kindly shared by the author.

79. "F. W. Schnirring Makes Constructive Suggestions on Phonograph Advertising," *TMW* XXII, 11 (Nov. 1926): 78.

80. *TMW* XXII, 10 (Oct. 1926): 78–79.

81. *TMW* XVII, 1 (Jan. 1921): 171.

82. Ted Curzon, "Cupid and a Gramophone," *TMJ* XVI, 5 (May 1924): 25.

83. Hazel V. Carby, "It Jus Be's Dat Way Sometime": The Sexual Politics of Women's Blues," in *Unequal Sisters: A Multicultural Reader in U.S. Woman's History*, ed. Vicki L. Ruiz and Ellen Carol DuBois (N.Y.: Routledge, 1994), 330–41.

84. Michael W. Harris, *The Rise of Gospel Blues* (N.Y.: Oxford University Press, 1992), 83.

85. *Phonograph & Talking Machine Weekly* XXXVI, 16 (Oct. 18, 1933): 8; John F. Ditzell, "Now for the Good New Days for the Record Business," *Radio & Electrical Appliance Journal* XXXV, 5 (Nov. 1933): 27.

86. *P&TMW* XXXVI, 16 (Oct. 18, 1933): 8.

87. *R&EAJ* XXXV, 5 (Nov. 1933): 27.

Chapter Six

1. Lawrence W. Levine, *Black Culture and Black Consciousness: Afro-American Folk Thought from Slavery to Freedom* (N.Y.: Oxford University Press, 1978), ch. 4.

2. Robert M. W. Dixon and John Godrich, *Recording the Blues* (N.Y.: Stein and Day, 1970); Derrick Stewart-Baxter, *Ma Rainey and the Classic Blues Singers* (N.Y.: Stein and Day, 1970); Nelson George, *The Death of Rhythm and Blues* (N.Y.: Pantheon, 1988); A.J. Millard, *America on Record: A History of Recorded Sound* (Cambridge: Cambridge University Press, 1995), 247–48. Ronald Clifford Foreman, Jr., "Jazz and Race Records, 1920–32: Their Origins and Their Significance for the Record Industry and Society," Ph.D. diss., University of Illinois, 1968.

3. J. Fred MacDonald, *Don't Touch that Dial! Radio Programming in American Life, 1920–1960* (Chicago: Nelson-Hall, 1979), 327–29.

4. Foreman, "Jazz and Race Records, 116–18.

5. John N. Ingham and Lynne B. Feldman, eds., *African-American Business Leaders* (Westport, Conn.: Greenwood Press, 1994), 183.

6. Brian Rust, *Jazz Records, 1897–1942* (Chigwell, Eng.: Storyville Pub., 1970), 1606; L. Kunstadt and B. Cotton, "Daddy of the Clarinet: Wilbur Sweatman," *Record Research* XXIV (1959): 3.

7. "'Fattening Frogs for Snakes': Blues and the Music Industry," *Popular Music and Society* 14, 2 (1990), 15.

8. "Concerning the Black Race and Blue Records," *Talking Machine*

World IX, 9 (1913): 26. My thanks to Gene Deanna of the Library of Congress for bringing this article to my attention.

9. Reid Badger, *A Life in Ragtime: A Biography of James Reese Europe* (N.Y.: Oxford University Press, 1995), 89.

10. Chicago *Defender*, Oct. 14, 1914, p. 4.

11. W. C. Handy, *Father of the Blues: An Autobiography* (N.Y.: Macmillan, 1941), 200; Harry H. Pace to Roi Ottley, Nov. 17, 1939 in Ottley and William J. Weatherby, *The Negro in New York: An Informal Social History, 1626–1940* (N.Y.: Praeger, 1967), 232.

12. *Born with the Blues: Perry Bradford's Own Story* (New York: Oak Publications, 1965), 116.

13. Handy, *Father of the Blues*, 200.

14. Borgeson Interview with Peer.

15. Bradford, *Born with the Blues*, 48–49.

16. *TMW* (Oct. 15, 1919): 156.

17. *TMW* XVIII, 12 (Dec. 1922): 93; *Phonograph & Talking Machine Journal* XIV (Dec. 6, 1922): 1, 38.

18. *TMW* XII, 9 (Sept. 1916): 45.

19. *TMW* XI, 7 (July 1915): 30; ibid. XVIII, 12 (Dec. 1922): 93.

20. *TMW* (Oct. 1919): 27. Ralph Peer, who worked for Heinemann as a talent scout for the Okeh label in the 1920s, identified him as a "Jewish fellow" in Lillian Borgeson, "Interviews with Ralph Peer" (Jan.–May 1959), as quoted in Nolan Porterfield, *Jimmie Rodgers: The Life and Times of America's Blue Yodler* (Urbana: University of Illinois Press, 1979), 95.

21. Brian Rust, *The American Record Label Book* (N.Y.: Da Capo, 1984), 47–52, 226–29, 318–24.

22. Rust, The American Record Label Book.

23. *TMW* XIV, 5 (May 1918): 95.

24. John Cromelin, "Period of Unparalleled Popularity for Phonograph," *TMW* XIV, 12 (Dec. 1918): 94–95; Rust, *The American Record Label Book*, 213–14.

25. *The Phonograph* II, 12 (Dec. 27, 1916), 10.

26. Cromelin, "Period of Unparalleled Popularity, 94. His claims are supported by Lizabeth Cohen, *Making a New Deal: Industrial Workers in Chicago, 1919–1939* (Cambridge: Cambridge University Press, 1990), 103–5.

27. Peer Interview.

28. Jeff Todd Titon, *Early Downhome Blues: A Musical and Cultural Analysis* (Urbana: University of Illinois Press, 1977), 204.

29. Bradford, *Born with the Blues*, 119.

30. Emphasis added.

31. Bradford, *Born with the Blues*, 117–18; Stephen Calt, "The Anatomy of a Race Label, Part II: The Mayo Williams Era," *78 Quarterly* I, 4 (1989): 11.

32. *TMW* 5-15-23, 150; Bradford, *Born with the Blues*, 28. Correspondence between Harry Pace and Robert Vann, editor of the Pittsburgh *Courier* reveals the process whereby at least one record entrepreneur traded stock in his company for newspaper articles promoting his products. Percival Prattis Papers, Moorland Spingarn Research Center, Howard University, Washington, D.C.

33. See William Howland Kenney, *Chicago Jazz: A Cultural History, 1904–1930* (N.Y.: Oxford University Press, 1993), 123–25.

34. Bradford, *Born with the Blues*, 48.

35. Stewart-Baxter, *Ma Rainey*, 12. Perry Bradford Vertical File, IJS; the entry for Smith in Guy A. Marco, ed., *Encyclopedia of Recorded Sound in the*

United States (N.Y.: Garland, 1993), 629 claims that "Crazy Blues" sold one million copies in six months.

36. Blues vocalist Big Bill Broonzy and his friends systematically bought copies of his records in order to ensure good sales figures: Broonzy and Yannick Bruynoghe, *Big Bill Blues: William Broonzy's Story* (London: Cassell & Co., 1955), 20–21.

37. Kerry Seagrave, *Payola in the Music Industry: A History, 1880–1991* (Jefferson, N.C.: McFarland & Co., 1994), 18; Foreman, "Jazz and Race Records," 159.

38. W. C. Handy's version slightly changed Perry Bradford's protest to "Perry Bradford waives only the American flag and that not too hard."

39. Millard, *America on Record*, 77; John Hammond, "An Experience in Jazz History," in Dominique-René de Lerma, ed., *Black Music in Our Culture* (Kent, Ohio: Kent State University Press, 1970), 59.

40. "Frank B. Walker; Disk Biz Pioneer, Dies in L.I. at 73," *Variety* (Oct. 23, 1963); Charles Wolfe, "Columbia Records and Old-Time Music," *John Edwards Memorial Foundation Quarterly* (Fall 1978): 119.

41. Barlow, "'Fattening Frogs . . . , '" 23.

42. Chris Albertson, *Bessie* (N.Y.: Stein & Day, 1972), 62.

43. Hammond, "An Experience in Jazz History," 59; Levine, *Black Culture and Black Consciousness*, 225–26; Paul Oliver, *Bessie Smith* (N.Y.: Barnes, 1961), passim.

44. William Barlow, *"Looking Up at Down": The Emergence of Blues Culture* (Philadelphia: Temple Univ. Press, 1989), 130.

45. Columbia Record executive George Avakian singled out Walker for particular praise for having, as he quotes his fellow Columbia executive John Hammond, "put aside upwards of twenty thousand dollars in royalties for his protegee." in *The Art of Jazz" Essays on the Nature and Development of Jazz*, ed. Martin T. Williams (N.Y.: Oxford University Press, 1959), 76n.

46. Russell Sanjek, *American Popular Music and Its Business: The First Four Hundred Years*, vol. III (N.Y.: Oxford University Press, 1988), 64.

47. Sanjek, *American Popular Music*, III, 62–63. Heinemann stoutly defended the 75¢ record in *Talking Machine Journal* XI, 6 (Dec. 1921): 7. Between the two sums lay considerable company expenses for advertising and price discounts to jobbers.

48. "Okeh Jobbers Meet in Chicago Prior to Record Carnival," *P&TMW* 21 (Mar. 3, 1926): 3.

49. *TMW* XXII, 6 (June 1926): 6.

50. "Okeh Cabaret & Style Show," *TMW* XXII, 6 (June 1926): 6.

51. Interview with Peer.

52. On Harry H. Pace, see: Ingham & Feldman, eds., *African-American Business Leaders*, 501–17. Extensive documentation on the pioneering race company appears in Helge Thygesen, Mark Berresford and Russ Shor, *Black Swan: The Record Label of the Harlem Renaissance* (Nottingham, Eng.: VJM Pub., 1996).

53. Marco, ed., *Encyclopedia of Recorded Sound*, 56–66; Handy, *Father of the Blues*, 202; Rust, *American Record Label Book*, 35–37; George, *Death of Rhythm and Blues*, 10.

54. As quoted in Ingham and Feldman, eds., *African American Business Leaders*, 510.

55. Robert Vann to Harry H. Pace, July 7, 1922, ts., Percival Prattis Papers, Box 144–29, folder 28, Moorland-Spingarn Research Center, Howard University.

56. As quoted in Dixon and Godrich, *Recording the Blues*, 9.

57. Chicago *Broad Ax*, May 7, 1921, 1; "Black Swan Phonograph Company Celebrates Second Anniversary," New York *Amsterdam News* June 6, 1923, 7.

58. As quoted in African *American Business Leaders*, 510.

59. Pace to Ottley, Nov. 17, 1939, in Ottley and William J. Weatherby, *The Negro in New York*, 232–35.

60. Chicago *Broad Ax*, Jan. 19, 1921, 1.

61. Handy, *Father of the Blues*, 202–3; Ingham and Feldman, eds., *African-American Business Leaders*, 509.

62. Barlow, "'Fattening Frogs for Snakes,'" 21.

63. Mayo Williams's opinion of Pace appears in Stephan Calt, "The Anatomy of a 'Race' Label, Part II: The Mayo Williams Era," *78 Quarterly* I, 4 (1989), 12.

64. James R. Grossman, *Land of Hope: Chicago, Black Southerners, and the Great Migration* (Chicago: University of Chicago Press, 1989), 146–55.

65. Bruce Bastin, "Truckin' My Blues Away: East Coast Piedmont Styles," in Lawrence Cohn, ed., *Nothing But the Blues: The Music and Musicians* (N.Y.: Abbeville Press, 1993), 205–31.

66. Foreman, "Jazz and Race Records," 202 gives the higher figure; also see, Samuel B. Charters, *The Country Blues* (N.Y.: Rinehart & Co., 1959), 49–52.

67. Calt, "Anatomy of a Race Label," 12.

68. As quoted in ibid., 13.

69. Ruth Glasser, *My Music Is My Flag: Puerto Rican Musicians and Their New York Communities, 1917–1940* (Berkeley: University of California Press, 1995), 148–49. Charters, *The Country Blues*, 51, says that Williams worked as a theatrical agent for many of his singers, thus justifying his recording fees.

70. Calt, "Anatomy of a Race Label, Part II," 15–17. Broonzy and Bruynoghe, *Big Bill Blues*, 21, reveals how easy it was to fail to inform the ignorant of their copyrights or to get performers drunk after the session and more easily convince them to "just sign this paper."

71. Frank C. Taylor with Gerald Cook, *Alberta Hunter: A Celebration in Blues* (N.Y.: McGraw Hill, 1987), 65–66.

72. Kip Lornell & Ted Mealor, "A & R Men and the Geography of Piedmont Blues Recordings from 1924–1941," *ARSC Journal* 26 (1995), 1–22; Bruce Bastin, *Red River Blues: The Blues Tradition in the Southeast* (Urbana: University of Illinois Press, 1986), ch. 3.

73. Stephen Calt and Gayle Dean Wardlow, "The Buying and Selling of Paramounts," *78 Quarterly* I, 5 (1990): 10–11.

74. Calt and Wardlow, "The Buying and Selling of Paramounts," 18–22.

75. As quoted in Levine, *Black Culture and Black Consciousness*, 227.

76. MacDonald, *Don't Touch That Dial*, ch. 7.

77. Paul Oliver, *Songsters and Saints: Vocal Traditions on Race Records* (Cambridge: Cambridge University Press, 1984), 273–74.

78. Country Blues record producer H. C. Speir As quoted in Gayle Dean Wardlow, "The Talent Scouts: H. C. Speir (1895–1972)," *78 Quarterly* I, 8 (1993): 13.

79. Dane Yorke, "Rise and Fall of the Phonograph," *American Mercury* 27 (Sept. 1932): 1–12.

80. Jeff Todd Titon, *Early Downhome Blues*, 204.

81. Titon, *Early Downhome Blues*, "Appendix A: Patterns of Record Purchasing and Listening," 271–76.

82. Richard A. Peterson, "Measured Markets and Unknown Audiences: Case Studies from the Production and Consumption of Music," in *Audience Making: How the Media Create the Audience* (Thousand Oaks, CA.: Sage Pub., 1994), ch. 10;

83. As quoted in Mike Seeger, "Who Chose These Records?: A Look Into the Life, Tastes, and Procedures of Frank Walker," in *Anthology of American Folk Music*, ed. John Dunson and Ethel Raim (N.Y.: Oak Publications, 1973), 15–16.

84. Seeger, "Who Chose These Records?" 17.

85. Seeger, "Who Chose These Records?" 8–17; Norm Cohen, "'I'm a Record Man': Uncle Art Reminisces," *John Edwards Memorial Foundation Quarterly* 8 (1972): 18–22; Charles K. Wolfe, "Ralph Peer at Work: The Victor 1927 Bristol Sessions," *Old Time Music*, No. 5, ed. Tony Russell (London: 1972), 10–15; David Evans, "Interview with H. C. Speir, *JEMF Quarterly* 8 (1972): 72; Paul Oliver, "Special Agents: How the Blues Got on Record," in Oliver, *Blues Off the Record* (N.Y.: Hippocrene Books, 1984), 48–56.

86. David Evans, "An Interview with H.C. Speir," *JEMF Qtly.* 8 (1972): 119.

87. Foreman, "Jazz and Race Records," 161.

88. Paul Oliver, "Special Agents," 55.

89. Evans, "Interview with H.C. Speir," 119.

90. Norm Cohen, "'I'm a Record Man': Uncle Art Reminisces," *JEMF Qtly* 8 (1972), 19.

91. Levine, *Black Culture and Consciousness*, 228.

92. Evens, "Interview with H. C. Speir," 120.

93. Ibid., and Porterfield, *Jimmie Rodgers*, 96–99.

94. Peer Interview, Southern Folklife Center. Alan Lomax, *The Land Where the Blues Began* (N.Y.: Pantheon Books, 1993), argues that race record producers insisted on more of what had already sold well and "cheap novelty" blues, "the sillier, the better." 446.

95. Foreman, "Jazz and Race Records," 175–77, 201.

96. Charters, *Country Blues*, 183; Benjamin Filene, "Romancing the Folk: Public Memory and American Vernacular Music in the Twentieth Century," Ph.D. diss., Yale University, 1995, 116–19.

97. Paul Oliver, "The Blues," in Oliver, Max Harrison, and William Bolcom, *The New Grove Gospel, Blues and Jazz* (N.Y.: W.W. Norton, 1986), 116–17.

98. Willie Dixon with Don Snowden, *I Am The Blues: The Willie Dixon Story* (N.Y.: Da Capo 1989), 62.

Chapter Seven

1. Bill C. Malone, *Singing Cowboys and Musical Mountaineers: Southern Culture and the Roots of Country Music* (Athens: University of Georgia Press, 1993), ch. 3; Bill C. Malone, *Country Music U.S.A.: A Fifty-Year History* (Austin: University of Texas Press, 1968), 3–78; D. K. Wilgus, "Country-Western Music and the Urban Hillbilly," *Journal of American Folklore* 83 (1970), 157–76.

2. Edward L. Ayers, *The Promise of the New South: Life After Reconstruction* (N.Y.: Oxford University Press, 1993), 104.

3. The interpretation of the southern economy as essentially colonized from without has been established by C. Vann Woodward, *Origins of the New South, 1877–1913* (Baton Rouge: Louisiana State University Press, 1951) and Gavin Wright, *Old South, New South: Revolutions in the Southern Economy Since the Civil War* (N.Y.: Basic Books, 1986).

4. Daniel Boorstin, *The Americans: The Democratic Experience* (N.Y.: Vintage Books, 1974), 133.

5. "Nation-wide Survey of Phonographs and Radios in Homes," *Talking Machine World* (hereafter, *TMW*) XXIII (April 1927), 10.

6. *TMW* XVIII (Oct 1921): 8.

7. "Rural Dwellers Make Excellent Prospects," *TMW* XIX (Dec. 1923): 26.

8. "The Phonograph in Country Towns," *Phonogram* I, 10 (1891): 221–23.

9. Daniel Boorstin, *The Americans: the Democratic Experience*.

10. "Small City Dealer Harvests Rural Trade," *TMW* XXI (June 1925): 4.

11. Ayers, *The Promise of the New South*, 19–20.

12. As quoted in Tony Russell, *Blacks, Whites and Blues* (N.Y.: Stein & Day, 1970), 26.

13. Kip Lornell and Ted Mealor, "A&R Men and the Geography of Piedmont Blues Recordings from 1924–1941," *ARSC Journal* XXVI (1995): 1–22.

14. Rupert B. Vance, *Human Geography of the South: A Study in Regional Resources and Human Adequacy* (Chapel Hill: University of North Carolina Press, 1932), ch. 12.

15. Ronald D. Eller, *Miners, Millhands and Mountaineers: Industrialization of the Appalachian South, 1880–1930* (Knoxville: University of Tennessee Press, 1982), 232.

16. Ralph Peer, "Discovery of the First Hillbilly Great," *Billboard* LXV (1953): 20; Bill C. Malone, *Country Music U.S.A.*, 41–42.

17. "The Brakeman Auditions for Ralph Peer: A Milestone in Country Music," *Billboard's World of Country Music* (Nov. 2, 1963): 31–32.

18. "Ralph Peer Dies at 67: Pioneered Global Music Publishing Concept," *Variety* (Jan. 27, 1960); Nolan Porterfield, *Jimmie Rodgers: The Life and Times of America's Blue Yodler* (Urbana: University of Illinois Press, 1979), 90–92.

19. Alfred M. Shafter, *Musical Copyright* (Chicago: Callaghan & Co., 1932), 228–32, 234–38, 244–45.

20. James P. Kraft, *Stage to Studio: Musicians and the Sound Revolution, 1890–1950* (Baltimore: Johns Hopkins University Press, 1966), 63, 77.

21. Shafter, *Musical Copyright*, 241–45; Herman Finkelstein, "Public Performance Rights in Music and Performance Rights Societies," in *7 Copyright Problems Analyzed* (N.Y.: Federal Bar Assoc., 1952), 69–85.

22. John W. Ryan, "Organizations, Environment and Cultural Change: The ASCAP–BMI Controversy," Ph.D. diss. Vanderbilt University, 1982.

23. Ryan, "Organizations, Environment and Cultural Change," 60–69.

24. Shafter, *Musical Copyright*; Paula Dranov, *Inside the Music Publishing Industry* (White Plains, N.Y.: Knowledge Industry Publications, Inc., 1980); note John Ryan's comments on the groping efforts of Jelly Roll Morton and Gene Autry to learn about ASCAP and secure membership. As this book was going to press, advertisements for Richard A. Peterson, *Creating Country Music: Fabricating Authenticity* (Chicago: University of Chicago Press, 1997), began to appear. I would like to thank Sara Leopold of the University of Chicago Press for sending me an advance copy of this fine work that makes in its second and third chapters many of the same points as this chapter.

25. He surely exaggerated here since A. P. Carter refused to sign a recording contract that omitted all copyright royalties.

26. Malone, *Country Music U.S.A.*, 41.

27. On Carson, see Norm Cohen, "'Fiddlin' John Carson: An appreciation and a Discography," *John Edwards Memorial Foundation Quarterly* x: 138–56; Bob Coltman, "Look Out! Here Comes, Fiddlin' John Carson: One of a Kind and Twice as Feisty," *Old Time Music* 9 (1973): 16–21; Gene Wiggins, *Fiddlin' Georgia Crazy: Fiddlin' John Carson, His Real World, and the World of*

His Songs (Urbana: University of Illinois Press, 1987); Malone & McCullah, *Stars of Country Music*; and interviews of Polk Brockman conducted by Ed Kahn and Archie Green, SFC, UNCCH.

28. Kraft, *Stage to Studio*, 65.

29. Wayne W. Daniel, *Pickin' on Peachtree: A History of Country Music in Atlanta, Georgia* (Urbana: University of Illinois Press, 1990), 69.

30. Archie Green and Ed Kahn interview with Polk Brockman, Atanta, Ga., Aug. 11, 1961, ts., Brockman File, Southern Folklife Collection, University of North Carolina at Chapel Hill.

31. *Appalachia On Our Mind: The Southern Mountains and Mountaineers in the American Consciousness, 1870–1920* (Chapel Hill: University of North Carolina Press, 1978), esp. ch. 10.

32. Roger S. Brown, "Recording Pioneer: Polk Brockman," XXIII (1975), 31.

33. Malone, Country Music U.S.A., 34–35.

34. Archie Green, "Hillbilly Music: Source and Symbol," *Journal of American Folklore* 78 (1965): 204–27; Green and Kahn Interview with Brockman, op. cit.

35. Russell, *Blacks, Whites, & Blues*, 23.

36. Nearly all the "facts" of his early life have been disputed. See Wiggins, *Fiddlin' Georgia Crazy*, 3; Malone, *Singing Cowboys*, 75–77.

37. Wiggins, *Fiddlin' Georgia Crazy*, 1–61.

38. Ayers, *The Promise of the New South*, 393–396.

39. Green, "Hillbilly Music," 209.

40. C. A. McMahan, *The People of Atlanta: A Demographic Study of Georgia's Capital City* (Athens: University of Georgia Press, 1950), 203–4.

41. As quoted in Patrick Carr, ed., *The Illustrated History of Country Music* (Garden City, N.Y.: Doubleday & Co. 1979), 42–43.

42. Barton C. Shaw, *The Wool Hat Boys: Georgia's Populist Party* (Baton Rouge: Louisiana State University Press, 1984), 1.

43. C. Vann Woodward, *Tom Watson: Agrarian Rebel* (N.Y.: Rinehart, 1938).

44. William Anderson, *The Wild Man from Sugar Creek: The Political Career of Eugene Tallmadge* (Baton Rouge: Louisiana State University Press, 1975), 76, 78 as quoted in Daniel, Pickin' on Peachtree, 96.

45. Woodward, Tom Watson, 444.

46. Kahn-Green interview with Polk Brockman, Aug. 11, 1961, ts., SFC, UNCCH.

47. Irene S. Futrella to Archie Green, Aug. 8, 1957, SFC.

48. David E. Whisnant, *All That is Native and Fine: The Politics of Culture in an American Region* (Chapel Hill: University of North Carolina Press, 1983), 5–16, ch. 3.

49. Green and Kahn interview with Brockman, Aug. 11, 1961.

50. Noel Holston, "The Man from the South," Orlando *Sentinel-Star Magazine* Feb. 25, 1973, 17F, in Brockman file, Southern Folklife Col.

51. *Bluegrass Breakdown: The Making of the Old Southern Sound* (Urbana: University of Illinois Press, 1984), 191.

52. Irene Futrelle to Archie Green, Nov. 20, 1957, ts., SFC.

53. Wiggins, *Fiddlin' Georgia Crazy*, 95.

54. As quoted in Charles Wolfe, "Columbia Records and Old-Time Music," *JEMFQ* 5 (1978), 118–25.

55. Cohen, "The Skillet Lickers: A Study of a Hillbilly String Band and Its Repertoire," *Journal of American Folklore* 78 (1965): 229–44 as quoted in Whisnant, *All That is Native and Fine*, 309, ft. 4.

56. Green and Kahn interview with Brockman, Aug. 11, 1961.

57. Wiggins, *Fiddlin' Georgia Crazy*, 80.

58. Wolfe, "The Birth of an Industry," in Patrick Carr, ed., *Illustrated History of Country Music* (Garden City, N.J.: Doubleday & Co., 1979), 57.

59. "Victor Machine Company's Recording Crew Arrives in Bristol to Make Records," reprinted in Charles K. Wolfe, "The Discovery of Jimmie Rodgers: A Further Note," *Old Time Music* 9 (1973): 24.

60. John Atkins, "The Carter Family," in *Stars of Country Music: Uncle Dave Macon to Johnny Rodriguez* (Urbana: University of Illinois Press, [1975]), 95–119; Malone, *Country Music U.S.A.*, 62–67.

61. Whisnant, *All That is Native and Fine*, 183.

62. Maybelle Carter interview with Ed Kahn and Archie Green, Aug. 31, 1961, ts., Cater File, SFC, UNCCH.

63. Ed Kahn Interview with Sara Carter Bayes and Coy Bayes, Angels Camp, CA., June 3, 1961, ts., SFC, UNCCH; Ed Kahn interview with Sara Carter Bayes, Angels Camp, CA., Apr. 16, 1962, ts., SFC, UNCCH.

64. Ed Kahn and Archie Green Interview with Maybelle Carter, ts., Aug. 31, 1961, SFC—UNCCH; Ed Kahn interview with Sara Carter Bayes, Coy Bayes, ts., June 3, 1961, SFC—UNCCH; Ed Kahn interview with Sara Carter Bayes, ts., April 16, 1962, SFC—UNCCH.

65. On Rodgers, the best book is Nolan Porterfield's beautifully written and thoroughly researched *Jimmie Rodgers: The Life & Times of America's Blue Yodler* (Urbana: University of Illinois Press, 1979), but Mike Paris and Chris Comber, *Jimmie the Kid: the Life of Jimmie Rodgers* (N.Y.: Da Capo, 1977), contains useful perspectives.

66. Bergeson interview with Peer; Porterfield, *Rodgers*, ch. 7, 383–83.

67. "Ralph Peer," in Phil Hardy and Dave Laing, *The Faber Companion to 20th Century Popular Music* (London, Eng.: Faber and Faber, 1990), 618–19.

68. *Variety*, Jan. 27, 1960, 2; "Ralph Peer," in Colin Larkin, ed., *The Guiness Encyclopedia of Popular Music* (Middlesex, Eng.: Guiness Publishing Ltd., 1995), 3215.

Chapter Eight

1. Michael Denning, *The Cultural Front: The Laboring of American Culture in the Twentieth Century* (N.Y.: Verso, 1996), ch. 9.

2. Andre Millard, *America on Record: A History of Recorded Sound* (Cambridge: Cambridge University Press, 1995), ch. 8.

3. Leonard B. Meyer, "On Rehearing Music," in Meyer, *Music, the Arts, and Ideas: Patterns and Predictions in Twentieth-century Culture* (Chicago: University of Chicago Press, 1994), 42–53.

4. Interview with Dave Kapp, November 1959, typed and transcribed by the Oral History Research Office, Columbia University, p. 24.

5. Telephone interview with Michael Kapp, Nov. 3, 1997; Russell Sanjek, *American Popular Music and Its Business* (N.Y.: Oxford University Press, 1988), 126.

6. Lester Velie, "Vocal Boy Makes Good," *Colliers* (Dec. 13, 1947): 24–25, 122–25; "Jack Kapp, Headed Decca Records, 47," New York Times (Mar. 26, 1949), 17.

7. Dave Kapp Interview, 1, 3, 15–16.

8. Talking Machine World, (hereafter *TMW*) XVIV, 7 (1923): 137; *Phonograph & Talking Machine Weekly* (hereafter *P&TMW*) XVIII, 23 (Dec. 3, 1924): 3.

9. "Negro Records: Booming Field Discovered, Developed, and Led by Okeh," *Talking Machine Journal* (hereafter *TMJ*) XV, 1 (1923): 65.

10. *TMW* XXII, 6 (1926): 84, 103.

11. *TMW* XXIII, 1 (1927): 6.

12. Robert M. W. Dixon & John Goodrich, *Recording the Blues* (N.Y.: Stein & Day, 1970), 32–33.

13. *TMW* XXII, 4 (1926): 63.

14. *TMJ* XI, 5 (1921): 58.

15. Hennion, "The Production of Success: An Antimusicology of the Pop Song," in Simon Frith and Andrew Goodwin, eds., *On Record: Rock, Pop, and the Written Word* (N.Y.: Pantheon Books, 1990), 185–206.

16. Dave Kapp Interview, 9–10. Michael Kapp disagrees, insisting that the record producer does not make a record for some imagined type of person but rather works to realize a record that he has already heard in his head. Interview with Michael Kapp, Nov. 3, 1997.

17. Jack Kapp, "Reasons for Popularity of Certain Selections and their Effect on Sales," *TMW* XIX, 3 (1923): 162a-162b.

18. "Jack Kapp, Headed Decca Records, 47," New York *Times* (Mar. 26, 1949), 17, claims that the record sold 2,000,000 copies while Sanjek, *American Popular Music*, computes a figure at half that amount. The higher figure might have reflected worldwide sales over a different time span.

19. *TMW* XXIV, 2 (1928): 94.

20. *TMW* II, 7 (1906): 5.

21. "Record Profits in Turnover, Says Parsons," *TMW* XXI, 5 (1925): 8, 11.

22. *TMW* XIV, 12 (1918): 3.

23. Howard Whitman, "Profiles: 'Pulse on the Public,'" *New Yorker* XVI (Aug. 24, 1940): 22–26.

24. Roland Gelatt, *The Fabulous Phonograph, From Tin Foil to High Fidelity* (Philadelphia: J. B. Lippincott, 1955), 255; J. Krivine, *Juke Box Saturday Night* (London: New England Library, 1977), 20.

25. Millard, *America on Record*, 166.

26. Whitman, "'Pulse on the Public,'" 22.

27. P&TMW XXXVI, 3 (July 19, 1933): 3; ibid. XXXVI, 17 (Oct. 25, 1933): 3; ibid. XXXVII, 9 (Feb. 28, 1934): 7.

28. *P&TMW* XV, 5 (Jan. 31, 1923): 3; ibid. XXII, 3 (July 21, 1926): 5.

29. "Dealers Urged to Big Film Tie-Up," *P&TMW* XIV, 16 (Oct. 18, 1922): 5; ibid. XV, 8 (May 2, 1923): 36.

30. Larry F. Kiner and Philip R. Evans, *Al Jolson: A Bio-Discography* (Metuchen, N.J.: Scarecrow Press, 1992), 110.

31. E. R. Lewis, *No C.I.C.* (London: Universal Royalties, 1956), 41.

32. N. Y. *Times* (Mar. 26, 1949), 17.

33. Lewis, *No C.I.C.*, 56–57.

34. Gelatt, *Fabulous Phonograph: From Tin Foil to High Fidelity*, 272; Sanjek, *American Popular Music*, III, 127.

35. Velie, "Vocal Boy Makes Good," op. cit.

36. "Jack Kapp, Symbol of Americanism, Plugged in Congressional Record," *Variety* 174 (Mar. 30, 1949): 37.

37. 26 (Mar. 7, 1949), 12.

38. "Pulse on the Public," 24.

39. *Radio & Electrical Appliance Journal* XXXVI, 2 (Feb. 1934): 9: XXXVI, 3 (March 1934): 6.

40. A. W. Calder, "Phono-growtho," *R&EAJ* XXXVIII, 3 (Mar. 1935): 14; ibid. XL, 10 (Oct. 1936): 28.

41. Frank Adams, *Wurlitzer Jukeboxes and Other Nice Things* II (Seattle, Wash.: AMR Pub. Co., 1983), 1.

42. "Sale of Good Old Beer Ditties," *Talking Machine & R Weekly* XXXV, 17 (Apr. 26, 1933): 8; "Beer Gardens Will Buy," *R&EAJ* XXXIV, 5 (May 1933): 11.

43. J. Krivine, *Juke Box Saturday Night*, 20–36; Sanjek, *American Popular Music*, III, 132.

44. "America's Jukebox Craze: Coin Phonographs Reap Harvest of Hot Tunes and Nickels," *Newsweek* XV, 23 (June 3, 1940): 49–50; Samuel Brylawski, "Cartoons for the Record: The Jack Kapp Collection," in Iris Newsom, ed., *Wonderful Inventions: Motion Pictures, Broadcasting, and Recorded Sound at the Library of Congress* (Washington, D.C.: Library of Congress, 1985), 361–73.

45. Vincent Lynch and Bill Hankin, *Jukebox: The Golden Age* (N.Y.: Perigee Books, 1981), 10.

46. Oliver Read and Walter L. Welch, *From Tin Foil to Stereo: Evolution of the Phonograph* (Indianapolis, Ind.: Bobbs-Merrill, 1959), 318.

47. Sanjek, *American Popular Music*, III, 143.

48. Herman Finkelstein, "Public Performance Rights in Music and Performance Right Societies," *7 Copyright Problems Analyzed* (N.Y.: Federal Bar Assoc., 1952), 69–85.

49. Ibid., 71.

50. *No C.I.C.*, 62.

51. Victor R. Greene, "Friendly Entertainers: Dance Bandleaders and Singers in the Depression, 1929–1935," *Prospects: An Annual of American Cultural Studies* 20 (Cambridge: Cambridge University Press, 1995), 181–207.

52. Guy Lombardo with Jack Altshul, *Auld Acquaintance* (Garden City, N.Y.: Doubleday & Co., 1975), 80.

53. Ibid., 82.

54. Mrs. Ruth Kapp to Gerry Gibson, Oct. 31, 1978, ms., Division of Recorded Sound, Library of Congress. Interview with Myra Kapp Levitt, Nov. 3, 1997.

55. "Ruth Etting," in Phil Hardy and Dave Laing, *The Faber Companion to 20th-Century Popular Music* (London: Faber and Faber, 1990), 248–49.

56. As quoted in Henry Pleasants, *The Great American Popular Singers* (N.Y.: Simon & Schuster, 1974), 136.

57. Bing Crosby as told to Pete Martin, *Call Me Lucky* (N.Y.: Simon & Schuster, 1953), 148–49.

58. Thanks to Lewis A. Erenberg, Professor of History and American Studies at Loyola University of Chicago for sharing with me his analysis of the cultural significance of Bing Crosby's 1930s recordings.

59. *Riding a Blue Note: Jazz & American Pop* (N.Y.: Oxford University Press, 1981), 18.

60. "Mixing Genres and Reaching the Public: the Production of Popular Music," *Social Science Information* 19, 1 (1980), 100.

61. *Call Me Lucky*, 150–51.

62. Hennion, "The Production of Success," 193.

63. Lawrence W. Levine, "American Culture and the Great Depression," *Yale Review* 74, 2 (1985), 196–223.

64. "*Easy to Remember*": Bing Crosby (1931–36) Saville SVL190; *Brother Can You Spare a Dime?: American Song During the Great Depression*, New World Records NW270.

65. *R&EAJ* XL, 1 (Jan. 1936): 24.

66. Arnold Shaw, *The Street That Never Slept: New York's Fabled 52nd Street* (N.Y.: Coward, McCann, & Geoghegan, 1971), 69.

67. *Time* XXXIV, 10 (Sept. 4, 1939): 36.

68. "Decca Plans to Create New Record Buyers," *R&EAJ* XXXVII, 5 (Nov. 1934): 28.

69. *R&EAJ* XXXVII, 6 (Dec. 1934): 30.

70. *R&EAJ* XXXVIII, 1 (Jan. 1935): 9.

71. "Selling Records to the Collegians," *TMW* XXIV, 6 (1928): 8.

72. John Hammond with Irving Townsend, *John Hammond On Record* (N.Y.: Summit Books, 1977), 1–38, 343; David W. Stowe, *Swing Changes: Big-Band Jazz in New Deal America* (Cambridge, Mass.: Harvard University Press, 1994), 50–64.

73. Irving Kolodin, "Number One Swing Man," *Harper's Magazine* 179 (Sept. 1939): 431–40.

74. E. J. Kahn, Jr., "Young Man with a Viola," *New Yorker* XV (July 29, 1939): 19–24.

75. On corporate liberalism, see: George Lipsitz, *Class and Culture in Cold War America: "A Rainbow at Midnight"* (N.Y.: Praeger, 1981), 5–8, 139; for a discussion of its connections to Popular Front politics, see Denning, *The Culture Front*, ch. 2.

76. Hammond with Townsend, *John Hammond on Record*, 63–64.

77. Benny Goodman and Irving Kolodin, *The Kingdom of Swing* (N.Y.: Frederick Ungar, 1939), 122–30; Hammond with Townsend, *John Hammond On Record*, 105–12.

78. Interview with Willard Alexander, Popular Arts Project, Third Series, Volume IV, Music, Oral History Research Files, Columbia University, 1960.

79. Gunther Schuller, *The Swing Era: The Development of Jazz, 1930–1945* (N.Y.: Oxford University Press, 1989), 18–20; John Hammond, *John Hammond On Record*, 139–48; Goodman and Kolodin, *Kingdom of Swing*, 133.

80. Brian Rust, *The American Record Label Book*, 39; Hammond, *John Hammond On Record*, 210–21.

81. *The Swing Era*, 31–32.

82. Henry Johnson (John Hammond), "Music Sold for Less than a Song," *New Masses* XX (July 7, 1936): 29.

83. John Hammond, *On Record*, 187.

84. Count Basie as told to Albert Murray, *Good Morning Blues: The Autobiography of Count Basie* (N.Y.: Random House, 1985), 165–66.

85. *Good Morning Blues*, 295–96.

86. Henry Johnson, "Phonographic Music," *New Masses* 23 (April 20, 1937): 35–36.

87. Kolodin, "Number One Swing Man," 432.

88. Paul Lopes, "The Creation of a Jazz Art World and the Modern Jazz Renaissance," Ph.D. diss., Department of Sociology, University of California, Berkeley, 1994.

89. Millard, America on Record ch. 8; James P. Kraft, *Stage to Studio: Musicians and the Sound Revolution, 1890–1950* (Baltimore: Johns Hopkins University Press, 1996). Avakian vertical file, IJS.

90. "How Popular Is Popular Music?: Youth and Diversification of Musical Preferences," *Popular Music and Society* II, 2 (1973): 145–54.

91. William E. Hall and Judith R. Blau, "The Taste for Popular Music: An Analysis of Class and Cultural Demand," *Popular Music and Society* 11, 1 (1987), 31–49.

92. Philip K. Eberly, *Music in the Air: America's Changing Tastes in Popular Music, 1920–1980* (N.Y.: Hastings House, 1982), ch. 2, 76–99.

93. Michael Chanan, *Repeated Takes: A Short History of Recording and Its Effects on Music* (London: Verso, 1995), 15.

Chapter Nine

1. George Lipsitz, *Class and Culture in Cold War America: "A Rainbow at Midnight"* (N.Y.: Praeger, 1981), 204.

2. Lipsitz, *Class and Culture*, 5–8.

3. James P. Kraft, *Stage to Studio: Musicians and the Sound Revolution, 1890–1950* (Baltimore: Johns Hopkins University Press, 1996), 69–72.

4. *American Popular Music and Its Business: From 1900–1984* (N.Y.: Oxford University Press, 1988), 87, 165–67.

5. Marc Hugunin, "ASCAP, BMI and the Democratization of American Popular Music," *Popular Music and Society*

6. Hugunin, "ASCAP, BMI," 13; Bill C. Malone, *Country Music U.S.A.* (Austin: University of Texas Press, 1968), 188.

7. Robert W. McChesney, "Conflict, Not Consensus: The Debate over Broadcast Communication Policy, 1930–1935," in William S. Solomon and Robert W. McChesney, eds., *Ruthless Criticism: New Perspectives in U.S. Communication History* (Minneapolis: University of Minnesota Press, 1993), ch. 10.

8. The best secondary discussion of the underdeveloped subject of electrical transcriptions is in Kraft, *Stage to Studio*, 78–80; Guy A. Marco, ed., *Encyclopedia of Recorded Sound in the United States* (New York: Garland Publishing, 1993), "Vitaphone Corp.," 751–52; and Philip K. Eberly, *Music in the Air: America's Changing Tastes in Popular Music, 1920–1980* (N.Y.: Hastings House, 1982), 76–79, 178–94.

9. Russell Sanjek, *American Popular Music and Its Business: The First Four Hundred Years*, vol. III (N.Y.: Oxford University Press, 1988), 121–22, 128–30.

10. *Waring v. WDAS Broadcasting Station, Inc.*, Oct. 8, 1937, *Pennsylvania Reporter*, vol. 327, 433–52; Kraft, *Stage to Studio*, 86–87; Sanjek, *American Popular Music*, 121–22.

11. *Frank Crumit, Plaintiff V. Marcus Loew Booking Agency and Others, Defendants*, Supreme Court of New York, Special Term, New York County, December 23, 1936.

12. Roland Gelatt, *The Fabulous Phonograph: From Edison to Stereo*, rev. ed. (N.Y.: Appleton Century, 1965), 276–77.

13. Kraft, *From Stage to Studio*, 135, 161.

14. "Trade's Reaction to Petrillo's Disc Plan Is Surprise at Elimination of Radio," *Variety* (Feb. 17, 1943): 33.

15. Kraft, *Stage to Studio*, 84, 121, 125.

16. See chapter three, 122.

17. *Variety* Aug. 11, 1943, 37.

18. *Variety* Oct. 6, 1943, 46.

19. *Talking Machine World* (hereafter *TMW*) X, 9 (Sept. 15, 1914), 14; also ibid., XIII, 4 (Apr. 15, 1917): 62.

20. *TMW* XIII, 10 (1917): 3, 121.

21. *TMW* XIII, 8 (Aug. 15, 1917): 8.

22. "Utilizing the War as an Advertising Medium," *TMW* X (1914): 28.

23. "Our Motto Is 'Business as Usual,'" *TMW* X, 9 (1914): 47.

24. Howard Taylor Middleton, "How the Talking Machine Dealers Can Best Do Their Duty to the Flag," *TMW* XIII 5 (1917): 14; ibid., XIII, 6 (1917): 45.

25. *TMW* VIII (Aug. 15, 1917): 57; VIII, 11 (Nov. 15, 1917): 126.

26. Waldon Fawcett, "Providing Talking Machines and Records for Uncle Sam's Fighting Forces," *TMW* XIII, 8 (1917): 11.

27. "Pleasant Thoughts of Home and the Dear Ones Left Behind," *TMW* VIII 3 (Mar. 15, 1918): 19.

28. "Talking Machines Popular in Military Cantonments," *TMW* XIII, 10 (1917): 3.

29. *TMW* XIV, 4 (1918): 79.

30. *TMW* XIII, 8 (1917): 11, 45, 114.

31. *TMW* XIII, 6 (1917): 45; ibid., XIII, 10 (1917): 3; ibid., XIV, 3 (1918): 16; ibid., XIV, 4 (1918): 79.

32. *TMW* XIII, 10 (1917): 3.

33. *TMW* VIII, 4 (Apr. 15, 1918): 50

34. "Music & Patriotism Combined Prove a Profitable Venture," *TMW* XIV, 7 (July 15, 1918): 3.

35. Victor cut phonograph production by 50% in order to make airplane and hydroplane parts for the government during World War I: *The Phonograph* VI, 9 (Aug. 28, 1918): 3. The company also undertook "very intricate and important [secret]" tasks as well, ibid., VI, 13 (Sept. 25, 1918): 3.

36. *Talking Machine World* Jan. 15, 1918: 4.

37. "U.S. Troops have 12-Station Web" describes the initial installation of the Armed Forces Radio Network first in England and then in Northern Africa. *Variety* (Sept. 8, 1943): 29.

38. Lewis A. Erenberg, "Swing Goes to War: Glenn Miller & the Popular Music of World War II," in Erenberg and Susan E. Hirsch, eds., *The War in American Culture: Society & Consciousness during World War II* (Chicago: University of Chicago Press, 1996), 161.

39. Richard S. Sears, *V-Discs: A History and Discography* (Westport, Conn.: Greenwood Press, 1980), Sears, xxxi.

40. Sears, *V-Discs*, xxvii-xxix.

41. Douglas E. Collar, "'Hello Posterity': The Life and Times of G. Robert Vincent, Founder of the National Voice Library," Ph.D. diss. Michigan State University, 1988, 5–55.

42. Collar, "'Hello Posterity,'" 135–54.

43. Sears, *V-Discs*, xxiii; "V-Discs Spin Out to G.I. Audiences At Rate of 2,000,000 Annually," *Variety* May 10, 1944, p.27; Interview with Lieutenant Commander D. G. Digiannantonio, Feb. 6, 1997. I am grateful to Mr. Digiannantonio for sharing important information on V-Discs with me.

44. Erenberg, "Swing Goes to War," 150.

45. E. P. DiGiannantonio, "The V Disc Program Backgrounder," ts., kindly supplied by its author.

46. "Prelude," in Sears, *V-Discs*, xxvi.

47. Collar, "'Hello, Posterity,'" 169.

48. Undated tape-recorded interview with G. Robert Vincent, kindly supplied by E. P. Digiannantonio, 2/6/97.

49. Collar, "'Hello, Posterity,'" 172.

50. "Celebrating V-Disc: A Musical Contribution by America's Best for Our Armed Forces Overseas," CD#1, kindly supplied by E. P. DiGiannantonio.

51. Pratt to Erenberg, July 1994, pp. 2–3. My thanks to Professor Erenberg for sharing this document with me.

52. Simon puts the words in Carney's and Brown's mouths in Sears, *V-discs*, xv.

53. By far the best discussion of the independent labels of the late thirties and early forties is Scott Deveaux, *The Birth of Bebop: A Social and Musical History* (Berkeley: University of California Press, 1997), 301–6.

INDEX

Armstrong Orchestra, 123
Arnold, Thurmond, 191
art music. *See* European art music
Artophone Talking Machines, 129
Ashcraft, "Squirrel," 19
Asian immigrants, 127
Asian records, 70, 71–73
Atheneum Building (Chicago), 79
Atlanta, 153
　Carson performances in, 145,
　　147, 148
　field recording in, 143, 144, 151
　outskirts of, 130
　population of, 146
　talent scouting in, 141
Atlanta *Journal*, 144, 146, 147
Atlantic Coast. *See* East Coast
Austin High School Gang, 14–15
Austria, 18, 115
Austrian immigrants, 67, 79
Automatic Music Instrument
　Company, 166
Autry, Gene, 226n24
Avakian, George, 180, 223n45
Ayers, Edward L., 136

Baer department store
　(Pittsburgh), 82
Baez, Joan, 153
Baird estate (Philadelphia), 56
ballads, 135, 148, 149, 171, 181
Baltimore, 199
band records. *See* military music
　records
Banner records, 128. *See also* Plaza
　records
Barker, Danny, 127
Barker Brothers department store
　(Los Angeles), 99
Barraud, Francis, 54, 55
Barrientos, Maria, 50
Barroso, Ary, 157
Barth, Jane, 98
Basie, William ("Count")
　European fans of, 20
　Hammond and, 172, 175, 178,
　　179, 180
　V-Discs of, 198
Basie's Band, 177, 178, 179
Bass, Roger, 16
Bayes, Nora, 102

Bean, A. G., 115
bebop music, 176, 177, 201
Bechet, Sidney, 20
Beecham, Thomas, xiii
Beiderbecke, Leon ("Bix"), 15–16,
　21
Benjamin, Walter, 30
Benny Goodman Orchestra, 64,
　176, 177, 179
Benson, Edgar, 64
Benson, George, 180
Benson, Susan Porter, 95
Benson Orchestra, 64
Berlin, 114
Berlin, Irving, 186
Berliner, Emile, 46, 47, 55
　emigration by, 68
　European records of, 67
　E. Johnson and, 48
　Owen and, 65
　trademark term of, 203n1
Berliner, Paul F., 21
Berliner Gramophone Company,
　39, 47
Berlin Opera, 93
Bernay, Eric, 174, 201
Bettini, Gianni, 68
Bierling, John H., 32
big band swing. *See* swing music
Big Joe's store (New York), 18
Binford, Jessie, 92
Bingham, W. V., 6
Bishop, Joe, 164
Biwa vocal music, 72
Black Bottom (dance), 104
Black character sketches, 35, 38
Black journalists, 21, 118
Black Label records, 31–32, 54, 61–
　62, 64, 214n92
Black musicians. *See also* blues
　　records; jazz records; race
　　records; ragtime music
　in depression era, 133
　European fans of, 20
　female, 106, 117
　Hager and, 115, 123
　Hammond and, 175–76, 179
　Marion Harris and, 102
　minstrelsy and, 39
　operatic, 124
　Pace and, 125

Heinemann operations in, 115
music magazines of, 175
Peer operations in, 156
phonograph design in, 50
terminology in, 203n1
British Columbia (firm). *See*
Columbia Graphophone
Company (U.K.); Gramophone
Company
British Decca (firm). *See* Decca
Record Company (U.K.)
British Flag (Oldham pub), 35
British songs, 8. *See also* English
songs; Irish songs; Scottish
songs
Broadcast Music, Incorporated,
186–87
Broadway show tunes, 108
Brockman, Polk C., 141, 144
Carson and, 138, 145, 147, 148
Jenkins and, 149, 150
talent scouting by, 131, 151
Bronson, Howard, 198
Bronx, 18
Brooklyn, 18
Broonzy, "Big Bill," 111, 121, 126,
133, 223n36
Brousek, Anton, 80
Brown, Anita Patti, 124
Brown, Lawrence, 200
Brown, Robert ("Washboard
Sam"), 133
Brown University, 126
Brunswick-Balke-Collender
Company, 160
Brunswick Records, 14. *See also*
Vocalion records
Black, 111, 162
Carter Family and, 154
Crosby and, 163, 168, 171
ethnic, 79
Hammond and, 175
Marion Harris and, 107–8
J. Kapp and, 160, 161–62, 163,
164, 167
star performers of, 168, 169–70
youth identity and, 19
Buenos Aires, 70
Buffalo (N.Y.), 27–28
"Bumble Bee Slim" (A. Easton),
133

Burchenal, Elizabeth, 81–82
Butterbeans and Suzie (comedy
team), 122

Cabbagetown (Ga.), 145
Cable Hall (Atlanta), 148
Café Society (New York club), 175,
179
Calaway, H. C., 141
Calcutta, 71, 72
Calvé, Emma, 52
Camden (N.J.), 48, 49, 80
Campbell, Olive Dame, 148
Canada, 149
C & S Records, 111
Canton (China), 72
Cantor, Eddie, 145
Cantwell, Robert, 148
Capehart, Homer E., 166
Capehart Company, 166
Carby, Hazel C., 106
Caribbean area, 194
Carle, Frankie, 200
Carl Lindstrom A. G., 68, 114
Carmen (film), 94
Carmichael, Hoagy, 102, 156
Carnegie Hall (New York), 50
Carnegie Institute of Technology
(Pittsburgh), 6
Carney, Harry, 200
Carroll, Lewis, 56
Carson, "Fiddlin' John," 145–47,
151, 152
copyrights of, 148
"discovery" of, 138
first recordings of, 143
Carter, A. P. ("Doc"), 152, 153–54,
226n25
Carter, Benny, 18, 175
Carter, "Big Tom," 154
Carter, Ezra J., 153
Carter, Maybelle Addington, 152,
153
Carter, Sara, 152, 153–54
Carter Family, 138–39, 151, 152–54
Caruso, Enrico
accent of, 85
in advertising, 52, 53
concert by, 60
Farrar and, 93
Gelatt on, xiii

Rockwell, T. G. ("Tommy"), 160
Rodgers, Carrie, 155, 156
Rodgers, Jimmie, 138–39, 183, 187
  contract with, 155–56
  discovery of, 151
  letter from, 152
Roell, Craig, 57
Roman Catholicism, 80
Romanian records, 82
Roosevelt, Eleanor, 197
Roosevelt, Franklin D., 174, 197
Roosevelt, Theodore, 28, 73, 139,
  196
Roosevelt Hotel (New York), 168
Roseland Ballroom (New York),
  178
Rothwell, Walter, 57
Royal Canadians (band), 168–69
Royal Opera (Berlin), 93
Rudolph Wurlitzer Company, 166
Rural Free Delivery, 137
Russell, Ross, 19
Russian immigrants, 67
Russian music, 71
Russian musicians, 77
Russian music records, 68, 74, 82
Rutgers University Institute of Jazz
  Studies, 16, 18
Ruthenian records, 82
Ryan, John, 226n24

sacred music records. *See* religious
  music records
St. Louis, 32, 104
St. Louis Music Company, 129
St. Louis Summer Opera, 38
St. Paul Symphony, 57
St. Valentine's Day, 105
Sajewski, Wladyslaw, 76, 77, 78,
  80
San Francisco, 73
San Francisco Symphony, 143
Sanjek, Russell, 19, 121, 167, 186
Sante, Luc, 33–34
Sargeant, Winthrop, 17
Sarna, Jonathan, 207n31
Satherley, Art, 131, 141
Saturday Evening Post, 52
Saturday Review of Literature, 174
Sauter, Eddie, 177
Savoy records, 201

scat songs, 170
Schaap, Walter, 18–19
Schipa, Tito, 100
Schnirring, F. W., 105
"School House" Victrolas, 58,
  194
Schuller, Gunther, 176, 177, 179
Schumann-Heink, Ernestine, 59
Scott County (Va.), 153
Scotti, Antonio, 59
Scottish musicians, 77
Scottish music records, 12, 13
Scottish songs, 8, 13, 17
Scottsboro Nine (defendants), 175
Scull, John, 47
Seeburg Company, 166
Seeley, Blossom, 102
Sembrich, Marcella, 59
Servian records, 82
Shanghai, 72
Shapiro, Henry D., 144
Sharp, Cecil, 148
Shaw, Artie, 17, 198
Sherman Antitrust Act (1890),
  189, 191
Shils, Edward, xviii
Shimmie (dance), 104
Shing Chong, 72
Sholes, Steve, 198
Shore, Dinah, 199
show tunes, 108
Sicilians, 13, 85
Siefert, Marsha, 54
Signature records, 201
"Silk Hats" (city slickers), 146
Silver, Monroe, 82, 83
Simon, George, 198, 200
Sinatra, Frank, 193, 198, 199
Singing Fool, The (film), 164
Sixta, B., 77
Skipper, James K., 180
Slovak immigrants, 80
Slovenian immigrants, 80
Smith, Bessie, 111
  Pace and, 124
  popularity of, 119, 121
  revenues of, 106, 120
  E. Waters and, 171, 175–76
Smith, Charles Edward, 17
Smith, Chris, 116, 117
Smith, Clara, 106

Sweatman, Wilbur, 111, 116, 117
  "Down Home Blues," 124
  "hill-and-dale" records of, 112,
    113
Sweden, 18
Swedish records, 82
swing music
  Black musicians and, 177
  class conflict in, 180
  Hammond and, 172, 173, 179
  invention of, 184
  Morgenstern and, 18
  Schaap and, 19
  Stearns and, 16, 17
  types of, 181
  Victor and, 64
swing music records
  bebop and, 201
  critics of, 179
  Hammond and, 175–76, 179
  technological innovations and,
    180
  on V-Discs, 197–98, 199, 200
Swiss records, 82
Switzerland, 115
symphonic music. *See* European
    art music
Syracuse University, 16

Taft, William Howard, 51, 194
Taggert, Blind Joe, 160
Tagini, Jose, 69–70
Talking Machine World (periodical),
    xii, 23
  on Blacks, 111–12
  on foreign records, 75
  on jazz records, 63
  on opera, 68–69
  on social acceptance, 44
  on women, 91
Tallmadge, Eugene, 146, 147
"Tampa Red" (H. Whittaker),
    133
Tango, 62
Teddy Wilson-Billie Holiday
    Orchestra, 175, 176, 179
Tempo (periodical), 16
Tennessee, 130, 152, 153, 199
Teschmacher, Frank, 14
Theater Owners' Booking
    Association, 131

Thiele, Bob, 201
Thomas A. Edison, Inc. *See also*
    New Jersey
    Phonograph.Company
  advertisements of, 55
  aesthetic offense of, 51
  automatic phonographs of, 26–
    28
  Black market and, 112
  competitive position of, 48
  conservative customers of, 183
  dissolution of, 163
  female retailers and, 97
  on foreign music, 68
  "gold moulded" cylinders of, 42
  "hearth and home" records of, 4,
    10, 11
  Hebrew records of, 66
  O. Heinemann and, 115
  A. Jones and, 35
  local ethnic musicians and, 80
  "lowbrow" recordings of, 31
  Mexican records of, 70
  middle-class market and, 45
  military phonograph of, 194
  new competitors of, 14, 63, 79
  passive customers of, 16
  piano accompaniments for, 41
  Silver and, 83
  Spanish records of, 69
  survey by, 5–14, 17, 205–6n7
  Victorian values and, 14, 17, 19,
    55
Thompson, William Hale, 121
Three Suns (musical group), 198
Thursby, Emma, 94
Time (periodical), 172, 180
Tipling (Lauter employee), 104
Titon, Jeff Todd, 129, 130
Tommy Dorsey Orchestra, 171
Toscanini, Arturo, 198
Tough, Davey, 176
Townsend, Edward, 34
Trachtenberg, Alan, 55, 213nn55,
    59
Tracy, Bill, 117
Treaty Ports (China), 73
Tréville, Yvonne de, 42
Trumbauer, Frank, 21, 64
Tucker, Sophie, 102, 111, 171
Turkey Trot (dance), 62